GHETTOSIDE

GHETTOSIDE

Investigating a Homicide Epidemic

JILL LEOVY

THE BODLEY HEAD
LONDON

Published by The Bodley Head 2015

1 3 5 7 9 10 8 6 4 2

First published in Great Britain in 2015 by
The Bodley Head
20 Vauxhall Bridge Road,
London SW1V 2SA

A Penguin Random House company

www.penguinrandomhouse.com
www.vintage-books.co.uk

A CIP catalogue record for this book
is available from the British Library

ISBN 9781847923622 (Hardback)
ISBN 9781847923356 (Trade Paperback)

Printed and bound in Great Britain by
Clays Ltd, St Ives plc

Penguin Random House is committed to a sustainable
future for our business, our readers and our planet.
This book is made from Forest Stewardship
Council® certified paper.

For Christopher

When you see the suffering and pain that it brings, you'd have to be blind, mad, or a coward to resign yourself to the plague.

ALBERT CAMUS, The Plague

CONTENTS

PART I

THE PLAGUE

A CIRCLE OF GRIEF

Los Angeles Police Det. John Skaggs carried the shoebox aloft like a waiter bearing a platter.

The box contained a pair of high-top sneakers that once belonged to a black teenage boy named Dovon Harris. Dovon, fifteen, had been murdered the previous June, and the shoes had been sitting in an evidence locker for nearly a year.

Skaggs, forty-four, was the lead investigator on the case about to go to trial.

At six foot four, he was a conspicuous sight in Watts, the southeast corner of the vast city of Los Angeles, a big blondish man with a loping stride in an expensive light-colored suit.

He stepped out of the bright morning light, turned down a narrow walkway along a wall topped with a coil of razor wire, and approached a heavy-duty steel "ghetto door"—a security door with a perforated metal screen of the kind that, along with stucco walls and barred windows, represented one of L.A.'s most distinctive architectural features. He knocked and, without waiting for an answer, pushed the door open.

On the other side of the threshold stood a stout, dark-skinned woman. Skaggs walked in and placed the open shoebox in her hands.

The woman stared at the shoes, choked and speechless. Skaggs's eyes caught her stricken face as he walked past her. "Hi, Barbara," he said. "Having a bad day today?"

This was Skaggs's way, disdaining preliminaries, getting right to the point.

His every move was infused with energy and purpose. In conversation, he jingled his keys, swung his arms, or bounced on the balls of his feet. The movements were not fidgety so much as rhythmic and relaxed, like those of a runner warming up. Forced to hold still in a court proceeding or a meeting, Skaggs would freeze in the posture of a man enduring an ordeal, a knuckle pressed to his lips, a pose that conveyed his bunched-up vigor more than any restless tic.

Now, having deposited the shoes in Barbara Pritchett's hands—and having received no answer to his question—he came to a halt in the middle of the living room carpet. Pritchett remained silent, head bowed, eyes fixed on the contents of the shoebox.

She was forty-two, in poor health. She had recently been diagnosed with diabetes, and her doctor had urged her to get out and walk more. But her son had been shot to death a few blocks away, and Pritchett was too frightened to venture out. She spent days lying in the dark, unable to will herself to move or speak. That morning, as always, she was wearing a big loose T-shirt with Dovon's picture on it. All around her, in the tiny living room, were mementos of her murdered son. Sports trophies, photos, sympathy cards, certificates, stuffed animals.

With great care, Pritchett perched the shoebox on the arm of a vinyl armchair by the door and slowly lifted one shoe. It was worn, black, dusted with red Watts dirt. It was not quite big enough to be a man's shoe, not small enough to be a child's. She leaned against the wall, pressed the open top of the shoe against her mouth and nose, and inhaled its scent with a long, deep breath. Then she closed her eyes and wept.

Skaggs stood back. Pritchett's knees gave out. Skaggs watched her slide down the wall in slow motion, her face still pressed into the shoe.

She landed with a thump on the green carpet. One of her orange slippers came off. On the TV across the room, the Fox 11 morning anchors pattered brightly over the sound of her sobs.

Skaggs had been a homicide detective for twenty years. In that time, he had been in a thousand living rooms like this one—each with its large TV, Afrocentric knickknacks, and imponderable grief.

They made a strange picture, the two of them: the tall white cop and the weeping black woman. Skaggs, like most LAPD cops, was a Republican. He would vote for John McCain for president that year. His annual pay was in the six figures, and he lived in a suburban house with a pool. It might be said of him that he was not just white, but a Caucasian archetype with his blond-and-pink coloring and Scots-Irish features. Watts had twice risen in revolt against such an icon—the white occupier-cum-police-officer—and so Skaggs's presence in this neighborhood was all the more conspicuous for the historical associations it evoked.

Pritchett had a background typical of Watts residents. She was the granddaughter of a Louisiana cotton picker. Her mother had followed the path of tens of thousands of black Louisianans who migrated west in the 1960s, and Pritchett was born in L.A. a few months after the Watts riots. She lived in a federally subsidized rental apartment, and she was a Democrat who would weep in front of CNN later that fall when Barack Obama won the presidential election, wishing her mother were still alive to see it.

Despite their differences, they were kin of a sort—members of a small circle of Americans whose lives, in different ways, had been molded by a bizarre phenomenon: a plague of murders among black men.

Homicide had ravaged the country's black population for a century or more. But it was at best a curiosity to the mainstream. The raw agony it visited on thousands of ordinary people was mostly invisible. The consequences were only superficially discussed, the costs seldom tallied.

Society's efforts to combat this mostly black-on-black murder epidemic were inept, fragmented, underfunded, contorted by a variety of ideological, political, and racial sensitivities. When homicide did get attention, the focus seemed to be on spectacles—mass shootings, celebrity murders—a step removed from the people who were doing most of the dying: black men.

They were the nation's number one crime victims. They were the people hurt most badly and most often, just 6 percent of the country's population but nearly 40 percent of those murdered. People talked a lot about crime in America, but they tended to gloss over this aspect—that a plurality of those killed were not women, children, infants, elders, nor victims of workplace or school shootings. Rather, they were legions of America's black men, many of them unemployed and criminally involved. They were murdered every day, in every city, their bodies stacking up by the thousands, year after year.

Dovon Harris was typical of these unseen victims. His murder received little media attention and was of the kind least likely to be solved. John Skaggs's Watts precinct kept records of scores of such homicides dating back years—shelves and shelves of blue binders filled with the names of dead black men and boys. Most had been killed by other black men and boys who still roamed free.

According to the old unwritten code of the Los Angeles Police Department, Dovon's was a nothing murder. "NHI—No Human Involved," the cops used to say. It was only the newest shorthand for the idea that murders of blacks somehow didn't count. "Nigger life's cheap now," a white Tennessean offered during Reconstruction, when asked to explain why black-on-black killing drew so little notice.

A congressional witness a few years later reported that when black men in Louisiana were killed, "a simple mention is made of it, perhaps orally or in print, and nothing is done. There is no investigation made." A late-nineteenth-century Louisiana newspaper editorial said, "If negroes continue to slaughter each other, we will have to conclude that Providence has chosen to exterminate them in this way." In 1915, a

South Carolina official explained the pardon of a black man who had killed another black: "This is a case of one negro killing another—the old familiar song." In 1930s Mississippi, the anthropologist Hortense Powdermaker examined the workings of criminal justice and concluded that "the attitude of the Whites and of the courts . . . is one of complaisance toward violence among the Negroes." Studying Natchez, Mississippi, in the same period, a racially mixed team of social anthropologists observed that "the injury or death of a Negro is not considered by the whites to be a serious matter." An Alabama sheriff of the era was more concise: "One less nigger," he said. In 1968, a New York journalist testifying as part of the Kerner Commission's investigation of riots across the country said that "for decades, little if any law enforcement has prevailed among Negroes in America. . . . If a black man kills a black man, the law is generally enforced at its minimum."

Carter Spikes, once a member of the black Businessman Gang in South Central Los Angeles, recalled that through the seventies police "didn't care what black people did to each other. A nigger killing another nigger was no big deal."

John Skaggs stood in opposition to this inheritance. His whole working life was devoted to one end: making black lives expensive. Expensive, and worth answering for, with all the force and persistence the state could muster. Skaggs had treated the murder of Dovon Harris like the hottest celebrity crime in town. He had applied every resource he possessed, worked every angle of the system, and solved it swiftly, unequivocally.

In doing so, he bucked an age-old injustice. Forty years after the civil rights movement, impunity for the murder of black men remained America's great, though mostly invisible, race problem. The institutions of criminal justice, so remorseless in other ways in an era of get-tough sentencing and "preventive" policing, remained feeble when it came to answering for the lives of black murder victims. Few experts examined what was evident every day of John Skaggs's working life: that the state's inability to catch and punish even a bare majority of murderers in black enclaves such as Watts was itself a root cause of the violence, and that this was a terrible problem—perhaps the most terrible thing in contemporary American life. The system's failure to catch killers effectively made black lives cheap.

To that unseen problem, John Skaggs was the antidote.

Had Dovon's case been assigned to another detective, it might easily have gone unsolved like hundreds of others—just another blue binder on a shelf. But in Skaggs's hands, it had become a relentless campaign for justice.

And Dovon's mother knew it. That was the basis of their kinship.

So now Skaggs stood with one hand in his pocket, one on his hip, regarding Pritchett on the floor, and did what years of homicide work had taught him to do: he waited, silent and unhurried.

Not the least embarrassed, Pritchett closed her eyes as if she were alone, pressed her face into the shoe of her dead son, and sobbed.

This is a book about a very simple idea: where the criminal justice system fails to respond vigorously to violent injury and death, homicide becomes endemic.

African Americans have suffered from just such a lack of effective criminal justice, and this, more than anything, is the reason for the nation's long-standing plague of black homicides. Specifically, black America has not benefited from what Max Weber called a *state monopoly on violence*—the government's exclusive right to exercise legitimate force. A monopoly provides citizens with legal autonomy, the liberating knowledge that the government will pursue anyone who violates their personal safety. But slavery, Jim Crow, and conditions across much of black America for generations after worked against the formation of such a monopoly. Since personal violence inevitably flares where the state's monopoly is absent, this situation results in the deaths of thousands of Americans each year.

The failure of the law to stand up for black people when they are hurt or killed by others has been masked by a whole universe of ruth-less, relatively cheap and easy "preventive" strategies. Our fragmented and underfunded police forces have historically preoccupied them-selves with control, prevention, and nuisance abatement rather than re-sponding to victims of violence. This left ample room for vigilantism—especially in the South, to which most black Americans trace their ori-gins. Hortense Powdermaker was among a handful of Jim Crow–era anthropologists who noted that the Southern legal system of the 1930s hammered black men for such petty crimes as stealing and vagrancy, yet was often lenient toward those who murdered other blacks. In Jim Crow Mississippi, killers of black people were convicted at a rate that was only a little lower than the rate that prevailed half a century later in L.A.—30 percent then versus about 36 percent in Los Angeles County in the early 1990s. "The mildness of the courts where offenses of Negroes against Negroes are concerned," Powdermaker concluded, "is only part of the whole situation which places the Negro outside the law." Gener-ations later, far from the cotton fields where she made her observations, black people in poor sections of Los Angeles still endured a share of that old misery.

This is not an easy argument to make in these times. Many critics today complain that the criminal justice system is heavy-handed and unfair to minorities. We hear a great deal about capital punishment, excessively punitive drug laws, supposed misuse of eyewitness evidence, troublingly high levels of black male incarceration, and so forth.

So to assert that black Americans suffer from too *little* application of the law, not too much, seems at odds with common perception. But the perceived harshness of American criminal justice and its fundamental weakness are in reality two sides of a coin, the former a kind of poor compensation for the latter. Like the schoolyard bully, our criminal jus-tice system harasses people on small pretexts but is exposed as a coward before murder. It hauls masses of black men through its machinery but fails to protect them from bodily injury and death. It is at once oppres-sive and inadequate.

America has long been more violent than other developed nations, and black-on-black homicide is much of the reason. This is not new. Measurements are problematic, since few official efforts were made to track black homicide before 1950. But historians have traced disproportionately high black homicide rates all the way back to the late nineteenth century, and in the early twentieth, "nonwhite" homicide rates exceeded those of whites in all cities that reported federal data. In the 1920s, a scholar concluded that black death rates from homicide nationwide were about seven times white rates. In the 1930s, Southern observers also noticed startling rates of black violence, and in the 1940s, a Philadelphia study found that black men died from homicide at twelve times the white rate. When the U.S. government began publishing data specific to blacks in 1950, it revealed that same gap nationwide. The black homicide death rate remained as much as ten times higher than the white rate in 1960 and 1970, and has been five to seven times higher for most of the past thirty years.

Mysteriously, in modern-day Los Angeles, young black men are murdered two to four times more frequently than young Hispanic men, though blacks and Hispanics live in the same neighborhoods. This stands out because L.A., unlike well-known murder centers such as Detroit, has a relatively small black population, and it is in decline. By Skaggs's time, there were few solidly black neighborhoods left; most black residents of South Los Angeles lived in majority-Hispanic neighborhoods. Yet black men died here as they died in cities with large and concentrated black populations, like New Orleans, Washington, D.C., and Chicago—more often than anyone else, and nearly always at the hands of black assailants. In L.A., it was strange how all those bullets seemed to find their black targets in such an ethnically jumbled place; it was, as one young man put it, as if black men had bull's-eyes on their backs.

Violent crime was plummeting in Los Angeles County, as it was across the country, by the spring of 2007, when Dovon Harris was murdered. But the disparity between black male death rates and those of everybody else remained nearly as large as ever. No matter how much crime dropped, the American homicide problem remained maddeningly, mystifyingly, disproportionately black.

Despite so much evidence of a particularly black homicide problem, however, there was relatively little research or activism specific to black-on-black murder. That gruesome history of Southern racism made the topic an uncomfortable one for many Americans. One of the enduring tropes of racist lore had been the "black beast," the inferior black man who could not control his impulses and was prone to violence. By the early twenty-first century, popular consensus held that any emphasis on high rates of black criminality risked invoking the stigma of white racism. So people were careful about how they spoke of it.

Researchers describe skirting the subject for fear of being labeled racist. Activists have sought to minimize it. "When the discussion turns to violent crime," legal scholar James Forman, Jr., has pointed out, "progressives tend to avoid or change the subject." Privately, some black civil-rights advocates describe feeling embarrassed and baffled by the stubborn persistence of the problem. "Like incest," is how one L.A. street activist, Najee Ali, put it, talking of the shame and secrecy the issue evokes. Other concerned blacks cite their fear of inflaming white racism: Why emphasize what seems sure to be used against them?

Yet the statistical truth was undeniable, and most Americans understood it intuitively even if they didn't talk about it in polite company. There was something in the way the nation acquiesced in shootings and stabbings among "inner city" black men that suggested these men were expendable—or, worse, that perhaps the nation was better off without them.

To John Skaggs, the nation's collective shrug toward homicide was incomprehensible. He sensed also that public indifference made his job more difficult. He might have found some support from none other than the black legal scholar Randall Kennedy. "It does no good to pretend that blacks and whites are similarly situated with respect to either rates of perpetration or rates of victimization. They are not," Kennedy wrote. "The familiar dismal statistics and the countless tragedies behind them are not figments of some Negrophobe's imagination."

Explicitly confronting the reality of how murder happens in America is the first step toward deciding that it is not acceptable, and that for too long black men have lived inadequately protected by the laws of their own country.

2

A KILLING

It was a warm Friday evening in Los Angeles, about a month before Dovon Harris was murdered.

Sea breezes rattle the dry palm trees in this part of town. It was about 6:15 P.M., a time when homeowners turn on sprinklers, filling the air with a watery hiss. The springtime sun had not yet set; it hovered about 20 degrees above the horizon, a white dime-sized disk in a blinding sky.

Two young black men walked down West Eightieth Street at the western edge of the Los Angeles Police Department's Seventy-seventh Street precinct area, a few miles away from where Dovon Harris lived. One was tall with light brown skin, the other shorter, slight, and dark.

The shorter of the two young men, Walter Lee Bridges, was in his late teens. He was wiry and fit. His neck was tattooed and his face wore the mournful, jumpy look common to young men in South Central who have known danger. His low walk and light build suggested he could move like lightning if he had to.

His companion, wearing a baseball cap and pushing a bicycle, appeared more relaxed, more oblivious. Bryant Tennelle was eighteen years old. He was tall and slim, with a smooth caramel complexion and what was called "good hair," smooth and wavy. His eyes tilted down a little at the corners, giving his face a gentle puppy look. The two young men were neighbors who whiled away hours together tinkering with bicycles.

They were strolling on the south side of Eightieth. Bryant carried in one hand an unopened A&W root beer he had just bought. Thirties-era Spanish-style houses—updated with vinyl windows—lined the street, set back a few feet from the sidewalk. Each had a tiny lawn mowed so short it seemed to blend with the pavement. Buses roared by on Western Avenue. Crows squawked and planes whistled overhead as they descended into Los Angeles International Airport, close enough to read the logos on their tails. Groups of teenagers loitered at each end of the street. An elegant magnolia loomed near the end of the block, and across the street hunched a thick overgrown Modesto ash.

The ash tree stood in front of a tidy corner house. Behind that house, in the backyard on the other side of the fence, another man was cleaning out a tile cutter. He had just retiled his mother's bathroom.

Walter and Bryant were taking their time walking down Eightieth chatting, their long shadows stretching behind them. They walked in sunshine, though dusk engulfed the other side of the street. Three friends emerged from a house at the end of the block behind them and called out a greeting. Walter stopped and turned to yell something back. Bryant kept walking toward the ash. A black Chevrolet Suburban pulled up to the curb around the corner, on the cross street, St. Andrews. A door opened and a young man jumped out. He pulled on gloves, ran a few steps, and halted under the tree, holding a gloved hand straight out, gripping a firearm. *Pap. Pap-pap.*

Walter reacted instantly. He saw the muzzle flashes, saw the gunman—white T-shirt, dark complexion, gloves—even as he sprinted. The man with the tile cutter was still behind the fence. He couldn't see the shooter. But he heard the blasts and dropped instinctively. He was forty, had grown up a black man in South Central and had the same battle-ready reflexes as Walter. He lay flat on the ground as gunfire boomed in his ears.

Bryant's reflexes were slower. Or perhaps it was because he was looking straight into the setting sun. To him, the gunman was a dark silhouette. Bryant staggered, then reeled and fell on a patch of lawn overhung by a bird-of-paradise bush. Silence. The tile cutter drew himself to his feet, crept to the fence, and peeked over.

The shooter stood a few feet away, next to the ash tree on the other side of the fence.

He was still holding the gun. The tile cutter watched as he walked a few paces, then broke into a run: there must be a getaway car nearby. The tile cutter made a brave decision: he followed the shooter, watched him jump back into the Suburban, and tried to read the license plate as it sped away. He turned and saw Bryant lying on the grass.

Teenagers were converging from three directions. One young man dropped to his knees next to Bryant. Joshua Henry was a close friend. He took Bryant's hand and gripped it. With relief, he felt Bryant squeeze back. "I'm tired, I'm tired," Bryant told him. He wanted to sleep. Josh could see only a little blood on his head. Just a graze, he thought. Then Bryant turned his head. A quarter of his skull had been ripped away.

Josh stared at the wound. Only then did his eyes register Bryant's cap, lying on the ground nearby, full of blood and tissue. He heard his own voice chattering cheerfully to Bryant, telling him he would be okay.

Standing over them, the man with the tile cutter was pleading with a 911 dispatcher on the phone, straining to keep the details straight as his eyes took in the scene. "Eightieth and Saint Andrews!" He took a breath and muttered hoarsely: "Oh my god."

He put away the phone. He turned Bryant over. He administered CPR. All around him, teenagers were screaming. Someone thrust a towel at him. He tried to blot it against Bryant's shattered head, wondering what he was supposed to do. Bryant vomited. His mouth was filled with blood. The man with the tile cutter, too, found himself staring at the brain matter—flecks of gray and yellow. Yellow? With one part of his mind he recorded his own bewilderment: Why was it yellow? With another part, he fought to stay calm.

One thought kept crowding out the others: *Please don't let this kid die.*

"Ambulance shooting."

Officer Greg De La Rosa, P-3, LAPD Seventy-seventh Street Division, was cruising around Fifty-fourth Street at the north end of the station area when his radio buzzed.

"Ambulance shooting" was the generic way most South L.A. murders and attempted murders came to the attention of police over their radios. In the three station areas that encompassed most of South Los Angeles—Seventy-seventh Street Division, Southwest Division, and Southeast Division—such calls, at least in this year, came more than once a day, on average.

The location of the shooting was almost thirty blocks south from where he was. De La Rosa went "Code 3," lights flashing, down Western Avenue, and got there first. It was warm, and still light.

He took in the scene. A chrome BMX bike down on the sidewalk. A baseball cap. A victim on the lawn. Male black. Late teens. Medium complexion. De La Rosa was on autopilot, filling out the police report in his head. He had been called to so many shootings just like this one. So many "male black," he could barely distinguish one from another. De La Rosa pondered the bike, cap, and victim, arranged in a straight line on the sidewalk and grass. The young man must have dropped the bike and run for the shelter of a porch, De La Rosa thought. A few more steps and he would have made it.

De La Rosa had grown up in an English-speaking family of Mexican descent in mostly Hispanic Panorama City, a rough patch of the San Fernando Valley, and was Los Angeles to the core: his great-grandfather had been evicted from Chavez Ravine when they built Dodger Stadium. He was also an Army veteran. He was still unprepared for what he found when he was assigned to the Seventy-seventh a dozen years before. The station area lay between Watts and Inglewood and spanned the heart of what many locals still called South Central, though the name was officially changed to South Los Angeles in 2003 to erase its supposed stigma. But people on the streets didn't use the new name much, nor the polite new city designations for its various sections—"Vermont Knolls," for instance. Instead, people said "eastside" and "westside" to denote the old race-restrictive covenant boundary along Main Street, and retained South Central for the whole. Florence and Normandie, the intersection where the 1992 riots broke out, was in the Seventy-seventh Street Division, near where De La Rosa now stood.

Over time, De La Rosa had grown used to the texture of life here, but it still baffled him. In the Seventy-seventh, everyone seemed to be related somehow. Rumors traveled at lightning speed. Sometimes it seemed that you couldn't slap handcuffs on anyone in the division without their relatives instantly pouring out of their houses, hollering at the police. De La Rosa's old home of Panorama City was also poor, but it didn't have the same homicide problem, the same resentment of police. He found that he avoided talking to outsiders about his job. He didn't want to waste his breath on people who didn't know what the Seventy-seventh was like and wouldn't understand even if he tried to explain it.

The tasks he walked through that evening were so familiar they were almost muscle memory: Secure the perimeter. Secure witnesses. Hold the scene for detectives. Get out the field interview cards. And get ready: onlookers would soon swarm them, asking questions.

De La Rosa remembered these "ambulance shootings" only if something exceptional occurred. Like the time he had been called to Florence and Broadway, right in front of Louisiana Fried Chicken. The victim, an older black man, had a small hole in his skin, the kind that often hides severe internal bleeding. "Get the fuck away from me!" the wounded man had snarled. De La Rosa tried to help him anyway. The man fought. In the end, De La Rosa and his fellow officers tackled him, four cops piling on, a team takedown of a possibly mortally wounded shooting victim. Even in the midst of the chaos, De La Rosa registered the absurdity, the black humor, so typical of life in the Seventy-seventh.

Black humor helped. But it still got to him—the attitude of black residents down here. They were shooting each other but still seemed to think the police were the problem. *"Po-Po,"* they sneered. Once, De La Rosa had to stand guard over the body of a black man until paramedics arrived. An angry crowd closed in on him, accusing him of disrespecting the murdered man's body. Some of them tried to drag the corpse away. The police used an official term for this occasional hazard: "lynching." Some felt uncomfortable saying it. They associated the word with the noose, not the mobs that once yanked people from police to kill or rescue them. De La Rosa held back the crowd. "You don't care because he's a black man!" someone yelled. De La Rosa was stunned. Why did they think race was a part of this? Sometimes, in the Seventy-seventh, De La Rosa had the sense that he was no longer in America. As if he had pulled off the freeway into another world.

That May night unfolded in the midst of an unexceptional period of violence in the traditionally black neighborhoods of South Los Angeles County. All across the ten square miles that stretched from Slauson Avenue to the north end of Long Beach, black men were shot and stabbed every few days.

About a month before Bryant Tennelle was shot on May 11, 2007, Fabian Cooper, twenty-one, was shot to death leaving a party in Athens. With him was his neighbor and lifelong friend Salvador Arredondo, nineteen, a young Hispanic man, who was also killed.

A week later, on April 15, twenty-two-year-old Mark Webster walked out of a biker club on Fifty-fourth Street near Second Avenue and was fatally shot by someone who opened fire from a distance. It seems unlikely that the attacker knew who he was.

That same night, some black men caught up with Marquise Alexander, also twenty-two, at a Shell gas station at the nearby intersection of Crenshaw and Slauson avenues and shot him dead. Four days later, on April 19, forty-one-year-old Maurice Hill was hanging out in his usual spot in front of a liquor store at Sixty-fourth and Vermont Avenue at about 10:30 P.M. when a gunman killed him; Hill, who had lived in the area all his life, spent most of his time sitting on a grassy median on Vermont Avenue drinking beer. The same day Hill died, Isaac Tobias, twenty-three, succumbed to his wounds at St. Francis Hospital in Lynwood, several days after being shot during an argument with two other black men near 120th Street and Willowbrook Avenue.

Three days later, in Long Beach, Eric Mandeville, twenty, was shot and killed while walking outside, almost certainly targeted by black gang members because he was young, black, male, and looked like one of their rivals. Mandeville was a McDonald's employee, clean-cut and well liked, a former foster child who had overcome a difficult childhood. Hours after his death, Alfred Henderson, forty-seven, was killed nearby. The next day, on April 23, eighteen-year-old Kenneth Frison died at California Hospital after lingering on life support for three weeks. He had been shot in the head at the corner of Ninety-fourth Street and Gramercy on April 1. Four days after Frison's death, Wilbert Jackson, sixteen, was sprayed by a lethal volley of bullets from a passing car as he stood in front of a fish store on Figueroa Avenue south of Fifty-first Street. Early the next day, April 28, thirty-four-year-old Robert Hunter was attending the funeral at Missionary Baptist Church on Adams Boulevard for his cousin—Isaac Tobias, one of the young murder victims mentioned above. An argument broke out at the church; Hunter was shot dead and two other mourners were wounded. Later that same day, Ralph Hope, twenty-eight, was shot and killed in Inglewood.

The next day, April 29, Aubrey Gibson, twenty-three, was found dead in his apartment at Sixty-fourth Street and Brynhurst. Three days later, some black men burst into an apartment at Third Avenue and Forty-second Street and shot fifty-four-year-old Melvin James in the chest. The same day, two other black men were killed: Donald Stevens, forty-four, died in a shooting in Willowbrook, and Larry Scott, twenty-five, was stabbed in the chest by a neighbor in a fight on Western Avenue at 100th Street.

Three days after that, on May 5, Mario Jackson, forty-five, and Tierney Yates, thirty-six, were shot to death at a motorcycle club on 109th Street and Broadway in Watts during a fight that broke out during a viewing of a televised boxing match. Jackson had moved away from his native Watts and done well in the entertainment industry, but some of his old friends from the neighborhood resented it. Responding police officers briefly detained some twenty people who had been present for the fight, crowded together inside the motorcycle club; every single one of them claimed to have seen nothing. Marco Smith, forty-one, was shot next, killed in Hawthorne the day after.

Carl Dixon, thirty-four, was shot and killed in Florence three days later, on May 9. That shooting also seriously wounded three other people; it is the only one of the attacks described here in which the suspects were Hispanic, not black. Bernard McGee, thirty-seven, was sitting next to Dixon when the shots rang out. He described watching his friend die, and how the red fabric of Dixon's shirt whipped as the bullets struck him as if yanked by a strong breeze.

Two days later, a gunman fired on Bryant Tennelle on Eightieth Street.

As De La Rosa looked closer at the victim, he realized that the young man before him was dying. Something about his breathing. De La Rosa also had seen this many times before. He had no medical training. He had simply gained an intuitive understanding of the stages of death from so much exposure. He was familiar with that deep unconsciousness that stole over dying men, that stillness, the way their breath came very slow. An ambulance arrived.

De La Rosa worked the shooting scene all through that night, under black palm trees against a red sky, porch lights glowing up and down the street. At some point, someone passed along a rumor—that the victim was the son of an LAPD homicide detective. De La Rosa wondered idly if he had also been a gang member.

The rumor was true. Bryant Tennelle was the son of an LAPD homicide detective. Wallace Tennelle, "Wally" to his peers, was a dozen years older than John Skaggs.

The two men were not acquainted. Tennelle worked downtown in

the Robbery-Homicide Division. The LAPD's personnel are scattered
across 470 square miles and scores of functions. Its social life is so bal-
kanized that people working in separate cubicles in the same squad
room sometimes do not know one another's names, and Skaggs and
Tennelle had never even worked in the same bureau. Nevertheless, they
were linked by a shared dark legacy and a battle to put things right.
Long before they met, a malignant wave, generations in the making,
had swept both of them up in its path, carrying them forward to the
moment when the son of one would be shot at the corner of Eightieth
and St. Andrews and the other would be called on to find the killer.

GHETTOSIDE

John Skaggs had been a redhead in his youth.

He was born in 1964 and was raised in a modest 1950s home in a Long Beach, California, subdivision that resembled those he would patrol as a cop later in Watts—one-story houses with single-car garages along streets lined with sycamores. His father was a Long Beach homicide detective, but his parents split when he was in elementary school. Skaggs was raised mostly by his mother.

Janice Skaggs was a coal miner's daughter from Nebraska, affectionate but stern. She placed great emphasis on fortitude and self-control in public. She had three other children to raise, and not much money. All four worked from an early age to help with family expenses. Without being asked, Skaggs paid rent for his bedroom as soon as he turned eighteen.

He was the youngest child and the only boy. He had been extremely competitive even as a child, a fervent athlete, especially in baseball. Winning had always been important to John Skaggs. His mother did not discourage this. But she had made it clear that the Skaggs children were always to appear mild, sportsmanlike, and well behaved. No matter how determined they were to prevail, they were to appear easygoing and civil.

He went to California State University at Long Beach but dropped out after one year. He found sitting in a classroom unbearable. Eventually, he followed his father's path into the police force. As Skaggs grew older, his mother's admonition stayed with him; he remained outwardly placid and inwardly exacting. Beneath his amiable grin lurked a perfectionist of the first order. He knew what would serve and what wouldn't. He didn't subject his insights to much examination. He didn't argue. He simply acted casual and bulldozed ahead.

By his forties, his thick, short-cropped hair was turning white, and the only clue that it had once been red was a tint of auburn in his eyebrows. Together with his pale blue eyes and pink complexion, it made him look like a natural blond—a beachy blond like someone who spent a lot of time in the California sun. His friends railed at the injustice. They got balder or grayer; Skaggs just got blonder. It was typical of the way good fortune seemed to follow him.

He had sharp cheekbones, a small round chin with a slight cleft, a furrow between his eyes, and big hands. His tall, rangy build hadn't changed much since his days on the uniform side of the LAPD ranks. More luck: middle-aged LAPD detectives were supposed to get portly, but John Skaggs still looked like "someone right out of *GQ* magazine," as one of his LAPD superiors put it. Skaggs occasionally put on the standard LAPD detective weight. But with the same discipline he applied to everything in his life, he cut back on eating, exercised more, and lost twenty pounds. What was hard about it? He never understood why other people had difficulty dieting.

He never called in sick. He never went to the doctor. His perfect physical condition went with the rest of it—the perfect children (a girl and a boy, naturally) and his wife, Theresa, who was as blond and beautiful as he was, the nice suburban house, the pool, the RV, the surfboards. Theresa was a legal secretary who managed a law office. As a couple they were organized, wholesome, mildly religious, and nice to each other; Skaggs had a rule against allowing antagonism of any kind to taint his family relationships. As for Theresa, she was strong-minded enough to hold her own against Skaggs's breezy certainty. "John is

John" is how she summed him up, an affectionate appraisal that comprehended how her husband's greatest strength—his incapacity for self-doubt—was also his greatest weakness.

Skaggs's confidence was limitless. But on paper, his career path did not seem especially distinguished. An uncle who was an LAPD deputy chief viewed him as a laggard. For years, he had faulted Skaggs's career choices, upbraiding his nephew over the phone. Why didn't he aspire to higher posts? Why had Skaggs allowed himself to stall out as a detective in the city's south end?

Los Angeles's nineteen police precincts were called divisions. It was understood that to advance, officers had to move beyond divisions to elite centralized units or administrative functions at the LAPD's downtown headquarters, Parker Center in those days, or "PAB," as the cops said—police administration building. Officers who stayed in the station houses were assumed to have less ambition, especially if they remained stuck in the south end.

At the level above divisions, the LAPD was divided into administrative quadrants. South Bureau was such a quadrant. It sat below an unofficial boundary—Interstate 10, the east-west freeway that stretched across the city—and encompassed the Southwest, Seventy-seventh Street, and Southeast stations. A Central Bureau division called Newton also sat mostly south of the Ten and bordered the Seventy-seventh to the north, along Florence Avenue. Together, these four stations covered the expanse of South Central.

For a police officer to work in any of those four stations was to be a little marginalized. They were L.A.'s poorest divisions, and they nearly always led the city in violent crime. Cops knew these places for their boxy apartments, chain-link fences, converted garages, bad dogs with no collars, and Chevy Caprices. They knew them for the men riding bicycles in street clothes, for the family-owned mortuaries, the flyers for hair braiding, the murals depicting Clorox bleach bottles, the shabby shops with exuberant names: Mantrap Nails, Sexy Donuts, Vanessa's Positive Energy. They knew what it meant to work in such neighborhoods. Many preferred not to.

Officers who chose to work south of the Ten were respected for their toughness. But the type of policing they did was not considered a launching pad for an ambitious career. In fact, hard-core south end cops were often seen as damaged goods in the LAPD, ruined for other work by the large number of complaints they generated and the narrow arena of policing they were perceived to occupy. Skaggs's uncle felt his nephew had limited himself by remaining in Watts.

Worst of all, in his uncle's view, Skaggs appeared content to remain a detective. This meant he languished for years at a professional grade equal to that of the lowest-level field sergeant. It meant he had voluntarily severed himself from the proudest traditions of the department. The LAPD had long measured its worth in patrol innovations, not investigative prowess. The TV drama *Adam-12* in the 1970s captured the LAPD's emblematic self-image—clean-cut, professional men in blue uniforms zipping around in their cars answering radio calls, sirens wailing. The LAPD uniform was saturated with meaning. It was a very dark, monochromatic navy blue—almost black—a regal shade. Departmental culture required that the uniform be worn like raiment, celestially clean and pressed with mirror-bright shoes and belts. Officers put a premium on looking sleek and fit; some even had the uniform custom-tailored to cling to sculpted biceps.

Detectives weren't part of this culture. Many workaday divisional detectives wore frumpy polo shirts and khakis. They were known for being out of shape. Homicide detectives such as Skaggs wore suits, of course. But late-night callouts kept them from getting enough sleep, so they often put on weight. Patrol officers were sometimes openly contemptuous of their plainclothes colleagues.

The structure and resource distribution of the department seemed to echo this contempt. In station houses, certain uniformed officers— gang specialists and so-called senior leads who specialized in community policing—occupied an elevated place, while detectives were consigned to backwater status, their desks placed alongside those of burglary detectives, competing for resources with curfew task forces and vice squads.

A few LAPD detectives worked in elite jobs downtown and enjoyed clout and prestige. An obvious choice for Skaggs might have been the Robbery-Homicide Division, or RHD. Housed at headquarters, RHD investigated cases deemed unusually complex or likely to draw media interest, including celebrity cases, massacres, and arson murders. RHD detectives were considered the department's best. They enjoyed low caseloads and were instantly recognizable in their elegant business attire. Their unit had been the subject of various books and television dramas.

But RHD tended to pass on the so-called ordinary street murders that Skaggs considered his specialty. Street murders constituted the bulk of black-on-black killings. So RHD's criteria ensured that black victims were less likely to get elite treatment from the LAPD. This was subtly offensive to detectives such as Skaggs, who did not view these murders as lacking in complexity. The policy offended his sense of fairness, too, for it seemed to confirm the accusation that every south end officer heard routinely from residents: "You don't care because he's a black man!"

Skaggs, of course, didn't say that this was why he had never applied for a promotion to RHD. In this and other matters, his innermost thoughts could only be deduced from his actions. When people suggested he go to RHD, he scoffed.

Cops who worked south of the Ten often seemed to revel in their underdog status. They looked down on cops from other bureaus, called them flabby and soft, and considered themselves of a higher order. One of Skaggs's colleagues picked up a word a Watts gang member used to describe his neighborhood: *ghettoside*. The term captured the situation nicely, mixing geography and status with the hustler's poetic precision and perverse conceit. It was both a place and a predicament, and gave a name to that otherworldly seclusion that all the violent black pockets of the county had in common—Athens, Willowbrook, parts of Long Beach, Watts. There was a sameness to these places, and the policing that went on in them. John Skaggs was ghettoside all the way. He never bothered to explain to his uncle how he felt. If other cops didn't see why his work mattered, why he was justified in being so very sure of himself, then Skaggs had no use for them. "It's Skaggs's world," his longtime partner Chris Barling would say with a roll of his eyes.

That phrase captured many of Skaggs's signature qualities—his dismissiveness, his self-contained optimism, his stark certainty that others sometimes took as arrogance. Most of all, it captured his internal ethos about policing, which allowed him to decide that real success was not the same as that defined by his police department, the public, society at large. To other cops, ghettoside was where patrol cars were dinged, computer keyboards sticky, workdays long, and staph infections antibiotic-resistant. To work down there was to feel a sense of futility, forgo promotions, and deal with all those stressful, dreary, depressing problems poor black people had. But to Skaggs, ghettoside was the place to be, the place where there was real work to be done. He radiated contentment as he worked its streets. He wheeled down filthy alleys in his crisp shirts and expensive ties, always rested, his sedan always freshly washed and vacuumed.

It was not because he relished difficulty that Skaggs embraced ghettoside work. He was not a lonely Marlowe and had no noir in his makeup. He was a sports enthusiast, a surfer, sunny and optimistic, a happily married family man. On weekends, he easily switched his focus to the family's RV and his desert racing bike. Skaggs preferred Watts for other reasons: he liked to be busy, and he believed his work there mattered and should be done well. He descended into the most horrifying crevasse of American violence like a carpenter going to work, hammer in one hand, lunch pail in the other, whistling all the way. He had molded his life around an urgent problem seldom recognized, and he was unshaken—perhaps even encouraged—by the fact that so many others didn't get it. He had a steady faith that things could improve with the right kind of effort.

That faith never left him, even after his work turned unexpectedly personal.

SCHOOL OF CATASTROPHE

Wally Tennelle was born in the coal-mining region of Jasper, Alabama, in 1954. Family lore held that an ancestor had been the illegitimate daughter of a house slave and a white plantation owner; that's where the family got their copper brown skin and hair.

His mother Dera's family was originally from Mississippi, but she spent her childhood in that Alabama coal country, always in near-complete segregation from whites. Wally's father, Baron Tennelle, aspired to better things. He and Dera were high school sweethearts. They married, had two sons, and headed out west in 1963, just before John Skaggs was born, part of the second great black migration from the South. Tennelle's father was high-energy, a hard worker and a natural salesman. In California, he parlayed a low-level job in the airline industry into a sales post. The family prospered. A third child, a daughter, was born in L.A.

From earliest childhood, Wally, the middle child, was decisive and organized, a stickler for neatness. To his mother's surprise, he would fold all his clothes, or tidy his room, without being asked. Dera felt deprived of the opportunity to nag him as a mother was supposed to.

Wally's cleanliness sprang from an inward orderliness of spirit that would define him all his life.

Wally finished high school and decided not to go to college. Instead, he joined the Marines and set his heart on a combat post in Vietnam. It was the last days of the war. He missed the window for combat deployment when his mother—not by accident, he realized later—took too long to send him the required certificate of baptism. He took another Marine post: a position as a guard at the U.S. embassy in Costa Rica.

Three weeks after he arrived in San Jose, Costa Rica, he entered a coffee shop across the street from the embassy and made one of the snap decisions that typified his life.

The Costa Rican girl at the counter was sixteen years old. Yadira Alvarado was from a farming family. Tennelle, then eighteen, spoke no Spanish, she no English. One of her coworkers had to ask her out for him. That first night at the movies, Yadira's thoughts were spinning. How to fill the silence? But Tennelle didn't seem to care. At the end of the evening, he dropped her off at the bus stop at her request. The next day, two dozen red roses were waiting for her at the coffee shop. On their next date, Tennelle surprised her with a few words of Spanish. They dated three years, and by the end of their courtship, he spoke Spanish fluently. She was nineteen when they married. He was twenty-two.

Their first home together was a military base in Cherry Point, South Carolina. Costa Rica had a racial context different from that of the United States. Yadira had no sense that she and Wally were what was called in the States a "biracial couple" until she noticed strange looks when they went out together. It was her first lesson in what she would later sum up as "this whole thing"—race in America.

After his run in the military was over, Wally and Yadira returned to his hometown, Los Angeles, where he found work as a Kmart security guard. He got a better job with his father's employer, United Airlines, lost it in a strike, and devised a new way to get by. He enrolled in El Camino Community College mainly for the financial aid check—he had little interest in being a student—and used the check to pay the rent and buy a lawn mower. He began working as a gardener.

Wally Tennelle would later say his decision in 1980 to become a police officer was just to earn a living. But Yadira remembers it differently. While she was still in Costa Rica, she said, Wally warned her that he wanted to be a police officer. He was giving her a chance to object. Yadira knew nothing of murder, nothing of the black asphalt war zone of South Central Los Angeles. But she probably wouldn't have objected anyway. Years later, their eldest daughter would observe that Wally and Yadira's mutual respect and independence were hallmarks of their very successful marriage. At home, they passed companionable hours, he more often outside, she within, each immersed in their separate occupations.

Wally and Yadira's first house in South Los Angeles was like their marriage: orderly and idyllic. In Costa Rica, Yadira saw young women courted by charming men who revealed a domineering side after marriage. Not Wally. Many people who knew him would remark on his consistency of character: he was the same person no matter the situation. Their house was pleasant and uncluttered. They never fought. Their daughter, named Dera for Wally's mother but known as DeeDee, knew how unlikely this sounded. But it was the truth: never had she seen her parents quarrel.

There were three children in all. After DeeDee came a son, Wallace, Jr., and then Bryant, born in September 1988. Yadira took a job in the kitchen at a Kaiser Permanente Hospital, working from 5:00 A.M. to 1:30 P.M. She remained there year after year, rising in the dark to put on her kitchen aide's smock. To her friends, it seemed a start-up job. They urged her to get her nursing degree. But Yadira loved the work, loved cooking, loved keeping busy.

The kids teased their parents for being boring. Privately, though, DeeDee had another word for them—*wholesome*. The word made her cringe. But it fit. They were like the Brady Bunch. Or, no, DeeDee corrected herself with a laugh: like "the Cosbys." After all, they were black. Sort of.

Racial identity was rarely discussed in the house. Wally Tennelle had somehow managed to grow up in South Central without ever having had a brush with violence or a negative encounter with police. He had been prevented by his mother from even wearing an Afro—and almost never talked of race. His conservative views on personal responsibility and self-improvement were typical of LAPD officers. To hear Wally Tennelle talk of the African American U.S. Rep. Maxine Waters, a frequent LAPD critic, was to hear the same frustrated grievances aired by just about every other cop in the city. In this respect, Wally Tennelle was blue before black.

In appearance, all three children bore strong resemblances to both their parents. But they looked different from one another. DeeDee was porcelain-skinned, with a dusting of light brown freckles over her nose, huge brown eyes, full lips, and wavy brown hair. She looked so white that, alone among the family members, she deliberately mispronounced her last name as "Te-NELL" instead of "Te-NELL-ee." That way, people would not assume she was of Italian descent.

Wally Jr. was darker-skinned, "copper tan" like his father, with clear dark eyes and dark brown hair. He spoke Spanish well and considered himself half Latino. "But if I'm in a hurry, I just say I'm black," he said.

Bryant was lighter than his brother, not as light as DeeDee. He was tall and slim, and his smooth complexion was the envy of his brother, who battled acne. But like Wally Jr., Bryant generally identified as black on the fly. In the end, because of where they grew up, because of some unspoken comprehension of a complex racial history, and because most of the biracial kids they knew did the same, all the children considered themselves black.

After a brief LAPD apprenticeship in Southeast, Wally Tennelle "wheeled" to jail division, then to narcotics, spending less time in patrol than is typical for new officers. He ended up in the Central Bureau CRASH unit in the early eighties. CRASH stood for "community resources against street hoodlums," a name that belonged to a bygone era of the LAPD, before reform efforts attempted to scrub out hints of wildness and bravado. The progression of gang squad names charted this evolution: an early special team of this type in the Seventy-seventh had been called PATRIOT. Then came the citywide units dubbed CRASH. Then, after a federal civil rights consent decree, they were relabeled with the anodyne GIT—"gang impact teams."

Tennelle's stint as a gang officer came in the midst of the great American homicide wave of the early eighties. It was the era of crack cocaine and rock houses and open-air drug markets. The young Marine veteran was in heaven. There could be nothing better than wearing that dark blue uniform, driving fast cars, and chasing gangsters around all night. He didn't want to do anything else—certainly not detective work. Everyone knew detectives were "a bunch of slugs," Tennelle recalled. He and his peers had a motto: "P-2 forever," for Police Officer II—that is, the die-hard street cops.

Then, in 1984, Tennelle was among a group of gang officers loaned out to the homicide unit to handle the high murder caseload, and he got his first homicide.

The qualities that make great homicide detectives are different from the qualities that make great patrol cops. But they are related. Wally Tennelle had a baseline of attributes that steer many young people toward police work. Although he was not college-educated, he was smart and energetic. Police work can be a haven for brainy, action-oriented people who do not, for some reason, gravitate toward formal education—the type afflicted with what DeeDee Tennelle diagnosed in her whole family as "a touch of ADD."

It made them uniquely suited for a job that was carried out almost entirely out of doors and involved sleepless nights, relentless bursts of activity, and the ability to move from one situation to the next quickly without leaving too much behind. A great cop—or a great detective— needed to be smart and quick, but not necessarily bookish or terribly analytical. A good memory, a talent for improvisation, a keen interest in people, and a buoyancy of spirit—one had to like "capering"—ensured that the hyperactive flourished in a job that left others wilting with stress.

Wally Tennelle had all these traits. But he had a few others that gave him an edge on even the better class of south-of-the-Ten cops. They were the same qualities that his mother had once noted: the preternatural neatness, the ability to control himself and the space around him, and the quiet certainty of his whole mien. Tennelle was an orderly thinker; he loved detail and was almost pathologically hardworking. He was also happy and had few if any personal demons. This latter trait was especially important. It gave him steadiness of purpose and stamina. Not surprisingly, when he worked that first homicide case, he was swept with the sense of certainty people experience when they discover what they were meant for in life. *Yeah,* he thought. *This is what I want to do.*

Tennelle worked as a homicide detective for Central Bureau CRASH until the late 1980s, and then he transferred to a divisional detective job in Newton. He worked as they all worked in those days—hammered by new cases, trying to slam together investigations that would stand up in court before the next one overwhelmed them, hoping they wouldn't founder in plea deals, which were much more common then. One weekend in the late 1980s, Tennelle was called to four murder scenes. Only at the fifth, he recalled, did the brass agree to summon a fresh team.

Along the way, Tennelle learned the homicide detective's creed from an early partner standing over the body of a murdered prostitute. "She ain't a whore no more," he said. "She's some daddy's baby." Wally Tennelle loved that philosophy. Whatever the wider world's response, the homicide detective's call was to treat each victim, no matter how deep their criminal involvement, as the purest angel. The murdered were inviolate. They all deserved the same justice. They were all *some daddy's baby.*

The city was entering what veteran detectives would thereafter refer to as "the Big Years." Homicides hit a high point in 1980, waned, then surged to a second peak in the early 1990s. In raw numbers, nothing like it had ever been seen before (though per capita rates of homicide were actually higher during the previous decade). In 1992, the homicide death rate for all Americans exceeded nine hundred per hundred thousand people. That is higher than in almost any other developed country. Among blacks, the picture was even starker: they died at about six times the rate of whites—just as they had in earlier eras and as they would after the Big Years. At the peak, the rate for the highest-risk blacks was off the charts. In 1993, black men in their early twenties in Los Angeles County died by homicide at a rate of 368 per 100,000 population, similar to the per capita rate of death for U.S. soldiers deployed to Iraq in the aftermath of the 2003 invasion.

Wally Tennelle earned the detective rank in 1990, right on the shoulder of the great wave. To "work homicide" in South Central L.A. in those days was to dwell in a demimonde the outside world could not comprehend.

It's one matter to contemplate what the scholar Randall Kennedy calls the "dismal statistics" related to black homicide—war zone death rates ten minutes from peaceful suburbs. It was another to watch the catastrophe unfold firsthand, as Tennelle would over the ensuing decade.

South Central then felt like another city, enclosed in invisible walls. The very air bore a tincture of grief. "Indescribable" was a word people used a lot: "So hard to describe, and even then, you can't smell it," a Watts detective said.

Choked silence, accompanied by that flat gaze one police chaplain called "homicide eyes," was perhaps the signature response people offered when asked to describe their experiences with violence. Eyes would stray midway through an explanation of a father's sudden obliteration, or a husband's slow, excruciating demise. An apologetic shake of the head would cut short an account of a son's maiming. Survivors who escaped gunfire trailed off into vanquished silence when talking of the friends who didn't. "There are no words," people often said.

Karen Hamilton, a bookkeeper from Jefferson Park, had still not spoken of her son's murder seven years after his death. She tried, drawing deep breaths, her hands shaking, but no voice came. Homicide grief may be a kind of living death. Survivors slog on, diminished, disfigured by loss and incomprehension.

For many family members, the nightmare begins with experiences most Americans associate only with war: the sudden, violent death of a loved one on the street outside your home. Parents and siblings are often first on the scene.

When eighteen-year-old Jamaal Nelson was shot, his mother ran outside, fell on her knees, and lifted his shirt to see his torso riddled with bullet holes. He rasped loudly and died in her arms.

Bobby Hamilton found his teenage son unconscious on the ground in a nearby park. The boy was breathing heavily, a bullet in the back of his head. Hamilton scooped him up like a baby and drove him to a fire station, where he died.

Other loved ones learned of the deaths from phone calls, or visits from police. A friend called Wanda Bickham to tell her that her nineteen-year-old son, Tyronn, had been shot and killed. Bickham slammed down the receiver, unable to hear it. Lewis Wright learned of his son's murder when an official at the coroner's office slid a photo across the table to him facedown. Heart pounding, he flipped it over to see his son's face. Sharon Brown spent the last moments of her thirteen-year-old son's life sitting still on a park bench outside the recreation center where he'd been shot, staying out of the paramedics' way. Later, she regretted it.

Immediately after the murders, many of the bereaved describe feeling mechanical and numb, their minds spinning, reflexively pushing agony away. At a funeral, one mother walked from her pew to her son's open casket like a robot, lifting each foot as if it carried a hundred-pound weight.

Realization comes slowly. Some people describe their worst spells of grief two, or five, or twenty years after the murder. "It's after. It's after.

It's after," Barbara Pritchett said, clenching her fists with anguish two years after Dovon's murder. Many people report being consumed by anger. "The whys," one bereaved father called it.

Some give in to despair. In the months after forty-two-year-old Charles Yarbrough was murdered, his mother, Anita McKiry, spent entire nights lying facedown, spread-eagled, on his grave. A Compton woman who had lost not one but two sons to homicide described herself as just "waiting to die." Carlton Mitchell, whose brother Paul was killed, took to walking dangerous streets hoping that he would be struck by gunfire like his brother.

Homicide could make pariahs of the bereaved. Family members described being shunned, as if their misfortune were catching. Sometimes it seemed that the closer people were to the problem, the more potent their distancing mechanisms. This distance could be heard in the evasive and often callous language used in black South Central to describe the phenomenon. One almost never heard the word "murder" on the streets. Euphemisms served instead: "puttin' in work," to "serve" someone, to "smoke" him, to "lay him out," to "light him up," to "take care of business"—the list went on. Bloods, Crips, and Hoovers had their own trademark verbs for attacking and hurting other human beings— "swoopin'," "movin'," "groovin'." The ubiquitous "whoopdee-woo-woo" and its many variations were all-purpose ellipses equally applicable to a minor spat or a massacre, depending on the context.

Chaotic public scenes of grief on streets and sidewalks were common. Mothers and grandmothers tried to bust through police tape. They threw themselves on victims' bodies, pummeling officers who held them back. Mini-riots sometimes broke out at crime scenes. Use-of-force cases erupted when police officers tussled with hysterical family members. In one case in Watts, a woman's son and relatives pressed around the car where she lay dying from a gunshot wound; officers pushed the mourners back by force, striking several with batons.

Outside the walled city, there prevailed a blander yet even more virulent form of callousness. It permeated officialdom, the media, the public rhetoric surrounding homicide. Very few of the bereaved were spared the sense that a wider world viewed their loss indifferently. "Nobody cares" was a universal lament south of the Ten during the Big Years, and for many years after. A threadbare, dismal, bureaucratic sense of routine surrounded the handling of homicides and related crimes. Officials were rushed and overburdened. One mother described learning of her son's death from a clerk in the hospital's property room who wordlessly handed her his shoes.

Very few murders were covered in the media. Television stations covered more than the papers, but without any particular consistency, and many, many deaths received no mention by any media outlet, especially if the victims were black. It rankled deeply. The lack of media coverage seemed to convey that black-on-black homicide was "small potatoes" in the eyes of the world, said a father who lost a daughter. "Nothing on the news!" a mother cried, weeping, at the sight of a journalist the day after her son was murdered. "*Please* write about it! *Please!*"

Even when cases got some public attention, the tilt often seemed off. Gangs were a big topic, but atrocity, trauma, and lifelong sorrow were not part of the public's vocabulary about black-on-black violence. Somehow, mainstream America had managed to make a fetish of South Central murders yet still ignore them. The principal aspect of the plague—agony—was constantly underrated.

Here, too, language was a battleground. More than one bereaved parent objected to terms such as "gang violence" as euphemistic, its purpose being to label their loved ones as throwaway people or otherwise diminish their standing as "innocent victims." Homicide activist LaWanda Hawkins, whose son was killed, summed up the objection: "'Gang member' is the new N-word," she said. Phrases such as "at risk" were worse, rolling victims and perpetrators into one indistinguishable mass. Vicky Lindsay grew so tired of palliating terms that she had a sticker made for her rear windshield: "My son was *murdered*," it declared.

Det. Brent Josephson, who worked in the Seventy-seventh Street station through the Big Years of the late 1980s and early 1990s, gave a name to the syndrome that ravaged the lives of many residents of South Bureau: he called it "the Monster." The name supplied a shorthand for

the whole mess—not just the pileup of homicides among a small group
of people, mostly black, and the unseen savagery of these crimes, but
also the indifference with which the world seemed to view them.

LAPD detectives had probably never been staffed adequately to handle the high levels of violence south of the Ten. But during the Big
Years, caseloads swelled to the point of ridiculousness, with so few detectives handling so many cases that the job came to resemble battlefield
surgery. Caseloads were at least twice what experts recommended for
many of those years, and ten times what RHD detectives would be assigned a decade and a half later. What detectives such as Tennelle did
during those years would never be repeated; his generation of homicide
detectives remains, to this day, unique in their exposure to the Monster.

They toiled ceaselessly, racking up overtime and divorces. Strokes
and heart attacks proliferated in their ranks. One detective in South
Bureau in the 1990s collapsed in the office. Yet the mountain of backlogged cases kept growing. "New cases piled on, and new cases piled
on," a detective named Jerry Pirro recalled a decade after the Big Years
peaked. "It got to the point where we were pretty much living at the
station. The phone would ring, and you'd cringe."

It was hard not to take it personally. Detectives felt they were fighting
an invisible war. By then, the notion of a lot of black and Latino drug
dealers and gangsters shooting each other down in the 'hood had become normal. It was often not news. "I remember a banner headline in
the *Los Angeles Times* one weekend," recalled a detective named Paul
Mize. "A bomb in Beirut had killed six people. We had nine murders
that weekend, and not a one of them made the paper. Not one." It was
aggravating, crazy-making. "You were dealing with problems and people that the majority of society doesn't want to think about—doesn't
want to deal with their tragedy and grief," a detective named John Gar-
cia recalled in the early 2000s, talking of his years in the Newton Division and South Bureau. "They are not the ones who have to knock on
that front door at two A.M. and say, 'Your loved one has been killed.'"

No one seemed to care. Mize recalled writing "poison-pen activities
reports" to superiors, begging for more resources. "I used to fly off the

handle and throw stuff around the room," he said. "I couldn't believe the decisions being made in Parker Center" by top police officials.

But to brass, detective work was "strictly reactive," as one high-ranking officer called it, dismissing the whole function. Crime prevention was seen as more progressive, and so competing priorities always seemed to win out over investigations: preventive patrol projects, gang sweeps. "Just all upside down," said a Newton homicide detective named Johnny Villa.

Law, of course, isn't like hygiene, and crime "prevention" inevitably leads to stereotyping people as potential threats. But "proactive" patrol work sounded better. Prevention carried an added bonus, as legal scholar Carol Steiker has noted: it gave police wide latitude, since the Constitution places many constraints on legal procedure *after* a crime, far fewer before it.

Despite the obstacles, many detectives brought battlefield dedication to the job in those years. But it was inevitable that the work would suffer. Cases were butchered; investigations were rushed, cursory, abandoned midway through. "You could have cases with viable leads, but you didn't have time to work them because fresh stuff was coming in," said a detective named Rick Marks, whose career spanned more than 160 cases.

The only thing that can be said for the crush was that it created a few unrivaled experts. Only a select number of homicide detectives in the country could claim the familiarity with homicide that the LAPD's South Bureau and Central Bureau "homicide experts" could. There were perhaps such detectives in New York, Detroit, Washington, D.C.— people who had learned their trade over years and scores of murders. Such detectives were experts less because of the variety of cases they worked than their sameness.

High-homicide environments are alike. The setting is usually a minority enclave or disputed territory where people distrust legal authority, as in South Los Angeles, where law had broken down in the Big Years and murder flourished. The killings typically arise from arguments. A large share of them can be described in two words: *Men fighting.* The fights might be spontaneous, part of some long-running feud, or the culmination of "some drama," as Skaggs would put it. These male "dramas," he observed, were not so different from those among quarreling women of the projects. In fact, they were often extensions of them. "Women work through men by agitating them to homicide," observed an anthropologist studying Mayan villages in Mexico. The observation fit scores of killings in L.A. that cops chalked up to "female problems."

The smallest ghettoside spat seemed to escalate to violence, as if absent law, people were left with no other means of bringing a dispute to a close. Debts and competition over goods and women—especially women—drove many killings. But insults, snitching, drunken antics, and the classic—unwanted party guests—also were common homicide motives. Small conflicts divided people into hostile camps and triggered lasting feuds. Every grudge seemed to harbor explosive potential. It would ignite when antagonists met by chance, gunfire erupting in streets or liquor stores. Vengeance was a staple motive. In some circles, retaliation for murder was considered all but mandatory. It was striking how openly people discussed it, even debating the merits from the pulpit at funerals.

From antiquity, the "men fighting" problem—men killing one another to settle disputes or exact revenge in the absence of a trusted legal authority—has confounded thinking people.

It would be too sweeping to assert that lawless peoples are all alike. But it's impossible to ignore that across historic and cultural settings, there appears to be a common palette of adaptations to lawlessness.

Loose talk and rumors are particular aggravators. Canadian Inuits fought over "chronic lying," the Sudanese over "volatile conversation," and Jim Crow blacks over "gossip and whispering." Revenge and jealousy murders are standard. So are reprisals against snitches who serve a distrusted state—"touts" kneecapped in Northern Ireland, informants necklaced in South Africa. Gangs that declare an order-keeping role— like the murderous neighborhood watches of Ghana—are another sure sign that a vacuum of legitimate authority has been filled by extralegal violence. So is the habit of grabbing one's friends from police, as people do in South African townships.

Witnesses in such contexts are scared. Men act touchy. They fixate on honor and respect—a result of lawlessness, not a cause. Petty quarrels grow lethal, and may mask deeper antagonisms. And arson, for some reason, gets a starring role—in czarist Russia, gold rush settlements in Alaska, and the sharecropping regions of the South.

In the dim early stirrings of civilization, many scholars believe, law itself was developed as a response to legal "self-help": people's desire to settle their own scores. Rough justice slowly gave way to organized state monopolies on violence. The low homicide rates of some modern democracies are, perhaps, an aberration in human history. They were built, as the scholar Eric Monkkonen said, not by any formal act, but "by a much longer developmental process whereby individuals willingly give up their implicit power to the state."

There are many challenges to this viewpoint, and many variations on it. But history shows us that lawlessness is *its own kind of order.* Murder outbreaks, seen this way, are more than just the proliferation of discrete crimes. They are part of a whole system of interactions determined by the absence of law. European history offers a panoply of rough justice systems based on personal vengeance, blood feuds, shaming rituals, and sundry forms of retributive and clan violence. Frequent homicide was a part of this picture. High homicide rates have also been recorded among hunter-gatherer peoples and other societies without elaborate legal structures.

Tellingly, the syndrome also crops up among isolated minorities alienated from the state, frontiersmen, and occupied peoples—any place, really, where formal authority is patchy or distrusted. Thus, some Indian tribes in Canada and the U.S. have disproportionate homicide rates, as do ethnic and immigrant enclaves in Switzerland, England, Wales, and Italy. In the peaceful Netherlands, non-Dutch ethnics suffer many times the homicide rate of their Dutch compatriots. Eighteenth-century rates among settlers on the wild edge of the American colonies were almost exactly those of South Central blacks in the twenty-first century. In the town of Tira, Israel, today, Arab citizens of Israel also suffer a homicide rate similar to that of black South Central. They blame the Israeli police in terms that would sound familiar to John Skaggs: "As long as it's Arabs killing Arabs, they just don't care," one resident said.

It's like a default setting. Wherever human beings are forced to deal with each other under conditions of weak legal authority, the Monster lurks. The ancient Greeks wrote of the Furies, hideous black gorgons who held grudges and rasped, "Get him, get him, get him." They could be subdued only by law.

To solve cases in such contexts, homicide detectives had to be schooled in folkways. They had to understand secret slang and symbolic affronts and maneuver through the endless nicknames and aliases. They had to understand people's fear of being labeled "snitches." They had to be able to unravel the tangle of relationships surrounding each case— that dense weave of homeys, "fiancés," baby daddies, and road dogs.

The homicide detectives had to learn how to pull bureaucratic levers rusted shut from years of indifference, had to work fast and effectively, juggling multiple cases. Putting together a ghettoside murder case wasn't a linear task—one clue leading to another, then another, like in all those TV shows. It required investigators to move side to side and backtrack, like spiders weaving webs. Witnesses lied, recanted, or disappeared. Their stories were usually inconsistent. Successful cases were spun from intersecting points of corroboration, not straight-line narratives.

Finally, the detectives who learned their craft in those years came to know the profound grief of homicide, the most specialized knowledge of all. They knew the way the bereaved struggled to function hour by hour. They knew about good days and bad days. Good detectives said to family members, "I can't possibly know how you feel." The best didn't have to say it. Years of such work endowed practitioners with an almost spiritual understanding of their craft. A detective named Rick Gordon, for example, still working in South Bureau as of this writing, had come to view the moral dimensions of his cases so profoundly that he talked of them in almost religious terms, talked as if their outcomes were predestined. Something *put* witnesses there, Gordon would say— something bigger than themselves. Humility was his doctrine—the ability to remain open, to let evidence speak. To discern liars but also to trust those who appeared to be lying but weren't.

Wally Tennelle would become one of this elite, the small, unrecognized cadre of superdetectives schooled by catastrophe.

At Newton, Wally Tennelle was paired with Kelle Baitx, a gruff black-Irish midcareer man from Orange County.

Baitx and Tennelle established a division of labor. Baitx would process the crime scene. Tennelle, with his fluent Spanish, would melt away into the crowd, migrating to the fringes of the crime scene or into adjoining streets. Inevitably, he would talk to someone the patrol officers had missed, would hit upon some tidbit of information that everyone else had overlooked. Baitx thought Tennelle's ability to canvass was uncanny. He would hardly notice his partner's perambulations, but somehow, at the end of the day, witnesses would be flushed from the brambles.

Tennelle projected competence without being intimidating. He was compact, not tall but broad-shouldered, with guileless brown eyes and a lined forehead. The lines formed a series of arches to his hairline and lent his whole face a kindly look. Altogether, in a job that was all about people skills—finding witnesses, persuading them to talk—he excelled.

The dizzying homicide peak of 1992 was upon them. Baitx and Tennelle worked an astonishing twenty-eight cases that year, almost three times the recommended caseload. Tennelle thrived on it, loving the adrenaline, loving the hard work. Baitx noticed something else about Tennelle: when other cops went out drinking after work, Tennelle would go home to his family. Baitx and Tennelle were close, but Baitx only rarely saw Tennelle's wife and his three young children. Baitx understood that when Tennelle wasn't working, he preferred his home life, wanted to be with Yadira and the kids, puttering around the house. Tennelle rarely talked about work. At home, DeeDee Tennelle was hardly aware that her father was a homicide detective until once, as a child, she made a secret discovery of autopsy photos in a drawer.

CLEARANCE

John Skaggs was twenty-two when he entered the police academy in 1987, starting out as Tennelle was entering his journeyman years.

After the academy, Skaggs was assigned to the Seventy-seventh Street Division for a mandatory probation period as a patrol officer. He would spend most of the rest of his career either in South Bureau or gaming the system to try to return to a post in South Bureau. He was in his element in those violent years, a tall, athletic, red-haired officer with easy confidence and a serene temperament who immersed himself in learning the politics of street life.

Wally Tennelle had been conscripted as a young gang officer to clean up after the first great wave a decade before. Now John Skaggs was conscripted to clean up after the second. In the first three years of the 1990s, that savage period spanning the riots, more than six thousand people died from homicides in Los Angeles County.

In 1994, Skaggs was recruited "on loan" as an officer trainee over at South Bureau Homicide. Skaggs was not a detective. He was a P-3 then, or field training officer. This is still done in the LAPD: patrol and gang officers are recruited to fill slots as homicide detectives without the rank. The written and oral tests used to promote officers to detective emphasize general procedures and departmental policies, not the singular abilities that distinguish good homicide investigators. Those cannot be measured by formal exams, and cops who tested well often had no talent for working murders. So homicide supervisors, weary of being stuck with underperforming employees, preferred to bypass the official promotion system and scout their own talent.

It was not surprising that John Skaggs would be tapped. He was the kind of energetic young officer who typically did well in homicide units. But when asked to work South Bureau Homicide, the combined squad that then covered Southwest, Southeast, and the Seventy-seventh, Skaggs resisted. He did not want to work as a homicide detective, even temporarily. He loved his hard-charging job as a gang officer. Detectives were washouts. But it would have looked bad to refuse.

Years later, asked why he had known from his first days as a homicide detective that he never wanted to do anything else, Skaggs gave a curious answer. He did not say he loved investigating homicides. He simply said that when one discovers one is good at a task at which few others excel, one has no choice.

"I could do it," Skaggs said when pressed. "*I could do it.* Who else can?"

Skaggs's father had always said little about his choices. Now he had just one comment for the son who set out to follow his own path to homicide work: "Be careful," he told Skaggs. "Because nothing else matters after working murders." Only later would Skaggs comprehend the full weight of this remark.

Skaggs was paired with a training officer. But the high workload broke down the usual conventions, and Skaggs, though often an acting detective, was often relegated to working on his own. He solved his first case. Then the next. Each taught him a little more.

Early on, he was given a six-month-old "cold case" and asked to see if he could breathe new life into it. (In those days, "cold" could mean a case only weeks old.) The victim was Leo Massey, a workingman who had stopped by a liquor store on his way home from work. He was panhandled for beer by another black man. Massey refused the panhandler, who attacked him as he walked out. The panhandler shot Massey through the leg and Massey bled to death.

Massey was a father and husband. By the time Skaggs got the case, Massey's wife, Glory, was furious. She had heard rumors about the killer within days. Everyone seemed to know who did it. Everyone except the police, that is. Glory Massey had no doubt in her mind that if Leo had been white instead of black, the police would have solved his murder.

Skaggs met her in the bureau's office at the Crenshaw Mall. Massey had developed piercing back pain from grief. She was angry. She believed the authorities didn't care, and she feared that one of her teenage sons—or some other young man from their neighborhood—would be tempted to retaliate. Now here was yet another LAPD detective claiming interest in the case. Massey was losing patience with it—these people called themselves professionals, yet they allowed teenage boys to do their work for them, to seek justice where the state had failed to secure it.

She sized up Skaggs. Great, another tall white LAPD cop—"nine foot eight or something!" Massey said later—and she was determined not to be intimidated. She brought her face as close as she could to his despite her own small stature. It meant looking almost straight up at him. Then she let him have it, all her pent-up frustration. "He's just another fuckin' black man now, right?" Massey screamed at Skaggs. *"Just another fuckin' black man down!"*

Skaggs didn't protest. He just listened.

When she ran out of breath, he began asking questions. Later, he came to see her again. He called, and came again, checking up on her, asking about her children.

Glory was not the only one who sensed that many people knew the killer. "Everybody knows" was one of the most common phrases voiced about homicides in South Central. Lots of people had heard about the shooting, and some recognized the suspect, who was a regular around the neighborhood. But even when Skaggs pressed, they offered conflicting names. "Jamal," some said. "Jabar," said others. No one seemed to know who the violent panhandler really was or where he lived.

Skaggs walked and knocked, asked and asked. He ended up searching a garage where a man who fit the panhandler's description was "staying." He noticed a fingerprint on a mirror and got lucky. His longtime partner Chris Barling would later observe how often it seemed that Skaggs made his own luck. Skaggs yanked at the mirror, and a driver's license with the man's picture, birth date, and full name—Jabbar Stroud—dropped from behind it. It remained only to have the witnesses confirm it.

Skaggs drove Glory Massey to the trial himself and warned her to leave the chambers before gruesome photos were displayed. She had grown to like him, and he her. He was so unperturbed by her initial rage that he didn't remember it afterward. By then he was long used to being admonished as a callous white racist cop. He had already heard many versions of "another black man down." It was part of the job—an enduring theme of ghettoside work   and he shrugged it off. They always thought he didn't care.

The sense that the police—and the larger city—didn't care was not just a cliché. It was the lived experience of South L.A.'s black residents, quantified by data. Society had changed a great deal during the civil rights movement and the decades that followed it. Criminal justice had changed, too. But the speed and certainty of adequate punishment for the murderers of black men remained a weak point.

Historically, the nation had never been very good at punishing murderers, no matter the victim. In nineteenth-century New York only about a tenth of all murders resulted in a conviction. Less than half did in Philadelphia and Chicago at the end of that century. These patterns probably continued well into the twentieth century. In Los Angeles, for example, a suspiciously large percentage of homicides—more than a

quarter of them—were not even counted for purposes of criminal investigation in the 1920s and 1930s. Some were probably killings by police. Other cases seem to have been shelved due to dead or absolved
suspects. Standards were clearly different: a 1925 *Los Angeles Times* arti-
cle applauded two killers who had hunted down a mugger after the fact,
noting approvingly that police did not think the act merited arrest. The
killers "had merely taken the law into their own hands," the paper
opined.

In subsequent decades, officials claimed to solve homicide cases at
very high rates. But California prison rolls tell a different story. During
the 1960s, the number of people sent to prison for criminal homicide
was less than half the number of homicides. The disparity grew more
pronounced during the 1970s, when there were three times more people
killed than killers convicted and imprisoned. There seems to be no other
conclusion but that thousands of murders went unpunished.

Federally reported clearance rates—the rate of cases solved per
crimes committed—are inflated, partly because they combine arrests
with cases LAPD cops called "cleared other," investigations declared
closed although no one has been prosecuted. Cases could be "cleared"
because the suspects were dead, sometimes killed in revenge murders.
Even with this inflation, by the 1990s, the reported rate for urban areas
had fallen to about 50 percent. Not surprisingly, a *Los Angeles Times* investigation found that the real rate was even lower. The study, based on
case-by-case analysis of 9,400 Los Angeles County cases in the early
nineties, concluded suspects were convicted of manslaughter or murder
in only about one in three killings. Clearance rates varied by race, with
cases involving black and Hispanic victims somewhat less likely to be
solved than those involving white victims. Killers of whites received the
harshest penalties. These findings echoed those of other research into
"victim discounting." Death penalty studies, for example, have found
that the race of defendants matters less than the race of victims. People
who kill whites are more likely to be sentenced to death; people who kill
blacks get lighter penalties.

The pattern persisted after the crime drop. From 1994 to 2006, a suspect was arrested in 38 percent of the 2,677 killings involving black male victims in the city of Los Angeles, according to the police department's own data. Even with "cleared others" included in the count, solve rates remain less than half. In L.A. County, a much larger area, similar patterns prevailed. The result was that unsolved homicides in South L.A. numbered in the thousands—an average of more than 40 per square mile piled up during the decade and a half between the late 1980s and early 2000s.

Maiming people offered even better odds. There were about four or five injury shootings for every fatal one in South Los Angeles. A waggish colleague of Skaggs called these shootings—which injured but did not kill their victims—*almocides*, for "almost homicides." High-crime precincts were racked by them. Some thirty almocides occurred each month in the nine square miles of the Southeast Division in the early 2000s, for instance. People—disproportionately black men—were left paralyzed, comatose, brain injured, or forced to spend the rest of their lives using colostomy bags. Officially, some 40 percent of these aggravated assaults were "cleared." But half of those were not arrests. They were "cleared others," usually because victims refused to testify. Among "category one" assaults in Watts in 2004, for example—serious injury cases—only about 17 percent ended with an assailant convicted.

The atmosphere this created was in the air Glory Massey breathed. Beneath the most serious unsolved and unprosecuted assaults thrummed an ocean of lesser crimes, often unreported ones. People were punched and kicked. Cars were shot up. Apartments were ransacked. Molotov cocktails were thrown into houses—a legal act for all practical purposes: overburdened fire department investigators recorded hundreds of arsons a year in Los Angeles in the late 2000s.

Verbal threats were rampant. Symbolic affronts and sexually tinged humiliations reinforced them. Petty burglaries, "pocket checks," the breaking of gold chains, the pulling down of pants—such acts carried a tacit threat of mortal violence to those who didn't heed their messages. Being "jumped" and "beat down" were part of the everyday vocabulary of the streets. "Caught slippin'" meant letting your guard down—a momentary slip could kill you. "Catch a fade" meant a fight. The gang term "DP" was an acronym for "discipline." It meant roughing someone up to punish him for something.

These crimes set the stage for later murders. "It's on Grape! I'll be back!" a girl yelled upon fleeing an unreported beat-down. Three weeks later, one of the men who had punched her was murdered, and the Grape Street Crips were the suspects. An out-of-bounds ball on a basketball court sparked a fight; afterward the loser's friends pressured him: "You need to drop that fool," they said. "Take care of business!" He obeyed, and days later killed the victor.

Black residents in the area had long complained not just of mistreatment by police, but also that the cops did little to catch the killers and violent assailants in their midst. It was a historic grievance. When the Swedish social scientist Gunnar Myrdal studied the black South in the 1940s, he found that, despite rampant complaints about law enforcement, black Southerners everywhere also said they wanted *more* policing—to protect them from other black people.

South Bureau officers heard some version of the lament several times a day: "It ain't like I'm out here doin' something. I'm just cruisin'!" a young woman named Tamala Brown sputtered, facing down a pair of Seventy-seventh officers who caught her driving without a seatbelt in 2005. "What about all these other people out actually *doin'* something?" No one seemed to hear that last part—no matter how urgently black people said it. Legal scholar Randall Kennedy was a lonely voice among his peers when he asserted that "the principal injury suffered by African-Americans in relation to criminal matters is not overenforcement but underenforcement of the laws." Glory Massey did not need to be told.

Years later, describing the experience of having Skaggs investigate her husband's death, she said that when Skaggs took over the case, "it was like how your own brothers would go and look for the guy, you know?" In her mind, Skaggs had substituted the state's intervention for communal justice, and Massey was deeply grateful. She believed Skaggs's aggressive work on her husband's case had probably averted another homicide.

Seven years later, Glory Massey's eldest son, Damon, was also murdered.

In the depths of her grief, Glory Massey thought about John Skaggs. Skaggs had been assigned elsewhere by then. No suspect was arrested in Damon's case. Years went by; no one contacted Glory. Her son's murder remains unsolved as of this writing. In response to inquiries, a man on her street said simply: "Someone took care of it."

6

THE CIRCUMSTANTIAL CASE

As young John Skaggs was trying out as a South Bureau trainee, Wally Tennelle remained working on the north side of the invisible administrative boundary of Florence Avenue. He was well on his way to becoming one of the Central Bureau's master craftsmen. Tennelle had by then worked scores of cases.

Tennelle and Baitx worked as partners for five years in the Newton Division. Up at RHD—the prestige division downtown—supervisors in search of talent homed in on Tennelle. They tried to recruit him. But Tennelle refused an RHD assignment on principle. He was still at heart a hard-driving south end copper who loved to be busy. On some level, he knew he was born to chase the lowly, frustrating gang cases they disdained up at headquarters.

And there was something else: a question of fairness. Wally Tennelle was no leftist, but the phrase "some daddy's baby" translated to an issue of social justice that he couldn't help taking to heart. The well-heeled had superior policing, he believed. "The poor people down here never get anything, and they need good detectives," he said.

The LAPD, however, did not have the same priorities. The institution was not geared to channeling its best talent to detective tables down in the Newton Division. Talented municipal employees are expected to advance. Plus, Tennelle was due for a pay raise and had three kids in private school. Without really understanding all its implications, he allowed himself to go through the process of oral and written exams and was boosted to the rank of D-3, detective III, or supervisor.

Promotion requires transfer in the LAPD. Tennelle was shifted out of homicide and into a supervisory position in a different unit in Newton, overseeing a "table" of detectives investigating domestic violence and rape cases. Ostensibly, such detective tables are supposed to conduct interviews and track down suspects. But in the ghettoside divisions of the LAPD, investigation of relatively low-level crime was afforded so little manpower that, in essence, these jobs become paper pushing. Detectives have no time to interview people, and in the arena of domestic violence and rape—the latter, like the former, overwhelmingly committed within families or among acquaintances—huge numbers of victims refused to testify in court. The detectives under Tennelle's command were mostly reduced to filling out forms and meeting administrative deadlines. Tennelle had inadvertently trapped himself in the most dreaded assignment imaginable, a desk job. His whole nature rebelled.

"You could just tell he was miserable," Baitx recalled. He had never before heard his old partner complain. Tennelle told his old boss he was thinking of quitting. The boss urged him to hang in there—he would get used to it. But Tennelle knew his own mind.

He endured six months for appearance's sake. Then he learned of one homicide D-2 spot open. It meant a demotion—he would lose his D-3 rank—and it was in RHD, where he had never wanted to be. But at least it was a real investigative job, not one that just went through the motions.

To the annoyance of his captain, Tennelle took the demotion, and in 1999—in horrified flight from the stacks of paper that piled up on the sex crimes table—he ended up at RHD.

He had accepted a 7 percent pay cut to make the switch. It took him seven years to work his way back. But it was worth it: he was back in an action-focused investigative job chasing killers, and he was happy again.

Baitx was amazed. He had never known anyone in the money-obsessed ranks to willingly take a demotion and pay cut.

Except for the voluntary demotion, Tennelle's ascent through the department in those years paralleled the experience of many south end cops. In one respect, however, Wally Tennelle was idiosyncratic, even a little radical. He lived in the Seventy-seventh Division.

Among LAPD officers, the proscription against living in the city of Los Angeles went without saying. It was something that had long annoyed various liberal critics of the department. For years, most officers in the department had refused to live in the city they policed and instead commuted into the city from distant suburbs. They formed little red-state bastions sprinkled around the five-county area of Southern California—Santa Clarita and Simi Valley to the north, Chino and as far as Temecula to the east, and Orange County to the south. But with a few exceptions, such as San Pedro, a historic enclave of ethnic whites, Los Angeles was considered off-limits, the length and breadth of this beautiful city disdained by its police.

Of course, for many stripes of public employees, including teachers and firefighters, living in Los Angeles was difficult because the city had developed a stark rich-poor split, and moderately priced homes in low-crime neighborhoods were hard to come by. LAPD cops worked odd hours, so the long freeway drives that would have been prohibitive for rush-hour commuters were feasible for them.

How much racial prejudice weighed into this choice depended on what was meant by the term, since a majority of officers were themselves minorities. Anyway, their attitudes were too paradoxical for such a coarse summation: LAPD cops had a tendency to voice disgust about the neighborhoods of central Los Angeles, then defend them in the next breath.

Mostly, though, officers understood what outsiders did not: that nearly every part of their jobs involved conflict, very personal conflict. To police the 'hood was to encounter a daily barrage of wrath. The idea of being followed home or confronted in one's own neighborhood was terrifying. So for years the department's critics complained that cops didn't live in the city, and for years the cops declined to do so.

But not Wally Tennelle. He lived not just in the city, but in the Seventy-seventh Division. While it was true that the Seventy-seventh—unlike Southeast—had many pockets of nice middle-class homes, it remained either the first or second most violent division in the city, year in and year out, and its eleven square miles included the territories of several of the city's most violent black street gangs. The fact that Wally Tennelle chose to live there was a source of wonderment to his colleagues, and fueled sotto voce commentary behind his back: "It was common knowledge" that Tennelle lived in the Seventy-seventh, said his RHD lieutenant, Lyle Prideaux, "and a lot of people didn't think it was real wise." Kelle Baitx, however, resented it whenever he heard that kind of talk. He had visited Tennelle's home, knew how well kept and comfortable it was, and saw that the neighborhood was also "nice." He himself had bought a house in El Sereno—another "nice" but distinctly urban, and mostly Hispanic, neighborhood near the city's core—and sent his children to private school, just as Tennelle did. Baitx had traveled once with Tennelle to Alabama in pursuit of a suspect, and Tennelle had used the occasion to visit his family's old home, a six-hundred-square-foot box with wood siding used, at the time of their visit, as a crack house. Baitx knew how poor Tennelle's parents had been, how humble his roots, and how far the family had come. Tennelle should be able to live wherever he wanted, Baitx thought.

For Tennelle, the choice was easy. The neighborhood was home; it was near where he grew up, where his mother still lived. He had bought a home he could afford when he was a young cop, and had what he called "a wild-ass dream: that my children only know one home."

Not that there weren't difficulties. When the Tennelles first moved in, an apartment building down the street was a hub for drug deals. A dealer once stood in Tennelle's driveway and conducted a transaction as Tennelle, who had served briefly as a narcotics cop, was mowing the grass a few feet away. Perhaps the dealer had a faulty antenna for cop detection; more likely he was caught slippin' because it had never occurred to him that a cop would live on his street. Tennelle called 911 and had him arrested.

Later, Tennelle wrote a 3.18 narcotics report on the building and offered his home as an "OP," or observation post, and the problem swiftly abated. After that, the Tennelles enjoyed the area. They were fond of their neighbors. Tennelle's commute was a neighborhood hop—few Angelenos have it so good. Tennelle could respond to homicide callouts in Newton division within minutes, unlike most detectives who lost most of the first critical hour because it took them so long to get there. His neighborhood had sidewalks, mature trees, well-tended yards, and adorable 1930s-vintage homes—some of them gingerbread style. Fresh sea breezes waft through this part of L.A., palm trees sway, and although the section lies in the flight path of LAX, it's far enough from the runway that the sound of descending planes is not too bothersome. You didn't have to be from the Frisco side of Jasper, Alabama, to appreciate this neighborhood; it was objectively and inarguably, as Baitx put it, "nice."

Tennelle's neighbors knew he worked for the LAPD. He did not apologize for being a cop; he had always treated people with deliberate respect, on the job and off, and he defied the world to make him ashamed. "I've run into my share of people I've arrested," he said, "and I can look them in the eye." Shirking off to live in the suburbs felt somehow dishonorable to Wally Tennelle. "I'm home here. I'm not gonna let anybody run me out," he said.

And more people wanted him there than not—this was made quickly clear. When word got around that there was a cop on the block, neighbors came to his doorstep with all kinds of troubles. Cops didn't live in the neighborhoods they policed because they feared all those suspects. But perhaps what they should really have feared was all the *victims*. Wally Tennelle soon discovered that his neighborhood embraced him— perhaps more than he bargained for—but he accepted the role with good grace and did his best to help his neighbors with their problems.

*   *   *

About the same time that Wally Tennelle went to RHD, John Skaggs was finally earning a promotion to the lowest rank of detective, D-1.

Skaggs was subject to the same promotional rules as Tennelle. Thus, earning the rank to do what he was already doing meant he would no longer be allowed to do it. Just as Tennelle's reward for advancement was a sentence on the Newton sex crime table, Skaggs was transferred out of homicide and sentenced to a narcotics table in the LAPD's Pacific Division in Venice, a low-crime area along the beach.

It was unendurable.

At last, a post opened for a "gang" detective on a South Bureau task force in the Seventy-seventh Street Division. It was not quite what Skaggs wanted. But at least it was south of the Ten, investigating crimes involving human victims, and unlike Tennelle, he didn't have to demote himself to make the switch.

A reprieve came with a new boss: Detective Sal La Barbera, a homicide supervisor who had first noticed Skaggs when the latter was still a young red-haired gang officer. La Barbera was just seven years older than Skaggs, but he had been a detective a lot longer. He had remained in ghettoside units longer than almost anyone he knew, passing on promotions and watching his peers advance. Dark-haired, with rawboned Italian good looks and a spray of acne scars over each cheek, La Barbera cut a romantic figure, an image he deliberately cultivated. He was not the devil-may-care loner he pretended to be. He did not do well alone, nor was he indifferent to the opinions of others. La Barbera was moody, easily hurt, forever trusting someone only to feel betrayed later. Various relationships had foundered in bad blood.

Over the years, the job had burdened La Barbera with a hounded, slightly paranoid demeanor. He'd gone on so many late-night homicide callouts that he had lost the ability to sleep through the night. His family relations were stressed, perhaps fatally so. He suffered from depression. Some colleagues disliked him, calling him two-faced. His manner didn't

help. He appeared most easygoing when he was put out, and he pretended to be joking when he wasn't. But he wasn't a liar. La Barbera said
what he meant most of the time—just in a very quiet voice. If you paid
close attention, you weren't deceived.

La Barbera's fractured personal life and internal contradictions
came oddly packaged with inimitable professional consistency. He had
a vision. He believed in his craft—believed unreservedly in the idea of
homicide investigation as a cause. He believed that the state articulated
its response to violence by apprehending those who committed it, and
that failing to do so sent an unmistakable message the other way—that
violence was tolerated, especially when the victims were poor black
men.

His theory was, he admitted, "a circumstantial case." But La Barbera's observations over the years in South Los Angeles had convinced
him that catching killers *built law*—that successful homicide investigations were the most direct means at the cops' disposal of countering the
informal self-policing and street justice that was the scourge of urban
black populations. La Barbera had character flaws. But his views on
homicide belonged to an elevated plane of ethical reasoning.

This made him an oddity. In truth, a lot of police had only the fuzz-
iest idea what they were there for, aside from the most basic, traditional
function of answering calls, dealing with them, and going "Code Four"
on the radio—"situation under control." There was amazingly little discussion of the craft of policing, and no consensus on what constituted
good police work versus bad.

Cops were told they were supposed to "be proactive," focus on "suppression," or practice "crime control." Showered in such nonsensical
orders and jargon, they couldn't really be blamed for struggling to
find purpose in their work. Officers drove around, conducted consent
searches, ran license plates, drove some more. It could feel quite pointless. It didn't help that even as they were supposedly held to high standards and expected to display the skill and initiative of trained
professionals, many so-called innovative policing strategies tended to
reduce them to cogs.

There was a lot of emphasis on police being "visible" and on strategically deploying them to targeted neighborhoods based on crime trends. But exactly what officers were supposed to do once they got to a so-called target neighborhood was left a little vague. The omission contained a disturbing implication: that a bunch of blue uniforms stuffed with straw might be able to perform the same function rather well, and for a lot less money.

New LAPD directives in the 2000s drove this home. One involved planting "decoy" patrol cars on high-crime streets. The empty, parked black-and-whites were supposed to scare would-be criminals into thinking actual officers might be nearby. Even worse for self-respecting police officers, the brass instituted a practice of assigning a pair of officers to drive around aimlessly in a patrol car with red lights flashing. Higher-ups viewed this as clever and progressive. The idea was to give criminals a sense that cops were on high alert. But when officers learned in roll call that their shift duties would involve no real work—that instead, they were to toodle around ridiculously under a flashing red light—their faces registered unmistakable insult.

If you asked most LAPD patrol officers why they chose to be cops, they would shrug and answer vaguely: "To help people." It was a little poignant. Cops enjoyed good pay and lavish pensions. But many seemed to really want to be do-gooders without really knowing how.

Sal La Barbera did not have this problem. He had a clarity of purpose that guided all his actions. Because of what he believed, he knew precisely what his mission was and why it was important every single day of his working life. He managed an array of priorities, all of which were harmonized in his mind with clear, long-term goals and a deep understanding of the problem he sought to conquer. All in all, he represented a consistency and integrity that was missing from the criminal justice system he worked within. And if he didn't seem to be the sort of man to carry that standard, well, that only confirmed Rick Gordon's doctrine that sometimes the people who appear least truthful are the ones telling the starkest truths.

The decade of the 1990s was over. Crime was dropping. South Bureau Homicide was disbanded and replaced by divisional homicide squads in each of three South Bureau station houses. La Barbera was put in charge of one of them: the Southeast Homicide squad in Watts.

Over the years, he had watched Skaggs develop as an investigator.

The two men did not work together directly at South Bureau Homicide, but La Barbera was familiar with Skaggs's style. He knew Skaggs did not procrastinate or putter around the office, spending too much time on computers. He was nearly always outside, moving, talking, making face-to-face connections with people, confronting them over and over, returning to places where he had been roughly turned away. Shortly after settling into his new unit, La Barbera recruited Skaggs.

Skaggs, for his part, sensed in La Barbera someone who believed in the work and its higher purpose. He leaped at the opportunity. So began the next phase of his career, at last a full-fledged homicide detective.

7

GOOD PEOPLE AND KNUCKLEHEADS

In 2000, the nine square miles of Watts were home to about 130,000 people, 39 percent of them black. Nearly everyone else in the Southeast Division was Hispanic, including many brand-new Mexican, Salvadoran, and Guatemalan immigrants.

Black people had inhabited the swampy bottoms of Watts since its earliest days. In the late 1920s, when Watts was an independent town, blacks became the town's majority, and might have elected its first black mayor. But outnumbered whites—claiming water-supply issues—staved this off: they got the City of Los Angeles to annex it instead. In the second of the great black migrations, after World War II, black people poured into Watts from the South and soon made it notorious among the country's "inner-city" black neighborhoods. "An infected pocket of misery, unemployment and despair where new arrivals from the South congregate," the political writer Theodore H. White called it in 1965, after the riots.

Every factor that predicted violence was concentrated in Southeast. The division was the poorest one in South Bureau. It was home to a cluster of public housing projects, including Jordan Downs and Imperial Courts, places made notorious by rap musicians. Older men dawdled in front of liquor stores or jaywalked with gaits of languid contempt. Police cataloged a score of black gangs there, some with imaginative and poetic names: Fudgetown Mafia, Hard Time Hustlers, Bounty Hunters. Bone-thin addicts with bad teeth rattled shopping carts down its boulevards.

Yet for all its notoriety, the landscape of Watts was not as formidable as its reputation. This was not a no-man's-land of high-rise slums. Trees and lawns adorned tiny detached one-story houses set off by waist-high chain-link fences. Sidewalks were crowded with kids walking home in their school uniforms and mothers pushing strollers. Teenagers practiced dance steps at bus stops. The housing projects boasted gracious touches. Nickerson Gardens, where curved streets wound around black-and-white row houses, had been designed by the famous black architect Paul Williams and reflected his deepest values—California living and "a passion for small homes for everyday people"—according to his Memphis archivist, Deborah Brackstone. Sunlight streamed through the windows of Nickerson's cozy, private units. Ground-level doors opened on geraniums and sloping green lawns.

And, of course, Watts claimed an equal share of the city's best attributes. It was Mediterranean and golden, with air that was soft in summer and crisp in winter. Gardens there burst with bird-of-paradise flowers and purple-blooming jacarandas. Palm trees lined streets, their glossy fronds flashing in the sun. There were still paddocks in Compton and a stable in Athens, and people rode horses up the grassy median of Broadway. They sat on couches on front porches, barbecued in their driveways on summer evenings as their children played.

The setting made much of the literature about the urban "underclass" based on observations in places such as Philadelphia, Baltimore, and the Bronx seem like some dark fantasy. A foreign visitor in 2008 said she was surprised by the pleasant surroundings; referencing George Kelling and James Q. Wilson's famous essay, she noted that there were no broken windows at all.

. . .

Most blacks in Los Angeles had Southern origins. But folklore held that Watts had drawn the poorest and last of the black migrants—refugees from rural Louisiana and East Texas, many from sharecropping and subsistence farming backgrounds. A bit of Watts mythology even held that its blacks were "darker complected" than blacks elsewhere in L.A. This notion was doubtful, and impossible to prove in any case, but it was of a piece with Watts's reputation for extreme black disadvantage.

That history was still in evidence when Skaggs came to work in Watts in 2001. Newcomers from the South still came, and transplants went back and forth to ancestral towns. In the roll call room of the station hung a large painted sign. It bore the logo of the Louisiana Hotel, a local establishment once considered a notorious nest of vice. The police had somehow pilfered the sign when the motel was demolished, and it was clear why they coveted it: "Louisiana Hotel" was shorthand for the neighborhood. Many of these sons and daughters of Louisiana still interacted as if living in a rural Southern village. Weekends brought big family cookfests and jovial church breakfasts. Everyone seemed to know everyone.

The uniformed gang enforcement officers in Skaggs's station house had a running joke about Slidell, Louisiana, a town that could appear to have been uprooted and replanted on the streets of Watts. Sometimes it seemed half the black gangsters in the division hailed from there. But Shreveport, Lake Charles, Natchitoches, and New Orleans were also well represented.

Only people who weren't familiar with this kind of "inner-city" environment would attribute its problems to alienation or lack of community solidarity. The truth was that "community spirit" in the sense of both local pride and connections among neighbors was far more in evidence in Watts than elsewhere. It was one of the defining aspects of the ghettoside setting: a substantial portion of the area's residents were related to each other through extended family ties, marriage, or other intimate connections. Relatives who were only nominally related by blood often saw each other daily, ate together, celebrated together, quarreled and comforted each other. They shared food, money, and living quarters. They raised each other's children. They traded off transportation and housework.

Even people who were not related were networked into this complex mosaic. Common-law romantic relationships—the myriad "baby daddy" and "baby mama" connections—not only constituted their own distinct category of familial bonds, they roped in a lot of other blood relations, too. And if people had no claim to family ties at all, they invented them. Terms such as "play sister" and "play cousin" were ubiquitous all over South Central and had an important role in organizing social life. Even friendships in Watts often appeared more intimate than elsewhere. In contrast to wealthier neighborhoods, where most people worked at day jobs and neighbors knew each other in passing or not at all, the unemployed people of these places were home all day, hanging out together, confined to a few blocks. It lent the constant calls for "the community to come together" a touch of absurdity. Watts already had more togetherness than most Americans could tolerate.

Among officers in the division, the company line was that most of South Bureau's population were "good people." But a minority—some cops put it at 1 percent, some as high as 15 percent—were "knuckleheads." This term referred to unemployed, criminally involved men, and gang members, especially black ones.

Blacks "could better their lives, but they don't," said one officer of Hispanic ethnicity. "They love it. They love selling drugs. They love forcing old people out of their homes so they can sell drugs there." Said a white officer: "The true victims are Hispanic. Black suspects prey on Hispanic victims." There was plenty of Hispanic crime and "gang activity," too. But the hard-core underclass in Watts was black, and it was impossible for patrol cops not to see that. All day long, their radios buzzed with familiar suspect descriptions. "Male black, five-six to six-two, eighteen to thirty-five, white shirt, black pants," a gang officer intoned drily, reading aloud from a report in the Watts station one day. All the cops present laughed, for they all sought the same suspect. But even as officers laughed, some cops also searched their souls, trying to figure out how to accommodate their experiences at work with the antiracism they shared with most of their countrymen.

They sometimes wrestled with race in disarming ways. No one in the wider world seemed to want to talk about it, but black residents, to many officers, appeared more violent than Hispanics. Their own eyes told them so. Statistics backed them up. Few officers wanted to believe that black people were somehow intrinsically wired for violence.

"Maybe the stereotype is true," said Francis Coughlin, a white gang detective who would play an important role in Skaggs's story. "I don't know! I like to think it is a choice. Even in this environment, you have a choice!" His voice betrayed a touch of anguish—the whole issue so delicate and painful.

"Choices" rhetoric helped officers ascribe the violence of Watts to individuals, and thus avoid explanations that felt like group generalizations of black people. But talk of "choices" also inevitably raised questions of blame. And since blame also served as a satisfying distancing mechanism, officers ended by blaming not just suspects but victims for the "choices" they'd made.

Some version of "good riddance" summed up much of the cops' private response to the violence there. "There are no victims here" was a tired cliché seemingly echoed by half the officers in Southeast. "You take your values and put them in the backseat while you are here," said gang sergeant Sean Colomey, who worked in Southeast in the aughts. "Then you go back to where you are from and get your values again."

A white Southeast officer called a successfully prosecuted gang homicide "two for the price of one," because one gang member had been killed and a second imprisoned. Another white officer, of supervisory rank, scanned a report about a black gang member who had barely survived a bullet to the head: "Why couldn't it have just taken care of the problem we are dealing with here?" she asked caustically.

A telling bit of cop slang that expressed this philosophy was the word *righteous*. Officers used "righteous" to distinguish people they considered real victims—innocent and worthy of sympathy—from victims only in a strict legal sense. A *righteous* victim might be the hardworking neighbor struck by a stray bullet. It went without saying that there were few *righteous* victims among the black men of Watts.

But officers could not be condemned wholesale for their strong emotional responses to violence. The anger of many Southeast cops was complicated—shot through with outrage and horror. Even as they spouted callous, shopworn rhetoric, some Southeast officers also displayed deep engagement with problems they encountered in Watts—problems that often seemed to be ignored by a wider world.

A gang detective in Watts named Patrick Flaherty was typical. He worked twelve serious shootings a month—far too many to solve. Flaherty, to his credit, hated "cleared other," and he worked hard. But few victims would testify. Once, a wounded gang member said "Fuck you" to Flaherty's request for information—his dying words.

Another time, he investigated the case of a fourteen-year-old boy paralyzed by gunfire. The boy's mother, against all evidence, insisted the perpetrator couldn't have been a black man. Flaherty offered this story as an example of perverse denial among blacks. His views appeared harsh and condemnatory: "The whole culture of the black community is crime!" he said. Yet in the same interview, Flaherty kept returning to this fourteen-year-old, whose story never made the news. Flaherty worked the case diligently, driven by a sincere, sympathetic response to the boy's ordeal, and he persuaded him to testify. He got to know the family, stayed in touch. And every time they went to court, he carried the boy down the steps of the family's apartment himself.

When Skaggs came to work in Southeast Homicide, the countywide homicide death rate for black men in their twenties was about forty-eight times the average for all Americans. Southeast had always been among the five most violent LAPD precincts, and sixty-five people were killed there the first year after Skaggs arrived, three quarters of them black. The next year, 2003, Southeast led the city in killings with seventy-seven people dead, two thirds of them black.

Skaggs occupied a corner in the back of the detective squad room, alongside his colleagues at what was called the homicide "table," for that is what it was—a handful of desks pushed together, the inauspiciousness of their function reinforced by the arrangement of office furniture, for the homicide table looked no different than the burglary table or the auto table.

After initially bouncing him around between partners, La Barbera eventually assigned Skaggs to work with Chris Barling, another Southern California native who had migrated from South Bureau Homicide. Barling was two years older than Skaggs, also white, and just as tall: the two men wore the same size suit. Barling looked fit, but astonished his health-obsessed colleagues with his diet of packaged burritos and Mountain Dew. Both men were of superior talent. At the point when they became partners, they had identical clearance rates: 75 percent.

The partnership clicked right away. Barling was analytical and talkative, with a flair for circumstantial cases. Skaggs saw that he was good at making sense of complex webs of evidence. For Barling, a denial was as good as a confession.

For his part, Barling admired Skaggs's style—how he attacked everything in sight, plunging after every scrap of information, going right at its source, refusing to take no for an answer. La Barbera sometimes assigned them extra cases just to juice the unit's end-of-year clearance rate.

Typically, La Barbera's little Watts squad had no more than four or five pairs of homicide detectives. These detectives carried the highest homicide caseloads in the city, double or triple those of colleagues in the wealthier San Fernando Valley and West bureaus. Twelve to fifteen cases per pair were typical in those years.

Homicide rates were on the wane, but homicide staffing had dropped, too, and clearing cases still wasn't seen as central to the department's crime-fighting strategy. So La Barbera faced the same old frustrations. It was a reprise of the Big Years: insufficient resources and upside-down priorities. Barling liked to say that they were "Don Quixotes, tilting at windmills." The unit was perennially short of cars and computers. La Barbera "took a complaint" once for stealing an extra, unused computer from the patrol officers because one of his investigators didn't have one, and he weathered the inevitable internal-affairs investigation. His detectives were not allowed to bring their police sedans home, unlike detectives in other units, such as "major crimes" at headquarters. They had no office in which to meet, unlike the station's community policing and data analysis units.

The homicide detectives also lacked sufficient space to interrogate people, since they shared the only available interview room with all the other officers in the station. The room had no recording equipment and no window, and it was always short of chairs and uncomfortably cold.

The detectives were not issued tape recorders, although prosecutors had begun to require recordings to file charges by that time. So they bought their own and, absent an interrogation room, devised ingenious ways to conceal them. One detective carried a heavy binder filled with paper. He cut out the center of the stack to make a secret hollow and hid his recorder in it. This qualified as high technology in ghettoside homicide.

La Barbera spent much of his time trying to secure adequate supplies and equipment. His detectives were not issued departmental cell phones; they bought their own. They did not have the capability to enhance or take stills from surveillance videos, or to videotape interrogations, so they persuaded a local appliance merchant to help them. They struggled for access to moving vans and surveillance cars. They waited for weeks to hear back from labs for reports on physical evidence. La Barbera purchased his own fax machine and printer for the office, and several pieces of furniture, including his own chair. The detectives made regular trips to Office Depot to buy pads, pencils, staplers, keyboards, calendars, and even the blue binders for the murder books.

La Barbera was forever setting goals and drafting plans, trying to improve things. His requests seemed pretty reasonable for a department that ran its own helicopter fleet: he wanted tinted windows in a sedan to ferry witnesses incognito, a locking cabinet for murder books, maybe a few digital cameras. Again and again, he was turned down.

The brass juggled other concerns—response times and suppression of lesser crimes, such as burglaries. These were more numerous and created more noticeable blips in crime statistics. Reporters, meanwhile, virtually never covered Southeast homicides. So there was little political pressure to address them.

Even within their own station house, Southeast Homicide detectives sometimes felt like lepers. They had to cajole their colleagues to help them with stakeouts and sweeps. La Barbera tried to improve this, too. He spoke to roll calls, quietly urging the uniforms to stop shooing people rudely from crime scenes and to treat bereaved families with compassion. The officers would roll their eyes, then bark at weeping relatives again, or smirk at witnesses—that smirk that some LAPD officers seemed to have learned at the academy. They still turned in field-interview cards that read like haiku. No one in charge seemed interested in impressing on the uniforms that it was appropriate for them to serve as a supporting cast for detectives. It was as if they policed on a completely different plane. Sometimes, patrol officers roared by fresh shrines on the street without a glance, unaware of the murders that had just happened there.

Just like Baitx and Tennelle a few years before, Skaggs and Barling worked the ghettoside way. Scores of cases, and not a moment to lose.

Skaggs rose at 3:30 A.M. Unlike the many LAPD officers who exhausted themselves working odd hours, Skaggs was disciplined enough to force himself to go to bed at eight o'clock every night, no matter what.

Each day began with a list of tasks, every moment booked, with delays for traffic and slow courthouse elevators carefully accounted for. He and Barling disdained colleagues who took long "Code 7's," driving as far as South Bay for restaurant lunches. Skaggs and Barling ate their lunches standing, brown bags spread out on the trunk of the sedan. Most days they worked twelve hours or more, with tasks stretching late into the night. Skaggs was a serious coffee addict; he drank it very black and by the pot, the last cup after dark; it did not affect his sleep at all. Overtime was his life. One of the office secretaries had dubbed the homicide squad "the green mile" because of all the green overtime forms they turned in. It was the one area in which divisional homicide squads were amply provided for: they usually didn't have enough detectives, but the ones they had could exploit contract provisions that treated them like factory labor and rewarded unceasing work. Skaggs earned $190,000 one year—his peak. Asked his base salary at the time, Skaggs could not pinpoint it. He had never bothered to learn his actual wage.

The squad was usually short on experience, with too many apprentices and too few veterans to train them. Ghettoside work was so draining that it required incompatible attributes, youthful energy and master craftsmanship. All the South L.A. homicide units suffered from high turnover, with young recruits often moving to easier and more rewarding positions as soon as they were able; this was also true of prosecutors down at Compton Courthouse. Short-handed South Bureau homicide units frequently accepted mediocre candidates to compensate. Two of La Barbera's detectives over the years were drummed out on misconduct allegations. Others solved no cases. La Barbera did his best to combat churn. He was a tireless talent scout and recruiter. But the best officers scoffed at his advances. "Hey, you want to work homicide?" La Barbera said brightly to one who passed his desk one morning. The officer guffawed and walked off, shaking his head.

La Barbera obsessed over every last detail of his management job, kept his own elaborate records, and studied his data in his spare time in search of best practices. He discovered that constantly training young recruits who didn't work out wasted time and hampered the progress of his best detectives. La Barbera looked at years of clearances and found it was better to keep strong detectives together than to partner them with apprentices. Strong pairs would solve more cases than the weak ones sacrificed. So he kept Barling and Skaggs together.

For Skaggs and Barling, this was a formative, golden period.

La Barbera demanded pride of appearance, and Skaggs always looked crisp in his business suits. He allowed himself the one indulgence of taking off his suit jacket as he worked Southeast's baking asphalt streets. But he kept the ties knotted and never rolled up the sleeves of the white dress shirts he always wore. He and Barling cleaned their sedan frequently so people would know at a glance they weren't just any plainclothes cops—they were homicide detectives. Skaggs loved it when Southeast residents, who studied their cops very carefully, recognized him as a homicide man.

In the office, Skaggs and his colleagues were obsessively neat. They kept bottles of Formula 409 spray at their desks. One day a trainee spilled coffee on Skaggs's desk. Appalled silence—then La Barbera quietly threatened to fire him. It wasn't clear that he was joking.

The cleanliness served a purpose. A stack of paper left on a desk meant a detective was falling behind, and with so many cases, that spelled disaster. Organization was survival. Detectives were always in danger of getting buried. Skaggs had pictures of his children under glass on his desk, but nothing else. He used scissors to cut out bits of text on printouts to keep track of his cases, Scotch-taped on 8-by-10 notebook sheets. When he solved a case, he highlighted it in yellow.

Nothing came easily in Southeast. But for Skaggs, the impediments—lack of sufficient manpower and equipment, no media coverage, little clout within the department—became motivators. Long before, he had begun to develop a subversive posture toward the status quo. Now, underdog pride suffused his work. Southeast detectives saw themselves as the equivalent of a military MASH unit—better and smarter craftsmen because they were forced to get things done fast.

Among the LAPD's legions of high-school-educated, second-generation cops in those years, Skaggs was not immediately recognizable as an outlier. He was smart, but not book-smart. Needing only language enough to convey favor and disfavor, he spoke simply in the vernacular of the avid California surfer he was. Skaggs began sentences with "See" or "All's I'm sayin'." When he praised things, he said "Sweet!" When he condemned them, he used bowdlerized profanity: "Shoot!" or "Flippin'!"

He had a favorite term of disparagement: *dumb-ass*. Skaggs found this term useful for dispensing with a long and varied list of annoyances in his life. Paperwork. Bad tattoos. Excessive drinking. They were all dumb-ass. Skaggs sometimes even referred to the high crime of murder as dumb-ass. It worked as a noun, too. Inconvenient bureaucrats could be dumb-asses. Killers could be dumb-asses.

Among cops, he fit right in—just another jock in the locker room—talking football and RVs and fitness regimens and the Baker to Vegas police relay race like all of them. His seeming ordinariness also served him working on the streets of Watts, where he mixed surfer slang and ghetto idioms so the latter seemed part of a natural vocabulary of found clichés. Skaggs could make reference to "snitch jackets" or "front street" without sounding affected. He was not like some South Bureau officers, who made a show of knowing gangster lingo. Skaggs believed he could speak to people he met in Watts just as he spoke to anyone else.

The ability to talk to anyone, anywhere, always using the same words and grammar, never talking down to people, never trying to impress some third party, was a curious matter of principle to him. It was part of a secret catalog of personal standards he had assembled around his work—a list of codes, seldom voiced, except in occasional flares of annoyance when he saw them transgressed.

His deceptively unsophisticated speaking style served another purpose as his career progressed: it was helpful in interrogations. Skaggs often played the goofy amateur. Suspects didn't comprehend the razor-sharp strategic intellect until it was too late. But it was not entirely an act. Skaggs was not someone who lost himself in deep analysis. He rarely felt the need to be any more precise or evocative than words like "sweet!" or "dumb-ass" permitted. He was not that interested in explanation. His reasoning style was strictly intuitive. His brain was full of data. The power of his mind lay in his ability to access it all instantaneously with great precision and to parlay it into swift, effortless decisions. "It's Skaggs's way," Chris Barling would say, "or it's dumb-ass."

His utilitarian outlook seemed to militate against soulfulness. But Skaggs must have had a little. He loved Steinbeck's *Cannery Row*. He loved the unappreciated landscapes of California, its creosote deserts and ponderosa plains. Of course, most Californians also loved the place. But Skaggs's passion was of a higher order. He'd been raised on Southern California's Elysian sunlight and rainbow mists. He couldn't imagine leaving. When Skaggs heard of cops retiring to other places—Idaho, or Gig Harbor, Washington—he shook his head in sympathy as if they'd been struck by illness. Poor souls. Living in that weather. They would never be able to get a foothold in the housing market again.

8

WITNESSES AND THE SHADOW SYSTEM

What one prosecutor called the "colossal" problem of ghettoside homicide cases was the difficulty in getting witnesses to talk. They were terrified they would be killed.

In Watts, if witnesses cooperated with police at all, they nearly always pleaded to have their statements kept anonymous. Many had to be chased down. After initial interviews, they would have to be subpoenaed to testify, then impeached on the stand because they lied about matters about which they had earlier displayed knowledge.

A witness's decision to testify was one of the most wrenching and emotional aspects of homicide prosecutions. Witnesses wept when confronted by detectives, then wept again on the stand. And that was when things went well. In many other cases, they denied what they had seen, or mysteriously vanished in the interval it took to schedule trial hearings.

The reluctance of witnesses to testify was the primary reason so many murder cases went unsolved. In 2008, lack of witness cooperation was the number one impediment to finding suspects in 108 homicide cases in the city of Los Angeles—or 40 percent of all cases in which witnesses played any role. In many other murders, reluctant witnesses may not have been the primary impediment but were still high among the reasons why cases were not solved. Barling liked to say that all the unsolved cases in Southeast were "just one witness away."

Street homicides offered few physical clues. Most were "scoop-and-carry" cases in which the wounded victim had been transported by ambulance to a hospital before being pronounced dead. Evidence consisted of a few shell casings, shoes, and ribbons of clothing left by paramedics' scissors.

Labs played little role in most street murder cases. It doesn't take a fancy scientific laboratory to determine that a man died because a bullet hit him.

Instead, cases were made on witnesses—and sometimes only witnesses. Since the sixties, the State of California had provided funds to help relocate witnesses to new apartments as a way of protecting them. The money was minimal—usually a few thousand dollars. The state program typically paid only for a move and a couple months' rent. There was no long-term assistance to help people start new lives in new places.

Moreover, the funds were approved for people only after they agreed to cooperate with prosecutions; detectives couldn't use them to get reluctant witnesses into a safe place before interviewing them. And moving relatives of witnesses was difficult. Witnesses often worried for the safety of elderly grandparents, who typically owned their homes and did not qualify for relocation.

Finally, the program did not fully comprehend the circumstances of the underworld denizens who were likely to be homicide witnesses. These included homeless people, addicts, prostitutes, gang members, and hustlers, who depended on a geographically specific black market—a corner to sell drugs, an alley to turn tricks. They weren't often noted for their responsible decision making.

For such tormented souls, witness relocation programs were not especially helpful. "Where do you relocate a homeless person? The next block?" said one former Southeast detective, Dan Myers. One of Myers's witnesses on a homicide case was a homeless crack addict. For years, he tried to keep track of her, hoping to keep her safe. Once, after a search, he caught up with her in an alley. She was half dressed, her hair disheveled, with nickel-sized blue bruises on her arm. She told Myers that gang members that week had grabbed her, shaken her, and threatened her about her testimony.

The extent of retaliation against witnesses was hard to measure. Detectives insisted retaliation was rare, especially after trials ended. But an average of about seven known murders of witnesses occurred countywide each year during Skaggs's first five years in Southeast, and the real figure was probably at least a dozen. This was a tiny fraction of total murders countywide. But a little murder goes a long way. Most rational people hesitate to do something that a dozen people a year get killed for doing in their county. There was so much fear that the twenty-five thousand dollar rewards offered for help on cases were virtually never collected.

Witnesses were also targets of intimidation that fell short of murder. Firebombs flew through their windows; drive-by shootings were conducted as they tried to relocate, bullets ricocheting near moving vans parked in the street. Some witnesses described being marked and harassed after testifying. Wearing a "snitch jacket"—a reputation for cooperating—meant being targeted for abuse. Police tended to have little sympathy for people tarred with this label, black gang members in particular. They appeared less inclined to offer relocation to young black men with criminal records. Some would even argue that witness safety was a nonissue because the only people who really needed to worry about retaliation were gang members—as if this made it less problematic. Threats and assaults against gang members were, of course, the very statistical heart of the problem, and so, in this respect, as in so many others, it was all upside down: the system's weakest point was exactly its statistical apex.

Police could be astonishingly parsimonious and presumptuous even with upstanding and fully cooperative witnesses. It was assumed that poor people could move at a moment's notice, that their ties to whatever place they called home were not equal to those of wealthier suburbanites. And some cops, steeped in right-wing rhetoric about the "nanny state," harbored deep philosophical objections to aiding witnesses with cash. One detective supervisor in Southeast during Skaggs's term said that she saw it as her duty to make sure they got as little state money as possible. She considered the division's poor to be welfare malingerers and did not want to abet their sponging ways.

Experienced homicide detectives did not share this view. They saw deeper into residents' lives, forged ties with them, and, most important, experienced their pain as more than a glancing inconvenience. Suffering was a teacher. There was a palpable difference between the exasperated posture of certain first responders—paramedics, patrol officers, some nurses, who dealt with people briefly and deflected their agony to stay sane—and the mute outrage of homicide detectives, doctors, and other workers who witnessed the long aftermath. The latter, such as Roosevelt Joseph, a Seventy-seventh Street Division homicide supervisor, often came to resent what they saw as callous judgments by the former. "They say these people should come forward—just because they work eight hours a day here and have a gun and a badge and go home to Orange County at night!" Work ghettoside long enough and one learned the hard way what could happen to witnesses. Brent Josephson, the Seventy-seventh Street detective, once relocated an eighteen-year-old witness named Yvette Rene Blue and remained friends with her. She would send him little notes and cards. But the young black woman visited her old neighborhood after testifying and was murdered. Josephson was never the same. He kept Blue's wallet-sized photograph taped to his computer terminal for years after.

Detectives made moral appeals to try to persuade people to cooperate despite their fear. But for many witnesses, testifying presented a quandary—they had to consider their own safety and that of friends and relatives against their duty to the state. Police and prosecutors, if they were perceptive, also felt this dilemma. One RHD detective described his uneasiness about using an older woman as a witness in a gang case: she had brushed his concerns for her safety aside, explaining that her son had been murdered years earlier, and she no longer cared if she died. In one Watts case, the main witness, a homeless prostitute, was cooperative because she loved the victim. But she refused relocation, probably in part because her desperate existence required her to remain where she was—living in her car, offering blow jobs to men in the projects. "She's not scared, but she should be," the detective said. "I'm scared for her."

Fear made collaborators even of people who committed no crimes. Many homicide witnesses shed tears when confronted by police. They would apologize as they yanked closed the curtains, or requested, in sheepish undertones, that police not come to their houses in daylight. Very often, police knew nothing of what witnesses were going through.

In one 2009 case in Watts, an important witness, who lived across the street from the driveway where a man was murdered, spent the next three nights sleeping on the kitchen floor with his family as men parked their cars outside and displayed guns or threw rocks at the house. He never reported the attacks: he was on felony probation for welfare fraud and had lied to his employer about it. He was afraid to deal with police for fear of exposure or being sent to prison.

Sometimes, the most down-and-out people showed epic courage. On another Watts case, a crack cocaine addict told police she had seen only enough to place the suspect at the scene. But when the day came for her to testify, she surprised the whole courtroom by looking the defendant in the eye and exclaiming, "You killed him! . . . I'm sorry, but you did!"

Another witness, Debra Johnson, testified against her attackers in a Nickerson Gardens massacre-style assault that left two people dead. Johnson—asthmatic, on parole, and addicted to drugs—was maimed by gunshots to the mouth and chest and could barely talk. But on the stand, she brimmed with spirit. "That's just how it was," she declared, and pointed an accusing finger at the shooters.

Both of these women were from the same neighborhoods as the kilers; they were both poor people indoctrinated in street codes. And both were very brave.

Yet although witness fear and safety was addressed periodically by the press and by policy makers, its centrality to the syndrome of black murders was massively underrated. In fact, journalistic and academic work related to witnesses tended to focus on their unreliability. The public could not be blamed for believing that these constituted primary problems in the justice system, since so many experts specialized in this issue, and so many grants were awarded for research about them. In Skaggs's time, there were regular calls to further restrict the use of eyewitness evidence in court—far fewer calls to better protect the mostly poor, frightened, and highly vulnerable people upon whose shoulders the state laid the burden of testifying.

The witness intimidation problem was just one aspect of the larger ghettoside problem: a shadow legal system that competed with formal law.

Each time he delved into a Southeast case, Skaggs had the sense that he was entering an underworld. For all the chaos, this world was organized, rule-bound. Black people in Watts were generally governed by a complex system of etiquette, backed by the threat of violence. This was the shadow that filled the vacuum of legitimate authority. One reason it existed was the neighborhood's vast underground economy. When your business dealings are illegal, you have no legal recourse. Many poor, "underclass" men of Watts had little to live on except a couple hundred dollars a month in county General Relief. They "cliqued up" for all sorts of illegal enterprises, not just selling drugs and pimping but also fraudulent check schemes, tax cons, unlicensed car repair businesses, or hair braiding. Some bounced from hustle to hustle. They bartered goods, struck deals, and shared proceeds, all off the books. Violence substituted for contract litigation. Young men in Watts frequently compared their participation in so-called gang culture to the way white-collar businesspeople sue customers, competitors, or suppliers in civil courts. They spoke of policing themselves, adjudicating their own disputes. Other people call police when they need help, explained an East Coast Crip gang member. "We pick up the phone and call our homeboys."

Gangs issued informal "passes"—essentially granting waivers that exempted people from the rules that governed everyone else. A star athlete in a gang neighborhood, for example, might be issued a "pass" that exempted him from participation in gang life. Or passes might be extended to people allowed to conduct illegal businesses in rival territories. "Selling without a pass" was an occasional homicide motive.

Gangs could seem pointlessly self-destructive, but the reason they existed was no mystery. Boys and men always tend to group together for protection. They seek advantage in numbers. Unchecked by a state monopoly on violence, such groupings fight, commit crimes, and ascend to factional dominance as conditions permit. Fundamentally gangs are a consequence of lawlessness, not a cause.

Some version of gangs has characterized lawless settings throughout history. In the nineteenth century, gangs ran the gamut: bandit groups among Russian peasants bearing catchy names like the "Steppe Devils"; Philadelphia volunteer firefighters who warred with each other and committed arson; New York City "voting gangs" who angrily confronted each other, fighting over what Monkkonen called the "nineteenth-century equivalent of cocaine—access to the jobs and graft political powers offered." In Georgia and Virginia in the early twentieth century, the "gang" mantle belonged to groups of black and white moonshiners who intimidated people and killed snitches.

The tendency for people to band together when state power is weak is so inevitable it can even seem innate. "The latent causes of faction," wrote founding father James Madison, are "sown in the nature of man." Without law, people use violence collectively to settle scores and right wrongs, and commonly refer to violence as their own law. Wherever law is absent or undeveloped—wherever it is shabby, ineffective, or disputed— some form of self-policing or communal justice usually emerges.

Police, prosecutors, and politicians in L.A. blamed gangs for the homicide problem. They portrayed gangs as formidable nations of organized crime or as an exotic new social disease. But among street officers in South Bureau, doubts sometimes surfaced, a sense that much of what

was breathlessly termed "gang culture" was pretty ordinary group behavior. Officers couldn't help noticing certain inconsistencies, like the
way so much gang crime seemed to involve just four or five guys "cliqu-
ing up," in the spirit of a high school locker room, or the way so few
gang homicides stemmed from drug deals—and so many from infighting. Some gang members showed signs of being unwilling draftees,
and many monikers sounded less like noms de guerre than like play-
ground taunts—"Cheeseburger," "Wheezy," "Klayhead," "Beer Can."
Petty arguments, insults, and women seemed to drive a lot of gang violence. One gang war in Southeast stemmed from the sale of a used car.
Gang members in Watts bragged of making large sums. But in the
morgue, the rolled wads of dollar bills found inside shoes contradicted
them: these were poor people. The black market is a desperate place.

The size of the stakes did not limit the reach of the shadow system,
however. Seemingly minor transgressions could bring severe reprisals.
Skaggs marveled that one of the highest offenses in the underground
was the simple act of "lying on" people, in the sense of spreading malicious gossip about them. But the prohibition that affected him most was
the one banning snitching—that is, cooperating with police. This was
not simply a criminal ethos. Snitching was sometimes seen as borderline
racial betrayal, a concession to a law enforcement system that had not
served blacks especially well. People in Watts would argue that street
justice was ethically superior. They would pressure homicide witnesses
to keep quiet so the victim's family would have a chance to strike back.

The snitching taboo was surprisingly nuanced. It was more like a standard of selective cooperation. Gang members sometimes turned in their
own for the killing of children, for example. This followed from the correct
assumption that such "innocent victim" cases would *bring out the heat*—
that is, provoke an aggressive police response. But moral repugnance also
played a role. Gang members who snitched in such cases sometimes did
so because they considered the mistake "out of bounds," or beyond the
pale. "They have their own idea of what's justifiable," Skaggs said.

Other killers were protected by a broad consensus, extending beyond
gang members. Murders of gang assailants inside enemy territory were

notoriously difficult to solve for this reason; the invader was seen to have had it coming. Detectives were also less likely to win cooperation in cases in which the victims were obnoxious or strangers. Skaggs described one case involving a victim who had been an annoyance to his neighbors: "Everyone in Nickerson says, 'That's no problem if he got killed! Why are you guys even bothering?'" he said.

Nearly every official who dealt closely with crime in Watts felt the same way. "They have their own businesses . . . their own law!" prosecutor Joe Porras said of the participants in the gang cases he tried in Compton Courthouse. "It's a parallel world, and you are trying to bring your law into it." Cops and prosecutors felt like door-to-door salesmen, trying to peddle a legal system no one wanted anything to do with. Prosecutor Grace Rai marveled at how much work it was just to get people to participate in proceedings at Compton Courthouse. To witnesses, jurors, and victims, "you can't just say, 'This is a violation of the law,'" Rai said. First, "you have to get them *behind* the law."

Testifying in Compton Courthouse in late 2009, one young black man explained why he had not reported a killing he had been present at. "The place I live at—there's *rules and regulations* behind living there," he said. He lived in the territory of the Bounty Hunter gang. Pressed for details, he did not say whose rules they were, or how he had come to learn them—simply that they existed for him unquestionably, enforced by an implied threat that surrounded him, as ever-present as the roar of traffic from the elevated freeways. An attorney asked what would happen if he violated these mysterious "rules and regulations." The young man answered with an impatient shrug: "Killed, shot—anything," he said.

Back in the 1930s, the anthropologist Hortense Powdermaker wrote of the proscriptions of Jim Crow in exactly such terms. Powdermaker noted a conversation with a black woman about her fear of socializing with a white man: "When asked what she is afraid of, she laughs and says: 'Don't you know it is against the law?' Further questions make it clear that she knows of no specific law . . . but the law to her is a vague and sinister force, transcending any body of definite rules."

The alternate ghettoside "law" in Watts was exactly like this—a vague and sinister force transcending any body of definite rules. The shadow system had long ago evolved to the point that a mere hard look or the sucking of a tooth conveyed its lethal force without further elaboration. People knew the "rules and regulations" and obeyed them.

At the same time, some Watts residents appeared to long for freedom from the oppressive menace of informal law. Many older gang members appeared miserable and talked constantly of "getting out." In the privacy of the interrogation room, many proved willing to turn on fellow gang members, telling detectives that they secretly disliked them. Residents would still holler "One time!" at the cops. The term derived from the memory of police touring black neighborhoods once a day, making no real effort to address crime. "One time" was a stock anticop insult, just like "po-po" and "blue-eyed devil." Yet it contained a plaintive note—a paradoxical suggestion that more times might be better.

And once in a while, street hustlers would make it clear that they would rather have formal justice if given the choice: they'd call 911. When the puzzled officers arrived, the hustlers would ask them to referee disputes: "My dope got ripped off! I want you to book him for robbery!"

Skaggs learned to think of his job as persuasion: selling formal law to people who distrusted it and who were answering to another authority— shadow law. The pitch had to be convincing and relentless. Ghettoside detective work was "ninety percent talking to people. Maybe a hundred percent," Skaggs said.

The challenge left no room for self-doubt, no room to equivocate. Skaggs was made for it. He went back again and again to the same streets, the same houses, knocking over and over, rousting witnesses at dawn or late at night. He learned certain patterns of life in Watts— where junkies loiter, which couch a drug dealer might call home.

Skaggs's manner of knocking was loud, persistent, and seemed to brook no opposition. He banged on windows using his department-issue flashlight, since most homes in Southeast had those steel security doors and it was hard to knock on their metal screens. If no one came, he banged some more. He moved to the next window and the next, banging and banging, as if he had all the time in the world. He might return several times that day. Sometimes people talked to him just to get him to go away.

"In the room" (which, in Southeast, literally meant a room, since there was no interrogation booth), Skaggs enveloped people with his conviction. Everything would be better once the truth came out—this was his axiom. His approach was neither coarse nor hostile. He simply bore down, relentless and businesslike. He talked of putting things right, of releasing burdens. He presented justice as psychological relief, even to suspects. He believed it was.

These were the skills that mattered because there were few mysteries among Southeast cases. The homicides were essentially public events— showy demonstrations of power meant to control and intimidate people. They took place on public streets, in daylight, often in front of lots of people.

Killers often bragged. Some were so brazen they posted public signs taking credit. Gloating graffiti was a common homicide clue. *DLB fallen star hahaha!!!* read one such public announcement in Watts. It had been spray-painted in an alley hours after a youth nicknamed Star was shot to death. (DLB stood for Denver Lane Bloods, who in this case were allied with the suspects from a neighboring gang.)

Families of the dead often heard rumors of who did it. Once in a while, a family member would report to police that the killers had attended the funeral, or paid them a menacing visit. An uncle in Southeast Division reported hearing the name of his nephew's killer from friends. But he was hoping police would discover the killer's identity without involving him. One mother in the Southwest Division reported that the killers of her son knocked on her door. They taunted her about her loss. If she told police, they would kill her too, they said.

"Everybody knows" was a phrase that cropped up a lot. Names buzzed on what Southeast detectives called the Ghetto Information Network—the GIN. But even when murders took place amid crowds of people, detectives were left with no witnesses. A score of people would see a murder; not one of them would testify.

To counter this, La Barbera taught his detectives to think of themselves as Madison Avenue impresarios. Their job wasn't deducing—it was sales. They had to "sell ice cubes to an Eskimo!" he would say. The elegant business attire was part of this ethos. "People say, oh, you think you're perfect," La Barbera said. "Well, yeah! We'd better be." He kept a whiteboard near his desk to track cases and leave messages. The salesman's credo, "ABC—Always Be Closing," was written at the top.

But it was not merely a sales job that detectives such as Skaggs perfected. Good ghettoside investigators projected something deeper to their wavering witnesses—something akin to pure conviction. It was no accident that the most successful among them were confident, reassuring. They made people feel they could handle their burdens.

In the early days of European law, the legal historian James Whitman said, state officials faced similar problems. Back when "vengeance cultures" permeated medieval society, murders often stemmed from feuds. Villages were small and, often, everyone knew who had committed the murder but no one wanted to speak in court. Whitman argues that many of our modern legal procedures, such as unanimous jury verdicts, actually began as efforts to coax cooperation—to provide safety and "moral comfort" to people who didn't want to testify and who feared retaliation.

Whitman's thesis has a medieval theological slant. But in other ways Skaggs and his colleagues personified the moral comfort he describes. They succeeded because South Central Los Angeles was a version of a medieval vengeance culture—a premodern setting, legally speaking. In the twelfth-century village, *fama*—rumors, in Latin—had already named a suspect. In Watts, the GIN usually had. In both, it was left to the state to confirm what everyone already knew. This was not a job for Sherlock Holmes. It was a job for a counselor—or prince.

THE NOTIFICATION

One winter morning in 2004, John Skaggs took the wheel of his sedan and headed out into the sun-washed streets of Watts. His mission was to tell a father that his son was dead.

With him was the most recent of a seemingly endless string of Southeast detective trainees, Mark Arenas, a thirty-four-year-old former gang officer raised in Downey. Arenas was trying to learn the ropes, and he was anxious not to appear the amateur. Arenas held a dim view of social dynamics in Watts. "The lack of responsibility!" he would exclaim in disgust. "Violence is *accepted* here."

Skaggs and Arenas had been at a homicide scene that morning, a black man killed in the driver's seat of his SUV. Skaggs had volunteered to tell the family. He took Arenas. "Ever done a notification?" Skaggs asked as he drove. Anything could happen during a notification. Loved ones of victims screamed, collapsed, or fainted. At the county hospitals, nurses were trained to prepare for being attacked. One colleague of Skaggs's would always remember the notification he made in the case of twenty-five-year-old Ronald Tyson, shot dead in an alley near Central Avenue in 2003. When he told Tyson's mother he had been murdered, she vomited.

Homicide notifications also carried some psychological risk for the people who carried them out. A coroner's investigator fumed that people she met were curious about dead bodies, as if that were the hard part. "It's not the gore. It's the grief," she said. Even if a notification went smoothly, "I walk out and I'm shaking and I'm suppressing the urge to cry," said Bryan Hubbard, a trauma surgeon at California Hospital. An image stayed with Hubbard for years: He brought a mother to view the body of her little boy, dead from gunshots. She spent several minutes shaking his small, lifeless form, trying to wake him up.

For Skaggs, notifications were one more task that required skills not taught in the academy. He considered this a serious part of a young detective's training. Arenas was feeling unsure and sought to impress Skaggs. So he cracked a joke, pretending he would deliver the news with tough-guy bravado: "Sorry to tell you—he took one to the head!" Arenas was still a gang officer at heart. In his milieu, a phrase such as "took one to the head" might mark one as cool. Skaggs stared ahead at the wheel. Arenas shot him a look, tried to apologize, and trailed off. After an excruciating silence, Skaggs changed the subject.

Three years had passed since Skaggs had come to Southeast. Skaggs and Barling had rocketed through dozens of cases, working closely with La Barbera. By then, they were helping run the squad, functioning almost as La Barbera's deputies. Shortages of manpower, supplies, and patrol and lab support still impeded investigations. Turnover remained high—Arenas was among the many recruits who would not remain in the unit long. But Skaggs, if anything, was more devoted to his craft than ever. He was dimly aware that the work had changed him, subtly reorienting his viewpoints on law enforcement and crime. He still spoke in the same vernacular as his cop friends. But his inward views had shifted.

It was something felt more than said—the culmination of scores of random observations that illuminated a moral dimension to homicide work that was absent from many other police functions. Skaggs now sensed his investigations addressed a deeper need in black neighborhoods than he had previously understood. This, in turn, colored other impressions. Arenas, for example, accused the division's black residents of inferior values. But Skaggs had concluded that many residents connected to Watts murder cases were ordinary people, trapped by conditions of lawlessness. Coercion and intimidation lay behind much of their apparent "acceptance" of violence, he thought. Sometimes, arresting a young man for murder, he would reflect that things might have turned out differently had the suspect "grown up just four blocks away."

Skaggs also saw that many victims had no role in provoking the attacks that killed them. His colleagues insisted Watts had no real victims. But years later, a trace of anguish would tinge Skaggs's voice when he talked of the many cases he'd handled in Southeast. His choice of words was telling: "All those innocent people!" he said.

Years before, the same accrual of understanding had prompted Wally Tennelle's reluctance to work at RHD, the phrase "some daddy's baby" ringing in his ears. Before that, it had prompted Skaggs's father to conclude that nothing matters after working homicide. And on this winter day, it prompted Skaggs's chill response to Arenas. He gave up on training for a moment. When they pulled up to the house, Skaggs walked ahead, and confronted a man in dress shoes on the porch.

He asked the man's name. He was the father they sought. Skaggs told him that his son had been killed—right there on the front porch. No buildup. No euphemisms. Just straight truth and clarity. The father sagged against the door frame: *"Oh my God."*

Skaggs followed him into the house. Spotless glass coffee table, red carpet, snow-white upholstery. The father, face wild with confusion, bent double as if punched, asked three or four more times, "He's dead? *Dead?*" And Skaggs answered patiently each time: "Yes, sir. Yes, sir."

The city's murder rate was dropping fast. But Southeast's homicides remained high. Seventy-two people would be killed in that small area in 2004. Sixty-five more would die in 2005, and sixty-nine in 2006, representing a per capita murder rate that was eight to ten times the national average. As always, the majority of the killings were black-on-black.

.   .   .

Skaggs and Barling remained partners, and in their first two years together, they cleared twenty-six of thirty-two cases—an 81 percent clearance rate. After that, clearing cold cases from previous years boosted
their rate even higher, and it remained high for the next three years.

They had developed an odd relationship. Though best friends, they
argued constantly. They argued about football, dinner plans, politics,
and every detail of their homicide cases—always without rancor. It
drove their colleagues up the wall. Barling was pedantic. Skaggs was
impish. Barling would wave his arms and spout malapropisms. "Con-
stringent" combined the words "contingent" and "constrained by"; "cy-
cular cycles" meant the persistence of inner-city problems. Skaggs
would shake his head, aping astonishment. Round and round they went.

Some of it was the result of a conscious policy the two had established: they agreed that only one of them would lead on each case. It
freed them to debate their investigations, knowing there was no real
danger of conflict. But for Skaggs, countering Barling's endless hand-
waving fulminations also may have served a subconscious need. It ensured that Barling would serve as the repository of outrage and left
Skaggs free to work.

Compassionate by nature, Barling was unafraid to air his distress
over the bloodshed in Watts. He was appalled by the Monster, tormented by what he perceived as the public's indifference and political
neglect, baffled by the black tilt to the stats. "It's either society's racism,
or something is *wrong* with them—something wrong just with black people. And I don't believe that!" Barling said, his voice rising in distress. "I
believe we are all created equally, men, women, all races! That's why I
cannot buy that."

Skaggs forced Barling to move on. His private views on homicide
remained buried at the level of intuition, surfacing now and then in
flickers—beats of awkward silence like the one that met Arenas's joke.
The rest of the time, he appeared carefree. It was key to his stamina.

Even the sordid misery of the streets rolled right off him. Skaggs by
that time had spent years amid drug addicts, prostitutes, and killers. Yet
he retained a squeaky-clean propriety. He was not morally rigid. But he

had a strong idea of what he considered a sensible life and was surprised by even minor lapses. Bad housekeeping scandalized him. Sleeping late was worse. As for the homicides, after a hundred cases, Skaggs would still shake his head, amazed someone could actually be so *dumb-ass* as to kill. In this way, he preserved what was not exactly innocence, but an unsullied spirit that allowed him to go home to his family each night psychologically intact.

Sal La Barbera never lost his high ambitions for the unit. He sought not just to perform adequately in his modest D-3 supervisory post, but to make of his job a great life project.

There was a touch of grandiosity to his attitude. But La Barbera had a rare combination of skills. As anyone who has worked in a professional environment knows, top practitioners don't always make effective managers. La Barbera was both workaday administrator and man of ideas. He would expound on some lofty crusade one minute, put the paperwork in good order the next.

At work, he displayed no anger, reserving his emotions for his various personal dramas. He emphasized team spirit. He taught his detectives to take pride in speaking for homicide victims, no matter who they had been in life. It was his version of Tennelle's "some daddy's baby." In Watts, the idea had particular relevance. "Innocent victims," in the conventional sense, were a minority. More often, victims in Watts murder cases were combatants, and everyday language in Watts reflected residents' sense that they lived in an unseen war zone. The LAPD was an "occupying army." Gang members called themselves "soldiers" and "warriors." And over on Broadway and Manchester, a protest banner announced the area's nickname: Little Baghdad—a pointed comparison to occupied Iraq.

As a result, victims in Watts cases were often suspects, too: fighters in a continuous flow of street skirmishes. Today's executioner might be tomorrow's victim. A detective might have a pretty good idea that a victim had been a "soldier," and even an exceptionally vicious one.

"Murderers are mean," as the historian Monkkonen said, and in Southeast, they seemed especially so. The meanest among them urinated on their victims, or blasted away as they lay dying and shielding their faces with their hands; punctured palms were a common homicide injury. But the creed dictated that the murder of a killer be treated as that of a child felled by a stray bullet. "They are all innocent angels when they get to me," La Barbera would say.

Most of all, La Barbera drummed into his detectives his conviction that virtually all the cases were solvable. The way he saw it, the perennially low ghettoside clearance rates were malfeasance. It was a theme he hammered away at in almost every staff meeting, and in a dozen quiet asides per day. He was not above goading his detectives: "These guys are sitting around smoking dope with no high school education!" went a typical refrain. "You guys are smart people. I think you can fucking figure out what happened!"

There was defiance in La Barbera's stance. It inspired loyalty. Skaggs and Barling absorbed his philosophy. They considered a respectable clearance rate to be 80 percent or higher. Ever the perfectionist, Skaggs took the notion even further. He coined a derisive term for detectives he considered mediocre. "Forty percenters," he called them.

Typically, the mix of South Bureau cases included a number of "self-solvers"—murder-suicides, simple domestic homicides, killings witnessed by police officers, cases in which suspects were caught running from the scene, and so forth. The prevalence of self-solvers meant police agencies had to solve a few additional challenging cases to produce a natural 30 to 40 percent clearance rate in official tallies. Given that reported rates were often not much higher than this across many of L.A. County's highest-crime areas, it could be inferred that Skaggs thought dimly of the whole system. Too often, he said, it seemed to him that detectives were "just going through the motions." Nothing annoyed him like low professional standards.

Skaggs and Barling became La Barbera's co-conspirators. They helped him hatch and execute little plots. One involved Southeast's old murder books—the blue binders detailing investigations.

Department policy dictated that the books were supposed to be stored away in a vault somewhere, even if the cases weren't solved. But La Barbera considered no case "cold." From his years in South Bureau Homicide, he knew how rushed detective work had been. He viewed "unsolved" cases as incomplete investigations. Sometimes, it took only a few days' work to clear them.

He also knew that many cases were not discrete crimes. In Southeast, murders sprang from a dense tangle of communal conflicts. Killings were often tied to previous murders, assaults, and arguments. Revenge cycles sometimes played out for years, with sons exacting retribution for fathers. "It's *aaall* connected" was one of the mottoes adopted by Watts detectives. Sometimes it was invoked several times a day. A witness to one murder might be a suspect on the next—or brother, or play cousin, to the previous victim. The murder books shed light on these links; La Barbera wanted them at his fingertips.

So La Barbera recruited Skaggs, Barling, and a few others. They took over an abandoned red construction trailer in the station's parking lot. They cleaned it and installed metal shelves from Home Depot. Then they quietly collected all the precinct's old murder books, in violation of department rules, to make a library. It took them three years to go through every book. In the end, the blue binders stood in organized rows—688 cases going back to 1978. Solved and unsolved cases were separated. The latter assessed for difficulty and labeled accordingly. The cramped rows of shelves made a disturbing monument to the Monster. Barling dubbed it the "Lost Souls Trailer."

But the project that most preoccupied La Barbera was legacy-building. He wanted to make sure the values he'd fostered in Southeast were preserved in the next generation.

Recruitment became an increasingly urgent focus. Skaggs and Barling helped. It was one of the few duties outside investigating in which Skaggs took interest. With each trainee who failed or moved on, La Barbera redoubled his efforts. He knew what he was looking for: the next John Skaggs.

Finally, in 2005, he found him.

. . .

Sam Marullo was thirty-four then, a gregarious Southeast gang officer from a big Italian American family in Mount Morris, New York. He was an exemplar of that species of smart attention-deficit cops who are drawn to ghettoside work. The son of a laborer, he had graduated from the Rochester Institute of Technology and attended law school for two months at the University of Albany before losing interest.

Marullo was exceptionally good-looking. He had dark brown hair, blue eyes with long curly lashes, and an excess of boyish charm. He excelled at cultivating street sources—"friendlies," as the cops called them—especially women.

He had his flaws. He was impatient and a little immature, and he was not a good listener. But he made up for it with generosity of spirit. He worked hard, cared about the people he policed, and was complimentary toward almost everyone he worked with. Plus, he loved his job with an intensity that bordered on the self-destructive. At least one marriage had fallen victim in part to his dedication to his work, according to his friends.

La Barbera saw in Marullo a rare incandescent talent. He recruited him as a detective trainee, just as Skaggs and Tennelle had once been.

Marullo wanted to bring a friend with him: Nathan Kouri, then a gang detective.

La Barbera was dubious. Kouri shaved his prematurely balding head; his round, puzzled hazel eyes peered from beneath a scrunched brow as if he were perpetually in deep thought. As is often the case with male friends, Kouri was Marullo's opposite; he was happily married with two special-needs kids, introverted, and always buried in work. He loved to read and to ask people questions. He devoured nonfiction books and newspapers. But he disliked talking. La Barbera agreed to train him at Marullo's insistence.

Mentorship is important in policing, and especially in ghettoside homicide work, an art form so underrated that it had been relegated mainly to an oral tradition. There were professional "homicide schools" for working officers. But much of the curriculum was irrelevant to ghettoside work. The classes focused on handling physical evidence, not on, say, keeping track of a witness with a substance abuse problem or responding to jurors threatened in the courthouse parking garage.

Professional organizations were likewise unhelpful. Skaggs and his colleagues attended a yearly conference organized by the California Homicide Investigators Association. But the agenda rarely touched on their daily work. "When the National Media Moves to Your Town" was the name of a typical seminar. By necessity, detectives learned on the job, older ones passing their craft to younger ones.

La Barbera assigned Skaggs to train Marullo. Skaggs was not a natural teacher. Young detectives who watched him work were forever influenced, but he was too intolerant of mistakes to be comfortable as a mentor. He could not lower his standards even for those starting out. Marullo's case was different. In this young gang officer, Skaggs, too, saw a talent worth the effort.

Skaggs and Marullo clicked. Early on, though, Skaggs had to curb Marullo's socializing. They'd return from some interview and Marullo would wander off to catch up with his gang unit friends. Skaggs scolded him. In homicide, there's no time to waste on office chatter. Marullo straightened out and soon proved his value. He was a great talker. Like Skaggs, he overwhelmed people with conviction.

Marullo, for his part, embraced Skaggs's style—that penchant for direct action, going after every clue right away, hitting it all head-on. "Get to the point, *get to the point*" is how Marullo summed up his mentor's philosophy. "Sometimes you only have one chance."

Skaggs and Marullo solved every one of their first eight cases during those busy months of 2005. Late that August, Marullo was given the lead on his first case.

Charles Williams was twenty-six years old and "on disability" due to psychological issues. He was black and poor and had never worked. His neighbors in the Grape Street Crips had allowed him to wear a purple Lakers outfit, the Grape Street color.

Gang members are often expected to "put in work." A bit of derogatory ghettoside slang condemned those who didn't: they were called "hood ornaments." But Williams, though a "hood ornament" of sorts, had been given a pass.

Williams liked to ride his bicycle around the neighborhood. He was standing in front of the counter of Watts Cyclery at 112th and Wilmington one day when an assailant burst through the door and shot him at close range, leaving him in a pool of blood on the floor. Williams's purple clothes had drawn the attack. The suspect was from Fudgetown Mafia, a Grape Street enemy. They took Williams for a combatant—or a good-enough proxy.

Marullo met with Christine Jackson, Williams's aunt. She had raised Charles from early childhood. His mother had died from illness, his father from an ice-pick homicide, never solved. Jackson worried that the police wouldn't take the case seriously. Her brother, Charles's uncle, had also been killed in a homicide, stabbed in the Nickerson Gardens housing project in 1983. That case, too, was unsolved. Jackson had sharp words for Marullo. She'd been through enough, she said. She was near crazed with grief; Charles's murder felt like the last straw. If police didn't solve it, "I will do what I'm gonna do   I will take care of business," she told him.

Anxious to prove himself, Marullo buried himself in the case. He got leads and was lied to. One witness, a Fudgetown gang member, said he knew the truth but couldn't speak it: his parole terms required that he remain in the neighborhood, and it would be too dangerous for him to remain as a snitch. Marullo turned his attention to the parole bureaucracy and succeeded in getting the man moved. Then he traveled to the witness's new home and convinced him to give a full statement.

A second witness was also a gang member. This young man had been a good student with a double life, a surprisingly common ghettoside story. He was riding in the car that day when a group of Fudgetown

Mafia gang members pulled up to the bicycle shop. An older gang member handed him a gun. *Get out and shoot that Grape Streeter,* the older man ordered.

But the younger one held back, horrified. The older man insisted. The younger refused to get out of the car. At last, the older gang member, in disgust, took the gun. He went into the bike shop where Williams waited, unsuspecting in his purple Laker gear.

It took several interviews for the young man to reveal this story. He lied, then recanted. At last, he confessed to Marullo that he was terrified. He feared the shooter, although ostensibly the two had been friends and "homeys." So-called gang loyalty is often like this: men go along to get along, as battered women go along with their abusers. Marullo's version of moral comfort was his earnest, boyish appeal: he persuaded the young man to testify despite his fear.

La Barbera was triumphant. He gave Marullo a nickname. Borrowing from gangster lingo, as cops love to do, he called him "Li'l Skaggs." La Barbera felt well on his way to assembling a crack team of homicide craftsmen, a group who might finally bring law to South Los Angeles.

PART II

THE CASE OF
BRYANT TENNELLE

10

SON OF THE CITY

It was a truth that all parents seemed to acknowledge: kids just come out different, no matter how much you try to treat them the same. Wally and Yadira Tennelle were not the first parents, and surely not the last, to be thrown off balance by their youngest child.

Both DeeDee and Wally Jr. had excelled in school. DeeDee had always been a reader. Wally Jr. had shown an abrupt intellectual bent as he got older, and he turned downright scholarly when he went to the University of California, Irvine. But Bryant was frisky, wiggly, and seemed unable to focus on his schoolwork. He misbehaved at school. He clowned and pulled pranks. He once sneaked into one of the nuns' offices with a bottle of stink spray—that sort of thing. He couldn't remember what his parents had told him five minutes before.

A psychologist told them he had attention deficit disorder—something more incapacitating than the milder form that DeeDee suspected afflicted the whole family—and that they should medicate him. Wally Tennelle resisted; at work he had seen so many junkies who had been medicated for similar disorders as children and it seemed to have done them no favors. He and Yadira spent thousands of dollars on tutoring for Bryant. Sylvan. Learning Tree. Wally Tennelle tallied it up once and realized it rivaled what they were spending on private school tuition. Year after year, they persevered, but the problems seemed to get no better. It took Bryant hours to do the simplest homework.

Bryant had abilities, just not academic ones. He loved animals. He cared for all kinds of pets, never losing interest in them. He maintained a tank full of exotic fish.

He was good with his hands. Wally Jr. marveled at how he seemed able to build anything. When Bryant's bicycle was stolen, he got interested in lowrider trikes. He restored an antique one, built a speaker box and battery cage for it, and wired the whole thing together. He designed and made clothes. He won his school's chili cook-off. He could reupholster car seats. He poured himself into what his older brother considered quirky, endearing little hobbies for a biracial kid from South Central L.A.

To be sure, as Bryant got older his interests widened to rap music, nice clothes, and all that. But rather than leave behind his world of childish interests, he simply developed them as he grew. He turned his cooking into a profitable enterprise, making brownies and cookies at home and selling them to classmates. He collaborated with his mother on a movie-set-quality Cat in the Hat costume for a party, designing and constructing its cylindrical felt hat himself. He took to raising his own chickens, producing what his father had to admit were "beautiful roosters" even though the crowing was keeping the family up and driving the neighbors nuts. Taking his mother's complaints about his music tastes to heart, he surprised her with homemade CDs containing elaborate mixes of "oldies" he knew she would like. And like his father he was organized— much more so than his older brother, whom Yadira had to chide to clean his room.

But school remained such drudgery—for Bryant, and for his parents. DeeDee and Wally Jr. were college-bound. DeeDee had such a crisp intellect for numbers that she became an accountant. Wally Jr. possessed a flair for the written word; he spent a semester in England studying British literature. But Bryant? Wally and Yadira were just hoping they could get him through high school. And even that modest goal sometimes seemed lofty. Despite the danger of ongoing combat in Afghanistan and Iraq, Wally Tennelle was secretly thinking that Bryant might find a career in the military.

Academics aside, Bryant was such "a good boy," as his father always said. He was relaxed, despite his need for constant movement. He was good-natured. He held no grudges. His parents would be angry with him one moment and completely disarmed by him the next: their youngest boy, so affectionate and responsive, tripping along behind wherever they went, wanting to help his mother in the kitchen or his father in the yard, always wanting to be friends.

What affected his father most was how Bryant tried and tried, never giving up, never letting constant failure embitter him. All those frustrating years of trying to succeed at school, something he was so ill-suited for—years of squirming before math problems that bewildered him and gazing into textbooks that seemed incomprehensible. Year after year, he tried and tried, with the same dismal results, scraping by in school, burning through his parents' money for remedial help, falling behind, staying behind, and yet "he never once complained," his father marveled. "He wanted to make us happy."

In his years of teaching, Brother Jim Reiter of St. Bernard High School in Westchester had discovered it was not necessarily students' academic prowess that won over their teachers. It was character—some combination of earnest effort, curiosity, and intrinsic goodness. Bryant Tennelle had it, despite his scholastic failings. "He was the type of student—you would do whatever you could to help him," said Reiter, who, besides his teaching duties, also volunteered as an on-call chaplain for the police department.

When Reiter encountered Bryant in high school, he saw how hard it was for him to focus. He was no longer, by that time, a behavior problem. He struck Reiter as introspective and aware of how much effort his parents had put into him. As frustrating as he found the schoolwork, "he wouldn't lash out," Reiter said. "He was bound and determined to make his parents proud of him."

Reiter, first as his teacher, then as his academic counselor, encouraged him. At last, after years of denying him a chance to participate in sports because of his studies, Wally and Yadira had given in to Bryant's pleas to play football. In his junior year he turned out for the team. He also did drama, dance—he was one of the only boys in the high school's large dance program—and extracurricular activities. Reiter secretly knew Bryant sold brownies and cookies at school for cash in defiance of the rules, and turned his back.

There had to be some way for Bryant to succeed in a world that had become so inhospitable to people whose strengths lay in manual arts. Bryant was so genuine—and so well liked. His teachers at St. Bernard, like his parents and DeeDee, were always on the lookout for the right path for him. Reiter and some others had talked about guiding him toward culinary school.

By then, Bryant had grown slim and taller than Wally Jr. With his honey-brown skin and shiny hair, he was a hit with girls, and his humor and inborn desire to please assured him close friends among boys as well. He was not mature for his age, Wally Jr. thought. Bryant still loved *Star Wars* and his Lego battleships. He still had stuffed animals all over his room. His favorite was a stuffed chicken, like those he raised. His father was still thinking about the Marines. But Bryant was not of this mind. He talked to his grandmother of his love for clothing, and to his mother of his love for mechanics. He took an adult course at Crenshaw High School repairing car interiors and thrived in it. He had reached the age to drive.

Driving gave Bryant the freedom to pursue hourly jobs. Wally Tennelle soon recognized in his youngest son his own proclivity toward constant work. Bryant got a job at a Togo's sandwich shop, and then Petco and Jamba Juice. Soon he was doubling up on jobs, shifting to better ones as they came along: Quiznos, Marie Callender's, Big Five. He was still just a high school kid. But at these hourly jobs, where academic skill was not at a premium—only energy, industriousness, and a drive to earn money—Bryant was in his element. Seeing him work so enthusiastically gratified his parents, who still wanted him to graduate but were pleased to see him finally excel. "He wanted to be like me," Wally Tennelle said. "Always out. Always working."

Senior year, Bryant flunked economics. It was a class required for graduation, and it meant his parents' dream of seeing him earn his diploma was thwarted. Reiter stepped in; Yadira and Wally were willing to try anything. They enrolled Bryant in an El Camino College class to make up the credits. But the class was too hard for him and required too much reading.

Privately, Wally Tennelle was worried. Those in the LAPD who suspected Tennelle was naïve for living in the Seventy-seventh were wrong. Tennelle knew the statistics; he knew the dynamics of gangs in his neighborhood, and understood the risks to his son better than most cops. It was always on his mind. But he also knew what many people don't—that risk for young black men remains high even when they leave Los Angeles. San Bernardino County, for example, was a popular destination for black families seeking to protect their sons from crime. But while in the first five years of the 2000s the homicide death rate for San Bernardino's young black men was indeed lower than for those in Los Angeles, it was still at least twenty times the national rate for Americans generally, and teenage rates there were rising fast. Tennelle's information was anecdotal, but he comprehended the bigger picture. "How many times have I heard, I moved my son to San Bernardino and he got killed?" he said. "Why not stand my ground here?"

Tennelle had lectured both his sons—told them how easy it was to be mistaken for someone else and caught by a gang shooting. "Where you from?" were the last words heard by many a murder victim in L.A. Wally Tennelle knew if you were fifteen to twenty-five years old and black or Hispanic, there was no right answer. He chided his sons for slipping, he instructed them in how to be careful. But Bryant, unlike his older brother, had a fearless temperament. Tennelle never connected the trait to his own personality. But like his father, Bryant refused to live with any trepidation. He did what he wanted, went where he wanted, and was friendly and guileless with everyone he met. It left his father cold with fear. He would check up on Bryant while working in his sedan.

He once came upon him walking at night at Seventy-ninth and Hall-dale. "Bryant, I want you home in an hour," he told him. Bryant was home at the appointed time. He was always like that—so good and willing, but still giving cause for worry.

Wally was not the only one worried. Wally Jr. was old enough to have experienced South Central at the end of the Big Years as only young black men did. The area wasn't as bad as its reputation. But when he was about seven years old, he was playing outside and saw a shooting down the block. He saw the shooter's Hawaiian shirt as he jumped out of the car, and he watched him shoot up a house. Another time, there was a party up the street—lots of Crips with blue bandanas walking up and down the street. Wally Jr. had been "where-you-fromed" several times. By high school he had developed a strategy: "I'm from nowhere. I don't bang." And keep walking. Sometimes the same gangster would hit him up two days in a row. *Don't you remember you just asked me?* Wally Jr. would silently fume. But it was not his daily reality. Sure, the boulevards around his neighborhood could be dangerous. And there was that apartment on the corner. But the Tennelles' neighborhood was also full of hardworking, friendly homeowners, families like theirs, and it was easy to keep a distance from the blue bandanas.

Much later, Wally Jr. would think about the great crime drop in Los Angeles, and the effect on his brother. Wally Jr. was only five years older than Bryant. But those five years were enough to have placed him in a different zone of fear. Wally Jr. and his friends had grown up in that brief span when South Central's gang members actually did wear col-ors openly—their blue, red, and orange bandanas spilling from back pockets—something that would later become uncommon. He and his friends knew the rules. They had felt the vulnerability. They had learned the codes. They instinctively watched their backs, studied cars as they passed, always aware if one doubled back or passed twice. They knew what streets to avoid and what clothes not to wear.

But Bryant was a child of a safer L.A. and was not schooled in the streets. He was much less cautious.

Wally Jr. saw this as an extension of his childish innocence. He sometimes tried to talk to Bryant about what colors to wear. He noticed how carefree his brother was, riding his bike while listening to his music. But Bryant didn't see the point of the rules. He even went to the Slauson Swap Meet on his bike, assuring his father it was all just fine. The Slauson Swap Meet. Every Seventy-seventh officer had answered calls there. Their father was angry—and concerned. He thought he saw a bruise on Bryant and wondered if he had gotten into a fight.

Bryant had been so sheltered and closely monitored by his parents that he knew only a few other kids in his neighborhood. But that, too, began to change as he grew older.

Joshua Henry had gone to Crenshaw High. He first met Bryant when he rolled by on his bike on one of his business ventures, selling homemade T-shirts and brownies. He shared Bryant's taste for dancing, music, and building bikes. They worked on the bicycles together and rode them around.

Josh adored Bryant for his humor and good nature and shook his head at what he considered his elite and eccentric ways—the private school education, the pet duck that Bryant kept into his late teens. Josh was not a gang member. But he knew the streets much better than did Bryant. As thirteen-year-old students at Audubon Middle School, Josh and his friends one day cut through an alley and found themselves facing men with guns. They ran as gunfire erupted and boarded a passing bus. On the bus Josh looked down and noticed the hole in his shirt. A bullet had gone right through without touching him. He felt sick, breathless with fear.

Another time, he was older, stopped in a car with a friend on Van Ness. A group of men surrounded them, trying to open the car doors. As they sped away, a bullet hit the car and Josh got that same sick feeling again. It was funny how in movies, shootings seemed exciting, he thought. In life, they weren't.

Josh considered Bryant "soft as a diaper" and thought he was crazy to go around the neighborhood so fearlessly. He, too, tried to teach Bryant the unwritten rules. Stay off Western, he'd say. "And watch yourself—no matter where you at." When Bryant didn't seem to get it, Josh tried to teach him lessons. He would see Bryant walking on the street—"walking with his head down!" he marveled later—and roll up on him in a bike or car. "See?" he'd say. "You just got caught slippin'!" Josh couldn't believe how naïve Bryant was. "He wasn't used to that environment," he said. "His parents raised him well."

Bryant, however, sampled some share of the black man's lot. He and Josh had a run-in with the LAPD while riding their bikes in the Kingdom Day Parade in celebration of Martin Luther King, Jr.'s birthday. Josh got mouthy. But Bryant told the officer his father was a detective and tried to reason with him, standing straight and talking quietly. Josh, watching, was impressed with his friend's self-control in a situation that left him fuming. It was a side of Bryant he hadn't seen before. The cop was not moved. Josh ended up with a ticket for blocking an alleyway that became a six-hundred-dollar fine.

Bryant Tennelle had entered that period of late adolescence when parents find their power reduced to suggestion and hope. Every parent goes through it; not every parent faces the lethal threat that bore down on young men in South Los Angeles.

That fall, Bryant turned eighteen. Legally, he was an adult. One day, he came home with an earring in one ear. "Why did you do that?" Yadira demanded. She knew her husband would be furious. Bryant kept his head turned so Wally couldn't see at first. But eventually Wally cried out: "What is that doing in your ear!" Soon Bryant had earrings in both ears.

Girls were coming around now. The family didn't like all of them. DeeDee, eight years older, took it upon herself to scold Bryant. "Pull your pants up!" she snapped. Bryant wore them looser than Wally Jr. had. He had developed a little hip-hop style, and it worried her.

Near the new year, Bryant got pulled over for speeding. It had happened before. This speeding ticket was the clincher: his driver's license was suspended. Bryant was effectively grounded. He still went to school. On his own initiative, he had appealed to Reiter to help him again after failing at El Camino, and was now trying to graduate through a public school program for adult students. He still worked, taking buses or getting rides from his mother. But now, Bryant found himself sitting at home, too old to be under his parents' thumb, without social options except those in the neighborhood.

Bryant had never mixed with many of the young people in his neighborhood before. His parents had carefully controlled his activities. It is one of the astonishing details of Bryant's story that despite having lived, as his father wanted, in the same house all his life, he was a stranger to kids living on the same block. Wally and Yadira had limited him to private school friends and the children of families they trusted. Bryant was extraordinarily sheltered.

But now he was on foot or on his bike around the neighborhood, and made his first acquaintance with some of the young people nearby. A short walk from his house was a shabby rental home where a family with gang ties lived. Older family members were more involved, a younger one, Christopher Wilson, less so, though compelled by his relations into some fellowship with the 8-Trey Gangster Crips. Walter Lee Bridges was a friend of Wilson's. With Josh Henry and some other young men, they formed a loose clique of what Josh would later call "affiliated" kids. Young men in South Central borrowed cop's jargon as readily as cops expropriated theirs: "affiliated" referred to youths who weren't necessarily criminal or violent but were inclined or obliged to be on friendly terms with the gang. None of Josh's friends were "hard-core" gang members. But they had all been in fights from time to time, and some had been shot at. They knew friends who had been murdered. They had an unwritten code of having each other's backs if need be.

Mostly, they just hung out together, fixed up their bicycles, smoked pot, and tried to figure out how to be cool and meet girls. Many white suburban teenage boys spent their time in much the same way. Asked later why Bryant had taken to wearing a baseball cap with the insignia of the Houston Astros on it—the covert symbol of the nearby 8-Trey

Hoover Criminals—Josh reacted as if the answer were self-evident. For the same reason they all wore such attire, he said: "To get girls!"

That spring, Bryant, Chris, Walter, and Josh began hanging out regularly. Their circle eventually expanded to Chris's girlfriend and her pretty cousin Arielle Walker from down the street. Arielle was black-eyed with a hint of ruddy cinnamon in her complexion. Her father was in prison for murder.

To the group, it was as if Bryant Tennelle were a visitor from some exotic shore. He was astoundingly naïve. He had never drunk alcohol, didn't fight, and knew nothing about gangs. He didn't even know how to kiss a girl. He had this nice home and proper family and an intimidating cop for a dad who puttered in the driveway with his cigars. And not only did Bryant work, he was *punctual,* something none of the rest of them were. Bryant would hang out, then cut it short to start his shifts. The others liked him and called him by his last name. But they didn't know what to make of him, with his beloved pet ducks and chickens and his gentle, sensitive ways. He wasn't aggressive. He wasn't loud. He sought to downplay conflicts. He wanted everyone to get along.

The last part was most novel of all. Lawless violence burdens black men as no one else. Walking with a bopping limp that suggests you have survived your share of street fights, yelling a lot, wheeling your eyes around angrily—these were learned behaviors among ghettoside men, affectations they adopted as preemptive defense against attack. Appearing weak was dangerous. Many men described having been robbed and threatened from childhood, relieved of their lunch money on the way to school, beaten up for backpacks and shoes, constantly called out to fight. Undersized boys were tormented, tall ones tested. It was frustrating and draining. Many black men were left with a version of the sickening sensation most males probably feel at some point in childhood, knowing a bully awaits them after school, wanting to fight. But the difference for these men was that the feeling was sharpened by fear of death and pervaded their adult lives. The stress wrought deep unhappiness. In the streets of the Seventy-seventh, men talked of suicide. Others were fatalistic and resigned. Lots of men, deep down, didn't want to fight. They tried to avoid it, acting tough to discourage challengers. They conveyed, with every mannerism and gesture, a message that said "Don't mess with me." It was an exhausting act to keep up. But it was worth it to feel safer.

Josh, Walter, and Chris wanted to toughen up Bryant. They threw play punches at him, trying to get him to jab and dodge. They tried to educate him in street codes. Bryant was too kind, raised too well. "He was nowhere near us," Chris said. So far above them, he meant.

Arielle was so unfamiliar with middle-class mores that she was amazed by the simple fact that Bryant got up early every morning. She knew hardly anyone who did that. "It changed us so much as a group," Arielle recalled. "We never had anyone like him around." Before long, she and Bryant were dating.

Bryant's family was less enthusiastic about his new social life. DeeDee had no patience for Bryant's "hanging out." She considered Arielle "a hoodrat" and the rest of the bunch "unsavory." She was worried. Bryant was a sponge, she observed—easily influenced. "If he doesn't get his act together, it will drive my parents crazy," she thought. She began job hunting for him, poring through lists of city openings in the hope of finding something more durable than the hourly, part-time work Bryant was doing.

For his part, Wally Tennelle was on high alert. At work, he increased his detours to check up on Bryant. The cop side of his brain was fully engaged. He studied his son's clothes and movements and scrutinized his friends. Bryant was too old for his parents to dictate his friendships. But Tennelle watched, all the time. He perceived the rough vibrations around Chris Wilson and Walter Lee Bridges. But he could also tell they were not "hard-core." He recognized them as that familiar, softer breed of "affiliated" kids. Both young men were intelligent and likable—good guys, there was no doubt about it. They couldn't help where they'd grown up. Tennelle knew that Bryant was mostly building bicycles with them. He knew that this pursuit meant a lot to Bryant. When he questioned him, Bryant assured him it was bicycles he liked, not gang-banging.

Yadira worried, too. But she never knew how deeply anxious her husband was over Bryant. Wally Tennelle would get up at 2:00 A.M. to check Bryant's room and make sure he was home. He churned with anxiety every time Bryant left the house. He harped on Bryant's whereabouts, nagged him about his social activities. Time after time, he gave the same lecture: "You walk like a duck, talk like a duck, and people gonna think you are a gangster." Despite the strains, the two remained close, collaborating on projects around the house.

Bryant showered in the bathroom off his parents' room because the main bathroom was kept clean for guests. It afforded Wally an opportunity to covertly examine his bare skin. One day, he caught a glimpse of Bryant's exposed back and saw what he dreaded: a new tattoo. It was not any symbol he recognized, no gang or neighborhood name. It was simply a logo of the city, the name "Los Angeles" with scrolls and angel wings. Wally confronted Bryant. There was another scene like the earring episode. But Tennelle was up against the fact that his youngest was no longer a child: "What can you do?" he said later. He had no legal right to demand that Bryant wear different clothes or have another girlfriend. "He is eighteen years old. You can't chain him down. You can't drive him out of the house."

At the same time, Wally Tennelle was an astute enough observer of gang life to perceive that his son was not like the gangsters he had spent his career arresting. Bryant held jobs and was obviously committed to them. He got up early, worked hard, and was always on time. He was studying hard to get his final credits to get his diploma. Most of all, Bryant remained the "good boy" his parents had always known him to be. There was no new shift in attitude. Bryant was never sullen. He was always good-natured, obedient even when he didn't have to be, loving to his mother, bonding with his father over various innocent pursuits—tropical fish and show-quality roosters—although neighbors' complaints finally forced the family to give up the birds. Wally Tennelle knew these were not the hallmarks of a gang-banging criminal. And when he confronted Bryant, all those years of protective parenting were turned back on him: "Daddy!" Bryant remonstrated. "You raised me better than that!"

All teenagers go through phases. Wally and Yadira hoped they would get Bryant back on track when he got his driver's license back. June 29 was the date they were waiting for.

By spring Bryant finished his class and at last he had the credits to get his diploma. It was cause for a family celebration. Wally and Yadira were so proud. Bryant told Arielle how happy he was. He told her how long he had been yearning to please his parents.

Yadira accompanied Bryant to pick up his diploma. Reiter and Bryant's other teachers were planning a party. And there was more good news: with DeeDee's help, Bryant had a secured a job with the City of Los Angeles Department of Recreation and Parks working with youths. DeeDee hoped this would turn into a career in public employment. She was now an accountant at LAX, working for the city, just like her father. Her aunt was also a municipal employee. DeeDee dubbed them "a city family." The parks job would give Bryant a chance to shine in a new arena as a mentor to kids. He would thrive, she thought.

It was Friday, May 11, before Mother's Day weekend. Bryant was to start his new job Monday. It seemed appropriate, like a Mother's Day gift to Yadira. She had been hoping for so long for all these pieces to fall in place—the high school diploma, the real job. Bryant was excited to show his parents he knew how much effort they'd poured into him, wanted to show them how much he appreciated it.

He told Arielle to expect him later that evening because he wanted to buy a Mother's Day basket for Yadira. Arielle was going to give him a lift.

The sun had not yet set. Bryant had some time on his hands. He bought a root beer with Walter and strolled along Eightieth Street pushing his bike.

11

"IT'S MY SON"

Wally and Yadira Tennelle did not hear the *pap-pap* of gunfire a short distance away.

As Walter Lee Bridges fled and Bryant collapsed, the couple were at home doing what they always did on Friday evenings—puttering, alone and together, doing their own thing. Yadira was in the shower. Wally was contemplating the cars in the driveway, about to move them.

At the shooting scene, Arielle Walker ran across the intersection to the cluster of screaming teenagers.

She saw Bryant on the ground, paramedics all around. Her eyes fixed on the cap full of blood.

She thought of Bryant's mother. She grabbed the cap and ran.

Wally Tennelle had begun to move the cars when he saw a young girl coming toward him, weeping. *Again,* he thought. *Now what?* He braced himself for his neighbors' latest drama.

Arielle quavered when she saw him. She was looking for Yadira. To Arielle, Bryant's mother had always seemed approachable, kind—everyone in the neighborhood loved Yadira. Arielle barely knew Wally. She knew he was a cop and was intimidated. It hadn't occurred to her that she might see him first. But he fixed her with his gentle eyes. She would remember his first words to her: "I can help you. What's wrong?"

Then his eyes dropped to her hand, to the blood-filled cap in her fingers.

Tennelle spoke before Arielle had a chance to, his eyes on the cap.

He knew that cap. "It's my son," he said.

The instant was all the notification he needed. He had not been a homicide detective all those years for nothing. As soon as he saw the hat, saw how much blood was on the cap, he understood that something irreversible had happened.

Tennelle thought of his wife inside. He called to her. She was still in the shower. He put Arielle in his car and drove over.

Josh, looking up, saw the big sedan zoom up and the door fly open. Tennelle hopped out while it was still rolling, its wheels coming to rest against the curb. He looked around. Bryant was on the grass surrounded by paramedics. The cops were putting up tape.

Tennelle noted his son's position and scanned the street. Later he would be able to describe the scene using the same tone and terminology as for a hundred other crime scenes. *Victim down. Feet facing west.*

He turned to one of the cops and motioned toward Arielle. *This witness,* he said, *needs to be secured.*

He carefully placed the cap on the ground near his son's head. Evidence. It belonged there.

He told the paramedics he would meet them at the hospital. He got back in his sedan and went to face Yadira.

Nearby, the man with the tile cutter was aware that a plainclothes cop with a professional bearing had arrived in a sedan. He assumed he was an LAPD detective sent to investigate. Only later did he learn who the detective was. He never heard him say a word.

"I think Bryant got shot."

That's how Yadira Tennelle remembers her husband putting it.

Please no, she had thought. When he got back, she was out of the shower, waiting.

By then, he had seen the cap full of blood and he had seen their son lying on the ground with his head half blown off. But Bryant still breathed. For Wally Tennelle, this task of telling his wife what had happened was traumatic in its own right. He fell into his old habit of understatement. Had he been someone else, the words he chose might have seemed deceptive. But because he was Wally Tennelle, they were simply of a piece with the calm, measured way he'd lived his whole life. Years later, the story of how he told Yadira remained nearly as painful to recount as the shooting itself. The worst notification he would ever make: how he hated breaking Yadira's heart. So all he said was that Bryant had been shot in the head, and they had to go to the hospital. He did not say that Bryant had been brutally maimed and was near death.

DeeDee went with them, and she understood even less about her brother's state than Yadira. She convinced herself that they were just going to the hospital to get some information. They were going to find out what was going on, that was all.

"It's in God's hands now," Wally told them in the car. Somewhere nearby a neighbor was screaming.

Security at the hospital was tight. DeeDee was frustrated. *Stupid paperwork,* she thought. Finally, they were admitted and were standing near the trauma bay. A nurse met them. She talked and talked. DeeDee didn't understand most of it. But one phrase stopped her short—*brain matter.* DeeDee's mind kept going back to the words—"brain matter." *Oh God.* She had a sense something terrible was about to happen but as yet had not admitted to herself what it was. Then she looked at her father's face.

They were sent to a waiting area. There were so many cops milling around the hospital that DeeDee wondered if there were any on the street. Her thoughts went to her grandmother. She conferred with her parents, then went to hold vigil with Dera Tennelle.

Bryant's brother was living in Encino. Wally Jr. and his wife, Ivory, were on Sepulveda Boulevard near the Skirball Center when Yadira called. Ivory answered. From the driver's seat Wally Jr. could hear his mother screaming into his wife's ear—heard the substance of what was happening—and made a U-turn in the middle of the big, wide boulevard. *Bryant shot.* Adrenaline exploded through his body as the news took shape in his mind; it had an almost physical impact, like the sensation of falling on pavement. California Hospital was clear across town. Between him and his injured brother stood the gridlocked interchange of the 405 freeway and the clogged midsection of the Ten. Wally Jr. and Ivory sat in traffic for an hour, anxiety consuming them, praying, fuming. Yadira called back once or twice. Then DeeDee. Wally Jr. took a call and heard his mother say the phrase "shot in the head." He must have misheard her, he thought, hanging up. She probably said "shot in the hand."

At the hospital, Wally Jr. spent fifteen minutes being cleared by security to enter. It didn't sit well with the soon-to-be college graduate, who was inclined to wonder whether part of the reason was that he was a young black man. "I just want to see my brother," he pleaded at one point. The security guard explained that the hospital had problems with gang rivals trying to enter the trauma center "and finish it." The explanation would stick with him.

Inside, the halls were packed with cops. He saw his dad's partner, but didn't immediately see his parents. Then he noticed a surgeon in the crowd, looking around as if searching for someone. His headgear suggested he had just come out of the surgical theater. Wally noticed that his face was tight. It was not the face of good news, he thought.

Brother Jim Reiter of St. Bernard High School had also been stuck in traffic. He had been summoned to the hospital as department chaplain. A murder in the Seventy-seventh, they told him. And the victim was a detective's son. Reiter knew nothing further. A shadow of an idea crept into his mind.

It's got to be Bryant, he thought. But then he chided himself for assuming. Tense and frustrated by the evening traffic crush, Reiter prayed the whole way to the hospital, the same prayer, *Please, don't let it be Bryant,* over and over. He missed the exit and had to go all the way to Western and double back, and he prayed some more. *Please, not Bryant.*

When he got to the hospital, he told himself his fears were baseless. He was being ridiculous. He told the clerks at the desk he was here for the detective's son. "Oh!" one said, matter-of-factly. "Tennelle?"

Reiter found the Tennelles sitting together in a small lounge with two other chaplains. All around there were officers, commanders, and various friends. Wally and Yadira sat together in chairs, facing the door. Reiter noticed how Wally kept his arm around Yadira's shoulders. The room was crowded. Reiter stayed in back, leaning against a cabinet, trying to be unobtrusive. He watched Bryant's father. Wally Tennelle seemed to be attending to everyone. He was playing caretaker. Did anyone need water? Anyone need to sit down? Reiter was amazed.

A doctor came and launched into what seemed to Wally Jr. to be a long and confusing explanation of Bryant's injuries. *He is going to say "we stabilized him,"* the brother kept thinking. He waited for it. Then he heard the words "brain injury" and "he went into cardiac arrest." Wally Jr. couldn't make sense of it. Instead, he stared at the doctor's face. He was a middle-aged black man with a flat sadness in his gaze. Later, describing how he finally understood that his brother had died, Wally Jr. remembered the expression on the doctor's face as much as the words he spoke. Yadira was weeping. *"I want Bryant,"* she cried. *"I want my son."*

Wally Jr. looked at his father. The elder Tennelle was nodding, calmly acknowledging the doctor's report. "Yeah," he said. "Okay."

The doctor was Bryan Hubbard, a veteran trauma surgeon of the Big Years. Hubbard and his colleagues were the medical equivalent of the Tennelles, Gordons, and Skaggses of the LAPD. They were high-energy perfectionists who had learned their craft in the age of the great homicide epidemic. For a while, the military had sent their medics to train with them.

Hubbard was a veteran of King-Drew Medical Center down in Willowbrook near Watts, closed a few years before. In the 1990s, gang fights outside the operating room there had been a problem. Surgeons could almost predict the timing of new trauma calls by watching friends of victims depart the waiting room, rushing out to take revenge. Soon after, surgeons would be summoned to another "Code Yellow."

Hubbard would tell family members a loved one was dead and sense they were planning vengeance. "I could see it in their eyes," he said. One man was more direct. "I'm tired of dealing with it the regular way." he said after Hubbard informed him his friend had died. "I have my own way of dealing with it." He pantomimed a gun with his fingers. *Please. Not while I'm on duty,* Hubbard thought.

Things were quieter by this time than they had been at King-Drew. But the nature of Hubbard's job remained the same. He had made scores of notifications just like the one he made to the Tennelles. It was the worst part of his job. He had to steel himself each time. He had never gotten much training in this aspect of his job. But he had learned from seeing others do it poorly. He knew that every word he said would be imprinted on the minds of his listeners, but that even so, they would find ways to block out the truth. He tried to be as blunt as possible. "Simple harsh truths" was the phrase he used to himself. "He passed," he tried to say, right away, as clearly as he could. The details could wait.

But people still didn't hear him. Or they couldn't comprehend it and remained confused. Or they fainted or fell on the floor, or cried out, as Yadira did. Told later that Wally Jr. understood that his brother was dead as much from Hubbard's expression as from his words, Hubbard nodded with weary recognition. It was often like that.

The Tennelles waited to view Bryant's body. The chaplains waited with them in the crowded little lounge. At last someone came. The body was ready.

They were escorted to a small area with curtains. Bryant's body was covered with blankets. A nurse pulled away enough cloth for them to see the smooth skin of his face. Yadira yearned to touch him, but the medical staff said no. Wally Jr. noted the seam across his brother's forehead where the wound had been sewn, and he hoped his mother didn't see it. He could barely look. He made himself gaze for a few seconds, then averted his eyes.

He shifted to observing his parents, worrying, wondering how they would handle this. At the same time, with some part of his mind, he observed himself, realizing that focusing on them was a form of self-protection. He shed few if any tears. Then he noticed his father. The detective was looking steadily at his youngest son's still form, studying the exposed portion of his face with an intent gaze.

A chaplain performed the conditional anointing, commending Bryant to God, brushing Bryant's forehead, hands, and chest with his thumb. They exited. On the way out of the hospital, Reiter was astonished again when Wally Tennelle turned and asked him if he needed a ride. He had assumed Tennelle had barely noted his presence.

At Bryant's grandmother's house, DeeDee was keeping vigil with Dera and a few other relatives. By every account, the Tennelle family had remained impressively calm throughout this ordeal, waiting patiently for the medical system to do its work—each member of the family focused on the others. But Dera Tennelle was not going to take it so quietly. When the call from the hospital came, she threw her walker across the living room and collapsed, wailing and rolling about. DeeDee and her cousins sprang up to yank the furniture out of the way. There was something faintly comic about it all, DeeDee found herself thinking as she scrambled around the floor, her grandmother screaming nearby. The next instant, she marveled at life's paradoxes, the way human nature perceives humor even at the height of disaster.

Wally Jr. had a similar insight: he woke up the next morning surprised to find that he had slept through the night. He was unfamiliar with the way a breathless, suspended state of shock precedes grief.

DeeDee Tennelle was wrong—not every cop in the city was at California Hospital. There was also a whole army on Eightieth Street. Chris Barling was among them, taking some satisfaction in the fact that, for once, he had beaten Sal La Barbera to the scene.

Barling spoke to Greg De La Rosa, got some leads on witnesses, and went to California Hospital to track down Arielle. There, he made his way through the throng of cops and somehow managed to find her. Arielle's eyes were red from crying and she was talking incoherently. Barling took her back to the police station for an interview. Before leaving the hospital, he caught a glimpse through the crowd of Tennelle, whom he did not know, and his wife. Barling read Tennelle's body language by reflex, as cops always do: Tennelle was making an effort to be strong, Barling thought. But you could see something off in his posture. His eyes had a desolate look that Barling recognized.

David Garrido, Sal La Barbera's counterpart in charge of Southwest Division's homicide unit, was also at the murder scene. It was already packed with brass, among them Lieutenant Lyle Prideaux of Robbery-Homicide Division, Charlie Beck, the future LAPD chief, and other higher-ups.

The sky was still bright where the setting sun had dropped, but darkness engulfed the street. Yellow lights shone from the houses. Spindly palms and a eucalyptus tree stood black against the sky and its few mottled clouds. Pretty houses, Garrido noted. Trimmed lawns. A bicycle overturned on the sidewalk.

Nearby was a pile of clothes. Garrido was used to that. The paramedics had ripped them off and left them there—blue Dickies, a white T-shirt, a black sweatshirt, and a pile of bloody towels. Patrol cars filled the street. A streetlamp illuminated a red biohazard bag and a white box that contained numbered placards. On the street-side grass median lay a dark Houston Astros baseball cap, a thick patch of red blood on the rim and a hole in the fabric tiny, half the size of a fingertip. Garrido drew near and noticed something on the ground. A piece of metal. He bent and picked it up. A little smashed projectile.

Pat Gannon, homicide commander in South Bureau, was in a hotel in Chicago, preparing to attend his son's graduation from Loyola, when his BlackBerry buzzed and he learned that Tennelle's son had been killed in the Seventy-seventh.

Gannon had known Wally Tennelle for two decades, knew him, as everyone did, as a quiet, unassuming detective who was "all about the work, all about solving the case and getting the job done." Gannon felt crushed. Tennelle, he thought, was probably one of the most beloved people in the department. Gannon knew he had a decision to make.

Already his phone was ringing and ringing, people giving him updates, wanting to know what to do. Emotions were running high. Several RHD detectives were arguing they should have the case, not lower-level detectives at the division. Gannon was getting an earful. Tempers were flaring. Some of his colleagues among the brass were fuming about "this arrogant DA"—a skinny guy who had turned up at the hospital and insisted that RHD get the case. Meanwhile, a Seventy-seventh detective supervisor named Matt Mahoney was moving ahead as if the case belonged to his group. They were "task-forcing" it in those first few hours, detectives fanning out all over "the westside."

Gannon knew that RHD had more expertise and manpower. But he also knew that the case did not exactly meet the criteria for elevation to RHD. Those criteria were, as he described it, "vague and flexible," but they usually were not stretched to encompass ordinary gang shootings with a single victim. Granted, special circumstances, such as extensive press coverage, could nudge a case into the RHD realm. But Gannon had worked in L.A. long enough to know that the Tennelle case probably wouldn't rise to that standard. Apart from the fact that the victim's father worked for the department, there was little to attract the media's interest. Bryant, after all, was a black male, eighteen years old, killed south of the Ten, and he'd been wearing a hat associated with a gang.

And there was court to consider. Any special treatment of the case by the police might be exploited by defense attorneys, Gannon thought. More to the point, he was anxious to separate the investigation from the emotions swirling among Tennelle's coworkers. Leaving the case with South Bureau detectives would ensure some detachment, since few people down there were personally connected to Tennelle. And it would serve another aim of interest to Gannon at that time: the brass had recently decided to recombine the three South Bureau divisional homicide squads into one unit, harking back to the old days of South Bureau Homicide. Success in clearing the Tennelle case would be validation for this new administrative setup, which would have one of the LAPD's bland new bureaucratic titles—Criminal Gang Homicide Group.

Gannon spoke at some point to Tennelle, but he didn't remember Tennelle giving any input on the question of who should take the case.

Tennelle recalled it differently. He took pains to show his approval of a divisional investigation. He, too, was worried that assigning the case to his coworkers at RHD might taint it. "I wanted the case to be clean," he said. But more than that, Wally Tennelle was still, in his heart, a ghettoside man, and he wanted the case to be investigated by ordinary station house homicide detectives down in South Bureau.

All those years in Newton had taught him how important it was to remain close to the street. He knew true craftsmanship in LAPD detective ranks wasn't represented by test results or departmental assignments. He knew how limited RHD could be—how small the detectives' caseloads, how rarefied their cases. "Our brass tells us, 'You're the best,'" he said, with typical frankness. "But I can name a bunch of detectives down there who are much sharper than the guys here."

He did not disparage his RHD colleagues. He respected them. But he had learned to see the world in a particular way. He had worked the Big Years. He had seen the Monster. And he knew how hard street shootings could be to solve. In Tennelle's opinion, RHD detectives didn't have the gang experience of their ghettoside counterparts. They were too far away from it, and they didn't have to work as hard and as fast. Tennelle included himself in this appraisal. "I am probably not as sharp as when I was in Newton," he said. So when Gannon made his decision, Tennelle privately rejoiced, even as his RHD colleagues fumed. The case would go to South Bureau. It was for the best, Tennelle thought. They would "have a better sense of it."

John Skaggs missed the entire drama of the Tennelle murder. He was out of town with his family on one of his desert racing weekends, camping out with the RV in the austere yellow terrain of the Mojave Desert near Ridgecrest. He was watching the sun set over the angular planes of that arid land—a beautiful sight—when Chris Barling buzzed him on the cell phone.

It was just before dinner. The sky was full of color. Skaggs was relaxed and enjoying himself. Barling told him he had just been at a crime scene, then that the victim was the son of Wally Tennelle of RHD.

Skaggs had one question: Who would take the case? Barling said he was pretty sure it would be the Seventy-seventh—Armando Bernal, perhaps.

A secret thought rose in Skaggs's mind, as clear as the horizon before his eyes: *They should give us that case. Me and Barling—we could solve it.*

But for Skaggs, it was a passing thought only. The killing of Bryant Tennelle was just a pulse in the din of murders that summer in the south end.

12

THE KILLING OF DOVON HARRIS

Three days after Bryant Tennelle died, twenty-six-year-old Carl Pickering Jr. was getting into a parked Chevrolet in front of Vertels liquor store near the block where Barbara Pritchett lived in Southeast Division. An assailant walked up and shot a bullet into his chest. Realizing he was dead, a girl stumbled screaming into the street in front of Vertels. Passing cars edged around her and kept going.

Eighteen-year-old Wilbert Mahone died next. He was standing outside in Compton at a relative's house later that same evening when a pair of drive-by shooters came roaring down the street. Wounded, he made it inside the house. He died holding the hand of his sixteen-year-old brother. Mahone's parents had moved him from Compton to Georgia in his youth because, they said, "we had sons and we didn't want them to be killed." Wilbert had returned to apply for a job.

Four days later, police found Christopher Davenport, thirty-six, lying dead on the sidewalk in San Pedro after neighbors reported hearing gunshots. The next day, LAPD narcotics officers in plain clothes killed Ronald Ball, sixty, in the Newton Division. The officers and their colleagues had detained a group of men they saw dealing drugs. Ball ran from them and hid under a car. When the officer tried to pull him out, Ball had a gun; the officer shot him.

Wayne McKinney, twenty-four, died a week later, on May 25, shot by a man or youth on the sidewalk while sitting in a car with a friend. Three days after that, eighteen-year-old Jamar Witherspoon was shot and killed by an LAPD officer at Eighty-ninth and Main streets. The officers were responding to a shooting call: Witherspoon, who police said was armed with a handgun, jumped a fence and ran—straight toward another officer, who shot him.

The next day, Carnell Ardoine, nineteen, was found dead in an alley near Eighty-first Street and Avalon Boulevard, shot in the mouth. Marcus Peters, also nineteen, died the next day in Long Beach in a walk-up shooting. Robert Lee, sixty-one, succumbed to wounds from a stabbing that occurred in the Newton Division soon after Peters's death. Stanley Daniels, thirty-one, argued with someone in the street at Thirty-ninth Street and Western Avenue. He was shot in the chest. No one called the police. Instead, by chance, LAPD officers on patrol found Daniels bleeding in the street. He died on June 2.

Irvin Carter, a disabled man in his sixties, died the following day after being slashed by a man walking with a knife in East Rancho Dominguez. And the next day, thirty-six-year-old Keith Hardy died at St. Francis Hospital after someone shot him many times in Compton. Christopher Rice, twenty-two—also shot in Compton—was also transported to St. Francis. He died four days after Hardy. The next day, June 10, Rodney Love, fifteen, was shot and killed on the street in the Seventy-seventh Street Division a block away from where Bryant Tennelle was shot. His mother ran outside just in time to watch her only child die as she dialed 911 over and over and got a busy signal.

Three days later, Detrick Ford, twenty, was said to have charged LAPD police officers with a knife in Watts, just east of where Barbara Pritchett lived on the same street. Officers shot and killed him. Dion Miles, nineteen, died that same day after being shot by some attacker in nearby Willowbrook. Miles was an art student at Cal State Northridge up in the San Fernando Valley and had no gang ties. He had gotten off a bus in an unfamiliar neighborhood, unwittingly wearing red in Crip territory.

With Watts's share of these criminal homicides—and others involving Hispanic victims—Skaggs and his colleagues were busy as ever that spring. Marullo was working with Skaggs as a full-fledged partner, though technically he was still a trainee and did not hold the rank of detective. Marullo had delivered on his early promise. He was passionate, effective, tireless. There was no question that he was the best young apprentice the unit had trained. He and Skaggs were working on a 100 percent clearance rate that year. They solved case after case.

Change was coming, however. Southeast would soon be incorporated into the newly reconstituted South Bureau homicide unit. Skaggs had sought a promotion to D-3, or supervisory detective. He was, as usual, playing the system to find a way to advance in rank yet remain working homicide in South Bureau.

Barling had taken a temporary supervisory nonhomicide job in the Seventy-seventh Street Division. Losing Barling was bad enough; La Barbera was dreading Skaggs's departure. But Marullo's performance was compensation.

Skaggs had a regret. He felt he had neglected Marullo's buddy Nathan Kouri, who had also been assigned to him as a trainee. The amount of time he and Marullo now spent in court left him little time to work with Kouri, the quiet former gang officer from Norwalk with the Lebanese surname whom Marullo had recommended so highly.

Neither La Barbera nor Skaggs had a sense of Kouri's abilities. Kouri was affable, well liked, and reassuringly square. He had been a Police Explorer in his teens and didn't drink. "Holy smokes!" he would say. "Geez Louise!" But he was an inept talker. He stumbled over words. No one could understand what he was working on, or follow the thread of his explanations. He avoided office banter. Theirs was a talking profession, but Kouri seemed more comfortable listening. He pestered colleagues and informants with questions, only occasionally interjecting a one-word response: "Inner-restin'!"

That spring, Skaggs renewed his efforts to focus on Kouri. His plan

was to work at least one case from start to finish with Kouri as his partner, keeping Marullo in the background. But then came a lapse in new
cases, and court hearings kept intervening. Kouri worked on bits of cases.
Skaggs knew this was not the same as handling a whole one. You had to
move with a case from start to finish—then follow it through court—to
really learn. You had to try it in your head as you worked the street.
Skaggs began to worry that Kouri would languish.

Then came Friday afternoon, June 15, graduation day at Centennial
High School in Compton.

Barbara Pritchett was thrilled. She had been waiting for this day. Her
second child, Dwaina, a senior, would be getting her diploma.

Barbara Pritchett's children were her life. She herself was the third
child of ten; her mother had had her first baby at age fourteen. The
mother had difficulties, and Pritchett was raised by her grandmother,
who had come west to California from Natchitoches, Louisiana. Once
grown, Pritchett had taken on the raising of her younger siblings herself. She brought up four of them, along with her own three children.
Among those still living with her was her littlest brother, Carlos, who
was several years younger than her youngest child, Dovon.

Their apartment was a rare subsidized unit with four bedrooms.
With so many children to raise, Pritchett held on to it for dear life. When
Pritchett was younger, her grandmother had helped keep her large
household afloat. More recently, her eldest son and daughter both
worked at hourly jobs. Pritchett was a home healthcare worker.

The family was close. Together, they made ends meet. Pritchett's
warmth and steady domesticity had made her the keystone of her entire
clan. Adult sisters, cousins, and longtime friends whom she called "cousins" constantly passed in and out of her living room, a center for social
life and holiday gatherings. Pritchett once spent four days preparing a
Thanksgiving feast for a couple dozen people, using smoked turkey instead of salt pork in the greens.

Pritchett had measured her life's success on getting all her charges through school and keeping them from gangs. Dovon, fifteen, was also at Centennial. Though only a tenth-grader, he, too, was released early because of the day's festivities.

He was in front of the school, about to catch a bus, when a fight broke out.

Centennial High School served students from Compton, Willow-brook, and Watts. Some of the most lethal gangs in Los Angeles County crossed paths in its hallways. Fights in and near the school were common. This one began with a fight between some girls. Kids started yelling at each other as they spilled outside, taking sides. A couple of boys yelled gang threats: "Bounty Hunters!" It was taken as a challenge to a rival gang—Westside Piru, another Blood gang sect. Police cleared the campus, hoping to avoid trouble.

Herded across the street, kids loitered in big knots. The argument mushroomed, girls and boys screaming at each other, menace in the air.

Dovon wanted to get away. With a group of other students, including a couple boys "affiliated" with the Bounty Hunters gang near his home, he boarded a Metro bus going north.

By then, news of the fight had spread thanks to girls calling on male protectors. Derrick Washington, the sixteen-year-old brother of one of the fighting girls, had gotten word that his sister was in trouble. He jumped into a Yukon with an older Piru gang member named Jason Keaton. They had a gun. The pair drove by the school just in time to see Dovon's group boarding the MTA bus headed north and gave chase. When Dovon and his friends got off on the outskirts of Nickerson Gardens in Watts, Bounty Hunter territory, the Yukon pulled up. Derrick fired. Everyone scattered. Dovon fell.

Skaggs got there after the ambulance was gone. Kouri wasn't with him. He was out of town on another case and due back that night. Skaggs surveyed the crime scene—for what it was worth.

As usual, not much. No body. Just an empty street, and a pair of dusty black tennis shoes strewn on the asphalt.

·   ·   ·

At Harbor-UCLA hospital, Barbara Pritchett found her youngest child on a ventilator, his face burned by gunpowder, his body swollen with fluid. Dovon had been shot in the head. His brain was destroyed. He would never awaken. But he remained on life support. Barbara touched his skin, still warm, and waited. Dovon's father, Duane Harris, had to fly in from out of town.

How long the victim remains alive after a declaration of brain death depends on several factors. In cases where organs are donated, it can take hours or days to arrange the transfer. And sometimes family members are not yet ready to accept the death. In Dovon's case, two days passed. Living at the hospital, Barbara proudly counted the number of Centennial High School faculty who visited him. The visits were validation of her efforts to raise her children well. Dovon had ADD and some troubles with academic work, but he had no criminal or gang involvement. He was unfailingly good-natured and affectionate, as was Barbara's whole family. Several of his teachers came and left weeping. Almost every visitor asked Barbara if anything had appeared on the news. It was a painful subject. There had been nothing on TV, nothing in the paper. Barbara kept up a brave face. It didn't matter, she told visitors. They all knew what Dovon's life had meant, even if the rest of the world seemed not to notice.

But Pritchett was secretly anxious. She suspected that her son's race and their circumstances would somehow stigmatize him in the eyes of the authorities. The lack of press coverage underscored this possibility. Dovon was, after all, just another black kid from Watts. Would police think he was just another gang member? Would they take the case seriously? Barbara, like most Watts residents, viewed the LAPD warily.

She sat by Dovon's still form and waited.

At length a tall white detective with blue eyes showed up at the hospital. Pritchett went out to see him. She made a point of looking him right in the eyes. "I want you to meet him," she said. "I want you to see his face."

She brought John Skaggs to Dovon's bedside. Dovon's body was still warm, still expanding with breath thanks to the ventilator. Barbara was hoping the sight would shake Skaggs from the indifference she presumed he harbored. Perhaps Dovon's physical presence might convince Skaggs that he was not just another young black man, "gunned down like he was nobody," as she would say later.

Skaggs humored Pritchett in his good-natured way. But he was not especially moved. He had been at many hospital bedsides, seen many swollen bodies. What Pritchett didn't know was how many scores of times he had already heard her version of the old lament—"just another black man down." Nor did she know that by this time, for Skaggs, the phrase was a battle cry.

The wider world might not view these homicides as earth-shattering. But to the detectives of the Southeast Division, they deserved every ounce of vigor the state could muster. By now, for Skaggs, this way of thinking was defining.

He and Marullo were already working in high gear. Kouri would join them soon. Skaggs wanted him to take a central role as soon as his plane landed.

By June 17, the doctors had explained the organ donation process to Barbara's uncomprehending family. Duane Harris, Dovon's father, could not accept it. He didn't understand: If organs could be donated, why couldn't Dovon receive some and then be saved? he asked. He offered his own: "Take my brain!" he begged. "Take my life!" The doctors had to explain it wasn't possible.

Duane Harris walked Dovon's gurney down a long hall at Harbor that last day to a pair of double doors. When they swung open automatically, Duane Harris stopped and the gurney rolled on without him. He stood in the hall as the doors closed, straining for a last glimpse of his son.

Within a few days, Skaggs and Kouri had traced the shooting that killed Dovon back to Centennial High. They had identified the players, and they cornered witnesses.

One episode in the investigation stood out. Skaggs interviewed Angela Washington, the teenage sister of sixteen-year-old suspect Derrick Washington. Skaggs had learned from other witnesses that Derrick had confessed the crime to Angela when he got home. Derrick, it turned out, knew Dovon, and even knew his nickname, "Poo-Poo." Derrick's defense attorneys would later argue that Derrick had been appalled to learn he had killed Dovon. Skaggs recognized Angela's value to the case. But when he and Kouri sat her down in the ice-cold interview room in the Southeast station, with its white walls and cheap wood veneer table, she denied her brother had ever confessed.

Angela, short, round, and with the same overbite as Derrick, spoke rapidly, and was emotional and angry. She was determined to protect her brother. Yes, she said, of course she had heard rumors that day. Everyone in the neighborhood was saying her brother had shot Poo-Poo. But "he looked me dead in the eye and said he didn't do it!" she insisted.

Skaggs let her ramble. His posture was relaxed, as if this were just a bit of unpleasant business to complete. At last he interrupted, speaking slowly, voice low. He said little. But his enunciation was deliberate, almost stately. His words marched into Angela's chatter like soldiers in formation.

"You and I," he said, "are going to be serious and honest."

Serious and honest. It wasn't clear whether it was his manner or his words that wrought the sudden change in Angela. Perhaps it was the set of his face or the dimension of moral comfort in his declaration. In any case, the interview abruptly shifted. With the word "honest" hanging in the air, the girl's head dropped into her hands. Several seconds passed in silence. When she raised her face, her cheeks were wet with tears.

"He told us to be quiet—" she began. And then she broke.

13

NOTHING WORSE

It was the strangest thing.

All the years that Wally Tennelle had been a cop, he'd participated in those quiet cop conversations: What would you do if it happened to you? If your worst fear came true, if some criminal raped your wife, killed your kid? When cops talked among themselves, the focus was anger and retribution. Would you wait for courts to exact justice? "I'd do it myself," the cops would assure each other.

But now that it had happened, Tennelle discovered something that astonished him: No matter how deeply he searched his soul, he felt no anger. And he felt no desire at all for retribution.

Instead, there was only pain. Inescapable pain. Tears ambushed him several times a day. He and Yadira kept Bryant's room exactly as he had left it: The Lego sculptures in their places. The *Star Wars* toys. The Cat in the Hat Halloween costume. They found solace in their religion, and in their conversations, Bryant's death became a matter of "God's will." This framework clarified the task that lay before them. After all, God's will was something to be accepted. And if you couldn't accept, the next best thing was to endure.

So they set about enduring.

DeeDee went back to work. She was pregnant, trying to raise a small son, and her marriage was breaking up. Months later she would admit that she had never really taken time to deal with her brother's death. It lurked at the edge of her thoughts. She held it at bay. She was angry at Bryant—angry at what she saw as his waywardness in recent years, which had put him at risk. At times, she allowed herself to think about the killers, whoever they were. Why had they done it? What were they thinking? She couldn't help but see the case in historical, racial dimensions. What did it mean that the civil rights struggle had landed black people here, knee-deep in murder? "After what our ancestors did," she thought, in silent argument with the perpetrators, "and you are going to go around killing each other?"

Yadira took an interest in Bryant's burial site at the mausoleum at Holy Cross Cemetery. She visited frequently. She cried freely and talked often to her husband about her grief. She found a television preacher she liked, and she tried to apply his lessons to her life. It helped her keep bitterness at bay.

She was stern with herself and policed her own self-pity. When she found herself thinking that she was the only one in the world suffering, she forcibly countered the thought. *Others also suffer,* she would remind herself.

Unlike many couples, who are thrust apart by grief, Wally and Yadira drew together. They resolved not to let the murder of their son darken their souls.

Yadira spoke of this resolution with passion: "We made up our minds," she would say, making a fist, "not to be depressed. Not to be angry!" But Yadira couldn't help wondering what they had done to deserve this. Her thoughts of Bryant were constant. She relived his entire life through memories, relived conversations. She worried that they hadn't told him enough that they loved him. But then she would check herself: of course Bryant knew.

When she, too, went back to work, she noticed how hard it was for people to know what to say. She sensed that they expected her to fall apart. But she didn't know how to fall apart.

She knew it was strange—she *looked* the same, despite this massive piece of herself that had gone missing. She acted the same. She went to work, greeted people, went home. Everything normal on the outside, except for occasional muffled crying on the job. At home, she wandered into Bryant's bedroom, out, then back in, everything in its place, just as it had been when he died. She placed his picture in a locket on a necklace and wore it at all times. She hung a plaque on the living room wall: "If love could have saved you," it read, "you would have lived forever."

For Wally Tennelle, the directive to endure fit easily into the internal monologue that had molded his whole life. He told himself to be strong, and to move on. Just keep moving. For Tennelle, there was no problem in life for which this answer did not suffice.

Tennelle's bosses urged him to take as much time off as possible. But he couldn't see the point. Work was going to keep him sane. So after three days at home, he went back. He needed to be there. He mounted a picture of Bryant on the dashboard of his detective sedan and dug back into his cases.

For his colleagues, it was not so simple. Tennelle's wounded presence around the office inflicted what can only be described as agonies of compassion. What could they do? The situation called for pity, in the ancient sense, without its modern patronizing stigma. In mythology, pity such as this would squeeze tears from bare rock. But in the workplace etiquette of Robbery-Homicide in 2007, the only permissible expression of pity was inadequate, mumbled repetitions of the phrase "I'm so sorry" and pointless offers of help that were ignored, as those who offered knew they would be.

It was an impossible state of affairs. Tennelle was so mild and impenetrable—so resolutely professional yet so obviously in anguish—that his friends could neither act normal nor reach out without feeling that they were brutalizing him somehow.

Death was bad enough. The death of a child, unbearable. But the murder of a child? There was nothing worse. Detectives' response was no different from that of the people in the neighborhoods of South Los Angeles. The killing of a human being anywhere is like a rock thrown in

a pond. Bitter waves emanate outward, washing over an ever-wider circle of friends, colleagues, and acquaintances, finally lapping against
those distant from the impact point, friends of friends, old classmates,
all, to some measure, sickened by the taint of this news—*murder,* so
awful, so unbelievable—no degree of separation big enough to neutralize its poison.

Some of Tennelle's colleagues had children about Bryant's age.
They had dealt with homicide bereavement all their careers. They knew
what it meant. Finally, Tennelle had to appeal to Lyle Prideaux, his
boss: "I just can't take any more people coming up to me," he said. "I
just need to be able to work." Quietly word went around, and they left
him alone.

But that doesn't mean they forgot. It's possible that Tennelle's stoic
and suppressed form of grieving produced a transference of emotion.
There was a great deal of acrimonious murmuring about the case going
to "divisional" detectives in the Seventy-seventh. The RHD crew felt
they could have solved it. Tennelle, of course, kept his opinions to himself. No one in RHD knew that he had secretly wanted the case to go
ghettoside.

Time passed. In his grief, Wally Jr., like his parents, went weeks without giving a thought to his brother's killers. He was looking for a job,
trying to put his UC Irvine degree to work.

Then, one day, he realized the killers were on his mind. He found
himself wondering who they were. What they looked like. Whether they
would ever be sorry. Whether he could forgive them if they were.

He became fixated on the question of whether the case would be
solved. He remembered his father telling him that the first forty-eight
hours truly were critical in getting people to talk—just like they said on
TV. After a month went by, he began to feel gnawing worry. He imag-
ined, with dread, his whole life going by and never knowing what had
happened to his brother. He developed a habit of praying before sleep.
Night after night, he closed his eyes with the same simple refrain: *Please
solve the case.*

. . .

The case had gone to Armando Bernal, one of the most experienced detectives in Seventy-seventh. Hired in 1981, Bernal had started in the mostly Hispanic Hollenbeck Division in the Boyle Heights neighborhood on the city's east boundary before migrating to the Seventy-seventh and eventually to South Bureau Homicide in 1989, where he learned a doctrine of maintaining a "clean, small" murder book.

Bernal did not describe himself as aggressive. He was deliberate and careful. He sought control. He wanted to prevent his cases from spinning out in "all different directions."

When the Big Years hit, Bernal experienced them as they all did—three-callout weekends, constant frustration, the indifference of the media a daily slap in the face. Bernal had a brooding demeanor. But he had his admirers in the Seventy-seventh. He was one of the most seasoned detectives in the relatively inexperienced unit, and he was considered a top practitioner.

But from an abundance of early leads from willing eyewitnesses at the scene, the case had quickly stalled. Bernal had a description of a black car and of a dark-skinned young shooter, but also a couple of accounts that contradicted these, and lots of street rumors. There were so many gangs whose territories converged in this part of Los Angeles that the field of potential suspects was very large. It was hard to know which rumors to credit. Bernal canceled his vacation and toiled through weekends to work the case. He was paired with Rocky Sato, another experienced hand, and given help by others in the unit. But after an initial flurry of interviews, Bernal was coming up empty-handed.

It was a familiar pattern. For years, more than half the "gang" homicide cases in the Seventy-seventh had foundered in similar ways, growing cold and ending up in storage. Pat Gannon, the commander, was secretly pained. He made a point of frequently asking for updates on the Tennelle case.

Privately, Gannon felt his position to be difficult. He was inclined to push, but he also knew that pressure from higher-ups could simply complicate matters further. He was aware of a simmering frustration building. It was bitterest up at RHD. But even in South Bureau, where few people knew Wally Tennelle personally, the case was an open sore. Gannon's newly consolidated South Bureau homicide group held weekly briefings. Week after week, the Tennelle case was brought up before all the homicide detectives in South Bureau. Week after week, the news was no news: there were no new leads to pursue.

Kelle Baitx, Tennelle's old partner and now homicide supervisor in the Newton Division, was partitioned off in another bureau. He only knew thirdhand of South Bureau hand-wringing over the Tennelle case. But Baitx couldn't help noticing as weeks passed. He knew hope was fading.

He was surprised. The killers, he assumed, were still living close by. You seldom went wrong by assuming they were within ten blocks of the crime scene. And the killing of a cop's son? It should have sent the GIN buzzing; Baitx was surprised that the Seventy-seventh wasn't hearing more rumors. Baitx had also heard the baleful murmurings emanating from RHD. But he knew how difficult gang cases were. Baitx willed himself not to second-guess Bernal.

Baitx knew Wally Tennelle well enough to be surprised that he had taken even three days off work. Tennelle had always been like that: not shy, not aloof, but just—Baitx would heave a deep sigh trying to describe it later—"just very, very matter-of-fact," he said.

He would call Tennelle, hoping to offer solace. But Wally maintained a fortresslike normalcy, parrying expertly. "Hey, Kelle!" Tennelle would exclaim, his tone bright, and before Baitx could get a word out, he peppered him with questions, beating back Baitx's solicitude with a steely wall of cheerful chatter. Baitx would find himself talking of his own life, bested by Tennelle's friendly interest. He would hang up thinking Tennelle had made him feel better, not the other way around.

Baitx was relegated to feeling protective of his old partner from a distance. One thing bothered him: the loose talk he heard around the department about Tennelle's choice to live in the Seventy-seventh.

Some cops seemed to think that Tennelle should have expected no better. "I thought it was shitty for them to say that," Baitx fumed. He piped up in defense of Tennelle. "It could have happened to any of us!" he insisted to colleagues. "I don't think where he lived was the cause of it."

Brother Jim Reiter of St. Bernard High School had a similar experience. As chaplain, he went on a ride-along in the Seventy-seventh Division shortly after Bryant's death. The killing came up at the roll call and elicited some discussion. "Why would anyone live in this neighborhood?" one officer asked the sergeant. The sergeant agreed. Reiter silently protested: *It's a* nice *neighborhood,* he thought. Why would anyone expect the Tennelles to move?

Reiter was raised in an Irish-German family on the northwest side of Chicago. He remembered people suggesting the family move out when blacks began moving in. And he remembered his father's reply: "I'll be damned if I am going to move out of this neighborhood." Reiter suspected Bryant's father was the same kind of man, and he was right. But even as his friends defended him, Wally Tennelle secretly questioned his choices. It had begun immediately. His eyes had filled with tears for an instant in front of his boss, Lt. Lyle Prideaux at California Hospital. "I blew it," he told Prideaux.

Again and again, in the weeks and months after, Wally Tennelle recalculated the impossible homicide odds of raising a black son anywhere in America. He wondered where he could have taken Bryant to keep him safe. He went back over his decisions, his stubbornness about the neighborhood he called home. He reconsidered his notion that kids should have just one house in which to pass their childhood.

Tennelle had remained in the Seventy-seventh for practical reasons, of course—the same ones that kept Baitx in El Sereno. But there was more to it. A secret reason, never voiced. It was a reason rooted in principle, the same one that had prompted him to refuse promotions to RHD for so long.

Wally Tennelle believed people in South Los Angeles deserved good cops. Committed cops. *Cops who were willing to live in their neighborhoods.* He held this belief so close that even his family members did not fully understand his views. It came out reluctantly, years later, only after he was repeatedly pressed.

Tennelle confessed that he had long been bothered by the way some of his fellow police officers behaved in ghettoside settings. He had concluded, "If you live sixty miles away, it's easier to disrespect people, to blow them off." He had not wanted to be that kind of cop. Tennelle was that rare officer who actually lived the philosophy so long advanced by LAPD critics: he had chosen to live in the city he policed out of valor and a sense of responsibility.

"I believe," he said in his understated way, "in watching over the community I live in."

Tennelle was the kind of ideal cop the city had long claimed it wanted. And now his son was dead. And the case was just another unsolved ghettoside murder.

THE ASSIGNMENT

June turned to July. Skaggs landed a rare nonsupervisory homicide D-3 spot in the Southwest Division around the University of Southern California, where he would work alongside Rick Gordon. He was preparing to leave Southeast and move to the Southwest station until the new Criminal Gang Homicide Group offices were ready in the Seventy-seventh Division. The three divisional units would then be combined in a large second-floor office in the ziggurat-style station house on Broadway, near Florence Avenue.

Meanwhile, black men kept getting killed south of the Ten. The pace of death was moderate by historic standards, but in the weeks after Dovon Harris's murder, a black man was killed in the zone about every three days.

Among the dead was Anthony Jenkins, forty-six.

Jenkins was a drug user—a "smoker" in street parlance. He was shot on the sidewalk behind Manual Arts High School in the Seventy-seventh Street Division in the early evening three days after the shooting of Dovon Harris. Jenkins lay bleeding for some time in plain view. Children rolled their skateboards past him. After a long interval, a passerby called 911. When Det. Jim Yoshida of the Seventy-seventh arrived, there was a crowd of people at the scene. As he and his colleagues began to investigate, "they were laughing at us," Yoshida reported later. "Laughing at us for going to the effort."

None of this came as a surprise to Yoshida, one of South Bureau's practiced hands. But he was in a low mood like lots of South Bureau detectives that benighted summer. Asked about the Jenkins case, Yoshida erupted. "Nobody cares!" he snapped. "*Nobody cares!* Nobody gives a shit!"

Then, late at night on July 11 came a break. Southeast officer Francis Coughlin was patrolling Bounty Hunter territory in Nickerson Gardens when he came across a group of young black men drinking.

Coughlin was a ten-year veteran of Southeast then a gang officer, pale as a midday marine layer, with thinning sandy-blond hair. He described his background as stereotypically Irish Catholic Bostonian. His flat Boston accent, like that of Chief William Bratton, had for some reason never dulled despite years in California.

Coughlin was among the more sophisticated breed of Southeast officers. He did not condemn vast swaths of residents as some of his colleagues did. He was fair-minded and discerning enough to put the "knucklehead" percentage in the very low single digits, and he liked many of the people he dealt with on the streets. And, like everyone else in the walled city, Coughlin was baffled and silenced by the bloodshed. "So *surreal*," he said. To believe it, "you have to see it."

The spot where Coughlin found the drinkers was "in the Nickersons"—that is, the Nickerson Gardens housing project, near where Dovon Harris had been shot. The drinkers saw Coughlin and ran. He chased them. One was in a wheelchair. He rolled away with short, strong bursts. Coughlin said he saw the wheelchair suspect toss a bag of marijuana. He was hoping to find an illegal gun. Coughlin didn't care about the marijuana. For him, and many of his colleagues, drugs were just a pretext to stop, search, and arrest gang members suspected of other, unsolved violent crimes.

This was how Coughlin did his job on many a night. Coughlin couldn't do much about all the shooters in Southeast who got away with it. But he could enforce drug laws, gang injunctions, and parole and probation terms relatively easily just by driving around and making "good obs"—good observations, cop lingo for catching, at a glance, a bulge under a shirt, a furtive motion of hands. A chase might ensue, and sometimes ended with the cops shutting down whole neighborhoods as the LAPD "airship," or helicopter, thumped overhead. Coughlin took extra risks to get guns—this was the gold standard.

Coughlin's methods were guaranteed to look like straight harassment to those on the receiving end. After all, how important was a bag of marijuana in a place where so many people were dying? But Coughlin's motivation wasn't to juke stats, boost his department "rating," or antagonize the neighborhood's young men. He had seen the Monster, and his conscience demanded that he do something. So he used what discretion he had to compensate for the state's lack of vigor in response to murder and assault.

This practice of using "proxy crimes" to substitute for more difficult and expensive investigations was widespread in American law enforcement. The legal scholar William J. Stuntz singled it out as a particularly damaging trend of recent decades. In California, proxy justice had transformed enforcement of parole and probation into a kind of shadow legal system, sparing the state the trouble of expensive prosecutions. State prisons, already saddled with sick and elderly inmates, were all the more crammed as a result.

But in the squad rooms of Southeast station, cops insisted that desperate measures were called for. They would hear the name of a shooter, only to find they couldn't "put a case" on him because no witnesses would testify. So they would write a narcotics warrant—or catch him dirty. "We can put them in jail for drugs a lot easier than on an assault. No one is going to give us information on an assault," explained Lou Leiker, who ran the detective table in Southeast in the early aughts. To them, proxy justice represented a principled stand against violence. It was like a personalized imposition of martial law.

That's why Coughlin went in hot pursuit of that pot dealer in a wheelchair. Coughlin caught and searched the man. He found a faded old revolver.

Coughlin understood why the man was carrying that gun. Black men who lived in Watts were in constant danger. Those who sold drugs were in more danger. And those who couldn't run away? One could almost say it was a matter of time before serious violence visited a drug dealer in a wheelchair. In fact, a man in a wheelchair from a gunshot injury had been murdered in the Nickersons near the very spot just a few years before.

Anywhere else, being struck by gunfire not once but twice would have seemed like extraordinarily unlikely chance. But at the coroner's office, medical examiners were used to seeing old scars from bullets alongside the new and fatal wound. It was like such men had been used for target practice, one coroner's examiner remarked. Like they were dying in slow motion. The first shots maimed or paralyzed them. The next ones, months or years later, finished them off.

This man carried that gun to defend himself. He wanted to survive. His legs had already been paralyzed by gunfire. If someone attacked him again, he wanted to be ready.

Coughlin sent him to jail. He sent his gun to the firearms lab.

Speedy, high-quality firearms analysis was the one kind of scientific investigation that mattered in solving street homicides. But in the LAPD, the firearms laboratory was drowning in backed-up work. It was overshadowed by the DNA lab, which got more media and public attention. Firearms analysts sometimes had to explain to their own colleagues what they did; journalists frequently confused firearms analysis with the science of ballistics, which deals with the angle and direction of projectiles, not which guns they come from.

The lab was run by a civilian named Doreen Hudson. Much of her job, like La Barbera's, consisted of devising schemes to compensate for lack of resources. Black-on-black violence south of the Ten swelled the lab's caseload. Detectives had to wait weeks for results. Hudson did what she could. She expedited work on certain cases, for example, based on detectives' discretion rather than political or bureaucratic priorities. Other battles she lost. Police agencies went on melting down seized firearms over her objection that they might constitute evidence. And she had to learn to live with the computerized federal imaging system the LAPD had adopted six years before, despite its limitations.

The National Integrated Ballistic Information database (NIBIN) catalogued digitized images of bullets and cartridge casings from crime scenes and seized guns. The database could be searched by an algorithm. This allowed fast, cheap searches, matching ammunition used in crimes to individual weapons. But Hudson knew the computer system was not as discerning as trained humans. It relied on simplified digital renderings of microscopic images produced through standardized procedures—a process that eliminated many telling nuances and contours.

Before, skilled technicians had taped Polaroid photos of bullets and cartridge casings to the wall and examined every microscopic dent and groove with the naked eye to match them to ammunition test-fired from individual firearms. This low-tech method was not efficient, but it yielded good results. The high-tech NIBIN system was a blunt instrument by comparison, and had one especially troubling limitation. Although the LAPD and many other agencies had dutifully entered test-fired bullets from hundreds of revolvers into its database for years, by the summer of 2007, the system had never successfully matched a bullet used in an L.A. crime to a revolver. Not once.

The gun used to kill Bryant was a revolver. Revolver matches are more difficult than other types of firearm analysis. They are performed by matching striations on bullets to tool marks inside the gun barrel, not cartridge casings to firing pins. Bullets are cylindrical, and the grooves and scratches they bear after being fired wrap around a curved surface. By contrast, breech face markings on the flat part of a cartridge case are relatively easy for a computer to read. So while the NIBIN system was adept at matching casings to semiautomatic pistols, it had proven useless at matching bullets to revolvers. It was an area in which humans remained superior to machines, but the lab was not staffed for such time-consuming expert labor.

Here again, the criminal justice system seemed to be doing its job when it wasn't. The NIBIN system appeared progressive and technologically advanced. But in this important area—about one-third of the

LAPD's seized firearms were revolvers—it was just going through the motions.

Hudson had known Tennelle for years and was heartsick. She was sick of all of it, she reflected—young men shot, cases unsolved, her technicians hampered by cheap, mechanical substitutes for craftsmanship. "I've seen way too much of this for way too long," she thought.

Rick Gordon was also familiar with the department's revolver problem. He was pushing for a different approach. So Hudson made a decision: They would bypass NIBIN. Her workers would continue submitting images to the database as required. But they also would quietly assemble their own duplicate database of test-fire exemplars from seized revolvers. This secret trove would be analyzed the old-fashioned way, with the human eye.

The eye belonged to criminalist Daniel Rubin, who had been trained as a chemist and whose accent betrayed his New York City upbringing. Rubin studied the bullet fragment that Garrido had found at the crime scene, and another recovered by the coroner from Bryant's head. They were most likely from a Ruger or Charter Arms weapon, he thought. It takes years for criminalists to be able to do this—determine a gun's manufacturer by the look of a fired bullet. But Rubin, too, had been trained by the Big Years, and he knew the telltale subtleties. He set up systems for diverting the guns that met his criteria, taking care to establish a reliable chain of custody for exemplar bullets. When the test-fires came in, he engraved each bullet with an identification number.

Presently, Rubin realized the standard copper-jacketed test-fire bullets required for NIBIN produced subtly different patterns than the discontinued, aluminum-jacketed ones used to kill Bryant. A colleague located a stockpile of the defunct ammunition at a local store. It was of a type that Rubin knew might fragment in the recovery tank. To avoid this, criminalists sometimes used paper clips to stuff putty in the hollow points, but that wouldn't work with these, Rubin thought—the aluminum jackets were too brittle. He inserted a tiny screw in each test-fire bullet to keep it intact—a method he'd learned from another analyst. He gripped the bullets with a piece of bicycle inner tube in place of pliers to avoid leaving marks.

It was all terribly time-consuming. Soon, Rubin was doing little else. LAPD officers seized more than twenty guns a day. Revolvers were starting to pile up. Rubin eliminated one, then another. By then, he had studied the two Tennelle bullet fragments side-by-side many times, memorizing the microscopic topography he was looking for. Eventually, Coughlin's seizure—revolver number 22—joined the backlog. But when Rubin looked up the file, he realized the weapon had never reached the crime lab; couriers had somehow neglected to pick it up. He reordered it, and eliminated more revolvers in the meantime.

Rubin had no hope. He would be searching for this needle in a haystack the rest of his career, he thought—engraving tiny numbers and screwing tiny screws until his last hour on the job. He told himself it could be worse. At least he was still paying his mortgage.

Then, on August 20, he picked up yet another three-by-five envelope. It contained the test-fire exemplars from revolver 22, an old Charter Arms Undercover, which had finally arrived by courier from the Southeast property room. Rubin sat down at the comparison 'scope. He tilted his favorite fluorescent light at an oblique angle and looked.

When the first set of grooves lined up, Rubin told himself it didn't mean anything. He'd been close before. He rotated the little thirty-eights and looked again, rotated and looked. Then he shut his eyes, drew a breath and exhaled.

A short while later, Rubin got out of his chair and left his workstation. He stood, hands on his hips, gazing into the distance. *No,* he told himself firmly, *it can't be.* He shook his head and went back to the scope. He spun the thirty-eights out of phase and began again, rotating them the other way this time.

Later that day, Rubin was outside, toiling in the hot sun near LAX. He'd been called out of the office to help process evidence from an officer-involved shooting. Hudson was there too. For more than an hour, Rubin had been trying to tell her something, but they were both busy working different parts of the scene. At last they crossed paths. Rubin spoke hurriedly.

Hudson listened, frowning. It might seem strange that she did not

rejoice upon learning that Coughlin's seized revolver was the murder
weapon. But hunting for a killer is frightening, the more so as a case
advances. Enforcing criminal law against violent offenders is one of the
most dangerous tasks a state can perform, and for frontline workers, the
danger is visceral. Skaggs speculated that some of his underperforming
colleagues were held back by subconscious fear. Each step toward an
arrest increased the pressure; not catching a killer could feel safer. When
Hudson learned of Rubin's match, she felt not triumph but dread and
anxiety.

There were other reasons to view Rubin's success with caution.
Street guns got passed around, especially "dirty" ones. Firearms analysts viewed a week or two as the maximum time lapse for valuable clues
to be gleaned from a match. Much longer than that, and too many
people would have handled the gun, making it too difficult to recon-
struct the chain of possession.

It was a little like trying to track down the source of counterfeit bills.
The guns used on the streets of South Los Angeles were, almost uni-
formly, unregistered illegal weapons, obtained from a swirling ocean of
cheap black market firearms. Many of these guns were pretty old, and
so far from point of purchase that it was impossible to trace their history.
Investigators in South L.A. were astonished when a gun used in a murder turned out to be legally owned; years would go by without such a
gun turning up. Despite California's relatively strict gun control laws,
the illegal market for street guns had persisted for decades. Older gang
members from the 1960s would recall buying guns in exactly the same
manner and for roughly the same prices as their counterparts fifty years
later. You could buy many street guns illegally for a hundred bucks, people said. Gangs usually had a stash.

This match did not mean the man in the wheelchair was a suspect.
Too much time had gone by for that to be likely. But it did mean he was
in a chain of people that led back to the shooter. It meant hope.

Or it seemed to. But the man in the wheelchair offered no helpful
information about the gun, and no other clues surfaced. Up at the firearms lab, Doreen Hudson was in a state of suspense, hoping the lab's

findings would lead to a quick arrest. "Instead, we had to accept it," she said. "It was the usual—another South Bureau homicide that would never be solved."

For his part, Tennelle was determined not to ask about the case. He never even looked up the case number on the computer. He didn't want to taint anything, and he didn't want the detectives to feel any pressure. But privately, the elation he had felt upon hearing they got a match on the gun faded into disappointment. He went on with his work. He thought about Bryant's case all the time.

Skaggs knew about the Tennelle case thirdhand—heard the briefings, noted the anguish it provoked among his colleagues. Skaggs had never spoken to Tennelle. But he knew him by sight. One day, he pulled up to the gas pumps at the Seventy-seventh Division and saw him there.

It was the first time Skaggs had seen Tennelle since Bryant's murder. He felt he should say something, but couldn't muster the courage. He suffered a failure of nerve, something that never afflicted him when he was working. But this was *personal*. A cop's kid had been killed and the case was still open. Skaggs hung back, feeling ashamed. He waited until Tennelle drove away. "I couldn't even look at him," he recalled bitterly later. "I felt bad about the frickin' case being open . . . I couldn't even fucking go up to him."

The collective shame probably did not extend much beyond the detective ranks. To officers such as De La Rosa, for example, the fact that an RHD detective's son had been killed over in the Eighties was of passing interest. But for homicide detectives, to whom clearance meant everything—or should have—the Tennelle case was a worm in the gut, hollowing out what remained of ghettoside morale.

Of course, they all understood the problem. The suspects probably thought they were targeting an enemy and got it wrong, as so often happened. No one who knew them was coming forward. It was all so numbingly routine. The whole maddening, familiar package: it was exactly what had been going on south of the Ten for a generation. Bryant Tennelle's murder was not much different from the murders of a score of black men in the surrounding area in the month before he died. It was

similar to the murder of Charles Williams, targeted for wearing the
wrong athletic gear, and of Dovon Harris, targeted because he was with
a group of other teenagers branded as enemy gang members by his assailant. It was no wonder the media covered so few of these cases.

But this time it was one of their own.

The sickening culpability afflicted even young detectives such as
Corey Farell, Skaggs's new partner in the Southwest Division. Farell had
never met Tennelle and had only recently joined the new bureau. Silent
with the rest of the young detectives in the weekly homicide briefings,
Farell sat in the back, listening to bleak updates on the case. He thought
about how little the so-called black community trusted the cops already.
"What does it say when we can't offer justice to one of our own?" he
wondered.

Lieutenant Lyle Prideaux was slim, with strawberry-blond hair going
gray.

He was one of the few people in the homicide detective ranks who
actually looked the part on days he was required to wear the blue uniform. The others teased him for this. Except for Skaggs and a few others, most detectives looked frumpy and uncomfortable in their old blues.

Everything about Prideaux, from his glance to his grin, was sharp-
edged and ironic. The LAPD's taste in humor ran more to the broad,
guffawing variety, and Prideaux was occasionally misunderstood.

Like Skaggs, like Tennelle, like so many of them, Prideaux might
have had another career were he not so hyperactive. His father was an
executive for United Airlines. Prideaux had grown up in Rolling Hills
Estates, an exclusive outpost on the Palos Verdes Peninsula, which had
one of the lowest violent crime rates in California.

But at a certain stage of youth, no office job seemed as appealing as
"driving around in fresh air and sunshine in police cars," and so there
he was, an LAPD career man since the age of twenty-one. By the time
of the Tennelle killing, he was in his midfifties. Anywhere else, he would
have been at the height of his career, rising through management. But he

was a policeman, so he was looking toward retirement. Although he did not have a deep background in homicide, and no ghettoside credentials at all, Prideaux was an able manager. He had won a place in Robbery-Homicide, and he was Wally Tennelle's boss when Bryant was shot.

He was out with his wife at Lido di Manhattan in Manhattan Beach, headed to the local light opera, when he got the call from Kyle Jackson, the unit's commander. As he drove toward California Hospital, arguments about who should handle the case were already zinging over the phone. At the hospital, he met with Jackson and some other brass, and then with Wally Tennelle. Years later, Prideaux's voice was still tight as he recalled the scene. Tennelle, he said, "came out and apologized for the inconvenience," Prideaux said. "He handed out bottles of water from a cart." Prideaux was in jeans and a sweater. He felt crushed, yet Tennelle kept addressing him as "Lieutenant."

The decision to give the case to the division was above his head. Prideaux was not involved. But like everyone in RHD, he marked the passing weeks. Still no suspects. Prideaux had learned the previous February that he would be reassigned as detectives' lieutenant in the new South Bureau Homicide. The Tennelle case remained unsolved.

Prideaux had ideas about it. By then, although it wasn't anywhere near what the LAPD technically called a cold case, it was getting cold by ghettoside standards. Every lead seemed to have been chased to oblivion, even the revolver. There had been no media coverage to speak of. It seemed to be a burning issue only within the LAPD, and even there, it was the preoccupation of a few—detectives such as Skaggs who cared about south-end homicides. And anyone who had ever met Wally Tennelle.

Prideaux believed the case needed a shake-up. He didn't know South Bureau well, so he performed what he called "some audio surveillance." He started asking around: Who was good? Who could solve cases in South Bureau? "Word came back to us: *Skaggs*," Prideaux recalled.

Prideaux had a vague memory of seeing John Skaggs as a young officer and remembered Chris Barling better—that quirky officer who always looked as if he were fifteen years old—but didn't know much about their record for clearing cases.

All he knew was that in those first weeks in South Bureau, he kept hearing their names. That top-of-the-line team in Southeast—Skaggs and Barling. Some of the talk was critical; not everyone liked Skaggs, who seemed to think rather highly of himself. Prideaux gathered he had a reputation, that he bulldozed over opposition and "like Sherman, he will burn down the forest to find what he's looking for," Prideaux said. It so happened Prideaux was looking for a Sherman.

He sought out confidants in the command ranks—trying to find anyone who knew Skaggs. Everyone who did told Prideaux the same thing: Skaggs works insane hours. He works days off and weekends. He solves all his cases. And he will cost you a fortune in overtime.

Prideaux and Skaggs never grew to know each other well. Skaggs was dismissive of Prideaux, whom he viewed as just another PAB bureaucrat (and being satisfied with this first assessment—and being Skaggs—he never revisited it). But Prideaux had a pretty good read on Skaggs from the beginning. Skaggs was successful, he later said, because he was organized and tenacious, had a great memory, and was "bright and insightful." But he also called Skaggs "a very hard man."

Asked what he meant by this, he explained that good homicide detectives were ruthless. They had to push day after day. They had to use whatever leverage they possessed to get people to talk. They had to interrogate people, pester them, relocate them, mess up their lives. They had to be remorseless. Prideaux said, "It takes a hard person to constantly work a case like that. It's tiring. It wears you out." Being hard, he said, "is a necessary attribute if you are going to be a homicide detective. I don't want it to sound negative. But they are harder than most people." Prideaux then repeated himself. "John Skaggs," he said, "is a *very* hard man."

Prideaux considered Tennelle another hard man, in the positive sense.

He was not the only one to notice certain similarities between Skaggs and Tennelle—those meticulous habits, the outward mildness matched with bunched-up energy, that obliqueness about their inward lives, that clean-hewn worldview, all right angles and straight lines. The two men were so clearly of a type.

That September, Prideaux called Skaggs in and told him he wanted him on the Tennelle case. Skaggs, ever the California surfer, had one thought: *Bitchin'*.

Prideaux briefed Skaggs on the case. But he also wanted Skaggs to know something about Tennelle—to understand what the case meant to Tennelle's colleagues who loved him. He wanted Skaggs to know about Tennelle's tenacity and energy, his honesty and high standards.

Seeking words to sum up Tennelle, Prideaux came up with the obvious ones: "He's *you*," he told Skaggs.

Prideaux did not simply hand over the case to Skaggs. He made Skaggs partner to Armando Bernal, the original Seventy-seventh Division detective on the case, who had gotten good leads yet appeared stalled.

When Skaggs learned he would have to work with Bernal, he refused. But Prideaux didn't give him the choice.

Prideaux defended the decision on the ground that as professionals, Skaggs and Bernal should be able to find a way to play nice. But he underestimated the seething intensity homicide detectives brought to their work, especially in South Bureau, where everyone felt a little persecuted—and especially on such an emotional case.

Prideaux's decision amounted to telling Bernal, the alpha detective of the Seventy-seventh, that he was being forced to work with Skaggs, the alpha detective from the rival Southeast, because his bosses felt he wasn't good enough. And it meant telling Skaggs that he could finally have the case he had been hankering for, but not on his terms.

It was a mess. Skaggs did not like Bernal and was not especially nice to him. Bernal was more circumspect, but it was clear he did not like Skaggs, either.

In Skaggs's account, the two had had some scrap early in their careers. It was an elaborate story from Skaggs's encyclopedic memory. The gist was that Skaggs had solved one of Bernal's cases for him and Bernal didn't like it. Bernal simply said their styles were inharmonious.

Prideaux was right that Skaggs was like Sherman. As soon as he got the case, he wanted to do what he had always done: plunge straight ahead as quickly as possible, get as many interviews as it took, use all the hours available, strip away false leads and lay bare the good ones. He wanted to attack. John Skaggs had no problem scorching some earth.

Bernal was much more careful. He was meticulous about documenting everything he did and anxious to avoid duplication—"shooting the gun in every direction," he called it, and thus stirring up a lot of false leads.

Bernal found Skaggs to be reckless, dashing off to do things without due planning and coordination; Skaggs, with his hatred of paperwork and desk-driven investigating, thought Bernal excessively process-oriented—a "checklist detective."

And there was another, especially lethal, flaw in this whole cursed scheme of Prideaux's. Neither detective was clearly the lead on the case, in violation of Skaggs's inflexible rule for partnerships.

Skaggs's first step was to page through the murder book to see what had already been done. Predictably, the book annoyed him.

Skaggs knew that the Seventy-seventh had been following street rumors that a gang called the Rollin' Sixties was involved in the murder. He saw that this was the angle that was being worked—though not worked in the way Skaggs would have worked it. Instead of taking to the field, knocking relentlessly, talking to anyone they could find, it seemed the detectives were waiting for calls to come in. Here again were violations of the craftsman's code he and Barling had established: You don't sit and wait. And you remain open, never allowing yourself to be seduced by assumptions or intriguing theories. "You never put all your peas in one basket," Skaggs would say.

The book itself wasn't as neat as Skaggs would have liked. It was "clustered," he thought. Only Skaggs knew exactly what he meant by that, but it had to do with his almost uncanny ability to build into his investigations powerful engines of progress instead of mere reports on efforts made here and there. Even when Skaggs was pursuing bad leads, he wasn't drifting—he was eliminating distractions.

Skaggs reacted most strongly to Bernal's meticulous scheduling and record keeping. Bernal made appointments by phone; Skaggs usually did not. He treated South Central like a twelfth-century village and simply walked around and talked to people, relying on serendipity and the power of face-to-face interactions. Bernal had taken care to note every incremental action. But to Skaggs, who considered fieldwork the only activity of investigative value, all those notes were the mark of hesitation and equivocation—sins, in his mind.

Bernal, for example, had noted phone calls that weren't returned and door knocks that no one answered. Skaggs considered that a lot of "filler." He would never load up a murder book with incidentals. If Skaggs knocked on a door and no one answered, he knew he would be back again, and again, and again, until someone answered. Woe be it to the occupants; they had no hope of evading the cop with a tie and no jacket. Skaggs would make a record in the book only of interviews he eventually conducted, not the door knocks that led up to them. To Skaggs, the only purpose of such notes was to make it appear that detectives were working busily should someone look over their shoulders.

There was a way of working—it was hard for him to put this into words, but he knew it when he saw it—a perfunctory way that met all the technical criteria for how a job was supposed to be done. It would be above reproach should any supervisor review the work, yet lacked some essential quality of passion, determination, velocity.

Checklist work and real work were not the same to him. You could get praise and a paycheck and fill your day with busy, important-seeming activities and never solve a case. In South L.A., Skaggs believed, murders got solved only through another level of vigor—when a detective was motivated by something greater than the promise of a good "rating" or promotion. There was a pro forma way to do the job, and there was the Southeast way—best described by the salesman's credo he had learned from Sal La Barbera. *Always be closing.* It was why he disliked it when detectives sat around in front of computers or ate lunch at restaurants.

Now Skaggs's whole outlook and career were rooted in the same aggrieved sense of injustice that had prompted Wally Tennelle to turn down RHD a decade before. He believed the victims of South Central deserved better than the *appearance* of a functioning justice system. They deserved professional practitioners who saw the full reality and horror of their fate and who brought to the job a personal stake in success and a battlefield sense of mission—not just a credible defense against a charge of malpractice. The Monster needed to be relentlessly pursued and routed, not just contained. Unconsciously, Skaggs saw in a murder book full of "filler" yet another expression of this tacit policy of passive containment. He did not like it at all.

Skaggs didn't know it, but his irritation was centuries in the making.

Criminal law in the United States has always displayed a tendency to go through the motions. From the nation's earliest moments, its legal system was fragmented and crude. Vigilantism and vendettas flourished in the legal vacuum. In the nineteenth and twentieth centuries, police compensated for the weakness of the courts by roughing up people to teach them lessons. As late as the 1950s, their work consisted largely of rounding up drunks in paddy wagons.

But where things got really bad was in the South. In that region's long, painful history of caste domination and counterrevolution lurks every factor that counters the formation of a state monopoly on violence.

From before Emancipation, Southern law was infirm. Slave owners wanted the power to discipline slaves without legal constraints. After the Civil War and Reconstruction, ex-Confederates murdered their way to control again, terrorizing emancipated black people and their white supporters into submission. This set the stage for the racist atrocities of Southern law that are somewhat better known to Americans—the stacked courts, fee systems, and chain gangs—abuses so systematic that, across the South, black people dismissed the whole framework as "the white man's court."

White conservatives favored legal systems that looked the part, but still achieved their racist intent—a "winking" system that, by design, just went through the motions. Southern legal institutions appeared to observe constitutional due process, but real power was held outside the law. Getting away with murder was key to the white-supremacist project. Impunity is a stencil of law; it outlines a shadow system. Southern legal institutions were, by turns, hypocritical, corrupt, partisan, ineffective, infected with vigilantism or too feeble to combat it. In this way, the South cultivated the Furies in all their dark horror. Its harvest was factionalism, informal systems of discipline and self-policing, terrifying etiquette restrictions, witness intimidation, vigilantism, rumors, arson, lynching, and a homemade system of order based on relationships that historian Mark Schultz dubbed "personalism"—the whole dreary cornucopia of informal justice.

For blacks, this system meant being killable. Blacks were "shot down for nothing" by whites. But that was not all. They murdered each other, too—in fields, labor camps, and at Saturday night gatherings where there was "so much cutting and killing going on." Their rates of death by homicide were similar to—and at times higher than—what they would be decades later in northern inner cities. In Atlanta in 1920, the rate hit 107 deaths per 100,000 people. In Memphis in 1915, it was 170. Black people even lynched each other, sometimes exacting mob justice against murder suspects whom white authorities had failed to prosecute.

White people "had the law," to quote a curious phrase that crops up in historic sources. Black people didn't. Formal law impinged on them only for purposes of control, not protection. Small crimes were crushed, big ones indulged—so long as the victims were black. John Dollard, a Mississippi researcher of the thirties, speculated that black infighting was the product of white design—or at least some intuitive consensus. "One cannot help wondering if it does not serve the ends of the white caste to have a high level of violence in the Negro group," he wrote.

It might not seem self-evident that impunity for white violence against blacks would engender black-on-black murder. But when people are stripped of legal protection and placed in desperate straits, they are more, not less, likely to turn on each other. Lawless settings are terrifying; if people can do whatever they want to each other, there are always enough bullies to make it ugly. Americans are nostalgic for the village setting and hold dear the notion of community, so the idea that the oppressed do not band together in solidarity is counter to our myths. But community spawns communal justice; the village gives rise to the feud. The condition of being thrown together just because they were the same color should be considered one of the injustices black people suffered in segregation.

Beyond this, white people saw to it that solidarity among black people was kept to a minimum. They enlisted blacks as spies, favored "their Negroes" over other black people, and used them as pawns in their battles with each other. For people of all colors, the South was a stew of factors that produce homicide—a place where law remained a contested prize in a low-level, unfinished revolution. But black people experienced law, both its action and inaction, as a systematic extension of the campaign of terrorist violence that had brought an end to Reconstruction and stripped them of their rights under the Constitution. For years after the Civil War, a taint of sectarian rivalry tinged black–police interactions. Nashville blacks declared they would not "submit to . . . arrest by any damned rebel police!" Black people fought police in street battles, and—just as in the Seventy-seventh a century later—they wrested friends from police hands. Later, as segregated enclaves formed in Southern cities—Nashville's "Black Bottom," Atlanta's "Darktown"— police avoided them. Officers "did not go through the areas where most Negro homicides occur, but rather stayed on the main thoroughfares." Black communities became, "at least to some extent, self-policing," a historian summed up.

This set up the great clash of the late twentieth century. A flood of black migrants, schooled by the lawless South, swept into cities such as Los Angeles. They brought with them their high homicide rates and their tendency for legal self-help. The police they met were not unlike those back home. LAPD officers shot and killed many people and were free with their fists. "I worked with one who took his gun belt off and said, 'You wanna fight?'" said Bernard Parks, the former chief, recalling his patrol days in the 1960s. But L.A. cops were different in important ways: there were more of them and they were a lot more intrusive. New professional standards meant deploying officers by mathematical formula based on frequency of crime. Since there was more crime in black neighborhoods, they got proportionally more police. In 1961, for example, the LAPD spent four times as much per capita in Newton Division as it did in West L.A. Southern black migrants had been used to police who ignored them. But these cops were ever-present, hounding them with aggravating "preventive" tactics.

The results were explosive. Watts burned, and so did Newark, Detroit, and other cities in the 1960s. From this turbulent brew the nation imbibed a deep skepticism toward bureaucratic justice that echoes to the present day. Black protest against overzealous police and prosecutors remains a cherished template for left-leaning critics of criminal justice. But another, profound grievance of the period went mostly ignored—the inadequacy of official response to black-on-black violence.

Instead of confronting the mounting death toll in the cities, the justice system took a permissive turn. It practiced victim-discounting on a mass scale just as black homicides surged. Prison terms per unit of crime in the U.S. hit rock bottom in the 1960s and 1970s, making this country one of the world's most lenient. Courts acquitted. Parole terms were generous. In the midseventies, only a third of California's convicted homicide perpetrators remained in prison after seven years, and the rough streets of South Bureau teemed with murderers newly released. Reformers focused on the rights of defendants, seemingly blind to the ravages of underenforcement.

The pendulum swung. Change in the 1980s was quick and ruthless. Get-tough policies became political winners. Prison populations soared. Change included longer prison terms for violence. But their impact was blurred by unreasonably harsh sentences for lots of lesser crimes. Cops began filing charges for "every Mickey Mouse thing," recalled defense attorney Seymour Applebaum. "And it's always a felony. Everything's a felony now." By 2007, parole violators returned to custody on technical violations made up the largest single category of new prison arrivals. But through it all, the basic weakness didn't change. In fact, homicide solve rates dropped.

Since it's not the harshness of punishment but its swiftness and certainty that deters crime, black people still had good reason to feel unprotected. Murderers still went free, while the new crime-suppression tactics bore more than a passing resemblance to the old Southern wink. Even after legal discrimination was abolished, the situation didn't change much from what black migrants had known in the South. Homicide wasn't just a bad habit black people couldn't break. Segregation, economic isolation, and the flawed workings of American criminal justice created the same conditions anew.

For white people, justice was almost as ineffective; homicide solve rates for all Americans still lag behind those of the safest European nations. But what might appear a tolerable level of incompetence to a relatively safe, dispersed, white majority felt different to black migrants from the embattled South. White people were more likely to have jobs, money, mobility—assets that compensate for criminal-justice failures by giving people other means to achieve independence and autonomy from each other. Not so the black people who fled to industrial centers in the twentieth century. For generations, black Southerners had experienced the weakness of criminal justice as a central feature of a system that kept them down. To them, the state's tendency to allow people to kill and face no consequences was an aspect of its enmity toward them. Blacks were like an occupied people. Especially in poor urban centers, they lived in minority enclaves and settled their scores outside the law.

By the late twentieth century, the criminal justice system was no longer very corrupt. Many police and prosecutors were sincere and professional, and legal outcomes were relatively color-blind. But because the reach of the system was so limited, the results were similar to those produced by masquerade justice. Even when criminal justice procedures were clean and fair, violent-crime investigations remained too ineffective and threadbare to counter the scale of black-on-black murder. Black people still had reason to doubt that the law would have their backs, and they reacted accordingly. This is the world that Skaggs lived in, although he didn't put it into this historic context. What Skaggs saw was simply this: the system looked busy, but didn't do its job.

. . .

It took just a few weeks for things to come to a head between Skaggs and Bernal. Bernal went out of town briefly and Skaggs got what he considered "a bullshit clue"—some report of a black SUV matching the description of the killers'. He did not touch base with Bernal about it. Instead, he simply marched up to the owner's house, knocked on the door, and immediately ascertained that the SUV belonged to Hispanics, not blacks, thus eliminating the clue. Upon his return, Bernal was annoyed. In Bernal's memory, Skaggs had duplicated something that had already been done and communicated poorly about it. In Skaggs's account, Bernal didn't want him pursuing leads alone and objected to his methods.

In any case, they had words.

Skaggs did not waste time arguing with Bernal. He made no effort to try to work things out with him. He was, as ever, blunt and unequivocal. He told Bernal he was walking into Prideaux's office to say the partnership could not work and to demand a change. Bernal tried to defuse the situation and hold him back, but Skaggs was not to be dissuaded. In this, as in everything, Skaggs sought to propel events to their conclusion as quickly as possible.

And so Lyle Prideaux found himself faced with the decision he had tried at first to avoid. There were Skaggs and Bernal, sitting before him in his office, obviously at a crisis point. Skaggs demanded that he be given the case to work free and clear or be taken off it.

Inwardly, Prideaux sighed. He was disappointed in the two of them for putting their personality problems before the case like that. But then again, he reflected, he had not brought Skaggs into this case because he was "some quiet little guy who was going to keep things under wraps." He had sought out Skaggs to burn down forests, and he could only blame himself that now here he was, squarely in the midst of a full-on Santa Ana blaze.

He told Bernal and Skaggs both to leave his office, then pondered his next move.

Prideaux didn't have to think long. In his mind, the Tennelle case was the number one priority of his new command. It was important for the future of the reconstituted homicide bureau, for the department's reputation in South L.A., and for the principle of the thing.

And it was important because of how Prideaux felt about it, deep down. Prideaux was like everyone else in the department who knew Tennelle: he could barely talk about the case without his eyes filling with tears. This was, Prideaux realized, a moment to earn his rank and pay.

So, in the next minute, he changed the course of the Tennelle case. He walked out of his office and told Skaggs he could have it.

Bernal was stunned. The decision was highly unusual, and a completely crushing condemnation of his work. Most of all, he was stung by the implicit suggestion that he had not given the Tennelle case his all.

Bernal was not the indifferent worker that Skaggs took him to be. After all, he had also worked the Big Years in South Central Los Angeles. He had also devoted his career to ghettoside work and felt a strong sense of duty about the neglected crimes there. He knew Tennelle a little, and he felt as they all did about Bryant's murder—namely, that it was unbearable, and that the case was a must-solve.

And on top of all this, Bernal had a personal stake in the case that went beyond his loyalty to Tennelle as a coworker. Unbeknownst to most of his colleagues, Bernal's nephew had been murdered in East L.A. over in the Los Angeles County Sheriff's territory a year and a half before Bryant's killing, and the case was never solved.

Christian Bernal was nineteen. He had been planning a career in law enforcement and had applied to join the Sheriff's Department. Like a lot of young would-be cops, he had a shaved head. Bernal's son was in the parked car with him when attackers came up on foot. It was like the Tennelle case. The cousins were not gang members. They were just young Hispanic men who the assailants assumed were gang rivals because of how they looked. The revolver blasts showered them both in broken glass.

Bernal was at home when his phone rang, and he picked it up to hear his son screaming hysterically—*"They shot him, they shot him, they shot*

him." Bernal's sister, Christian's mother, was devastated. At the time of
Bryant's death, the whole Bernal family was still reeling: Armando Bernal, like Wally Tennelle, had only experienced homicide as a police officer up until then. Now he knew how different it felt to have one's own
family ravaged by the Monster.

Rick Gordon thought highly of both Skaggs and Bernal and believed both men had contributed to the case in unique ways. Gordon
would point out later that various investigative styles were needed to
meet the demands of the South L.A. homicide environment. Cases dif-
fered, and not every investigator's style fitted every case. Bernal's approach might not have been the best fit for the Tennelle case, Gordon
said, but there had been many other cases in which his combination of
patience and meticulousness paid off.

Chris Barling had a similar take, despite being Skaggs's greatest fan.
Bernal was a tenacious investigator who "absorbs before he acts," he
said, but it just so happened that Skaggs was "the right detective at the
right time."

And it was not fair to suggest the case had languished in Bernal's
hands. In fact, huge inroads had been made. By the time Prideaux officially handed it off to Skaggs, the main eyewitnesses, the gun, the description of the car, and the most important street rumors had already
been cataloged, giving Skaggs plenty to pursue. Skaggs did not inherit a
hopeless case, but a stalled one. And there was no question that Bernal
cared deeply about it and had applied to it the comprehension that was
rooted in grief over his murdered nephew, just as Wally Tennelle was
then channeling his own grief into his RHD cases.

Finally, to Bernal's great credit under the circumstances, he handled
the fiasco with some grace in the end, swallowing his anger, going back
to work under the very lieutenant who had yanked this most important
of cases out of his grip, and pouring himself into his other duties with
set-jawed professionalism.

Skaggs, meanwhile, went to work.

15

EVERYBODY KNOW

To some of his detractors in the bureau, John Skaggs already had the partner he needed. There were sarcastic murmurs behind his back about the new detective team made up of "Skaggs and His Ego."

But Prideaux made Skaggs choose a flesh-and-blood second on the case. Skaggs would have liked Barling, but that was no longer realistic, since Barling was now a D-3. So Skaggs tapped his recent young partner from his tour in Southwest, Corey Farell.

True to form, he also did whatever was needed to get out and talk to people as much as possible. So one day, when Farell was tied up doing something else, he looked around the office to see who else was on hand. As the clear lead on the case, he could finally move as he wished, and he was in no mood to be held up by anything.

It happened that Rick Gordon was nearby. And so, on October 1, five months after Bryant's death, Skaggs—in need of a temporary partner—asked Gordon to accompany him. And that's how the two men—arguably the two finest ghettoside detectives in the city at that time—set out on a very particular mission.

. . .

The man Coughlin had caught with the revolver was a member of South Central's battalion of black men whose lower halves were crumpled in wheelchairs, propped on crutches, or crammed into leg braces. One saw these victims with regularity driving around South Central— young male gunshot victims, jarring collisions of health and debility, young faces and wasted limbs. Asked what happened, they gave the same answer this man later gave in court. One word: *"Shot."*

He looked younger than his twenty-eight years. He had a small mouth and a slim, narrow nose that widened at the base, skin very dark and smooth. A neat thread of beard framed his chin. His clothes were bright and pressed—even the pants that lay in a loose fold across his thighs. He was efficient in his wheelchair, propelling himself with athleticism. If a wheelchair could saunter that's what his did. He had not been quick enough to outrun Francis Coughlin. But Coughlin was faster than a lot of guys on foot.

The man had a quiet dignity despite his mask of gloom and wariness. He didn't seem deranged by trauma, as some gang members do past twenty-five. His manner of speaking was quiet and reasonable. He talked about *getting out* and said he wanted to go to school. It seemed he meant it. A number of Southeast officers knew him personally. "A gangster," they called him, but were quick to add, "he's not a bad guy." Some even said they liked him. The man in the wheelchair was a type— a normal guy somehow caught in the pathos of gang life.

He had been shot while walking home from a night game at his high school a dozen years before. A car rolled up and he heard someone yell "East Coast," then heard the shots. He'd been hit seven times but felt only the last three. He was surprised later to learn of the others. Knocked flat, he lay on the ground as a burning sensation rose through his body. That was all. Just a burn. The doctor came into his room at King-Drew Medical Center the next morning, after surgery. His spine was fractured. He would never walk again. He was seventeen.

After Francis Coughlin caught the man with the gun, Bernal immediately went and "hit" him: he visited him in custody and asked him where he got the gun. The man said he bought the gun from a "smoker"—a crack addict. The man appeared forthcoming. He gave details of the homeless man.

Still it was not helpful. A homeless guy would probably not have gang ties and so would be harder to track. Bernal returned with Rick Gordon. The man stuck to his story. After Skaggs was assigned to the case, he and Bernal returned together a third time. Same story.

When John Skaggs came to interview the man in the wheelchair at Twin Towers Jail on October 1, it was his fourth visit from investigators.

To Skaggs, it was obvious the man in the wheelchair was lying— obvious that he must be reinterviewed, again and again if necessary. He was to Skaggs simply a point of exertion: a rusty lever that would give once the right persistence was applied. The sort of persistence that was his specialty. Why was Skaggs so sure? Skaggs couldn't say. The man's dishonesty was so plain to him that it needed no explaining. This was part of the altered perspective of the craftsman: Skaggs saw lies the way a good contractor would notice a beam out of true.

Gordon and Skaggs sat with him in a small interview room in Twin Towers.

The man in the wheelchair already knew Gordon, so Skaggs let Gordon do the talking, observing the old Southeast rule of only one lead. Gordon began the conversation with a tone of familiarity, as if picking up a thread dropped moments before. Like Skaggs, Gordon conducted interrogations like business meetings. His style was subdued and apologetic, as if he were sorry for the trouble he brought.

The man in the wheelchair elaborated on his story of the crack addict who sold the gun once again. "That guy has a white beard. He is skinny. He is forty." When Gordon pressed for details of his hair, the man paused as if straining to be accurate: "More gray. Low haircut," he told Gordon.

Gordon turned up the pressure without changing his tone. By this time, the man had certainly guessed that he had been caught with a very, very dirty gun indeed. You don't get four visits from homicide detectives for just any gang killing.

Gordon suggested the man might be fingered for a serious crime. "I don't want to see a guy like you going to some shitty-ass pen," Gordon said. "You and me both!" the man rejoined quickly.

Gordon's voice remained gentle. But he bore down. "We want your cooperation, one hundred percent, and I feel like we have it, but . . ."

The man was silent. "What are you thinking?" Gordon asked. Silence. Gordon dropped his voice, called him by his first name. "Just like I told you before, you can erase everything you told us," he said. "If it's not the truth, I'd rather not be spinning my wheels."

Homicide detectives lie to suspects routinely and legally. But Gordon had an even more cunning tactic. He began telling the man the truth. His tone was as unadorned as if he were speaking to a colleague. "You don't even know how busy we are," he told him. "I got more murders I'm working than you can imagine. If it's not the truth, I'd rather follow real stuff. I'm not gonna be pissed off at you if all this was made up. I'm just looking for the truth."

Gordon said precisely what he really thought. He *did* have a lot of cases, and he really didn't want to waste time.

Skaggs was quiet. At last, the man insisted again that he bought the gun from "a smoker-type transient." He added the detail that the two had discussed swapping a stereo.

The detectives were getting nowhere. Gordon was dogged but not harsh. He kept asking the same question five different ways. Finally, seemingly defeated, he veered away into inconsequential chatter.

The detectives were preparing to leave. They asked after the man's family. They asked about his children. The man told them he had a new "little baby." His tone grew relaxed. "I'm not the jail type," he offered. "I just want to get out of here, start back my life, go back to school." The detectives were sympathetic. The conversation flowed. At last, Gordon and Skaggs made movements to go. Gordon tossed out one last question.

"Anything else?" Gordon asked. "Is there a way you can help us?" Gordon was trying to give the man an opening to drop a hint. Hints were common in such interviews. People who were afraid to testify would try to help detectives indirectly. Sometimes they would leave them anonymous messages, scrawled notes crammed under the wind-shield wipers of police sedans.

But the man in the wheelchair didn't hint. He threw open a curtain—suddenly, blindingly. His tone changed. He had sounded nonchalant. Now he was somber.

"Well, I'm just gonna go ahead and tell you officers," he said. "Actually, I got the gun from this dude."

The detectives froze, waiting. Then the man produced the key Skaggs knew he had had all along. "They call him *No Brains*," he said.

Gordon and Skaggs emerged with the case transformed. The man in the wheelchair had not bought the gun from a smoker. He had paid fifty dollars to a mysterious gang member with hazel eyes and curly hair called "No Brains" one day on the campus of Southwest College.

He said No Brains belonged to a gang called the One Hundred and Eleven Blocc Crips, a subset of the Rollin' Hundreds Blocc Crips. For a moment, both detectives were baffled. Despite all their years in South Bureau, neither Gordon nor Skaggs recognized the name of this gang. Gangs were so hyperlocal that the Rollin' Hundreds, located a few minutes' drive from the Seventy-seventh over in the sheriff's territory, might as well have been from a different country. No Brains had a teardrop under his eye, the man said, and the letter *B* tattooed on his arm.

No Brains hung out with a girl, the man said. *A girl*. Both detectives were doubly alert. Who was she? A homeless type? they asked. No, the man said: "She ain't that type. No drugs or gang."

A good girl? they asked. "Yeah," the man said.

When it was over, Gordon asked him why he hadn't leveled with them before. He gave the answer Gordon had heard a hundred times: "I got family out there . . . I don't want someone to blow my head off—my mama and kids shot."

They said they'd keep his name out of it. They lied.

In Skaggs's mind, an idea was taking shape.

A witness interviewed at the murder scene the night of Bryant's death had mentioned a rumor that a gang called *Rollin'-something* was involved in the crime. The word "Rollin'" was used in several gang names in L.A., including the Rollin' Sixties located to the north. But now the detail came back to Skaggs. He paired it with a flash of memory: new graffiti Skaggs had spotted shortly after Bryant was killed. He and Nathan Kouri had seen it while driving near the crime scene—the word "Bloccs" scrawled on a wall.

Skaggs was looking for an alternative to the Rollin' Sixties theory, which he felt had monopolized too much investigative effort and borne no fruit. Now here were two clues pointing to the Rollin' Hundreds Blocc Crips.

This was typical of how Skaggs went about his work. His capacious memory was engaged from the first minute on a case, filing away every detail—a stray comment, a graffiti tag scratched on a window. Such random impressions might seem meaningless to someone else. But Skaggs knew that down the line, a pattern would form. It was another reason he preferred fieldwork and put so much emphasis on face-to-face contact. Going back to the crime scene, revisiting homes of bereaved families, chatting up people he met on the street, might have seemed a waste of time to another detective. But to Skaggs, every moment in the field was an opportunity to load his memory with more grains of information. He knew that eventually one grain in the great sand pile would prove the diamond. Sometimes he would go back to the scene, park his sedan, and just wait, windows rolled down. He would call out to anyone who passed, "How you doin'?" and then chat.

Now he remembered that in one of the many reinterviews of witnesses on the cases, someone had mentioned a fight in the neighborhood not long after the murder. Chris Wilson and a brother of his, a gang member who had refused to speak to the police, had reputedly seen two strange teenagers on their street and thought they recognized Bryant's killers. Tellingly, they didn't call the police. They ran out, confronted them, and challenged them to fight—street justice for the killing of a police officer's son whom they considered a friend.

Reports held that one was a Rollin' Ninety. The brothers got beaten up. The Rollin' Ninety had pulled the elder's pants down—sexual humiliation being, like threats and low-level violence, an instrument of message-sending that was relatively common in the gang milieu. Skaggs knew how inaccurate the GIN could be, but this incident could help point toward other facts. In this case, it was clear that some gang members in Bryant's neighborhood believed that the attack had come from affiliates of the Rollin' Nineties, and the Nineties were allied with the adjacent Rollin' Hundreds Blocc Crips.

Since the talk with the man in the wheelchair, this remembered tidbit suddenly had new significance.

A warrant database search located by their gang monikers the pair of Nineties gang members the brothers had fought. It turned out that the young street fighter from the Rollin' Nineties was sixteen. He was on the run with a probation warrant. Gang officers were asked to keep an eye out.

A week went by. Then Skaggs got a call: the sixteen-year-old probationer who'd beaten Bryant's neighbors was in custody. He'd been brought in by a gang officer who recognized him at Jesse Owens Park. This youth was the son of a plumber from Hot Springs, Arkansas, who had come to L.A. three decades before during the great migration wave and stayed because it was beautiful. The plumber's family mostly had done well. One son worked for the Metropolitan Transportation Authority and the other for United Parcel Service. But his youngest was different.

The father had been struggling with his problems for several years at the time of the Tennelle case. Like many black parents in Los Angeles, he felt danger pressing in from all sides. Like Wally Tennelle, he was fearful that a gang might recruit his boy. But the father also viewed law enforcement warily and worried for his son's safety at the hand of the police. He believed many police officers conducted themselves poorly and had it out for black young men. He had sent his son all the way across the city to attend high school in Beverly Hills. But the son hid a friend's pellet gun in his locker and got caught, the father said.

The boy was suspended by the school and put on probation by a juvenile court. Once he entered the criminal justice system, things went downhill. He ended up violating his probation and going to juvenile camp. When he came out, he seemed to have taken on a new gang persona. Later, his father turned him in to a probation officer himself. It was an extreme step. But the father hoped that some jail time would straighten him out. Instead, his son came out tougher than ever.

The son had medium light brown skin, flat cheeks, and an angular chin. He looked a little older than he was and had a lean grace. That Tuesday evening, when Skaggs went to the Seventy-seventh to meet him, he had none of the swagger that might have been expected from a hardened Rollin' Nineties Crip. His eyes were full of tears.

Up until that point, Skaggs had thought this young probationer might be his killer. But once he had sized him up, he shifted gears. When he mentioned the intersection where Bryant was shot, the probationer responded readily: Was this about the killing of "the policeman's son"? Skaggs began by asking him why he was crying. "My pops, man," he said. He was going to miss his father's birthday once again—he had been in jail for every one of his father's birthdays since he was fourteen, and he was desperate to be available for this one.

Although his speech was laced with 'hood talk—words such as "cherp" and "nigga"—the probationer could turn it off when he wanted. Skaggs asked him to speak up because "my partner's not the smartest guy around."

Skaggs loved teasing Farell with this line in the interview room. He had used it many times, taking advantage of the younger detective's predicament: Farell had to sit by silently to observe the "one lead" rule.

The probationer proved a lucid interview subject. He seemed to have a good memory, and he even displayed a little literary flair, offering details that suggested he was a sharp observer. He made it clear he would help them so long as he never had to appear in court: "You say my name not gonna be in nothing. I believe you," he said.

"Everybody know."

This was the phrase the probationer used several times in the next half hour.

Everybody, he said—that is, dozens of people in the gang milieu—knew about Bryant's death. They knew who did it and for what gang. Everybody knew. Everybody was talking.

It was just as Kelle Baitx suspected—the young probationer's account suggested that the suspects lived within a few miles of the crime scene, and that they belonged to an underground network that was buzzing with gossip about the case. The case was like many others—more of a public murder than a secret one, a communal event. It was no mystery—except to the police.

The probationer said he had been back in Hot Springs visiting his grandmother in May when he got a "cherp" from a girl he called "Hollywood." "A tramp just got chipped," she told him. The probationer was happy—it meant a gang rival had been shot. "I was like, all right, *woo woo woo*," he said. But then one of the probationer's homeys called, alarmed. "A police officer's son got chipped somewhere off Normandie and the police is hot around here—*shit!*" The homey recommended he stay put in Arkansas.

The probationer got several more calls to the same effect. Everyone was talking about how the "tramp" had turned out to be a police officer's son and how cops were now scouring the neighborhood. People were scared they'd be swept up in a dragnet and "put up for that shit."

When the youth returned from Arkansas in early September, his friends were still abuzz. "Stay away from Bloccs," they warned. "They chip that nigga—police been over there, like, swarmin'."

People were mad about it. "That Baby Man from Bloccs is stupid," someone said.

Baby Man. The probationer knew him. "Oh, cuz did it?" the youth had replied. "That's crazy!" In the days that followed, he heard more and more. "Every day people talking about it!" he told Skaggs. "Everybody know!"

Ordinarily, gang members welcomed some demonstration of police concern as proof of the seriousness of their attacks. A bit of gang slang expressed this: "puttin' up tape" was a phrase used a little like "earning stripes." A member who "put up tape" had executed a successful mission—killing or maiming a rival with gunfire. Because police encircled shooting scenes with yellow tape only if someone had been seriously hurt or killed, tape signaled that the shooters hadn't missed or chickened out. It was a badge of honor.

But this was different. With most gang shootings, police intervention often did not go much beyond "putting up tape." But with an officer's son dead, police were "superhot." "Stay away from Bloccs," people said. "Stay away from Baby Man."

Push hard enough and eventually the current sweeps you downstream. Skaggs's case was moving swiftly now. He had two nicknames: "No Brains" and "Baby Man," both members of the Blocc Crips. There would be no more time wasted on the Sixties.

But the case still remained squarely in the arena of street rumors, where many gang cases foundered. "Everybody know" was a phrase that applied to a lot of unsolved murders south of the Ten.

Skaggs asked the probationer Baby Man's real name. He couldn't remember. "His real name is D-something . . . D . . . D . . ." The youth pondered.

What does he look like? Skaggs asked. "Dark skin. Funny-shaped head," the youth said. He said Baby Man was about seventeen years old, and he added one of his literary flourishes: "Dry rough hands."

The detectives kept pressing. What about his head? "It's, like, an oval shape, like an egg—a cracked egg!" the probationer said. Farell stifled a laugh, and the youth laughed, too. "When you see his picture, you gonna see what I mean," he promised.

There was more. The probationer had run into Baby Man in Jesse Owens Park at a gathering of gang members. "What's up, man? You shot that nigga? You shot that police officer's kid?" he had said in front of everyone.

Baby Man was aghast. People were mad about the trouble the case had caused. Baby Man denied his involvement before the group. After, he pulled the probationer aside, pleading: "Don' be sayin' that shit." He didn't admit or deny his involvement. He said he didn't know what to do and was scared. "Man, I'm gonna go to jail!" he had lamented.

The probationer still couldn't remember his name, except that it began with *D*.

He told the detectives Baby Man was not popular: "He has got something wrong with him," he said. "He's stupid."

Skaggs started to speak. But the probationer interrupted him. "Devin!" he exclaimed triumphantly. "That's his name—Devin!"

Devin Davis, sixteen years old at the time of Bryant's death, was then serving time in a juvenile camp after having been caught with two guns in less than a month. He was easy enough to identify from police records. He had been arrested more than once and had been entered into the gang database—his picture, his personal information, his gang name of Baby Man as well as three or four other monikers, and his membership in the Blocc Crips.

Hazel-eyed No Brains was a different story: Skaggs did not have enough detail to figure out who he really was. He had found no one matching his description in any record search. He was still searching when he got a call from a gang deputy at the Sheriff's Department.

The deputy's "friendly" knew exactly who No Brains was. He identified him as an older, light-skinned Blocc Crip with green eyes. He was in jail. But the friendly didn't know his real name.

The case now had not just direction, but momentum. Skaggs and Farell were working full tilt. In mid-November, they served a search warrant on Devin Davis's house. Skaggs met his mother. Sandra James, kind, religious, and proper, was very cooperative. She had other grown children who had done well in life, going to school and working, she told Skaggs. But Devin, her youngest, had ADD. He had thrown her off balance with his many problems.

In Devin's bedroom, Skaggs found what he was looking for: scribbles on notepaper celebrating the Blocc Crips and bearing the gang moniker Baby Man.

And one more find: a little white scrap of paper with a phone number scrawled on it, and a name: No Brains.

The two Blocc Crips were now linked. But No Brains remained elusive. Skaggs by then knew exactly which bed and jail module No Brains was assigned to. But he still could not get an accurate identification of him from the sheriff's deputies who manned the jail, and they couldn't seem to find him.

It took Skaggs two weeks of wrangling with the sheriff's jail bureaucracy to figure out exactly who and where No Brains was. At one point, he threatened to walk through the module himself—how hard could it be to spot a light-skinned, green-eyed gangster with Blocc Crip tattoos? At last, they came back to Skaggs with a name. The light-skinned inmate was Wright Lawrence.

The name didn't match any rap sheet. And the state fingerprint database had listed the inmate as "Lawrence Wright." Skaggs was exasperated—authorities could not even keep their mistakes straight— but he was not surprised. Given the abundance of nicknames, gang monikers, and fake names used by criminals, the problem of people being imprisoned under the wrong name was not uncommon in his experience. This extended to other records as well—homicide victims were frequently listed under different names in various public databases. Spanish names were a mess: Mexican immigrants typically had one or two first names and two last names—their father's followed by their mother's. But arrest forms insisted on English conventions, listing everyone as having a first name, middle name, and last name. As a result, Spanish names were often mangled in the booking process.

The names of black people who interacted with the system could present authorities with similar problems. Apart from the endless nicknames and aliases, there were many formal names with multiple variations, unconventional apostrophes, and unusual spellings, and these were frequently misstated or misspelled in public records, even death records. Officers relied on fingerprints and other elaborate cross-checking methods to keep track of who was who.

Skaggs went back to his computer and started over. He looked for records of light-skinned Blocc Crips and rap sheets that matched the inmate known as Wright Lawrence—dates, addresses, arrests—and, by cross-checking several databases, he arrived at the correct name: Derrick Starks.

He called the Sheriff's Department to inform them they were holding Starks under the wrong name. Months later, Skaggs checked to make sure they had corrected the error. They hadn't. Starks remained listed as jail inmate Wright Lawrence for months.

Derrick Starks, twenty-five years old at the time of Bryant's death, was a Blocc Crip with a typical gang rap sheet that included robbery and attempted burglary. He had been born in Louisiana, where his family's roots lay. His mother had been one of seventeen children. She was a real estate agent who devoted volunteer hours to helping families who had lost children to homicide. Starks had an older brother in college. He was the troubled younger brother. Raised in a neighborhood near Century Boulevard, he had joined the Blocc Crips in his late teens.

His current jail stint was related to a burglary charge and a parole violation in connection with a car crash. The car had collided with a telephone pole on May 15, four days after Bryant's death, and Starks had been arrested. The arrest report said Starks had been driving. He had a companion with him when he crashed: a girl.

The car was a black Chevrolet Suburban.

A Suburban, a girl. This last detail was a bonus: Skaggs had been hoping for a girl in the car. Ever since the man in the wheelchair had mentioned that No Brains hung out with a "good girl," Skaggs had been attuned to this possibility. A girl in a gang car might be an opening. Frequently, she was being dragged along—if not against her will, then at least with no particular choice in the matter. And girls were not subject to the relentless gang violence that boys were—at least not shootings—and so were easier to flip.

Skaggs had time on his side. Both suspects—Devin Davis in juvenile camp and now Derrick Starks—were in custody. They weren't going anywhere.

The arrest report had listed the girl in the car as Jessica Bailey. It was a false name, as Skaggs was sure it would be. He found an address for a *Jennifer* Bailey in the Hundreds Blocc vicinity from motor vehicle records. Jennifer Bailey had never been arrested. But Skaggs used her address to cross-check against criminal databases and came up with another name: Jessica *Midkiff*.

Jessica Midkiff was Jennifer Bailey's niece. She had a big rap sheet for prostitution, and a tattoo on her neck. Skaggs pulled up her picture. Midkiff was light-skinned and cute. The tattoo on her neck was large and garish. He nodded to himself. "I think this is my Jessica."

It was Friday, November 30, about 3:00 P.M. Skaggs saw the next few hours clearly. He wanted the LAPD's best surveillance team on Midkiff immediately as he ran "a ton of clues" seeking other connections. But it didn't quite work out that way. When he called headquarters, they balked. The SIS (Special Investigations Section) team downtown was too closely associated with RHD, someone said. Skaggs cursed to himself. He called the South Bureau surveillance team. They were assigned elsewhere. So Skaggs spent the next few hours making call after call to get someone to do surveillance and catch Jessica Midkiff. At last, South Bureau's team was reassigned. It was always like this, he reflected.

Everything, everything, was harder than you thought it would be.

He worked late into that night, then went home and waited.

16

THE WITNESS

The tattoo on the side of Jessica Midkiff's neck was an angel. It was so large it appeared to be straining to encircle her throat.

Skaggs first met her in a small detention cell in the basement of the Seventy-seventh Street station. She was twenty-two and petite, with very light skin, brown hair, a doll-like nose, and chestnut eyes that curved down at the corners. Her chin jutted slightly, and her black brows were arched and sculpted. She was in gray sweatpants and a teeny, light-weight top inappropriate for the December night. Her feet were bare. She was sniffling and sobbing with fear.

Earlier in the day the surveillance crew on the house had seen her come out and get into a car. The team followed the car and arrested her at a nearby gas station. Skaggs asked Midkiff if she knew why she was there. "No, I promise, I don't!" she stammered. Skaggs responded in his unhurried way, as relaxed as if they were discussing plans for dinner. "Okay," he said. "You and I are going to talk."

But Midkiff was already talking as fast as she could. She had "anxiety," she explained between sniffles—meaning some kind of disorder. She had recently emerged from "this program." She'd been trying "to do good." "I'm not gonna lie—I was a prostitute for years—and I checked myself into the rehab for that."

She was wide-eyed—afraid the arrest meant she was going back to jail. She wanted Skaggs to know she wasn't holding out. "I got a bench warrant from Compton. And I've been taking care of it." She was terrified of losing custody of her young daughter, she said. "It's a big thing to me. Whatever you guys want me to do, I'll do it!"

It would seem to have been an ideal situation. Midkiff seemed disposed to cooperate fully. But Skaggs was wary. She seemed a little *too* willing—too "cute," he would say later. She hung on his every word and gazed up at him with big teary eyes encircled by black lashes. His first instinct was to dismiss her presentation as an act.

Skaggs had thought Midkiff might be a suspect, the knowing getaway driver, and he was geared for an adversarial interview. He had planned to corner her, to force some slip that would put her at the crime scene. He had reviewed her long rap sheet. Clearly, she was an experienced prostitute and had been interviewed by many a police officer. She'd had abundant opportunity to hone this performance.

When he first walked into the cell, he had promised Midkiff that "a very important talk we are gonna have. Huge. Very big." Now, faced with her near hysteria, he dialed it back. He told her something had happened the previous May. "We are gonna sit down and have an easy talk, you and I." But at the mention of May, Midkiff instantly began babbling about her ex-boyfriend. "What's his name?" Skaggs demanded, suddenly sharp.

"Derrick," she said.

The case Skaggs had been chasing was now chasing him. Random details were spilling out of Midkiff, and they hadn't even sat down at a table yet. Derrick Starks clearly brought up all sorts of issues for her. She was talking fast, spinning in several directions. Skaggs barely had time to draw a breath before she had outlined all the major themes of her life:

She had been abused and had lived badly.

Derrick was among her abusers.

Now she was trying to change. "I'm just trying to get my life together the best way I know," she wept. "I don't really know how, but I'm tryin'!"

It seemed too good to be true. Skaggs remained suspicious. He had Farell take her upstairs to the interview room while he gathered his notes. In the interview room, he started off in his harshest tone.

Skaggs was not rough or threatening in interrogations. He never raised his voice. But he had a way of bearing down, of signaling impatience and resolve. His manner suggested he was comfortable with power and intended to demolish all opposition. This was true of him on duty and off. His was an easygoing personality, but not a compromising one. Corey Farell noticed this, and he thought it one of the traits that distinguished Skaggs. Some police officers felt they had to adopt a false persona at work; Skaggs, if anything, was more genuinely himself while working.

Skaggs bore down on Midkiff sternly. He sat very close to her, speaking slowly and allowing the timbre of his voice to dip. He was mildly profane. He was a homicide detective, he told her. He was going to talk to her about "some big, big shit. You gonna step up, or you gonna go down?"

"Step up," Midkiff said instantly.

Midkiff promised to tell the detectives whatever they wanted to know. "Honest to God, I'll do it," but "I don't want to go on nobody's stand," she added.

Before Skaggs could begin his questioning, she had laid out her objections to testifying in court without prompting. They were the usual ones. Her grandparents owned a home and could not afford to leave. "I know I messed up dealing with the wrong people—if I have to take it I'll take it—but I don't want my family jeopardized behind my stupidity!" she said.

Derrick Starks had been calling her from prison. She was in high anxiety about it. She broke down: "I just want to wash my hands of these people, and I can't get rid of them!" she wept.

"Yeah we can," Skaggs replied calmly.

This was exactly the point: getting rid of people. Seldom was it put this way. But one of the primary reasons to have a legal system is to take certain people out of the picture. It is what justifies the immense power the police hold. If you don't incapacitate violent actors, they keep pushing people around until someone makes them stop. When violent people are permitted to operate with impunity, they *get their way.* Advantage tilts to them. Others are forced to do their bidding.

No amount of "community" feeling or activism can eclipse this dynamic. People often assert that the solution to homicide is for the so-called community to "step up." It is a pernicious distortion. People like Jessica Midkiff cannot be expected to stand up to killers. They need safety, not stronger moral conviction. They need some powerful outside force to sweep in and take their tormentors away. That's what the criminal justice system is for. It was what Skaggs was for, and he knew it.

Skaggs began talking in generalities, using the same stern tone. It was the strategy he always used. He would talk with a voice full of meaning even though he was stalling. He nattered on. And with another part of his brain, he studied Midkiff. He was trying to figure out if she was lying.

Our job "is a simple one," Skaggs rambled. "We have one thing to do every time we come to work—find the truth. That's pretty easy. It's difficult in the neighborhood we work in, but that's kind of an easy concept. *Somebody got hurt. Somebody got killed.* We find out what happened to them."

Five minutes passed. Ten. Skaggs talked in circles. Like Rick Gordon, he resorted to telling Midkiff the truth, strategically. "I've never met you before, I don't know if you are putting on an act—if you're really good at turnin' on tears," he told her.

Through it all, Midkiff wept and professed her willingness to cooperate. Skaggs offered her water. She said she needed a cigarette to calm her nerves. He promised to take her outside for a smoke. They were going to have a big talk, very soon, he said. He tossed out vague phrases to explain what was happening.

Skaggs seemed to have an inexhaustible supply of clichés for this purpose. He never used the word "interrogation." "Something we need to get on the table," he said. "Something we all have to deal with," to "put in the right place."

Midkiff kept interrupting. She talked about her daughter and Derrick. By the time Skaggs had worked up to reading Midkiff her Miranda rights, his attitude toward her was beginning to shift. She still seemed a likely liar. But he wasn't seeing the usual signs. He couldn't read her.

His tone softened. He stopped swearing. He promised to talk to her about "big, big stuff," not "big shit" as before. "Look at me," he said. "We have not made any decision of what's gonna happen to you tonight." He read the rights to her, conversationally and easily, then got down to business.

But when Skaggs uttered the words "shooting off Western," Midkiff seemed confused. She didn't understand what they were talking about.

"Western?" she said. She thought that Skaggs was going to ask her about the time Starks crashed his mother's Suburban into a pole and got arrested. That hadn't happened on Western. He had crashed because of a car-to-car shooting, although the police report had not reflected this. Starks had also asked Midkiff to lie for him in a burglary investigation. All these episodes were in her mind. She was confused. So Skaggs clarified, focusing her on the events of May 11.

She hesitated, eyes brimming. "I don't want to die!" she whispered. "They are going to kill my family!"

"You have a promise from me that I will not leave your family hanging," Skaggs said.

Midkiff's hesitation was brief. She began: "I wanted to drive his truck, I was so eager to drive his frickin' truck—" At the memory, she suddenly laughed bitterly.

When she smiled, she had dimples in both cheeks.

More than half an hour of rambling talk had passed since Skaggs and Midkiff had first laid eyes on each other. Only now did he begin to ask his questions.

On the day Bryant Tennelle died, Midkiff had been in the Suburban

with Starks, she said. They picked up two dark-skinned teenage boys—
one of whom she later identified as Devin Davis. The other she didn't
know; he was never identified.

They drove north to "the Eighties" and Starks handed one of the
teenagers a gun. The boys jumped out and went around a corner. Midkiff heard gunshots. The car doors opened and the pair jumped back in.
Starks yanked her over his lap into the passenger seat and took the
wheel. They drove off. "I'm the man, cuz!" Devin Davis had crowed.

Skaggs wanted every detail. But eagerness was anathema to his tech-
nique. The ability to slow down when events reached fever pitch was
something Nathan Kouri admired in his mentor. It distinguished him as
a master interrogator, Kouri thought. "Us new guys want to go in for
the kill," he said. But Skaggs wasn't wired like that. After Midkiff finished her initial narration, he called a break. He left Midkiff to release
the crew of officers he'd assembled earlier for a search warrant. He no
longer needed them.

Jessica Midkiff had been born at Queen of Angels Hospital in Los
Angeles, but her family roots were in Texas and Alabama. She was biracial, half black and half white. Her father had been one of those rare
poor whites still living in South Central L.A. in the late 1980s. But like
most people of mixed race in her milieu, Midkiff considered herself
black.

Her parents had split while Jessica was young, and she said that an
abusive stepfather had raped her repeatedly. By the time she was eleven,
she was performing oral sex for cash, food, and clothes. She was turning
tricks in cars by fourteen.

Prostitutes such as Midkiff are effectively slaves. But they tend to spin
a narrative about their own lives that suggests more agency. Midkiff referred to various pimps over the years as "boyfriends." Some were
pimpier than others. In her mind, there existed the possibility of a man
being "kind of like a pimp." She had straight pimps who kept her with
a stable of other prostitutes and appropriated all her earnings. She also
had boyfriends like Derrick Starks, with whom she was paired as a couple but who also asked her to turn tricks now and then.

Her daughter's father, who had gotten Jessica pregnant while she was a student at Washington High, had been one of the few men in her life who was not abusive and didn't try to pimp her. But after his brother was murdered, he joined a gang and ended up in prison, she said.

While still an adolescent, Midkiff traveled as a prostitute. She worked in Los Angeles, Riverside, Las Vegas, and parts of Arizona. She worked Sunset Boulevard, peddling ten-minute intervals in cars: oral sex for $50, intercourse for $100, both for $150. She was hired by a professional football player and for pricey all-night parties, once earning $850 for a single trick. She'd also worked Figueroa Street—that dangerous bargain basement for prostitutes. You were down-and-out when you found yourself working the long murderous stretch that plunged southward along the Harbor Freeway. Years later, the thought of it still caused her to shudder. "I *hate* Figueroa," she said.

In between, she returned home from time to time. Her grandparents still lived stable, homebound lives. Her mother was raising her little girl. At one point, she enrolled in continuation school and was proud to be elected class secretary. But men always found Midkiff. There had been so many boyfriends-cum-pimps, so many beatings, girl fights, and rapes at gunpoint, so many misdemeanor arrests, that her prostitution years had a kaleidoscopic quality. Only she could keep it straight.

She slept all day and was up all night for years, her life a blur of shared motel rooms and fleeting, intense friendships that often ended in rancor. By the time she was twenty-one, she had never held a job, could barely read, and had no ability to conduct relationships with any maturity or control. She was brittle and constantly flew into rages. She had frequent fights with other women. And she suffered severe post-traumatic stress disorder that prompted anxiety attacks. Memories would sweep over her at unexpected moments, as real as if happening anew, the pain rivaling that of childbirth, she said.

One night, someone dropped her off on Lincoln Boulevard, another down-and-out open-air market. She was at the end. She asked a shopkeeper for change to use a pay phone. Instead, the man gave her sixty

or seventy bucks and a ride. For once she received help from someone
who asked for nothing in return. With his help she reunited with her
mother, who took her in. A short while later she enrolled in the Mary
Magdalene Project in the San Fernando Valley, a residential charity focused on treating prostitution like an addiction. Midkiff loved the program. But she fought with another woman and was ejected.

She came back to her mother's house in South Central, in the neighborhood of the Rollin' Hundreds Bloccs. As always, she drew male attention. One day walking back from a nail shop on Western and Imperial
to her grandparents' house, she met a gangster she knew named
"Thump." He had a light-skinned friend with him. The friend had massive shoulders and a cupid's-bow mouth. Derrick Starks had gotten out
of jail that April 3.

They talked. A sheriff's patrol car swooped in. Deputies put them all
in handcuffs, and searched them. They let Midkiff go but made the two
men sit in the cruiser. The pair joked with the deputies—"You messed
up our game!"

Derrick Starks would return to pull "his game" on Midkiff three days
later as she was walking to the store. She was reluctant to give him her
number. "But you can't really be too mean about it 'cause you don't
know what to expect," she later told Skaggs. Midkiff was accustomed to
romance shot through with mortal fear; she thought little of it. Shortly
after, she "hooked up" with him.

Midkiff's story was typical of south end prostitutes, that is, it was
sordid, dramatic, and monotonous. Such stories always seemed to begin
the same way—with a rape or molestation in childhood—and to end
with an aging prostitute accepting ever-lowlier tricks to feed a drug addiction. At the end of the line harrowed-looking homeless women with
missing teeth wandered the streets, offering blow jobs in alleys.

But Midkiff was atypical in some ways. Skaggs was beginning to see
this. For one thing, she was not a junkie. Midkiff was a chain-smoker
and binge drinker. But observing her over the next few hours, Skaggs
felt sure she was not a regular user of cocaine or methamphetamine.

She appeared bright despite her lack of formal education. "I can tell you are not a malicious person," she told Skaggs at one point. And she had an excellent memory.

What Skaggs couldn't see was that Midkiff actually was at one of those rare crossroads in life. She was telling the truth: she wanted to change, but she didn't know how. There would be no storybook ending for her. But this interview was a turning point. It would change everything for both of them.

"Code Four here!"

Skaggs was back in the squad room talking to one of his bureau colleagues on the cell phone during a break, his tone light with relief. He snapped the phone shut and surveyed his colleagues hovering nearby. One was readying six-packs—photo lineups for Jessica to identify the suspects. Another prepared to take Jessica out for a cigarette.

Prideaux also lingered. He had remained in the background, enduring spasms of anxiety as Skaggs spoke to Midkiff. By now, Prideaux knew he had made the right decision in selecting Skaggs for the case. He orbited the tall detective and waited for an opening.

"Hey John, you need anything?" Prideaux finally asked. He spoke with forced lightness. But his voice held a deferential note. Anyone listening would have thought Skaggs, not Prideaux, the superior officer.

"No, L.T.!" Skaggs told him. Securing Midkiff's cooperation was game-changing, Skaggs knew he was in the home stretch.

There is little celebrating in homicide units. Even La Barbera and his crew, long known for irreverence that bordered on inappropriateness, did not generally high-five each other or appear jubilant when they solved cases. They indulged in pranks and black humor, and they posed every year for a grisly homicide-themed Christmas card from the unit—a faux crime scene with a dead Santa, for example. But day to day, homicide remained just too depressing to permit much gaiety in their ranks. Detectives walked out of meetings with suspects, witnesses, and survivors looking somber and spent no matter how well the interviews had gone. Grim faces accompanied even the most dramatic investigative triumphs. It wasn't an affectation, it was a natural reaction to the cloud of agony that emanated from the Monster.

One could never feel good about solving a case. No sense of a mission accomplished could minimize the horror. Bryant's death, no matter what the detectives did, would remain sickening and unspeakably sad to everyone who had dealt with the case, forever after.

So although Prideaux had been waiting for weeks for this moment—waiting to see Skaggs emerge from a key interview with a look of success—he allowed himself just two words to express his feelings:

"Good job," he muttered.

Skaggs reflexively dropped his voice to match Prideaux's.

"Yeah," he said, and nodded. "It worked out."

Up until then, Skaggs had betrayed no emotion about the favorable turn the case had taken. But the tactful respect in Prideaux's voice seemed to catch him off guard.

Skaggs emitted a small sigh. Then he repeated his own words in a murmur, as if reassuring himself. "It worked out."

That evening stretched for hours. Skaggs interviewed Midkiff in detail, then drove her past the crime scene. He searched her mother's house. He became more and more certain that she was telling the truth. He was astonished by how well she remembered the sequence of events seven months before. He tested her, pretending he didn't know certain details so that she would supply them. He lied to her, telling her he had a conflicting statement from another occupant in the car. He wanted to see if she would improvise.

But she was unshakable. She stuck to her story. After her initial flurries of tears and anxiety attacks, Midkiff settled down and answered each question in a sad, matter-of-fact voice. She labored to find exactly the right terms and paused frequently to remember. When she couldn't, she said so and apologized.

She nailed everything. Skaggs could not find any holes. Her descriptions matched everything they already knew: the direction and location of the Suburban, the description of the shooter, his clothes, the style of gun, the number of shots. Skaggs finally tried accusing her of lying. She just wept, said "Well?" and kept repeating her story.

Skaggs had dealt with many people in his career with histories like Midkiff's. Prostitutes tended to be among the most dysfunctional people in the street environment, their problems intractable, their unreliability profound. But later, Skaggs would say that Jessica Midkiff was the only homicide witness he had ever interviewed who told the same story at every stage of the investigation and trial without a single detail changed, or a detectable lie.

It went against all his expectations but again confirmed Rick Gordon's doctrine. This jittery young prostitute with her cutesy affectations, angel tattoo, and bare feet would turn out to be the best witness Skaggs ever had.

As the night had gone on, Skaggs had extracted from Midkiff a detailed version of the broad outline she had told him at the beginning of their meeting. Midkiff said that she and Derrick Starks had spent the night before Bryant's murder in a motel called the Desert Inn on Century Boulevard. Neither had their own apartment. They stayed in cheap motels at least four times a week, sleeping late and drifting into the next day's activities. These usually involved hanging out with Starks's friends, the Rollin' Hundreds Blocc Crips. Members would "come outside and drink and party—that's what they do," she told Skaggs.

Jessica had wanted to drive Starks's black Suburban that day. She wasn't sure of the time. But she knew it wasn't morning—they were never up by morning. She was at the wheel when Starks got a call. He directed her to a spot on 111th Street to pick up two acquaintances wearing dark hoodies. Devin Davis was "hyped . . . antsy," she said. She thought he was disturbed. But she did not get a good look. "Derrick would not let me stare at his friends too long," she explained to Skaggs. "I would get in trouble, like, 'Oh you wanna fuck my homeys?'"

In the car, Davis taunted the quieter young man in the backseat: "You ain't no real crippin," he taunted. "You ain't no real man, you ain't ready to put in no work!" Starks was playing the same Crip song over and over on the car stereo. Davis gave her directions. They went down a side street. Starks turned down the music.

Davis told her to stop the car. Midkiff knew she was not allowed to obey another man. She waited until Starks echoed the command, then parked. Davis said: "I'm gonna go hang up some business."

Midkiff turned and saw him reposition a handgun in his waistband. The teenagers hopped out. She watched them glide into the eastbound street, out of sight. She sat in front with Starks. She had believed it was just another of Starks's outings. She had thought he was going to get girls for the two teenagers, find them weed, or buy liquor for them. But now, glimpsing the gun, she was alarmed. "What do you have me in?" she demanded. "I don't have you in nothin'!" he snapped.

Midkiff pleaded to be allowed to go home. Then, through the closed windows of the car, she heard—*pow . . . pow, pow.*

Davis said, "Go go go go go!" when they jumped in the car. After Starks yanked her into the passenger seat, Davis was "amped up" and bragging. "I'm proper!" he said. Starks hushed him and turned the music up. That night, they stayed in the motel again. A few days later, Midkiff was again in the Suburban with Starks when some rivals from the vicinity of the 80s spotted them. The gang rivals chased them, seeking retaliation. Starks crashed the car and got arrested. Midkiff gave the CHP officer an alias, using her aunt's name.

Midkiff's obedience to Starks was robotic by her account. He did not trust her, she said, and did not share his plans with her. But he expected blind obedience, and he mostly got it by merely implying the violence of which Midkiff knew he was capable. "Pretty much whatever he said, it went," Midkiff told Skaggs. "He is way bigger than what I am. He choked me out once till I damn near passed out . . . I'm not gonna sit there and go, Well, where the hell are we going? Because every time I get a smart mouth, I catch it. I fight back, but he is still a man and I am a small female."

She was five-one and weighed 113 pounds. Starks was of average height but strong and fit, with massive shoulders; he'd played football.

She'd not known they were headed to do a shooting. But even if she knew, "I'm not gonna ask him, just because I don't want to catch it. And I know that might be *punk* or whatever. But I don't want to get beat up."

She claimed she didn't know that someone died in the shooting. Skaggs challenged her on this point repeatedly. But in the end, her confusion convinced him.

There were scores and scores of gunshots fired in South L.A. that barely registered in the outside world. The events of May 11 didn't stand out for Midkiff because she considered it just another shooting of the type that happened "usually," as she put it.

"I know shots went off," she told Skaggs. But "people usually can shoot a lot and not hit somebody. Especially gang-bangers."

The man in the wheelchair had told Gordon and Skaggs that Midkiff was "a good girl," which she was not, in the conventional sense. But she was not a gang member. Starks viewed her as "a weak link." He shushed Davis because he didn't want her to know what was happening. He didn't trust her, she said.

He was right not to.

Midkiff had no appetite for murder. When Skaggs told her of Bryant Tennelle's death, she wept. "I feel bad behind it," she said. "That's wrong. I can see my mother thinking about me if I get laid out. Or if my child gets laid out."

At last, Skaggs asked her to testify in court. "I don't even care about me anymore, I'll do it," Midkiff said. She began to cry again, worried her family would be killed. "They'll do it!" she told Skaggs.

He told her that he would be scared, too, if it were him.

17

BABY MAN

Devin Davis was seventeen in the first weeks of 2008. He was an awkward-looking kid with a large head, high round cheeks, and very round, large brown eyes. He was afflicted with ADHD and high blood pressure—a diagnosis rare in teenagers but not uncommon in South Central. He had been struck by gunfire some months before that had injured his wrist.

Devin appeared to be constantly on the lookout for something to guffaw at, in the anxious way of teenagers who fear being left out of a joke. But Devin was not cheerful. His eyes had a plaintive expression. His affect was peevish and unhappy.

When the probationer first uttered Devin's moniker Baby Man to Skaggs, Skaggs was pretty sure Devin was the killer. Then Midkiff fingered his photo, identifying Devin as the "crazy boy" in the back of the Suburban, and Skaggs was certain. He intended to come right at Devin, plunging forward, as always, in the straightest possible line.

Devin's imprisonment gave him time to prepare. Skaggs wanted every advantage. The interrogation of Devin Davis would be the most important juncture in this most important of cases; it would be a pivotal moment in his whole career.

Skaggs knew what he wanted from Devin—a full confession. In his mind, he had already constructed the outlines of a case built solely on the accounts of the man in the wheelchair, the probationer, and Midkiff, supported by corroborating evidence. But he knew the case would be far stronger with a confession.

Skaggs had interrogated hundreds of murder suspects, and a striking number had confessed, at least partially. This was not entirely a tribute to Skaggs's talent: confessions were astonishingly common in ghettoside cases. Sal La Barbera maintained he'd gotten some version of a confession on almost every case he had ever cleared. Perhaps not in the actual interrogation, but in the long waits in between—during meals, or while being processed for arrest—young men nearly always let something slip. It was relatively rare for suspects in gang cases to invoke their right to an attorney.

Skaggs couldn't understand why suspects confessed. But La Barbera, who ascribed sentimental motives to everyone—even murderers—had a theory. He believed it was the burden of guilt. Murder, he suggested, had a kind of existential weight; one had to be very hardened indeed not to be bested by it. Other detectives had similar notions. Brent Josephson, the old ghettoside hand from the previous generation, had a memorable story from the peak years. It involved a scoop-and-carry homicide case in a park. Assigned after the fact, with the evidence cleared away and no witnesses, Josephson was standing helplessly at the scene, thinking he didn't have a prayer of solving the case, when he noticed a skinny Hispanic youth in the distance. Josephson called out to him, thinking the kid might have some pointers. Thunderstruck, the young man hung his head and shuffled over. "You got me," he told Josephson, and proceeded to confess. The specter of an LAPD detective beckoning from across the park had apparently been too much for him. It was like a summons from God.

All Skaggs knew was that, as common as confessions were, you couldn't count on getting one. Many gang members were interrogation experts. They knew the cops' methods. Older men in particular had the edge on the very young cops the South L.A. divisions attracted. These suspects had cunning and strategy. And just like the cops, they were smooth liars. So although there were those who refused to talk, or bailed midinterview, the more common scenario was a tense tit for tat in which suspects offered detectives bits of information in exchange for finding out what the police knew.

This approach was not as irrational as it seemed. Without an attorney present, gang suspects could get a sense not just of what the police were thinking, but also of what was happening on the streets. If your homeys had snitched, you wanted to know it. If it was in your best interests to snitch on them first, you wanted to know that, too. The cops were only part of the equation. The willingness of gang suspects to be interrogated demonstrated, again, how such men inhabited two legal structures—a formal one and an informal one. They had to negotiate both, and the LAPD interrogation room was a space to explore their options, play one side against the other.

There was possibly another reason suspects submitted to being interrogated: it was interesting. Few people can resist talking about something that really interests them with someone who shares that interest. For all these reasons, suspects talked. South end homicide interrogations by Skaggs's era lacked the brute terrorism of the old LAPD, and they were sometimes almost cordial. But they were nearly always elliptical games of cat and mouse in which the mouse was as curious as the cat. Skaggs was expecting that Devin would agree to talk a little. But that didn't mean he would get what he wanted.

On the afternoon of January 14, Corey Farell and a young detective named Vince Carreon picked up Devin from Challenger Youth Camp in northern Los Angeles County's Antelope Valley at the foot of the Mojave Desert and drove him back through the desert to the Seventy-seventh Street station, his hands cuffed in front of his body for the long journey.

When he arrived, Skaggs looked him over. Devin wore a blue jumpsuit and his hair was scruffy, in the manner of young men too long in jail without a haircut. He was dark-skinned, just as Midkiff remembered. His manner was petulant and anxious. Farell had told him nothing.

Skaggs wanted to secure an advantage over Devin from the start. He had devised a couple of ruses, driving Devin past the crime scene, suggesting to him that the police had evidence that didn't exist, including a fictitious video that Skaggs claimed had been shot by a security camera. The goal was "just to freak him out," he said later. He also wanted a read on Devin. By provoking an emotional reaction, Skaggs hoped to gather a sense of his state of mind, and to infer from that his susceptibility to questioning.

As they drove, Skaggs studied the teenager. Devin seemed immature for his age. He gave the impression of suffering from a mental or social disability. "Kinda weird," Skaggs thought. It was easy to see what the young probationer had suggested about Devin—that he had problems making friends. If Devin had been your average high school student somewhere else, he might have been just another misfit. But Skaggs thought Devin "a little bit on the tough side, not just on the dumb side." He had "a look." To Skaggs, suspects fell across a spectrum. Some were very violent, some less so. And some were so unused to violence that it left them badly shaken. Skaggs had dealt with suspects who started babbling the instant they sat, spinning defenses and "fronting out" their friends. But Devin's composure suggested that he would not crack easily.

They returned to the station house and climbed the back stairs to an interview room. Skaggs gave Devin a soda and asked if he wanted lunch. Devin said no. It was 2:30 P.M.

Over and over, through years of little rooms, cans of soda, mismatched chairs, and Styrofoam cups, Skaggs had felt his way through scores of interviews like this, learning through repetition. Skaggs used relatively little profanity and kept calm.

He sought, above all, to assure suspects that it was okay to talk—that if they would just tell the truth, it would be all right. Beyond that, it was pure improvisation. The interrogator had to think fast and react quickly, "reading" the suspect while appearing not to, shifting tactics as dynamics changed.

Sometimes Skaggs sought to break down suspects. Other times he tried to build them up. He would subtly insult them—"Do you take medication for psych problems?" And they would hasten to defend themselves. Or he would flatter them—"Dang! You still okay? I've heard your name on the street!" And they would puff up and start bragging. One of his favorite methods was to act distracted or bored until they became desperate for a reaction.

Skaggs and Farell now retreated to the hallway, leaving Devin in the room. Skaggs had no idea how he was going to proceed. Yet Farell could perceive nothing out of the ordinary in his manner. It was as if he were embarking on a weekend errand.

Skaggs prepped his tape recorder and noted the date and time. They headed back to the room. Skaggs sat down, not across from Devin, but on the same side of the table, pulling his chair so close that their knees almost touched. He always sat this way for interrogations. He was not being menacing in any way, yet he was violating Devin's personal space. This subtle breach was unsettling.

Skaggs began speaking, sounding mild and reasonable. "Okay, Devin," he said. "This is where we get to take care of all our business. Okay?"

Breezy. Businesslike. A light touch of regret. As if they were friends with an unpleasant matter to settle.

Devin was ready, in defensive mode. He had arranged himself in a posture signaling noncompliance, slumped way back, sullen, put out. "I'm gonna ask you to speak up. I'm a little hard of hearing," Skaggs said, his standard line. He told Devin to sit up straight. "Show a little respect . . . a little mutual respect . . . If you're sitting up straight, I know I have your attention! All right?" The last note was bright and lively.

Devin shifted in his seat and mumbled his assent—"Yes sir . . . yes sir," he said wearily. It was typical gangster-cop interplay—the affected politeness, excessive use of courtesy titles, and emphasis on "respect." The 'hood was perhaps the only context in America outside the military where the word "sir" was still appended sentence by sentence in conversational speech. Devin, it was clear, had spoken to many a cop.

Skaggs went on, oversimplifying. "My name is John Skaggs. This is my partner Corey Farell. We work homicide. Do you know what that means?"

"No," Devin replied. Skaggs played it straight. "Homicide investigators investigate people who get killed," he explained dutifully. "Not shot at. Not jumped on. Not robbed. When somebody gets killed on the streets, they call us, and we go to work."

Skaggs launched his attack. He began talking aimlessly about the investigation. He started in the middle, digressed, and doubled back. He hinted at a Very Serious Talk about to occur. But instead of starting it, he burrowed into technicalities. He declared his intention to be upfront. Then he wandered. He promised to get to the point. Then he didn't. He peppered his speech with various throat-clearing asides— "Are you with me?" "So, listen!" "We'll get to that!" But he never got anywhere. Every gesture and inflection assured Devin that he was being clear and direct. But the words delivered only discursiveness and confusion.

It was infuriating—and effective. The tactic had served Skaggs well for years. Ordinarily, Skaggs was a man who never procrastinated, never went in circles. But in interrogations, circling was his weapon of choice.

"Your name came up in a murder investigation," Skaggs told Devin gravely. "Flat out." He paused, letting the flat-out-ness of his statement sink in. Then he was not flat out. He digressed, droning on about the video camera and its fictional video, its quality.

Then, finally: "So here's what happens. Back in May, okay? You know the months of the year?" Devin was silent. Skaggs continued: "So kind of at the end of winter. The start of good weather . . ." And Skaggs riffed on weather.

Devin released a long sigh. "Some people loaded up . . ." Skaggs went on, using the same tone as he had used describing the sunny day in May. But Devin interrupted him, in revolt against Skaggs's intrusive knees.

"Mind if I move my legs?" he said.

Skaggs was genial. "You can put 'em anywhere! Just don't kick me!" he said. Devin shifted heavily as Skaggs talked some more. "I'm going to give you the opportunity to say what's on your mind," he said. "But let me talk for about five minutes." Skaggs nodded toward the fat murder book he held. "This is what I want to talk to you about today." He wandered again, and then finally, speaking fast, almost collegially, returned to the investigation. He presented it as if it were a problem he expected Devin to help him fix:

"So, what I know is a black Suburban gets on Saint Andrews, a dude gets out, and somebody gets killed, okay?" he said. "And you're in that video. Not only that, I got the Suburban. The Suburban is in custody. I will show you photos of it. I'm gonna show you everything so that you can see I'm not talking out of my ass."

Here Devin interrupted again, for some reason objecting, not to the idea that he might have committed murder, but to the suggestion that he didn't trust Skaggs. "I'm not trippin' on you! I'm listening to you!" he said, his voice high and indignant.

Skaggs continued, his tone conciliatory. "We all know how there's stories about cops who try to pull a fast one and stuff like that. I want to be up-front with you."

Devin kept insisting that he wasn't, as he put it, "trippin'." Skaggs got him to calm down, then said: "This is the real deal. And this is the only—the one and only time—you will ever have a chance to talk to the two guys who investigated that murder."

"Can I ask you a question?" Devin said.

"Absolutely!" Skaggs sounded downright buoyant.

"This is not going to affect my time in camp, right?"

He had been asking some version of this question over and over, in different forms, all afternoon. "That is a ridiculous question," Skaggs said, sounding exasperated. Davis objected, sputtering. Skaggs raised his voice: "Let me talk!"

"That's what we are talking about," Skaggs said, when he had Devin's attention again. "*We are talking about your future.* So, we will get to that part of your future when it comes up."

Devin was beginning to whine. Skaggs scolded him to "act like a man." Then his voice softened and he promised he would soon address

Devin's concerns. Once again he hinted at the Very Serious Talk that was about to start.

"We are going to see what's in your mind, whether you are going to be straight up," he said. "So we'll get to that."

Skaggs was back in his mild, businesslike tone, spinning wool in the guise of being forthcoming. He told Devin that snitches "put him on Front Street" and called him by his gang name, Baby Man.

"I ain' no Baby Man," Devin said, drawling a little. "We'll get to that, we'll get to that," Skaggs said. Always promising, never delivering.

Devin was starting to fray. *Tell me!* he pleaded. "You say you'll be up-front! Well then lemme know everything."

"Absolutely!" Skaggs said. Bright and helpful.

Then he returned to his obfuscations. He made reference to Starks, saying Starks was "a bitch." Devin thought Skaggs was referring to a woman; street slang could be confusing even to seasoned users. Skaggs corrected him. He'd meant that Starks had broken down easily. Devin chortled.

Skaggs said he had found Starks's phone number on a slip of paper in Devin's bedroom. Devin demanded to see it.

Skaggs obliged, producing a page of the murder book. "That way you know what's happening," he said. Devin looked, and switched gears instantly: "I know him," he said. "I'm not going to lie to you . . . I'm an honest person," he said.

For several more minutes, Skaggs let Devin page selectively through the murder book on the pretext of demonstrating how up-front he was. He showed Devin a letter in which Devin declared he belonged to One Hundred and Thirteen Blocc Crips. "I got put off of there, though," Devin objected. The gang had beaten him up and kicked him out, he said. "Hold on! Devin!" Skaggs said, interrupting him. "We're talking! You don't have to answer to nothing!"

"All right," Devin said, suddenly sounding weary. "Then I go back to camp after this?"

"You are going back to camp when we're done here," Skaggs said.

"And that's it," Devin said.

"What do you mean, 'that's it'?"

"I won't have to worry about hearing this never again," Devin said.

"I don't know. We ain't done talking about this, are we?" Skaggs said.

Devin emitted a pained laugh. "I'm not trying to make you mad or nuthin'," he said.

"You can't make me mad," Skaggs replied airily.

He began producing letters he alleged Devin had written and making reference to a fictitious handwriting analysis. The letters talked about killing "Snoovers," the derogatory term for Hoovers. At the word "Snoovers," Devin giggled.

Skaggs showed Devin a letter in which Devin referred to himself as Baby Man. "Oops!" Skaggs said sarcastically.

"I ain't from that shit no mo'," Devin whined. Skaggs grew sharp again: "Devin!"

"All right! They call me that. I guess." It was the second time Skaggs had forced Devin to backtrack. Skaggs acted exasperated. Devin asked again if he was going back to camp. Skaggs told him to stop asking. Devin turned back to the murder book, manhandling it.

"Hold it! Easy, tiger!" Skaggs said, keeping his hands on it. He showed Devin more pages. A picture of the Suburban. A picture of Midkiff. "Who the fuck is this bitch?" Devin said. He called the interview "bullshit" and demanded that Skaggs get around to his questions.

Skaggs calmly bade him to wait, flipping pages of the book. Outside, on the streets of the Seventy-seventh Division, a siren wailed.

"We're gonna do some talking," Skaggs said. "We'll get to the good talking in just a second."

"Can I get lunch? Please? I'm hungry," Devin said.

"We'll do that in a minute," Skaggs said.

"'Cause I'm ready, sir! I mean, I'm doing my time—"

This was danger. What Skaggs feared most was that Devin would abruptly back out and demand to be taken back to camp. He'd had interviews end that way before, with a suspect declaring: "I ain't sayin' shit! Fuck you!" Skaggs couldn't risk that now.

He shifted his tone, growing serious. "So here's, here's where we're at. Devin. There's some snitches from Bloccs, and there's some snitches from the nine-oh's."

The word "snitches" caught Devin's attention. Skaggs went back to talking about a killing, daylight, a video camera, witnesses.

"So I'm in big, big, trouble?" Devin interrupted.

Skaggs downplayed it: "Well, what I'm sayin' is, I've got people saying you shot a boy . . ."

Twenty minutes had passed and this was the most direct Skaggs had been about his suspicions. He introduced the murder accusation casually.

Devin, who for most of those twenty minutes had been exhorting Skaggs to get to the point, now seemed suddenly eager to turn him back. He cut Skaggs off, voice urgent:

"So, I—I'm getting in trouble for it, right?"

"Hold on! Eeeeasy, tiger!" Skaggs downplayed it. The heavier the mood, the lighter his tone.

But Devin got worked up. "I wish you'd just tell me the truth, sir!"

"There ain't no truth yet. We ain't done talking! When we're done talking, I'll answer anything you want. Okay? You with me?" Skaggs's voice held impatient humor, fatherly, reassuring, exasperated. It worked. "Yes, sir," Devin said.

Skaggs took a breath and then repeated his infuriating mantra: "Listen to me. We are gonna do some talkin'."

Rick Gordon had elicited evidence this way, too: breaking suspects down through a simple tactic he called Boring Them to Death. Skaggs returned to his meanderings, saying that snitches had said Devin had been put up to the crime by Starks, but then burying the allegation in lesser ones, saying Devin had done this and that. Devin was reduced to denying small allegations in pieces: "That's on my mom!" he exclaimed at one point, swearing on some denial. Skaggs used the occasion to open a discussion about Devin's mother for no reason. Devin took the bait. They digressed.

Then Skaggs mentioned Midkiff again. "She is not going to take a hit for you," he said.

"I'm not gonna take a hit for her!" Devin retorted hotly.

Skaggs pounced. "What she do?" he said swiftly.

But Devin saw it, and pedaled back. "Shi', I dunno . . . I'm not takin' a hit for nobody," he muttered.

Skaggs resumed as if nothing had happened. Devin protested. "It's just—you said you had more to tell me," he said. Skaggs assured Devin that he did. Devin needed only to listen.

"But I mean all the other stuff you're sayin', reee-ally makin' my blood pressure go up," Devin said.

"I bet it does," Skaggs said. "It'd make me fuckin' freak out."

Devin agreed. It certainly was making him freak out. "It should," Skaggs told Devin, suddenly quiet. "Someone just told you you've been fingered on a killing."

Devin mumbled something. Skaggs zeroed in. "Hmm?"

"Nothin'," Devin said. "I'm sayin' it to myself, just thinkin' out loud."

"That's cool!" Skaggs was light again, and he went on as if Devin's internal dialogue held no interest for him. He droned on about the evidence, this time inserting the phrase "killin' a cop's kid."

"Killin' a cop's kid!" Devin sounded shocked.

"Yeah," Skaggs said, suddenly sounding annoyed. "I don't expect you to admit to anything, Devin."

"I ain't lyin' to you, sir! I been honest with you the whole time!" Devin cried. Skaggs disagreed. An argument ensued. "You didn't even admit your name was frickin' Baby Man!" Skaggs said.

Devin's voice was tight. He retreated, pleading: "Can we just keep it low-low? Like, 'cause it's, like, I feel like you gettin' mad and stuff."

"Why would I get mad?" Skaggs's easy tone was back. Devin again asked him to move his legs. Skaggs acted surprised. He asked if Devin was "claustrophobic or something." Devin said he was. "Okay!" Skaggs said amiably. "I'll stay back."

He launched into his meandering talk again, getting nowhere. This time he assured Devin that "we are gonna get to some questions, but first I wanted to lay it all out for you." At one point, he stalled with the phrase, "As you know, we know our business—"

"I know! I'd put you up for a job! Truthfully!" Devin interrupted.

Skaggs ignored this endorsement and went on. Devin again cut him off. "Okay, but are you gonna tell me who is snitchin' on me?" he demanded.

"If this was to go to court, absolutely you are going to find out. But I ain't going to tell you today," Skaggs said.

Devin started. Going to court? He wasn't going to court, was he? People didn't usually go to court on something like this—did they? Skaggs told him that it was up to the DA. Only when they finished talking would they be "locked in," he said.

Devin got quiet. "What you mean by locked in?" he said.

Skaggs spoke very slowly. He would prepare his findings. The DA would decide what to do, he said. Then, "What do you think the DA's gonna do to the person that's in the video bustin' on some kid?"

Devin let out a sharp burst of air. "I'll be there for the rest of my life," he breathed, as if speaking to himself. He sounded resigned. Then he rebelled: "I got a baby on the way, though!"

They had been in the room for twenty-eight minutes. Devin began to cry. "You and I need to have a heart-to-heart talk," Skaggs said.

But Devin was working up to sobs. "I'm about to have a son. I won't see my own baby be born!"

Skaggs tried for calm. This was dicey. Devin seemed to be cracking. But he had not yet been Miranda-ized. "You and I are gonna have a real-deal talk here," Skaggs said, scrambling.

"It don't matter! I'm gonna go to jail anyway. I'm gonna sit in there for the rest of my life anyways. I ain't gonna never go home!" Devin wailed. "Fuckin' sucks!" Then the inevitable addendum: "'Scuse my language."

This was like the overuse of "sir." For some reason, swearing, then apologizing for it, was a common gang tic.

Skaggs downplayed Devin's tears and resumed talking about the case. Devin interrupted him.

"You already said—that *he put me up to it*," Devin said, then dissolved into a cascade of snuffles.

The statement was thunderous. But still not quite a confession. "Wait!" Skaggs sought to wind the conversation back. But Devin sharpened up again, pausing mid–whimper. "I'm not admittin' to it," he said.

Devin said he hoped the cops would help him. "I'm not here to hurt or help," Skaggs said. "I'm here to find the truth. That's why we need to get to the point."

The phrase seemed to send Devin around the bend. "That's what I'm askin'! Just *get to the point*!" He sounded desperate.

Skaggs was sympathetic and promised to get to his questions very soon. He made a seamless transition: "For me to ask you questions— well, you've had your rights read to you before, right?"

Devin had. This could be a scary moment for detectives. The reading of rights broke the mood. Skaggs spoke easily. He even made a game of it, asking Devin if he knew his rights well enough to recite them. Devin tried, then trailed off. He was in his own world, tears flowing, head bowed. "I'm never gonna go home," he wept.

Skaggs offered to read the rights for him, magnanimous, as if doing Devin a favor. Devin listened at first, sniffing, then interrupted: "I don't even want to hear it, sir. It's just gonna hurt me more," he said.

"Well," Skaggs said mildly, as if dispensing with unpleasant business, "I have to. So let me just go over them . . . And then we'll talk." He read the Miranda rights, slowly and clearly, stopping for Devin's "Yes, sir" after each line.

A pause. Devin still wept. "I feel for you, for the predicament you're in," Skaggs said softly.

He suggested they take a break. He offered Devin a tissue. He said he would steer the conversation away, give Devin a chance to relax. He brought up Devin's mother again. "Your mom is a very nice lady," Skaggs said. "I feel for your mom." This was true: Skaggs did think Sandra James was a nice lady.

Skaggs had separated the cuffs so Devin's hands were free, though he still wore the metal shackles and one was hurting his injured wrist. Skaggs helped him shift the cuffs to fit more comfortably. Then he circled back to the murder, talking about Devin in the third person. People were asking why Devin had done it, he said musingly. "He doesn't seem like that bad of a guy," Skaggs rambled. "What the hell happened?" Skaggs turned over more pages in the murder book, referring again to the case as being "the real deal." But his efforts to elicit a response from Devin failed. To everything, Devin replied, "It doesn't matter, sir, I'm already gonna go to jail." The teenager was talking to himself, lamenting that his friends had snitched.

He sat crumpled over the table, a desperate, ailing, injured seventeen-year-old boy—seemingly in real pain, weeping pitiably, crying that he wanted to go home. Faced with Devin's searing agony, Skaggs didn't flinch. His calm never wavered, but his tactics were without mercy. He came at Devin again and again. "I want to know why," Skaggs said.

Devin's head dropped.

Skaggs's eye caught the gesture. He froze, and time stood still. *Now,* he thought.

"He put me up to it," Devin said, his voice suddenly clear. Then something about how he had closed his eyes.

"Okay," said Skaggs, very quietly. "That's what we are gonna talk about. Go ahead and clean yourself up."

But Devin caught himself a second time. Again he backtracked. "I didn't do it," he said. He was taking back the confession he had just made. "I was thinking about something else," he said.

They had been in the room nearly forty-five minutes. A confession seemed close, yet remained out of reach. Corey Farell had barely moved. His notepad was before him but he had jotted only sparingly—afraid of doing anything that would break the flow. If Skaggs felt anxiety he didn't show it. In fact, he seemed calmer by the minute.

Watching from his corner, Farell felt the weight of the whole case beginning to fall into place, its separate pieces converging with the escalating tension in the room, rushing like streams to a river. But each time Devin backed off, the currents slackened.

"Okay!" Skaggs said easily when Devin took back his confession. "Ain't nobody mad!"

He gave the weeping teenager more tissues and coached him on how to use them, as if talking to a child.

Devin was getting hysterical again. He returned to sobbing—"I'm going to jail for life. I'm seventeen, and I'm goin' to the pen!" he said. "They gon' punch on me. I got one hand. I can't do nothin'!"

"Devin! Devin!" Skaggs was talking over him again, trying to bring him back. When Devin paused for air, Skaggs began talking nonsensically, buying time.

"Devin, you're seventeen. I'm—how old do I look?"

"Forty-seven," said Devin through sniffles, coming close.

Skaggs acted sheepish, laughing. "Yeah," he said. "I don't like to admit it, but . . ."

Then suddenly, Skaggs grew serious. He raised both hands. "So, listen," he intoned, and brought his hands together sharply. *Clap!*

For a moment, the sound hung in the air, just as Skaggs's words to Derrick Washington's sister had hovered before she dropped her head and started crying. Asked to explain this part of the interview, Skaggs had no insight to offer. He could not explain why, three quarters of an hour into the interrogation, he had suddenly resorted to clapping his hands like a kindergarten teacher.

Skaggs was trying to make Devin focus. But the clap was also an instinctive gesture, a flash of virtuosity from a man for whom establishing control was second nature. Skaggs clapped in Devin's face as if he knew exactly what was about to happen, then clapped twice more, reflexively, to lock it down. So simple and powerful was the device—three sharp reports shattering the air in the tiny room—that someone who didn't know the context might have assumed that Skaggs was engaged in black magic, calling forth an evil spirit with his hands.

"So, listen," Skaggs said. *Clap.* "What happened that day?" *Clap. Clap.* And Devin broke.

Suddenly, he was talking so fast the detectives couldn't keep up. He was stumbling to get the words out. He was giving them the whole case.

"He put me up to it," Devin said. "*Woo woo whoopdoobam.* He said we go over here, I was in the car . . . I was with the burner, all right. I got out of the car, closed my eyes, and I just started doing it, I don't know why! I was scared! . . . I didn't want nobody thinking of me as no bitch or nothin' . . . I just wanted to have friends! That's all I wanted. I didn't think you had to do all that!"

He paused for air. "Okay," Skaggs said mildly. "And that's what we're gonna talk about."

Two decades he'd been doing this, extracting confessions, some easily, some less so, and yet he was still surprised every time. He had gone into the interrogation hoping to get a confession from Devin—not needing it, not absolutely—but knowing it would tie up the case just as he wanted. Yet when the moment came, it was still breathtaking, like a shift in the astral alignment. Skaggs didn't pause to analyze. He buried his surprise and plunged forward in his distinctive way.

Devin was weeping. The tension was at its zenith.

Skaggs chose to retreat. It was as if his adrenaline flowed in reverse. This moment was surely one of the most explosively important of his working life, but he displayed no urgency. He downshifted.

He spoke in a relaxed way, as if what Devin had to say next held only perfunctory interest for him. His tone became light, almost careless: "I just need a few specifics before we go on," he said. "We'll take a break. Uh, throw a little food in your belly, get a snack—"

"Can I call my mom?" Devin snuffled.

"Yes, you can. Not right now." Devin was still crying.

Skaggs began. "Where did you get picked up?"

A pause, then Devin spoke, his voiced changed. His tone echoed Skaggs's. He was calm, sad, resigned. "I think a Hundred and tenth," he said.

For the next forty-five minutes he answered Skaggs's questions, one after another, employing his "Yes, sir" after Skaggs chided him for not speaking clearly. Skaggs spoke slowly and Farell scribbled freely on his notepad. The story emerged at a stately, somber pace. An afternoon in May. A blue-steel revolver so old and worn it appeared light gray. Skaggs was no longer meandering. One question followed another with crisp logic, as if he were turning over the pages of his immaculate binder in his mind. Horrifying details emerged, one following the other as they would later in court, each one linked in Skaggs's mind to a piece of corroborating evidence.

Devin's voice broke at times, but he offered no resistance, walking the path to his own destruction resolutely, with one obedient answer after another, sobbing in between, saying over and over that he knew he would spend the rest of his life in jail. Skaggs got him to construct the chronology in detail—to describe how he and Starks had cherped each other, said "Wha's up?" and somehow arrived at a plan to do a "beat-down" on gang rivals to the north.

He got him to relate how Midkiff and Starks picked him up, headed north to the eighties, and parked around the corner. Here, the conversation descended into the strange map-and-compass talk of ghettoside cases—that curious legal edifice built on corroborating points in lieu of truthful narratives from willing witnesses.

Because so many witnesses rolled back on their stories, or revealed them reluctantly, investigations were built from inadvertent slips or grudging admissions. Cases fell together when enough of these slips intersected with each other, or matched with random bits of evidence. The result was not a coherent tale of murder in the style of fiction. It was more like a superstructure of joints—made up of the linkages left standing after all the mistakes, lies, and obfuscations had been stripped away.

Devin said that, as Skaggs suspected, other gang members had been giving him a hard time for being a "punk" and he wanted to prove himself. He had taken an ecstasy pill early in the day, anticipating a party. "I was under the influence, and I listened to a jackass," he said. He seemed not to know Midkiff well. He thought she was white and called her "Jennifer." It was clear he knew Starks better. He acknowledged recognizing his picture, but he balked when asked to state his gang name, probably afraid of snitching.

He hinted at another reason: the moniker No Brains was intended to be pejorative, he suggested. Devin himself was sensitive to such slights, having been called insulting names. "I been like that. I don't ever call nobody by no name," he said.

Devin said that he recognized the neighborhood by the gang graffiti on the walls and that he put on gardening gloves as they drove, not wanting to "mess my hands up." When they parked, Devin said he saw a guy walking on the street wearing a Hoover hat, and Starks turned and stretched an arm toward him. In his hand was a .38 revolver. "Here," Starks said.

Skaggs hammered this point, returning to it again and again. Hadn't Starks said anything else? Let's smoke someone? Take care of business? Put a cap in someone? Fuck somebody up? Skaggs reeled off euphemisms. But Devin was emphatic. "None of that. It was just, like, *Here*. That's all I remember. He said, *Here*."

Devin said his heart raced at the sight of the gun. He claimed he had not reckoned on shooting anyone. He just thought they were there to fight. He stared at the gun in his gloved hand, thought: *Wha'? Fuck!* But he didn't want anyone to think he was a punk. He took it, and got out of the Suburban.

Did he know who he was shooting at? Skaggs asked.

"I didn't get to, like, really see him," Devin said. "All I know is that he was black."

He said it simply, as if it were obvious. Axiomatic, even. And it was. A black assailant looking to kill a gang rival is looking, before anything else, for another black male. This was the fundamental fact of Bryant Tennelle's death. Other elements contributed—the neighborhood in which he lived, the company he chose to keep, the hat he was wearing that evening. But for all that—and for all the rhetoric about bad choices, senseless acts, at-risk behavior, and so forth—what killed Bryant was the one fact about himself that he could not change: he was black. As it happened, he wasn't even so very black: he was half Costa Rican. But it didn't matter. In the eyes of his killer, Bryant Tennelle was branded by history. He was a black man, a presumed combatant, conscripted into a dismal existence "outside the law" whether he wanted to be or not. Before anything else, Bryant was black. To Devin Davis, that meant he was killable.

Devin said he closed his eyes tight, fired, and ran. He said he didn't see Bryant fall. He didn't think he had hit him, he said—or, if he had, he convinced himself he had only wounded him. He made it clear that such nonfatal shootings were, to him, mundane. "I thought someone just got hit in the arm or something. Like, you know, a regular hit," he said.

Afterward, Devin said, "he didn't feel right." He made Starks drop him off at Jesse Owens Park. He went swimming. He denied boasting about the shooting and said he had been assailed by guilt. For months, he convinced himself that he had only wounded the guy he saw walking down the street near St. Andrews, he said. When he was shot in the wrist sometime after at Jesse Owens Park, he convinced himself that it was that same gang rival he'd blasted getting back at him. *We even,* he'd thought.

Devin's diminishment of his crime and his self-protective rationalizations reached heights of absurdity. He told Skaggs that he had not aimed at Bryant, but Bryant had walked into his gunfire. It was unclear at times whether his denial was for Skaggs's benefit or his own. When Skaggs asked him if he knew he had killed "a cop's kid," Devin played ignorant. "I killed a cop's son?" he wailed. "I really ain't gonna go home."

But soon after, he confessed that he already heard from the probationer that Bryant was a police officer's son. Then he wept even harder, saying, "I took somebody's child," and later, "I fucked up my whole life . . . I couldn't take it back."

Skaggs's questions continued, his tone neutral, his manner methodical and efficient. How had Devin felt when he learned he had killed someone? Devin sobbed. "I ain't never ever think I'd hurt somebody," he said, through gasps. "I ain't never did want to hurt nobody in this world. I always just wanted to be a person everyone was just cool with. Everybody just liking me! I never did want to, ever, ever, ever, ever, my whole life, never wanted to hurt nobody!" He said he disliked guns because his brother had been shot "and I know how my mama was."

As the interrogation wound down, Devin began asking for his mother. "I'm never gonna go home and see my mom again," he sobbed at one point. Skaggs handed him a tissue. "That I can't tell you," Skaggs said.

"I'm scared," Devin exclaimed a little later, weeping again. "I don't know what to do!"

"I don't blame you," Skaggs said quietly.

It was approaching 4:00 P.M. by the time Skaggs had walked Devin through his confession, looping back for clarification on a few points. By the end, Skaggs was down to minutiae—whether the yard had a fence, that sort of thing. Devin unloaded it all, his voice thick with resignation and a kind of suicidal despondence. Skaggs extracted the admissions drop by drop, corroborating nearly every detail of the mission, almost exactly as Midkiff had presented it and eyewitnesses had described. Skaggs's murder book now had a few additional photos, identifying the murder scene and Starks, and penned with the initials D.D.

At last, Skaggs turned to Devin and asked him if he wanted to view the nonexistent videotape. Devin said he didn't. "Shit," Devin said. "I'm already washed. I'm going to jail for the rest of my life."

He was weeping again. "I really don't even want to talk about it, sir! I already know how it is. I watch TV. I watch *Law and Order.* I know how it goes. I took somebody off the planet. Off the earth. There ain't no coming back. There ain't no bringing him back to life . . . Ain't never gonna see my baby. Ain't never gonna get no pussy. Ain't never gonna see my damn son. I can't do nothin'. I'm washed."

"Okay," Skaggs said quietly. "We're done, Devin." He offered Devin lunch.

Then Skaggs walked out. Exhaustion swept him. For ninety minutes, he had been in a hyperalert state—assessing, calculating, talking with one part of his brain and processing with the other, absorbing every word Devin uttered, every movement, every blink. He felt drained, as if he had just run a marathon. But he knew he'd done it. The case was cleared.

Farell felt the tension hit him much later, after he went home. He likened the feeling to his patrol days. He would chase armed suspects without a thought. Only much later would it strike him: *Oh, yeah, they could have shot me.*

As they walked him out of the building, Devin was back to whining. He wanted something—a soda. Skaggs turned, and for an instant, the calm, imperturbable patina he had maintained for two decades of working homicides slipped. Farell caught his look, surprised; he had never known Skaggs to be anything but easygoing and in control.

"Fuck you," Skaggs told Devin. "You killed a cop's kid."

After Devin Davis, the interrogation of Derrick Starks was anticlimactic.

It took place two days later. Skaggs and Farell took Starks out of jail, drove him by the crime scene, and interviewed him.

Starks struck Skaggs as more seasoned and wily than Davis. As Midkiff had suggested, he was a big young man, who must have loomed over her like a heavyweight boxer. He was only six feet tall, but solid. His thick neck had a crease in back, and he had a distinctive, saturnine face, like a Roman statue—sensitive cupid's-bow mouth, dimples, and straight, slim nose. His eyes tipped up at the corners under arched brows, the left one perennially cocked. He was light-skinned, with light brown hair and hazel eyes; except for his strong Louisiana accent, Starks could easily have passed for Hispanic.

Starks barely spoke on the drive. In the interview room, Skaggs did most of the talking. His approach was soft and casual. He got a cup of coffee for himself and a grape soda for Starks. He inverted his usual joke of insulting Farell. Skaggs's interrogations were like the theme and variations of a symphony. He used the same devices again and again but subtly reworked them each time. This time, instead of calling Farell dim-witted, he referred to his own supposed dim-wittedness and credited Farell with solving the case. Usually, cases weren't as easy as this one, he added.

Skaggs then launched into a recital of the evidence against Starks.

By now, he had the statement from the man in the wheelchair, Midkiff's account, Davis's confession, and the many corroborating points between them. He also had cell phone records that showed Starks's movements and placed him within nineteen blocks of the murder scene at the time of the murder.

He had confirmed through the California Highway Patrol that Starks was in possession of the black Suburban in custody and had been driving around with Midkiff a few days after the killing. Eyewitnesses had identified photos of the Suburban. Skaggs also had letters and recordings of tapped phone calls Starks had made to friends from jail, none of which amounted to a confession, but which made it amply clear he was deeply involved with the Bloccs and knew about the Tennelle case.

He presented Starks with true information, but he wove in some lies, too. For example, he told Starks the police had found his DNA on the gun. This was something that almost never happened in real life at that time. But it happened so much on TV that Skaggs had found it to be a useful deception. He wanted to convince Starks that the evidence against him was insurmountable.

The lies were just decorative touches, though. For Skaggs actually did, by now, have plenty of information, with or without statements from Starks. He was telling the truth again when, more than an hour into the interrogation, he told Starks sternly, "It doesn't matter what you say. Meaning I don't really have to get any statement from you at all." Already, Skaggs had enough evidence to seek murder charges, and his chief purpose in this meeting with Starks was to see whether Starks could present evidence to exonerate himself. Skaggs needed to be able to say "I did my job as a policeman and as a human, to give a man a chance," he said later. He made it clear to Starks that his window was closing. "Today is the last thing I have to do on this case. When you and I part"—Skaggs emitted a whistle—"done. Done. Go on to the next one." He snapped his fingers. Again, this was the truth.

Starks responded mostly with silences—one stretched for fifteen seconds—and deep sighs. Skaggs paused periodically to let him talk. When he didn't, Skaggs fell back on his usual meandering chatter, seeking an angle that might provoke Starks into loquaciousness. At one point, Skaggs unintentionally echoed Wally Tennelle in a revealing way: he told Starks he had always been able to look defendants in the face in court and had no fear of their anger. "Why? 'Cause all's I do is go in there and say what happened," Skaggs said. His words were almost identical to those Tennelle used when explaining why he was not afraid to run into people he'd arrested. Both men believed deeply in the straightforwardness of their craft. For all the deception that went into interrogations, they saw their work as a simple effort at truth seeking: they presented the facts as best they could ascertain them, turned them over to a court, and let go of the results. Skaggs was once asked to turn over the records of an investigation to authorities in Mexico who had extradited his suspect. He later described this as one of the worst moments of his career—being forced to cede control of the facts he had gathered to a foreign court that he neither understood nor trusted. For Skaggs, the American system was his safety net.

He never expressed resentment of Miranda or any other constraint of constitutional due process. He was used to the restraints and drew comfort from the knowledge that once he finished, his work would be painstakingly vetted by the defense, judge, and jury. "Just say what happened" was another of La Barbera's credos from the old Southeast homicide squad. Skaggs and Tennelle believed so wholeheartedly in this description of their role as law enforcement officers that they did not see how anyone could be mad at them. This was part of the emotional equipment of men capable of scorching earth.

Skaggs even went so far as to offer Starks a pretty good defense: he suggested that a question remained about whether he knew what Davis planned to do. Did he "just jump out of the car and do his own thing?" he asked.

Assigning intent to Davis alone would have been a potentially effective legal strategy for Starks, although it went against some evidence in the case. There was, for example, Midkiff's account of being yanked out of the driver's seat for the getaway so Starks could take the wheel. But Starks did not take the bait. "I'm overwhelmed. I don't have nothing to say," he said.

Skaggs worked every angle. He exhorted Starks to look him in the eye. "How come you don't look someone in the eyes when they're talking to you?"

"I don't know," Starks answered. "My dad—he says the same thing." It was the only exchange between them that day that revealed anything intimate.

The rest of the time, Starks spoke in monosyllables or short phrases. He gave no hint of weakening in the way Skaggs wanted him to. Starks suggested he couldn't be expected to remember events Skaggs mentioned because he had been "jumped" in 2002 and "my memory's been messed up ever since." He said people were lying about him. He said, "I weren't nowhere near it."

At last, Skaggs prodded Starks for "your side of the story," one last time.

Starks took his time, then answered slowly:

"I told you my side. *There is no side.* I wasn't there. I didn't do nothing," he said.

Skaggs exhaled in a long breath. It was over.

On February 19, 2008, the Los Angeles district attorney filed charges against Devin Davis and Derrick Starks in the murder of Bryant Tennelle.

Skaggs had barely spoken to Wally Tennelle through the whole course of these events.

He had made one mortifying visit to the Tennelle family early on. This was when he was still paired with Bernal. A supervisor from the bureau had come, too. Skaggs couldn't stand working this way. In Southeast, he had always sought quiet and intimate encounters with grieving families, but this felt like a conference of diplomatic envoys, and the conversation was stiff and formal. "We went three deep!" he exclaimed later in disgust.

But at some point, as the case broke open and Skaggs became sure it would be solved, he picked up the phone. For the first time, he spoke one-on-one to the RHD colleague he barely knew. He told Tennelle what had happened. Tennelle did not ask any questions. Skaggs said arrests were pending.

Then, as Skaggs had done so many times before, he fell silent and waited, listening as Tennelle wept at the other end of the line.

18

MUTUAL COMBAT

Sam Marullo stared at Sal La Barbera in disbelief.

It was the summer of 2008, several months after charges were filed in the Tennelle case. The trial was still more than a year away, and Skaggs's initial victory was fast fading from view.

Marullo was in T-shirt and jeans, having returned from a long day's stakeout. He stood in the new Southeast detectives' "pod" of cubicles, which was now part of South Bureau Criminal Gang Homicide Group, Gannon's combined South Bureau detective office at the Seventy-seventh Street station. In the LAPD, "innovation" often meant reverting to previous practice, and this new organizational structure was essentially a reprise of the old South Bureau Homicide unit that had launched Skaggs's career.

Marullo adhered to Skaggs's rule of putting every hour to use, including evenings. He had been about to leave in pursuit of a witness when La Barbera stopped him and told him to go home instead; he could not approve the overtime. La Barbera had just learned his overtime budget was to be cut by 57 percent.

In any world that made sense, homicide detectives would have been compensated with set salaries like other professional white-collar workers.

But in the anachronistic world of American policing, they were blue-collar workers paid by the hour, and prohibited by union rules from unpaid work after hours. So Marullo was effectively grounded. With all the other impediments, it seemed one more insult. Marullo was wavering.

Pat Gannon had hoped Skaggs's success on the Tennelle case would inspire the many young apprentices in his new consolidated "group." It had worked to some extent. One detective coined a noun in the aftermath of the arrests—a "John Skaggs Special." It meant a certain kind of investigation: aggressive, relentless, field-focused.

But new difficulties had already cropped up.

In the new office in the Seventy-seventh Street station, one-way windows to the interrogation rooms had been installed backward: suspects could observe police, but not the reverse; the windows had to be covered. The office phones didn't work. There weren't enough sedans. Supervisors were secretly hoarding "salvage" cars. One of the office secretaries had gone rogue. She had been ordered to ration office supplies but was secretly handing out pens and notepads anyway.

Gannon had moved on, and the group's new commander, Kyle Jackson, formerly of RHD, had never been a detective. His introduction had provoked dismayed murmurs. Jackson was on his last command before retirement and had a persnickety reputation. He believed, he said, in "dotting *i*'s and crossing *t*'s." Tall and thin with a long oval face, Jackson had introduced himself to the detectives by lecturing them on racial and gender bias, a gold bracelet flashing under his sleeve. As he talked, a bright patch of sunlight on the roll call tables faded and the detectives' faces grew progressively glummer.

Then word came that John Skaggs was leaving. Skaggs had been transferred to head up the new homicide unit in a new police station under construction north of the Ten.

Skaggs had been struggling since his promotion to D-3. His slot in Southwest had been temporary. He and Barling had been assigned to train new young Seventy-seventh Street detectives. But Skaggs itched to get back to investigating. The Tennelle case had boosted his visibility, and an ambitious new lieutenant in the new Olympic Division wanted him to head a very small unit by himself. Skaggs sensed an opportunity to take a more hands-on approach to cases. He felt, like Tennelle years before, that he was running out of good ghettoside options.

It left South Bureau, as always, short of master craftsmen. "That no-good rotten bastard Skaggs," Prideaux called him jokingly behind his back. He was miffed. Skaggs hadn't even bothered to tell Prideaux about the transfer. Prideaux tried to enlist Barling in his resentment. But Barling, ever loyal to Skaggs, just stared back at him blankly.

La Barbera remained in charge of Southeast but now worked under Prideaux. He hated reining in Sam Marullo, who, with Kouri as his partner, had continued to live up to his moniker "Li'l Skaggs." But the overtime restrictions were no joke. An economic recession had slammed an unprepared nation in late 2008, and local governments were reeling. La Barbera worried he'd use up his allotment for the week, then be swamped with new homicides. Now he told Marullo his interview would have to wait.

Marullo stared. La Barbera, he realized, was serious.

Marullo was enough like Skaggs and Tennelle not to appear angry. He had the good detective's gift of an unflappable demeanor. But he made it clear what he thought. This witness was key to solving the killing of a thirty-two-year-old black man: without him, the case might not be cleared. La Barbera remained firm. "Fine!" Marullo said at length, and spun away.

With Kouri later, Marullo fumed. What was the department thinking? Why didn't people care? Marullo was discovering anew, in 2008, what Wally Tennelle, Sal La Barbera, and John Skaggs had discovered years before: that, relative to the challenge, to work ghettoside homicide was to dwell in the weakest outpost of the criminal justice system.

Overtime reductions were, of course, a pay cut for homicide detectives. But it was the practical difficulties that stung Marullo, who might have earned overtime doing something else.

For ghettoside homicide detectives, the ability to work odd hours was essential. It was absurd to assume witnesses could be corralled via office-hours appointments made by phone. The whole job was ambushing people who sought to avoid cops—barging in on them, pleading with them, going back to plead again.

Aware that detectives were looking for her, one witness on a Southeast case left a decoy note on her door: *We'll be right back, we went to pay the gas bill,* it said. The note remained for days, growing soggy in the rain. At length, the detectives camped at her door until it opened and she grudgingly confessed to the ruse.

So when Prideaux had first announced the overtime reductions at the weekly meeting, *sheesh*es erupted from the benches. "We have seven hundred open cases!" Dave Garrido had protested. Chris Barling had cited the math: based on current caseloads, and assuming court procedures intervening, detectives would be left with only sixteen hours to work each case, he said.

Ever mindful of morale, La Barbera had tried to soften the blow by making light of the restrictions. One day, he wrote on the whiteboard: "Top Ten OT Reduction Strategies: (1) Drive faster (2) Wear running shoes" et cetera. But Marullo couldn't laugh.

Skaggs, Barling, and La Barbera were used to it—they had been tilting at windmills for years. But Marullo was growing increasingly frustrated. Although he had solved many cases, his few unsolveds ate at him.

In April, a black man named Nye Daniels, a John Skaggs witness in his early years at Southeast, had been murdered. Marullo had been assigned the case but had no leads. He had formed a bond with the mother of Daniels's two children, who was now raising them alone. The children's photos were taped to his computer terminal, their small faces gazing at him day after day.

As Skaggs had taught him, Marullo always gave his personal cell phone number to victims' family members, and sometimes even to the parents of suspects. For months now, he had been getting calls from the mother of Henry Henderson, an eighteen-year-old killed next to Barbara Pritchett's house. Pritchett had been startled by the gunshots. Venturing out, she had recoiled at the sight of the teenager's empty shoes. Henderson's mother would call Marullo drunk and distraught. In June, the trial of her son's alleged killer had ended in a hung jury.

•   •   •

The Los Angeles Superior Court's Compton satellite was built in 1978, the same year the LAPD broke off part of the Seventy-seventh Street Division to form the new Southeast Division in Watts.

Every grim and Kafkaesque aspect of the county's criminal justice system was at its worst at Compton Courthouse. It rose, a blank white tower, from the midst of jumbled squat buildings, the only high-rise in sight.

Exterior walls were scribbled with faded graffiti alongside the murals of Thurgood Marshall. Junkies and transients wandered the plaza. The lines at the metal detectors were four deep. The elevators were slow and creaky; the stairs were locked because some stabbing or other had occurred there. The courtrooms were a far cry from the posh federal ones in downtown L.A.: notices were posted with Scotch tape, wood veneer fixtures were chipped. Almost nothing that went on in Compton Courthouse ever made the news. Seymour Applebaum, a defense attorney who would soon figure in Skaggs's story, called it "the most insensitive piece of architecture ever built. It's a Crusaders' fort overlooking the Saracen plain."

John Skaggs had spent a good portion of his career inside the fort. Now, he made a last trip there before his transfer to the Olympic Division. He came for the trial of Derrick Washington, the sixteen-year-old defendant in the case of Dovon Harris, Barbara Pritchett's son.

Pritchett sat behind Skaggs through the trial, wearing a T-shirt with Dovon's picture inside out because the judge had told her she could not display his image in the courtroom. She had eaten nothing since the previous day, and she sat clasping and unclasping her hands, drawing deep breaths.

The prosecutor, Joe Porras, stood up. Pritchett began to weep.

Porras began by announcing that Dovon's death was "tragic. More so than normal gang violence we are so accustomed to." It was standard rhetoric to win sympathy for the victim, and Porras knew it was not exactly true—lots of the murders that people had grown "accustomed to" were also tragic—the public just didn't realize they were.

Outside the courtroom, Porras was the type of ghettoside worker who saw such nuances clearly. He could speak movingly of what he called "borderline gangsters" and the trauma they endured from watching their friends die. But today was about Dovon, and Porras was giving it his all.

A photo flashed of the murder scene, Dovon's black shoes in the foreground. Pritchett pressed a hand over her mouth.

On the stand, Derrick Washington's sister denied ever having met John Skaggs. The prosecutors impeached her. She jiggled in her seat as the video ran, then she yawned. Three days later, Pritchett bolted out of the courtroom. *Guilty, guilty, guilty.* The word echoed in her ears as she fled. The case was a John Skaggs Special. The jury barely deliberated an hour.

As Skaggs prepared to leave South Bureau, new killings kept pouring in. One night that July, Marullo and his partner, Nathan Kouri, were called to a homicide on a street called West Laconia Boulevard down in the Southeast "strip." A uniformed officer standing guard offered the sparsest of briefings at the tape. "It's a black guy," he said.

Actually, there were two. Raymond Requeña, twenty-four, moniker "Tigger," had been found dead in the street by paramedics. Requeña, a Belizean listed as Hispanic in some official reports and black in others, had a slew of arrests that began with taking a knife to school when he was barely entering adolescence and later included assault with a fire-arm. But of late, police interview cards had recorded him as an unemployed warehouse laborer on disability.

Several blocks away, at Vermont and 120th, police had also cordoned off a parked Dodge Neon with a "California Police Youth Charity" sticker on it—"Cops helping kids," read the slogan. The back window had been shot out. Inside, a Tinker Bell backpack spattered with blood lay on the backseat. Police or paramedics had removed a baby seat from the car. It was sitting on the asphalt near the Neon's rear wheel, flecked with brain matter.

Fifteen-year-old Daniel Johnson had been in the backseat of that car. He had been riding with two other youths about his age and a mother and her two small children. A bullet had smacked into the car. Daniel had slumped onto the shoulder of the friend next to him, bleeding from

a mortal wound, as Raymond Requeña was dying a few blocks away on
Laconia.

The killings happened after an argument between two women mushroomed, resulting in a face-off between two youths, both with gang ties.
The bigger youth threw a punch at the smaller one. The smaller one
left. He returned with his mother and stepfather and a group of friends,
loaded in several cars.

The parents later explained that they had wanted the two youths to
have a fistfight to settle the score. Such a response might seem crazy. But
in Southeast, cases of parents personally escorting their kids to "catch a
fade"—to fight—were not so unusual. Encouraging so-called fair fights was
seen as a hedge against homicide: parents sought to ensure that their sons
weren't labeled "punks," which might increase their risk of getting shot.

The results were predictable. The caravan rolled up the street—
"came in thick," as one witness later said. The local gang members
hollered, "Get outta the 'hood!" The intruders hollered back. More
yells. Then gunshots. Both of these hits were tag-alongs; neither had
been involved in the earlier fight.

Even La Barbera, when he first heard the details, thought Laconia
was a classic "cleared other—mutual combat." But Marullo and Kouri
were relentless. They worked through the night, the next day, then the
next, interviewing fearful witnesses. As they parsed events and talked to
traumatized survivors, they came to believe the gunfire was out of proportion to the threat. The smaller youth's entourage had carried no
visible weapons. They had shouted that they sought only a fistfight.
The driver of the car in which Daniel Johnson rode had fled to avoid
violence. Daniel had never even exited the car. The mothers of both
victims were devastated. At Daniel Johnson's funeral, his hysterical five-
year-old sister had to be pulled from the casket; she had tried to yank
out his body. Marullo was deeply affected by the families' grief.

The chief witness to the episode was a sad-faced mother of two in her
late thirties who was also a small-time marijuana dealer. The shooters
were her neighbors and sometime friends. She knew them well. She had
received a threatening phone call within hours of the killings, and she fled

to a motel in terror. She told the detectives she would not testify. She had elderly relatives in the neighborhood. "They gonna kill me," she said. She was actually shaking, her extremities trembling as if with cold.

"Just *please*," said Marullo, reduced to artless entreaty. "You gotta help us. *You're the one.*" In the end, Marullo and Kouri convinced her of the importance of giving evidence. Then they persuaded prosecutors to file murder charges on four Raymond Avenue gang members.

It was an impressive clearance of a case that, though it was a double homicide with a teenage victim, had received no media coverage. But Marullo felt exhausted and depressed afterward. The marijuana dealer was repeatedly threatened. She would end up being relocated several times. Daniel Johnson's young friends were terrified of testifying. Their parents were furious at the cops, convinced they would not be protected.

La Barbera redoubled his efforts to inspire Marullo and the rest of his squad. He devised corny morale-building activities—a squad barbecue, drinks out. He arranged a breakfast with a motivational speaker at the Police Academy in Elysian Park.

The speaker was an auburn-haired woman in a flowing pantsuit and pearl earrings. Shannell McMillan's business card read "Pursuit of Purpose, individual and team training." She brandished a felt-tip pen and flipped over pages on an easel, reading aloud such statements as "Values arc our strength in a team setting." The detectives shifted around in the cramped space, jostling each other, chuckling, pouring cups of coffee.

McMillan told them that people fell into four personality types: Wind, Fire, Water, and Earth. *Winds* sought attention and liked to talk. *Fires* liked results and risk. *Waters* were sensitive, compassionate, and open with their feelings. *Earths* were steady, quiet, and detail-oriented. "There are no Earths in jail," McMillan offered.

The detectives warmed to the exercise, especially after breakfast was served. They laughed and shouted their answers to McMillan's questions. Silverware clanged. Condiments were passed around—ketchup for the detectives from the East Coast and Midwest, *tapatio* for those from California. Marullo, a ketchup man, was in party mode, cutting up and laughing loudly. Only Nathan Kouri was quiet.

McMillan administered a personality test. Despite its New Age cheesiness, the exercise seemed to tap into something genuine. All the detectives fit into one of the categories, and no one quibbled with the results. Marullo was quickly determined to be a Fire. Skaggs, who was not present, was also classified as a Fire in absentia—everyone agreed.

McMillan offered that Fires are best when paired with Waters or Earths, who balance their shortcomings. The detectives nodded knowingly, remarking that this was why Skaggs and Barling—who all agreed was a Water—had worked so well together. Nathan Kouri was an Earth. La Barbera, not surprisingly, was the only person in the group whose personality type was indeterminate.

In the midst of the session, Kouri spilled a pitcher of coffee. He mopped frantically with napkins, turning bright red in the neck and sending his colleagues into transports of delight. "What happened there, Nate? Let's analyze it!" they cried. Kouri couldn't help playing into their hands. He embarked on some overly technical explanation of how the spill happened—how the coffee was coming out too slowly, how he had tried to adjust the lid, and so on, blushing and mopping as his friends laughed.

Kouri remained in Marullo's shadow. His methodical style balanced his partner's blazing energy. But deep down, Kouri considered his own skills inferior. He worried that he lacked the necessary gifts. Skaggs overwhelmed people with confidence, Marullo with charm. But Kouri was neither confident nor charming. His thoughts formed no thread; they skipped around in vast matrices of detail. Nor was Kouri intuitive. He could not "catch the feel of a case or a person" as Skaggs and Marullo did, nor anticipate people's reactions.

Kouri reproached himself frequently as he worked. In interviews, he would forget to ask questions and have to go back. He had concluded that he was "kind of a slow thinker," just the opposite of his mentor Skaggs. Privately, he resolved to compensate.

He would just have to work harder, he thought.

19

WITNESS WELFARE

Chances were a jury would find both Derrick Starks and Devin Davis guilty, Skaggs thought. But it was not a sure thing. Felony conviction rates in California were much higher by this time than they had been in the 1970s, when Skaggs's father was a detective and fewer than half of all felony arrests resulted in convictions. Conviction rates had risen over the same period that clearance rates had declined, so whether prosecutors failed to convict or investigators failed to win charges, the net result was the same. The system remained weak in terms of outcomes against killers. Cases were more likely to fall apart at a different point in the process, but that didn't change the overall result.

Skaggs professed confidence. But Phil Stirling, the assistant district attorney assigned the case, was worried.

Stirling was the "arrogant DA" from California Hospital. He was lean, with a touch of Ichabod Crane about him. He had a hook nose, a slight overbite, and a shock of straight dark hair. His hooded eyes were encircled by purple discoloration, as if he were in a perpetual state of exhaustion. His physique was like the balsawood frame of a kite: it curved and snapped with the constant motions of his limbs. His suit jackets always pulled askew, his collars loose. This was partly because he was skinny, but mostly because he never held still.

Stirling's unit dealt with crimes against police officers, an area that Wally Tennelle had specialized in as an investigator, and Stirling knew Tennelle from previous cases. Stirling had a reputation for being abrasive. But he was disarmingly open with his feelings and his saving grace was a healthy sense of humor about himself; he basically knew that he was a skinny guy who fidgeted all the time and could irritate people, and he was self-effacing about it.

His prosecuting partner was a younger attorney named John Colello, compact, with a buzz cut, a small chin, and blue eyes a little too close together. Colello was organized and goal-oriented. Skaggs approved of their partnership. Colello and Stirling were fire and water, and reminded him of himself and Barling: they always agreed on a lead for their cases, and they also argued about everything without antagonism.

Stirling was the lead in the Tennelle case and he was most worried about the case against Derrick Starks. Starks hadn't confessed. He hadn't fired the gun. He hadn't even seen the killing. The case against him rested heavily on the testimony of Midkiff and the fact that Davis's confession and other witness statements corroborated each other in so many details. But Midkiff might have reason to lie. She had a long criminal record. She might be unlikely to elicit a jury's trust.

Early on, a committee in the DA's office had declined to seek a death sentence. Their reasons, though unstated, were not hard to surmise. Davis, the triggerman in the killing, was a juvenile. Starks, who, as an adult, would have been the one eligible for the death penalty, was tied to the killing by more tenuous strands of intent. And he never got out of the car.

For all his confidence, Skaggs also knew that much work remained on the Tennelle case, so he immersed himself in trial preparations.

His first problem was Jessica Midkiff. From the moment Midkiff said she was willing to talk in the basement of the Seventy-seventh Street station, it was clear she would never again be able to return to her grandparents' home. But she was the kind of marginal person who could barely function outside the ghettoside world. She had never held a job. She stayed up all night and slept all morning, and got blind drunk on occasion. With her big tattoo and coquettish manners, she drew disreputable men wherever she went.

The detective got relocation funds to pay for a hotel stay of several weeks. Midkiff at first seemed settled. She brought her five-year-old daughter to visit and let her swim in the hotel pool—a rare treat for the little girl. But after about six weeks, Skaggs got a call from the hotel manager, complaining that Midkiff had taken up with a new guy and they were making noise. Skaggs had to find a new motel. Shortly after, the manager at that hotel called him, also wanting to kick her out.

Skaggs knew he needed a long-term solution. Police wiretaps of phones in jail were picking up threats against her. He needed to get her away from South Los Angeles and into an apartment. But witness relocation rules assumed that the witnesses could support themselves after moving. Midkiff had no means of support. She was always teetering on the edge of prostitution, a return to which would have been devastating to the Tennelle case as well as calamitous for her. Skaggs needed her safe, sober, and alive.

So he got involved in her problems.

There was no end to them—money, abusive boyfriends, family problems, her penchant for being drawn back into inappropriate relationships of various stripes. Her child's father, who remained in prison, was trying to get custody of the little girl, who was stable and happy, living with Midkiff's mother and excelling in school.

Skaggs didn't say it to Jessica, but he was deeply worried about her. If she went back to her old haunts, she could be murdered. Starks could order Jessica killed from prison.

So he monitored her carefully, checking up on her regularly and taking her to lunch when he could. True to his peculiar propriety, Skaggs always professed wonderment at Midkiff's dissolute ways. She went to bed at six in the morning and slept until the afternoon, "then does nothing for fourteen hours!" Skaggs marveled, as if he had not worked for years among people who passed their time in exactly this manner.

Jessica only seemed to be able to land one sort of job: brief stints lap dancing or stripping. Skaggs shook his head at the way she was always assuring him that she had some new project in mind—things that never seemed to come to fruition, like getting her GED and finding a job outside of strip clubs. Once when he took Jessica to visit her daughter, she thrust a frosty shake Skaggs had just bought her into his hands before exiting the car. She didn't want her daughter to see it, she explained to him primly, because she was trying to keep the child off sugar. Skaggs thought this absurd. The obvious doesn't seem to have occurred to him—that Jessica wanted to appear responsible to impress him.

She did whatever he wanted without question. It was disturbing: Skaggs recognized in it the same ferocious loyalty and obedience that he'd seen prostitutes show their pimps on the street. Through some kind of transference, his witness on the homicide case was now treating him like her pimp. He tried to make the most of it for the sake of the case and her well-being, gently prodding Midkiff to seek work that didn't involve stripping and steering her away from alcohol and the bad boyfriends who continued to parade through her life. And he used her obedience to try to keep her safe.

Skaggs was getting to know her better. Jessica called him on his cell phone whenever she had a problem, which was often. Theresa Skaggs, too, came to recognize Jessica's voice on the speaker of the family car phone, because her husband was compelled to take off-duty calls from the young woman so frequently.

Jessica was utterly alone, Skaggs realized. Her mother visited her only once. At this point Jessica rarely saw her daughter. On her birthday that February, Skaggs noticed that she got not a single call or visitor. She had lived for years crowded into motley groups—motel rooms with three or four other prostitutes, or shared houses—and she had passed countless days in the leisurely milieu of the South Central streets. Her life had appeared anything but solitary. But now, only a few miles from her old neighborhood, she was a castaway. At last, Skaggs gave in to her pleas to move back in with her mother briefly, since her apartment was not immediately in what he considered the danger zone.

In June, Skaggs's phone rang at 2:00 A.M. It was Jessica. She was on a street corner at Forty-second and Central Avenue in the Newton Division, the heart of old South Central where Wally Tennelle had learned his trade. She had been out drinking with some guy, and somehow the date ended with his beating her up. He had stolen her purse and jettisoned her on a street corner in a dangerous neighborhood in the middle of the night with no money. Skaggs prepared to go pick her up himself. But then his phone rang again. The guy had come back, acting nice and begging forgiveness. The old story. Skaggs hung up knowing that it wouldn't be long before her next crisis.

One heavily overcast morning that summer, Skaggs set off on one of his many witness welfare checks, worried by a new report from Jessica that she had been fired from her latest stripping job for fighting. He had been talking to her for a while now about her temper, but she wasn't getting the message.

Jessica's mother wanted her out of the house. Recently, Jessica's newest boyfriend had shown up drunk and caused a scene. Jessica's mother was alarmed. She had two little girls to raise, Jessica's daughter and her own youngest, who was near the same age. And the mother was, as Skaggs put it, "realistic" about the risks Jessica posed. If Jessica or her boyfriends caused some incident that got the family evicted from this $1,200-a-month apartment, it would be a disaster. They were living together in fragile comfort and security. Jessica's mother had bad credit and would have great difficulty finding similar housing.

Skaggs had one more issue on his mind that day: the preliminary hearing was drawing near. He could not be sure of the date, since it kept changing, but he knew it was close. He had barely spoken of this obligation to Jessica in the months since that first interview, deliberately downplaying it so as not to alarm her. But it was time for him to start delicately preparing Jessica to testify.

Skaggs pulled up to a neighborhood full of blooming bougainvillea and apricot roses and went to the door. A little dog yapped behind the screen door, and he tried to peer past it, calling over its barks: "Hello?" He could hear Jessica moving within. When she answered, her voice was creaky, clearly fresh from sleep.

"You just getting' up?" he called incredulously through the screen. "What happened to our eleven o'clock appointment?"

He agreed to wait while Jessica dressed and retreated, muttering, to his sedan. "Twenty-two years old and sleeping at eleven-fifteen!" he said. "Come *on!*"

At last, Jessica emerged in a zip-up jacket with a fake fur hood, wearing long, translucent apricot nails and jeweled white sandals, slight as ever, the ends of her long hair dyed a lighter shade. Her demeanor with Skaggs had changed since that first interview. She was happy to see him, eyes crinkling with delight, down-turned mouth giving out a throaty, embarrassed giggle as he chided her for sleeping in. She endured his fatherly grilling with a playful jut of the chin, readily answering questions she was clearly expecting.

"What about the boyfriend?"

"He's gone."

"Promise?"

"Yeah."

Skaggs by then knew the names of all her family members and their acquaintances. He asked about them one by one.

Jessica treated him as a confidant. Skaggs was always struck by the way she easily blended everyday minutiae with horrifying revelations, using the same inconsequential tone for both. She would talk about being raped one moment and her last manicure the next. She shifted easily from topic to topic, chatting about the family dog, an acquaintance's abortion, her grandmother, her last drinking binge, and her plans to vote for the first time in the upcoming election for Barack Obama because she disapproved of the wars.

She related it all in the same easy monotone. Skaggs scolded her perfunctorily for drinking, and for supporting Obama. But otherwise, he absorbed all her varied tales with his usual blend of easygoing humor and affectionate teasing. Only once did she manage to penetrate his equanimity. He had asked her about a male friend they both knew and she reported indifferently that "he said something to the sheriffs, and they kicked the crap out of him. He's paralyzed now." Skaggs, face expressionless, flipped off the air conditioner and fell momentarily silent.

He took her to a pancake house. She told him she was smoking less, but then made him wait while she smoked a cigarette before entering the restaurant. Inside, she ordered as if starving. One plate of eggs and cheese—she made a big delicate fuss about the onions, telling the server she wanted them chopped very fine—and another plate of pancakes.

She continued chatting over breakfast, drawing up her shoulders when she laughed, dimples showing in both cheeks, waggling her shoulders and popping her neck just a little. She was still aiming to get the GED, she said. She had put in an application at a local drugstore. And now she was contemplating bartending school. Skaggs urged her to "put your goals on paper. Write 'em down."

For Jessica, it was not so easy. She didn't quite see that working in strip clubs came at the expense of developing other skills. She told herself it was an extension of her love of dancing, and she legitimatized the work in her own mind by setting absurdly prudish boundaries, vowing, for example, to stick to partial-strip dancing jobs where she was allowed to wear adhesive cups over her breasts. She had also ruled out lap dancing and was avoiding clubs where she knew her fellow dancers were turning tricks out back. She considered herself "clean" and did not want to fall off the wagon back into prostitution.

She knew enough of the world, however, to realize that she had never held what she called "a real, *real* job." She had a sense of what Skaggs was getting at, but no clue how to go about it. She was relying on him even more than he realized and was worried whether Skaggs would "stay friends" with her after she testified.

When he left, he reminded her of the approaching court date. "Don't get too nervous till it's time to be nervous," he told her lightly. Jessica made no reply. She gave him a polite one-armed hug, the Southern California version of a handshake.

. . .

Just before noon down on 118th Place and Avalon, Nathan Kouri's bald head shone in the ruthless August sun. He was wearing his puzzled look, brow furrowed, with his leather notebook in hand, knocking on doors to investigate the unit's newest murder. Marullo, nearby, looked untouched by the August heat, relaxed in his dark suit, sunglasses fashionably placed on the back of his head. Near them, La Barbera was processing the crime scene himself to save on overtime.

At the end of the street, a small crowd stood behind the yellow tape. "La'Mere!" someone cried. "They got La'Mere this time!" The speaker was a woman in yellow with an aluminum cane and a Goody comb stuck in her unkempt hair. She was the mother of Ronald Tyson, murdered nearly five years before, the same woman who had vomited when notified of his death. The victim had been a friend of hers. He was La'Mere Cook, Sr., an oil rig worker with six children and no gang ties.

A young woman came up to the tape, light-skinned and wearing a lavender kerchief. She said she was a relative of La'Mere Cook and wanted to join the rest of her family. She called out to the officers guarding the tape. They glanced toward her, smirked, and turned away. She stood in the sun and pleaded. They ignored her.

Marullo and Kouri left for the police station to conduct interviews; La Barbera remained behind, smoking cigarette after cigarette, sweating as he pushed the measuring wheel in the hot sun, sourly noting the uniformed officers standing by.

Marullo hurried to the roll call room at Southeast where several of Cook's family members waited. He leaned on his fingertips to speak to them over a desk. They were all talking at once. Cook's uncle was angry that they had been kept waiting. He took it as indifference. "I'll have it done my way!" he snapped at Marullo. "I can get it done!" The uncle had been a gang member back in the day. Now he was a portly, ordinary-looking man with missing teeth.

It doesn't get any plainer. A middle-aged uncle raising his voice in the roll call room of a municipal police department to declare to, of all people, a homicide detective that he was seriously contemplating a revenge murder. The Monster is hardly subtle. Marullo tried to calm him, doing his boyish-charm thing, eyes wide, eyebrows raised. "I'm sorry, sir! I know you're upset . . ." Across the room, some uniformed officers glanced toward them and went back to their chatter, unperturbed.

At length, Marullo led a woman from the family away. He thought she was Cook's aunt. But as he escorted the woman downstairs, her movements were slow and labored. She sat and rocked. She was short and ample with a honey-brown face and little gray braids. She laid a white 8-by-11 sheet of paper on the table. Marullo began with a reference to her "nephew," and she slumped. "My son, my son. Oh Jesus. My only son!" She was sobbing.

Marullo was caught off guard. He had not understood this was the victim's mother. He made a quick readjustment, pulling his chair around the table so as to sit next to her and softening his tone. He touched her shoulder very lightly. "I'm sorry," he said. Then: "I don't want to seem like I'm being insensitive. I have to ask you some questions here. We want to find who did this."

The woman was leaning heavily on the table, breathing hard. Her name was Joyce Cook. Marullo asked her to spell the name and she buried her head on the table, sobbing and incoherent.

Marullo persisted gently with his questions, leaning forward, nodding, trying to keep her on track. She told him what she knew. La'Mere had just gone outside. The killers had driven right up to the house in a van, and a young man or boy had jumped out and fired. There had been shots, then more shots—"So many bullets!" Joyce Cook said. She had opened the door at the sound of gunfire and watched her son's murder unfold.

Marullo, tense, balanced a pen between his fingers. "I know you are hurting," he said at one point. "And I can't imagine what that's like."

Cook wept. Marullo tried to get her to focus. But she collapsed and then erupted: *"Too late!"* she wailed. "Too late! You guys always come too late!"

Marullo stood accused. His eyes dropped. A ripple of emotion skimmed his face. "I wish I was there," he said to the tabletop. "I'd be there if I could." Joyce Cook seemed not to hear him. She had fallen forward, her head on the table, sobbing silently.

The paper she'd brought turned out to be a diagram. In the midst of chaos, having just watched the murder of her son, Joyce Cook had had the presence of mind to find a pencil and draw a picture of what she'd seen. Wobbly lines sketched the house, the van, the shooter. It was an astonishing record of the altered state of trauma, documented in real time. Scrawled here and there were snippets of thoughts, almost as if Joyce Cook had been writing in her sleep: "Didn't stop shuting till I open the door," she had written. "Still shuting." And, above, "La'Mere Cook, my only son."

The drawing was of little investigative value. The police already knew most of it, and Joyce Cook's tracings had a mad, rambling quality to them. Yet the diagram was a poignant artifact of the deep yearning for justice. Even as her son lay dying, Joyce Cook's thoughts had gone to the police investigation. Cops in South Bureau were constantly accusing "the community" of not caring enough to help them solve these crimes. Yet the cops themselves often seemed deaf to the community's pleas for their success.

To many officers, black residents of these ghettoside neighborhoods seemed so incomprehensibly perverse and hostile, so hell-bent on not making things better for themselves. And that same "community" bristled and postured in response. Yet beneath all this dysfunction, just as the cops yearned to be do-gooders who "helped people," the "community" yearned for their help.

But many officers couldn't pick up on it. Or perhaps the implications were just too painful if they did: after all, Joyce Cook was right. They were usually too late.

The Cook killing remains unsolved at this writing. The unit had many strong leads, and a few terrified but helpful witnesses. A suspect gang was identified: they lived on the same block as Barbara Pritchett. But after Marullo and Kouri passed the case on to colleagues, it stalled.

One witness was also, coincidentally, a witness on the Henry Henderson case, which Marullo was trying to get through court. The Cook suspects had seen her; a few days after, her house was ransacked. She recanted on the stand in the Henderson trial and disappeared.

Another witness refused to talk to the detectives at all. This was a sixteen-year-old black youth wearing blue who was on the street when the killers rolled up. He had seen them, and he was probably their intended target. But he was street-smart and quick as a gazelle; he escaped over a fence, leaving unsuspecting La'Mere Cook behind.

The previous February, this same sixteen-year-old had himself been shot by gang assailants. The bullet slammed into his trachea. It was a classic "almo-cide." The sixteen-year-old boy had nearly died. He had coughed blood, turned blue, and his throat had swelled. He was in intensive care for a week and required three surgeries, then remained hospitalized two more weeks, heavily sedated. Family members took turns at his bedside. La'Mere Cook came, too. The youth couldn't speak for weeks. The swelling caused his tongue to poke out of his mouth, a bizarre and horrifying sight.

He improved and went home. His mother was traumatized. She worried night and day. As with so many gun assaults in Southeast that did not end in death, the case remained unsolved. When Cook was shot, this mother rushed over, afraid it was her son again. Instead, she arrived to see that someone had rolled the dying Cook on his back. She saw a look of astonishment in his eyes. Then uniformed police arrived, and the first thing this mother saw them do was handcuff her son and demand to know if he was a gang member. When detectives came, much later, wanting her son to give a statement about what he'd seen, the mother refused to cooperate. She didn't see the point. To her, the police hadn't cared that her son had spent weeks in a hospital with his tongue sticking out. She didn't think they would solve La'Mere's case any more than they had solved her son's. "They never want to solve it if it is a young black man," she said. They seemed interested only in endangering her son further. And unbeknownst to the police, Joyce Cook had told her neighbors she did not expect them to put their children at risk because of La'Mere's killing. She did this out of compassion for them. To Cook, one dead son on the block was enough.

At La'Mere Cook's funeral, the sixteen-year-old boy pressed both hands against his face and sobbed like a child. He sat with the other pallbearers—black men and boys like him, their faces stricken with grief and bewilderment.

The pastor gripped the mike and looked at the pallbearers. "The devil is trying to make you think it is an honor to die for your 'hood!" he boomed. "The devil is trying to fool you!" The sixteen-year-old straightened and leaned forward, eyes fixed on the pastor, a look of deep thought on his face.

After the wake, several of Cook's friends gathered to mutter among themselves. The police would not solve the case, one said. To them, Cook's murder "is just another nigger dead," he said.

"We police our own," said another. "Soldiers are heroes. Why are we called gangsters?"

Joyce Cook was not surprised when her son's murder went unsolved. The same thing had happened when her husband, La'Mere Cook's father, was murdered back in New Orleans years before.

Cook did not allow family members to erect the usual shrine with candles on the spot where La'Mere had died. She was from New Orleans, where she'd been taught that candles would release the restless spirit of the murdered man into the air. Cook believed there were too many murdered spirits afoot in South Central already, and she was afraid.

The summer of 2008 also saw, at last, the preliminary hearing in the Tennelle case.

Devin Davis had become thickset during his six months in jail, and his hair was an unkempt bush growing down the back of his neck. He looked as boyish and awkward as ever with his big head and square face. His eyes roved around as he entered the courtroom, looking for his mother. Derrick Starks was mostly unchanged, big-shouldered as ever, hair cropped, hazel eyes alert, a suggestion of a mustache at the corners of his mouth.

The man in the wheelchair, now thirty-one, had been subpoenaed against his will. At first he had refused to come to court. Stirling had spent a half hour before the session fielding the man's concerns for his safety and that of his family. Now he sat in his wheelchair on the stand, sunk low. As Starks, seated a few feet away, surveyed him with an appraising look, the man recanted his statements to Skaggs and Gordon and asserted again that he had gotten the gun from a crack addict. Challenged, he insisted he'd been pressured by the investigators. He did not return Starks's gaze.

The prosecutors impeached him. As his own recorded voice filled the courtroom, laying out No Brains, the man pretended to study some papers in his lap. Then he looked angry. Then he started shifting in his seat. At last, he wilted in his wheelchair, abandoning all pretense with a hand over his mouth and a look of bleak terror in his eyes.

Pointing out that this man, who had barely survived a shooting, occupied the zenith of statistical homicide risk doesn't begin to describe the full dreadfulness of his situation. It wasn't just that he was already lucky to be alive and that he was now being exposed as a snitch before two accused gang murderers. He was also an "underclass" black man, one of society's outcasts. No newspaper was going to stop the presses if the man in the wheelchair got killed. No news station was going to cut into its regular programming. No detectives' supervisor was going to yank the case away from a veteran detective and reassign it if it didn't get solved.

The man in the wheelchair did not need any special powers to perceive his status. All his life, he had lived in the Southeast Division. Patrol officers there usually treated men like him three or four ticks more rudely than other people; the gradation between cold killers and paralyzed young men who sold marijuana for extra cash was not particularly well calibrated in their minds. If someone made yet another attempt to murder this witness and succeeded, he surely knew he wouldn't qualify as a "righteous" victim. But bullets had damaged his spine no less easily for that.

When the judge released him from testifying, he wheeled himself out of the courtroom so quickly that Skaggs did not have a chance to push him. Skaggs trailed out behind him. The man had been betrayed. Skaggs and Gordon had assured him that his statement was strictly anonymous. Perhaps this was in Skaggs's mind as he followed him out. Or perhaps Skaggs had simply worked Southeast long enough to comprehend how frightened the man must have been. "Hey. Sorry! You know I'm sorry!" Skaggs told him in the corridor. His manner was uncertain and oddly out of character. The man's eyes were full of despair. He did not respond.

The Beverly Hills High student turned probationer was similarly recalcitrant. He also denied his statements to Skaggs. He denied the interview had ever taken place. When they impeached him, he said it wasn't even his voice on the tape. The probationer's eyes locked briefly with Starks's as he was led out of the courtroom. Starks kept his eye on him. As he passed, Starks slowly rotated his chair and watched his retreating back—watched it all the way to the door. A long, hard stare.

Skaggs put Jessica Midkiff in a motel for the weekend for safety. Midkiff was excited about it. She had brought her daughter. The little girl was thrilled this time by the bathtub—they didn't have one at home. Midkiff let her sit in it and watch a movie. When Skaggs arrived to pick her up that morning at 6:15 A.M., she informed him that she had gone to bed at 6:00 A.M. and had slept for only fifteen minutes. Skaggs was appalled. He assumed it was her irresponsible ways again. But Midkiff had been too nervous about testifying to sleep.

She wore faded jeans, a nylon blouse with a floral pattern, high heels, and a ponytail, her half-lightened hair cascading down her back. She carried her black clutch purse to the stand and held it as she was sworn in.

Sitting on the stand to testify, Midkiff was ashen. Starks was watching her closely, swinging slightly back and forth, his chair twitching like a

cat's tail. Her eyes flicked toward him. Between them was some complicated electricity.

Midkiff launched into her story, then faltered, breathing deeply. She
kept hesitating and sighing, appearing to waver. "Give me a minute,"
she pleaded after one of Stirling's questions reduced her to stammering
confusion. Asked if she was driving, she said: "I believe I was." It was
nothing like her certainty in the interrogation. At last she waved a hand
over her heaving chest. "Sort of hard for me," she murmured.

Skaggs, on his bench, jiggled and flexed his fingers.

During the weeks that Skaggs had been preparing her to testify, Midkiff had made it clear that she felt bad about being, as she saw it, a
snitch. Moving away from the 'hood, she felt she had "lost her identity,"
and it was dawning on her that she had no real friends. She was more
desperate than ever that Skaggs not abandon her. She made weak jokes
about it to him, unable to approach the subject directly. "I thought you
said we'd be friends!"

Now, on the stand, she thought she'd seen Starks give her a "sexual
look" and for a moment entertained the notion that he might jump out
of his chair and grab her. Then she realized he was chained. Later, she
saw Starks's mother, Olitha Starks, among the onlookers and thought
she caught a hard stare. She was so rattled that the judge called a side-
bar.

Midkiff's nose itched as she testified; she didn't know what to do
about it. A defense attorney cross-examined her and she grew belliger-
ent, stretching her neck and laughing scornfully. Later, there was mention of her grandmother, who had passed away. Midkiff broke down
and made a scene. "'Scuse me!" Stirling brought her a tissue. Wally
Tennelle, who attended the entire hearing alone, watched this scene
unfold with a grim face, playing with a piece of Scotch tape adhered to
the bench.

The case cleared "prelim"—that is, the judge ruled there was sufficient evidence for the pair to stand trial. But Midkiff had not increased
Stirling's faith in her. The trial was months away. Stirling was really
worried now.

• • •

It wasn't the horror that burned out ghettoside detectives. It was the
frustration. Sam Marullo was beginning to drown in it. The day after
Southeast victim La'Mere Cook was buried, the second trial of the defendant accused of killing Henry Henderson outside Pritchett's front
door ended with another hung jury, despite Marullo's dogged work on
the case.

Then Marullo learned that he was unlikely to be promoted to the
rank of detective in recognition of the job he was already doing, despite
his many successes.

The overtime crunch was getting to him. Recently, he had been told
he could not attend a victim's funeral. Skaggs had taught him to always
attend funerals. "You have all the burden of the families who think
about nothing but this. And you can't do your best," Marullo said. "You
try to detach yourself as a coping mechanism . . . but then the family
breaks that down."

La Barbera still tried to crack bitter jokes about it. One evening
around 4:30 he pulled a wooden whistle from somewhere, blew it, and
yelled, "Fifteen minutes!" But he could see that Marullo was upset and
thinking hard about his future. Worried about losing Li'l Skaggs—"my
only Fire"—he called the squad for a meeting in mid-September to discuss the overtime restrictions. "I'm worried about the effect on you," La
Barbera said.

He was sitting in a low chair. His detectives sat on desks or leaned
against partitions. He had intended a pep talk. But someone pointed
out that officers assigned to Compstat—the fashionable management-
accountability program based on the mapping of crime statistics—had
been given take-home cars, unlike homicide detectives. Marullo jumped
in. Homicide worked to "restore faith in the community," he said. But
since the work was so undervalued, "it's hard to ask people to give up
their life for this." He gestured toward La Barbera. "Look what it's done
to you!"

There was a stunned silence, broken by nervous laughter. Marullo was, after all, speaking to a superior officer, and a friend. "I can't believe you said that!" someone murmured. Marullo broke off, abashed.

But La Barbera waved his hands. "No, no!" he said. "You're right . . . It's ruined my life!" It was impossible to tell if he was joking.

Marullo recovered and plowed on. Why were they struggling for resources when crime was low and the police force had expanded so much? Why? He stood with one hand on his head, eyes troubled. "I don't get it," he said at last. "Someone's missing it here."

Chris Barling went up to Marullo afterward. "I've been there—don't get me wrong. I've been as frustrated as you because of the constraints," Barling told him quietly. But "you keep pounding away! You keep fighting!" Barling waved his hands, talking and talking, urging Marullo not to give up.

Nathan Kouri was sitting nearby. He listened, a hand over his mouth.

But when Barling finished, Marullo tossed his empty coffee cup into a garbage can with a bang. "I've made a well-thought-out decision," he said, and turned away.

A short time later, La Barbera came into the office in a particularly morbid mood. "Sammy broke up with me via text!" he announced.

Marullo had taken a P-3 position in the Southeast gang unit—a uniformed job as a training officer focused on crime suppression. La Barbera, predictably, took Marullo's defection personally. Marullo "is not a Fire," he snapped. "He just thinks he's a Fire."

LOST SOULS

Skaggs hated multitasking. *One thing at a time, up against only today*—this was yet another of his maxims. But he had no choice but to start a new job while winding down his old one.

It required months of shifting back and forth between roles. He continued to prepare for the upcoming trial in the Tennelle case while setting up his new office in the soon-to-open Olympic Division. The new station would include parts of Koreatown and a section of the LAPD's Rampart Division.

Back in the day, an open-air drug market in MacArthur Park and a kind of sectarian war in exile among Central American immigrants had made Rampart a savagely violent place. Crime was still relatively high when the LAPD secured bond funds to add a new station there. But by the time the station was built, wealthy Koreans, in flight from crashing Asian stock markets in the late 1990s, had snapped up real estate in the area, and developers had built hip new lofts that attracted students and professionals. At the same time, homicides had plummeted among the area's remaining Spanish-speaking immigrants.

It was an astonishing change. Among the lessons to be drawn was that poverty does not necessarily engender homicide. Even after gentrification began to take hold, nearly 40 percent of Rampart residents remained below the poverty line. Many of these poor city dwellers were illegal immigrants crammed into shabby brick apartment buildings; the neighborhood was relatively dense by L.A. standards. Yet black residents in South L.A. had vastly higher death rates from homicide.

Scholars have made similar findings elsewhere. Despite their relative poverty, recent immigrants tend to have lower homicide rates than resident Hispanics and their descendants born in the United States. This is because homicide flares among people who are trapped and economically interdependent, not among people who are highly mobile.

Immigrants are, essentially, in transit. Those in Rampart in the 2000s had left old ties behind in their native lands. They were deracinated. Their new neighborhoods were not like the underground, isolated, highly networked, communal enclaves of South L.A. Instead, they were stopovers. Their inhabitants would soon decamp from MacArthur Park to Whittier or La Puente. Hispanics had a further advantage over blacks: despite their high poverty rate, they had long enjoyed better private-sector opportunities than black Angelenos. Los Angeles employers had shown an "unabashed preference" for Hispanic labor over black for generations, historian Josh Sides showed. The supply of Mexican labor was one of L.A.'s first selling points, used by boosters to lure manufacturers. In the twenties, many employers who relied on Mexican immigrants refused to hire blacks. Organized labor in the 1930s bypassed black workers and directed its campaigns at Hispanics. During World War II, blacks, unlike Hispanics, were excluded from employment in the shipyards and docks, or relegated to inferior jobs. It wasn't that Hispanic workers didn't suffer discrimination—they did. But often they were treated badly in jobs that black people couldn't get in the first place. A preference for Hispanic labor in the food and metal industries had become entrenched by the 1960s. Later, black men, unlike Hispanic men, lost out in the great Southern California aerospace boom. Barred by racism early on, they were later marooned by geography as the industry moved to suburbs where whites and Hispanics could more easily buy homes. Black people couldn't buy homes or rent in many of the new defense and aerospace hot spots, first because of restrictive real estate covenants, then because of de facto efforts to continue these covenants in defiance of court rulings. Blacks became trapped in a sunny version of Detroit, living among shuttered tire and auto plants as the rest of Southern California enjoyed a second manufacturing boom. Although public employment remained a bright spot, by the 2000s, black people in L.A. had lower labor-market participation than their Hispanic counterparts, who as a group were less educated, and they still lived largely separate from whites, crowded into their own private Rust Belts.

This fit a national pattern. Blacks lived in figurative walled cities; Hispanics did not. Black people had long been vastly more segregated from white people than Hispanics, and were more concentrated. In fact, black people had remained more crowded together and isolated much longer than any other racial or ethnic group in America. "Black segregation was permanent, across generations," said the sociologist Douglas Massey. No one else had it as bad—not even residents of the Little Italys or Polish or Jewish immigrants to eastern cities of the nineteenth century. Black people couldn't outrun segregation if they tried. It followed them, reinforced by invisible dynamics, like real estate steering. In the year 2000, decades after the courts struck down restrictive covenants, black people in Los Angeles were no more likely to have white neighbors than they had been in 1970.

Segregation concentrated the effects of impunity. This helped explain why relatively modest differences in homicide clearance rates by race produced such disparate outcomes. Indices of residential segregation are strong homicide predictors. Homicide thrives on intimacy, communal interactions, barter, and a shared sense of private rules. The intimacy part was also why homicide was so stubbornly intraracial. You had to be involved with people to want to kill them. You had to share space in a small, isolated world.

By contrast, America's lonely, atomized upper-middle-class white suburbs were not homicidal. Their highly mobile occupants were not much involved with each other. They didn't depend on one another to survive. The occasional condominium board meeting might get ugly, but mostly there was enough law in such places—enough expectation of a legal response to violence—to keep the occasional neighbor dispute from getting out of hand. And if there wasn't—for example, if a young man grew tired of his brawling high school chums—moving somewhere else was easy enough.

In Skaggs's time, Rampart, despite its poverty, had a murder rate equal to the citywide average—and similar divisions in the suburban San Fernando Valley. The new Olympic Division would not resemble any place Skaggs had worked in years. Nonetheless, he was preparing eagerly for the new station's opening, spending most of his time in the new offices, which were still under construction.

His old colleagues in South Bureau derided him as a "traffic cop." They called his new division "Mission or Midwilshire or whatever that station is"—a swipe at the area's low crime rates. Then they accused him of taking custodial supplies with him, including power strips and cans of Dust Destroyer. These were coveted items in homicide, where the most basic office products were rationed. Under interrogation by Barling, Skaggs broke. He copped to stealing the Dust Destroyer.

Finally, Skaggs made a last visit back for the South Bureau Christmas party —enduring jeers of "West Bureau!" when he walked in—and said goodbye.

By that time, he was ready for the new station to open. He had a large whiteboard installed in his new office to list cases, just like La Barbera's. He had it stenciled so it wouldn't look messy. At the top, he wrote the old Southeast mantra "Always Be Closing" in red letters. He bought a top-notch coffeemaker and apple-spice Febreze air freshener.

He laid claim to a closet the size of a room and had new shelving installed. Skaggs knew that for all the slowdown in crime, he was sitting on top of a vast dark stain of unsolved homicides from the Big Years in Rampart—back when the bodies floated in MacArthur Park lake. He planned to improve on the Lost Souls Trailer. He dug up the unsolved cases himself. There were 453 of them going back to 1966.

Before the lights and floors were installed, John Skaggs had already gone through scores of the old books, and by the time the new station opened, he had assessed and sorted every blue binder. They stood in rows in his new closet, marked with labels that said SUPERHOT, SEMIHOT, and so on, all the way to SUPERCOLD.

The work was interesting. The homicides were different from those he knew. There had been, for example, a spurt of killings of gay men in the 1980s, never solved. Some of the victims in those cases had lived secret promiscuous lives. Others were transvestites. This aspect of murder was familiar to Skaggs. Like homeless people, female prostitutes, and criminal-class black men, these victims were vulnerable because they were marginal: the Monster feasts on the despised. Skaggs was determined to secure belated justice for these victims.

There were also gang killings among Hispanics. Overburdened detectives in the Big Years had barely investigated some of them. Skaggs found one case where police took three hours to respond to a shots-fired call. They came at last to find a body and no clues.

But Skaggs was struck most of all by how many cases had strong leads. This was very different from Southeast. In many instances, he saw, Rampart detectives had received "righteous calls" from witnesses, people coming forward to report what they had seen. Even though many of the neighborhood's residents had entered the country illegally, they appeared more apt to cooperate with police than people in Watts. In all his years in Southeast, Skaggs had never once taken a clue over the phone. He was amazed.

In between, he worked on the Tennelle case. There were jail tapes to listen to, witnesses to track. Skaggs brought his old Southwest partner Corey Farell to the new station to help him with this part of his work.

Farell had just had a second child. He promised his wife he would be home to help in the evening. She rolled her eyes: "You working for Skaggs?" she asked. "Yeah, right."

Skaggs alone dealt with Jessica. He felt she would be safe so long as she stayed where she was. But she would call him, then disappear. Skaggs would be left desperately trying to reach her, stuffing down his worries. "Probably has some dumb-ass boyfriend," he would tell himself, dialing again and again.

If she was gone long enough, he would lose a day's work to check on her. Usually she reappeared soon, claiming illness or some problem with her cell phone, then would tell him her rent was late and she was out of money. Or that she hadn't eaten and had no food. Skaggs, who had two teenagers already, felt that he had acquired a new daughter, a "nightmare child."

Yadira Tennelle made regular visits to Holy Cross Cemetery to replace the flowers on her son's crypt in the cemetery's mausoleum where Bryant's cremated remains were inurned. She yearned for Bryant's physical presence. The mausoleum seemed to bring him closer, yet the visits were always, in the end, achingly unsatisfying.

Still, Yadira would aim her car every Friday after work toward that sunny hilltop, its crest revealing the expanse of the city stretching south and toward the bay. Wearing her turquoise hospital pinafore, white tights, and white sneakers, a basket of red carnations and yellow roses on her arm, she would make her way quickly across the parking lot, sharp white globes of sunlight reflected in the parked cars all around her and sea breezes rattling mini-palms in landscaped beds.

Ignoring the view, she would vanish into the velvety shadows of the big multistory mausoleum. Yadira had a ritual: She bought flowers at the hospital, unwrapped them at the mausoleum, then used a long staff to mount them on Bryant's high-placed crypt.

Yadira couldn't stop the habit of cherishing Bryant, of thinking about him constantly in the way a mother does, planning for his future, noticing activities he might like, opportunities that might be good for him, jobs that might suit him. DeeDee was the same way. Going to work at LAX, she would notice the various municipal employees around her—the facilities crews caught her eye—and she would think of the possibilities for Bryant. The crews of men worked outdoors all day in active, hands-on jobs with decent pay and benefits—a good possibility for Bryant, she thought. It didn't matter that he was gone: such were the folds of maternal concern that had swathed him through life; they could not be loosened. Yadira Tennelle had to force her mind to conform to this new, hard reality, to accept that Bryant's life had been lived, that he was now "a sentence with a period," as she put it.

It was a fact, just a fact. But it was astonishing how painful a fact could be. For Yadira, contending with this enormous, bobbing balloon of agony pushing its way into every instant of her life required exhausting effort. When it first happened, she had not cried much. The hurt was too great for crying—tears belonged to a realm of earthly physics, but the murder of her son had transcended the coordinates of her world.

Only later, when the fact took shape as a dimension of her daily life, did it penetrate her flesh like an illness. Then she cried, and felt it in her whole body; it affected her physical health in bearable but bothersome ways. Being "strong" was a principle important to both Wally and Yadira Tennelle, but Yadira sometimes felt under assault. Bitterness was a temptation that pressed close around her; she had to keep herself ever alert. "Why be mad? Let him rest in peace," she would tell herself. But then another voice would object: He did not suffer. She did. The dead rested. The ones who stayed behind did all the suffering . . . But no. Yadira sometimes had to stop her own thoughts. She would not be negative.

She turned to her ritual. In the shade of the big, open mausoleum, the fall sunshine streaming through, she trimmed the carnations and roses with the cutters they provided, jammed their plastic bag back in her basket, and padded across the cement floor, up and around, to where a plaque stood high on a wall with Bryant's photo. "In Memory of Our Beloved Son, 'Brownie Boy,' 1988–2007."

Yadira raised her eyes to it, leaned on the staff, and wept.

"Motherfuckers!"

Nathan Kouri was soldiering on without Marullo. His new partner was Tom Eiman, the former proprietor of a door and window installation service who had joined the LAPD as a second career.

Eiman had become an effective undercover narcotics officer. He was the perfect Everyman—stout and middle-aged, with wire-rimmed glasses and a watchful bearing.

It had been left to Kouri to shepherd to trial the Laconia double homicide, which Marullo had abandoned midstream. So, with Eiman in tow, Kouri had pulled over this woman, one of several reluctant witnesses, as she was leaving for work. He had reached through her car's open window and laid a subpoena on her passenger seat. Now, she was screaming. "Motherfuckers! You are harassin' me!" A crowd gathered.

It had been like this with nearly every witness on the case. Two people involved were so afraid they would be attacked for cooperating with police they started carrying guns. One of them, a juvenile, had been caught with the gun and now faced weapons charges. A third witness had run into an ex-girlfriend of one of the defendants: the woman had "jumped on her" and beaten her up for snitching. A fourth witness, also a teenager, rolled himself into a ball at the preliminary hearing in Compton Courthouse and refused to enter the courtroom. He had to be carried to the stand by two police officers, crying, his legs thrashing.

Next, Daniel Johnson's grieving mother was threatened by members of the defendant's gang in the corridor outside the courtroom. It was "in her best interest not to testify," they said. Finally, the boyfriend of another witness was threatened in the courtroom itself by an older man. The man used the graphic sexual language of gang intimidation: "I'm a real motherfuckin' Crip with HIV and I fuck a nigger in the ass," he said. When Eiman leaped out of his seat to confront him, the "real motherfuckin' Crip" revealed that he was a gang intervention worker paid a salary from public funds. Then he dialed the cell phone number of an LAPD commander and complained that Eiman was harassing him.

Now this woman was accusing Kouri of misconduct for serving her with a subpoena. She appealed to the crowd: "I don't have anything to do with nothin'!" she shouted.

"Unfortunately, you do," Kouri retorted. They handcuffed her and bundled her into their sedan.

"Can we *talk* about this?" Kouri pleaded.

Before deciding on police work, Kouri had attended nursing school, and even now his manner on the job was like that of a stern but warm-hearted nurse. He met hostility with disappointment, resistance with dismay. He administered a subpoena like a painful injection, briskly and sympathetically.

At length, he succeeded in calming the woman. They let her go, Kouri saluting her as if there had been no quarrel: "Take care!"

Marullo, meanwhile, was at the Southeast station, back in the Southeast gang-enforcement unit. He arrived for his first watch that fall, grinning. He tugged at his uncomfortably tight blue uniform, observing that it had mysteriously shrunk; a colleague rolled her eyes. His fellow gang detectives—muscles bulging under the short sleeves of their Class C's—mixed protein powder with bottled water as a sergeant discussed the night's tasks. Mostly, gang officers were supposed to drive around and make "obs" arrests—catch guys with drugs or guns. Or, as Marullo put it later, taking the wheel of his black-and-white, "that big ol' gang-suppression line you hear that no one knows the definition of." At Ninety-eighth and Main, his headlights swept the legs of a group of Main Streeters. He stopped. "Where you been?" one asked. One of the man's companions answered for Marullo. "He a homicide detective! He turned back over!" They eyed him, frowning. "Why you come back, man?"

The nights were mostly quiet that fall. Marullo got a pursuit or two. But mostly, he spent hours driving, talking up street sources, and revisiting his choices. By November, his grin had faded. He confessed to unease one night, heading back to Southeast through dark streets: "I feel bad sometimes—like I'm not contributing, you know?"

After John Skaggs returned Dovon's shoes, Barbara Pritchett had placed them in the center of her living room shrine.

It was early 2009, nearly two years after Dovon's death. But the shrine had, if anything, grown larger. The shoes stood on display between two teddy bears, surrounded by other tokens and balloons from Dovon's birthday party, which the family had held without him. Above them, Pritchett had affixed a map of homicides that had been printed in the *Los Angeles Times*.

Pritchett still could not speak of Dovon without weeping. But she was trying to keep it together for her thirteen-year-old brother, Carlos, the one she was raising as a son. She wanted to make sure he graduated. Her family rallied around her. Her children had pooled their resources recently and bought her a new couch and carpet.

Since Dovon's death, she had extended the motherly concern that came naturally to her to the police and prosecutors who entered her life during the ordeal. She called Skaggs often, and also Sam Marullo, Nathan Kouri, and Joe Porras, whom she had come to know through the case. She called them "family."

But this made no difference one spring morning at about 5:15 A.M. when a relative staying with her heard something outside. He looked and saw police surrounding their home.

It was Southeast officers, serving a search warrant. They were seeking another of Pritchett's five brothers on a robbery warrant. Pritchett was ordered outside. She had no shoes on and was wearing only a robe.

Among those staying in the house that night was a sister-in-law and her six-month-old baby. Pritchett's daughter emerged carrying the baby, upset because it was cold. The baby had been ill and she didn't have a blanket. She exchanged sharp words with an officer, who told her to put her hands up. Couldn't they see she was carrying a baby?

As officers stomped through their house, the family stood shivering next to the garbage can in the alley.

It turned out to have been a mistake. The warrant had named the wrong brother. The one they sought was not close to Pritchett and had a different address. Pritchett's daughter was furious. But Pritchett was just glad they hadn't ransacked the house. She resolved not to let the episode affect her newly favorable view of police.

Shortly after, a woman was nicked by gunfire down the street. Pritchett went out to see and spotted Sam Marullo in a blue uniform, no longer working as a detective. She knew by then that Skaggs had left South Bureau and Joe Porras had left Compton Courthouse—*all the good ones defecting except Kouri,* Pritchett thought.

Some months later, an acquaintance was killed in Nickerson Gardens. Among the mourners was a young black man who knew Pritchett, and who had also known Dovon. The young man confided his doubts that this new case would be solved.

"We need John Skaggs back," he told Pritchett. She agreed.

But Skaggs was off at Olympic, growing bored.

He had thrown himself into his new job. He made his new young detectives dress immaculately, and he set squad meetings at 7:00 A.M. to make sure they got up early. He sweated them if they left so much as a paper clip holder on their desks. But for all that, by spring, his whiteboard remained blank. Not a single homicide had occurred in the new division. Skaggs was suffering the unaccustomed discomfort of energy to spare.

The Tennelle case continued to occupy him. Since the preliminary hearing, the two uncooperative witnesses, the man in the wheelchair and the young probationer who had fought Bryant's neighbors, had disappeared. Farell was searching for them.

And there was new evidence. Jail recordings had caught Starks remonstrating with Davis while the two were housed together. Starks had declared himself out of the business of killing. But he added: "If I were to kill a copper, it'd be Detective Skagg. Tall white boy. Wears only a shirt with a tie and no jacket." Skaggs seemed pleased—confirmation that he stood out from other cops. But the tape was unlikely to be admitted in court.

Stirling, the prosecutor, continued to fret about the prospects of winning a guilty verdict. Skaggs, like many people, found Stirling hard to take. But he had decided to approve of him and so he humored him.

The pair made a prison visit that spring. They had hoped to interview a prisoner with additional evidence. The prisoner turned out to have nothing to contribute to the upcoming prosecution. But the long trip was not a waste. It helped Skaggs and Stirling cement their working relationship. Stirling sat in the passenger seat and gave very poor directions. Skaggs drove, displaying perfect confidence in his bearings even after they became thoroughly lost.

Skaggs enjoyed provoking Stirling. He was annoyed at Stirling's worries and teased him about them. Stirling was not above provoking Skaggs back. When Skaggs stopped to buy a black coffee with a shot of espresso in it—he liked a coffee flavor that Starbucks called "bold"—Stirling ordered a blended caramel Frappuccino with whipped cream. "Holy shit!" Skaggs sputtered when the frilly concoction arrived. He passed it to Stirling with disgust. Stirling smiled serenely.

A jumble of squat prison buildings appeared on the horizon, round coils of barbed wire gleaming silver in the hazy light. A guard in a tower lowered a key to them using a bucket and string, reminiscent of Dr. Seuss's *The Lorax*. No high technology had proved superior to this method.

A prison guard met them, a huge black walkie-talkie on his chest and blue and green tattoos covering his forearms. Skaggs and Stirling entered the prison, passing between circles of fences with dead space between them. Signs warned of high-voltage danger and bore silhouettes of human figures struck by lightning.

The pair waited in an office adorned with American flags as big as bedspreads. On the wall was a display of mug shots labeled "busted." The "busted," who included many women, were prison visitors caught trying to sneak in narcotics. Stirling chatted with the guards. One told about the prison's new push on indecent exposure: "They've been giving them twenty-five years to life for exposing themselves to female guards!" he said brightly. Another boasted of a big-time Mexican Mafia leader who resided there. Stirling was impressed. But under questioning, the prison employee conceded that the capo was actually in the hospital. "He has kidney problems. He's getting old," he said.

Skaggs remained silent throughout, fingers tapping. The prison guards' bearing had a touch of self-importance. They sauntered in and out wearing jumpsuits and black baseball caps. They appeared proud of their status as law enforcement professionals and behaved as though Skaggs were one of them. They talked of their "investigations" in the confidential manner of equals sharing shoptalk. But the thin line of Skaggs's mouth suggested he did not consider the prison guards of quite the same caliber as himself.

Stirling, who often talked too much, instantly adopted the guards' tone. He began spilling details about the Tennelle case. Skaggs's fingers grew still, and his mouth tightened into a frown. It was clear he was very displeased.

The inmate they had come to see was a black man with gang ties to South Central. He was young and athletic-looking. He had an engaging manner and his eyes conveyed clearheaded intelligence. It was easy to imagine him in another kind of life, as a popular high school football player or a promising college student. But in this life, he had been shot at and assaulted repeatedly. He had lost friends to homicide. He had attacked people and hurt but not killed them, he said. His family's house had been "shot up." A man had beaten him, broken his gold chain, then departed with the words, "I coulda killed you. No one would say anything about it."

The young man was going to be released soon. He was worried. Prison was safer than freedom for young black men in California, who were much more likely to be murdered outside than in. Some gang members even described incarceration as a reprieve—a temporary break from the terror of the streets, like a soldier's leave from battle.

The young man indicated his "gang identity" was a ploy to survive. "Gotta play the role," he told Skaggs. He spoke wistfully of a gang member he knew who had escaped the life, finding a job in construction far away. He was in love with a woman, and he wanted to do the same. But he had no money, and he knew his prison record would make it difficult to get a job or an apartment, even a credit card.

Skaggs had long been struck by how many gang members, like this young man, seemed to be pretty regular guys. They were gang members in *spite* of their normalness. They had joined gangs as thirteen- or fourteen-year-old boys. Some were forced. Others sought protection.

Still others were seduced by teenage enticements: Girls. Money. Adventure. A chance to brawl and "party." By their twenties, they were sick of it. They appeared despondent, as repelled by the violence as any sane person would be. They cried a lot. Their loyalties had shifted to girlfriends and kids. But they couldn't shake their adolescent ties.

There was, of course, a whole complex range of people in the ghettoside world. Some men liked hurting people. Some didn't. Some men started out not liking it but became brutalized and sadistic. Maybe the mix would differ in other groups of Americans. Maybe some other racial or ethnic cohort would contain a higher ratio of regular guys, or a lower ratio of men susceptible to becoming violent. Maybe the gnawing fear of getting murdered—estimated as high as one in thirty-five by a Justice Department report in the 1990s—would influence another group of men differently.

But this was hairsplitting. Take a bunch of teenage boys from the whitest, safest suburb in America and plunk them down in a place where their friends are murdered and they are constantly attacked and threatened. Signal that no one cares, and fail to solve murders. Limit their options for escape. Then see what happens. The young man turned on them somber, frightened eyes. He didn't want to be in prison and didn't want to die. He wanted out but couldn't find a way.

As Skaggs and Stirling went out through the prison gates, an alarm sounded. A guard waved a hand toward the window to show Stirling the cause—a house sparrow trapped between the fences. Birds "just blow up" when they touch the high-voltage wire, the guard explained. They'd flutter a few moments, then perish.

Stirling stopped to watch the sparrow trace its last desperate loops. "Poor little bird," he said, and walked on.

All through 2009, small motions played out in the Tennelle case. Skaggs and Stirling became acquainted with the two defense attorneys appointed for the defendants. Seymour Applebaum, Davis's attorney, had a deep voice seemingly made for addressing juries and could have been

credibly cast as Socrates, with his white hair spilling over his collar and a
white beard. Applebaum disdained computer gadgetry. He wrote with
pencil on paper and spoke from a lectern, making eye contact with his
listeners, not gazing toward a screen as so many prosecutors did. Ezekiel
Perlo, Starks's attorney, was built like a ship's mast despite being nearly
seventy years old. Perlo had an asymmetrical, humorous face and a slight
limp, and he had recently battled lymphoma. Both attorneys were high-
end. They had considerably more experience than the prosecutors and
were both qualified to try capital cases, which placed them among the elite
of defense attorneys locally. The pair had been chosen for the case before
the DA's decision not to seek the death penalty. Trial was set for 2010.

As the months wore on, Skaggs's new unit in Olympic finally got a
few homicides—a justifiable committed by a juvenile who hit his adult
attacker with his skateboard, a nineteen-year-old Latino youth killed in
a drive-by, and a drunken man who had died two weeks after receiving
a mysterious bump to the head.

Skaggs had been struck by how much more cooperative witnesses
were in Olympic than they had been in Southeast. "I've been out on two
shootings, and the wits didn't run off. They waited and talked to police!"
he said.

Roosevelt Joseph, one of the old-timers from Seventy-seventh homicide, had long held that witness cooperation varied according to crime
rates: "As homicide creeps up, witness cooperation drops off," he said. A
feedback loop exists between murder rates and ambient fear; Skaggs
was now seeing this firsthand.

Inwardly, he still chafed. He wasn't used to free time. He had started
running at 3:30 A.M. before work. In April, he ran the Boston Marathon
for charity. Friends had told him to start slow, to pace himself. Skaggs
complied, though this went against all his instincts. He was still fresh at
Mile 21 and finished in four hours, nine minutes, with energy to spare.
"Bad tactics," he thought. He'd violated his own creed: *Never hold back.*

He still enjoyed his job and his home life. But he felt tested in both.
His son had turned seventeen. Skaggs worried that the boy was prone to
"bad decisions" and fretted that he had not found a job. Skaggs had al-

ways worked, pulling weeds starting at age twelve. He gave his son ulti-
matums, threatened to take the car. Finally, he found the less he said, the
better. "Attitude!" Skaggs exclaimed. "He thinks he knows everything!"

Parenting a child in late adolescence is delicate work. For years,
much research and advocacy directed toward homicide had focused on
"youth violence." There were virtually no charity or government programs focused on adult male victims. But statistics suggested that it was
not youth but *leaving* it that heightened risk. Death rates for black men
peaked at ages eighteen to twenty-two, then remained relatively high
through the forties.

Black parents of homicide victims often felt criticized, as if their
child's murder somehow indicated a poor upbringing. But homicide risk
descends on young black men at exactly the moment when they shake
off parental authority. It's a moment that also throws many white parents. Skaggs's son presented different challenges than Bryant. But as the
father of a seventeen-year-old, Skaggs said he related "100 percent" to
Wally Tennelle's struggles.

Then there was his other, lately acquired nightmare child.

Jessica Midkiff still needed constant tending. One day, Skaggs fetched
her for a proceeding related to her probation. She came running out
with her hair wet, breathing hard, clutching her HIV-test certificate.
When she jumped into the car, Skaggs took off his sunglasses and gave
her a long look. "You look healthy!" he exclaimed. She beamed. "I try
to go to bed early," she said.

She was still dancing, making two hundred dollars a night. She still
smoked. She fell asleep in the backseat. But Skaggs was feeling encouraged. Midkiff had met, for once, a man whom he considered a nice guy,
a security guard at one of her clubs. And she was finally taking steps to
finish her GED.

As they drove by the University of Southern California campus,
Midkiff woke up. She peered at the college girls walking by: she had always wanted to see a university campus.

THE VICTIMS' SIDE

La Barbera badly missed Marullo. Four of his detectives defected that year, all for assignments that seemed to offer more perks and fewer frustrations. He was left once again with too many inexperienced detectives, and too few sure hands to train them.

The overtime pinch was hurting. And he remained unsure of Kouri, who never seemed to be able to explain what he was doing.

Kyle Jackson, the group's new commander, had not been popular with the ghettoside crew at first. But he was showing signs of absorbing their subversive perspective. He fought for resources. He expressed compassion for what he described as the "desperately helpless community" of South Bureau.

La Barbera was surprised, but perhaps he shouldn't have been. Jackson, who was black, had grown up in Watts. His mother had been on welfare and he had spent some of his childhood in Nickerson Gardens. His stepfather had built the notorious Louisiana Hotel, whose sign adorned the Southeast roll call room.

La Barbera was not in the office one evening when Jackson loomed over Kouri's desk, lamenting Marullo's decision to leave. He pointed at Kouri in his theatrical way. "But *you*? Do *you* want to stay?" he asked.

Caught off guard, Kouri answered without thinking: "*If* they let us work," he griped.

Then he realized his mistake.

Kouri had been noticing the ease with which unsolved cases slipped into oblivion. Sometimes it seemed to him that investigators gave up too easily. Giving up was not acceptable. When Eiman had groused that the gang intervention worker from the Laconia case was going to "beef" him—that is, file a complaint against him—Kouri had countered solemnly: "You can't let that stuff stop you. It would paralyze you."

Now Kouri's head snapped up to meet Jackson's gaze. He realized his commander was testing him. "Yes!" Kouri corrected himself with sudden intensity. He *did* want to remain in homicide. "Yes, I do!"

One strangely cool and misty afternoon in August 2009, a boy dressed up in "old school" gangster style with an orange bandana hanging out of his pocket ambled toward the corner of Broadway and Eighty-ninth Street across from the Celestial Church of Christ.

A dark-clad figure awaited him and raised a gun. He gripped it in both hands, braced his legs, and fired. The boy tried to run but fell mid-step and pitched forward. He lay still for a moment, lifted his head, then dropped it. He was crying. He raised his head once more. Above him, festive yellow and orange helium balloons promoting a neighborhood store bobbed in the wind.

A young woman ran to his side then rushed away, hands pressed to her face. A man carrying a baby stepped around the boy and went into the store.

Paramedics soon arrived, followed a minute later by a police car.

A big officer got out and glanced at the boy on the sidewalk, who was still moving. Then he turned away, pacing out a perimeter. He and his partner put up crime-scene tape and shooed the crowd away. The big officer paused, hand on hip, to bark something into his radio, then shooed some more, waving his arms, and turned to watch the paramedics remove the boy's clothing and shoes. By then, other officers had arrived. They, too, stood and watched. Not one knelt to talk to the boy. Not one asked him who did it.

A short while later, Nathan Kouri, colored pens jutting from his pocket, stood on the street next to small, discarded shoes. Nearby, La Barbera waved his arms to stop an approaching police sedan: a pair of gang detectives were driving right through the crime scene. *"Hey!"* La Barbera yelled, incredulous.

On the other side of the yellow tape, a small knot of people gathered. "They gonna clean the blood up?" said a young woman to no one in particular, wrinkling her nose. "They always leave it, and it smells."

The victim was a thirteen-year-old named Da'Quawn Allen. More than two years had passed since Bryant Tennelle's death, but the trial was still months away. In the intervening period, 545 black men and boys had been killed in Los Angeles County; Da'Quawn was the 546th.

Eiman was on vacation, and Kouri had been assigned to train the Southeast squad's newest recruit, a former gang officer with a master's degree in environmental science named Mike Levant. Kouri was still inexperienced. But La Barbera had no choice. Almost everyone else in the squad by this time had even less time in homicide.

Kouri and Levant jumped in their sedan, Kouri balancing his black folder on the dashboard. "Last few nights, Hoovers and Main Street been goin' at it!" he said into the phone, then snapped it shut. "A lotta movin' parts, buddy," he said to Levant. "Holy smokes."

They were on their way to Harbor-UCLA hospital, where Da'Quawn had been pronounced dead. Another shooting victim had come in to the trauma center at about the same time. Kouri thought the two shootings might be connected. He headed into the blinding late afternoon sun to the hospital, hoping to interview this survivor.

It turned out to be a false lead. The survivor was a young woman. She had been shot in the leg during an unrelated fight, which, by coincidence had unfolded at the same time as Kouri's case, just a few blocks away. The fight had involved a man's girlfriend, his ex-girlfriend, a baseball bat, and a stolen cell phone—what Skaggs would have summed up as "some drama." It was the sort of case that could easily have been a homicide had the bullet's angle been slightly different.

The woman greeted Kouri warmly from her hospital bed. She remembered him from her niece's murder case. The visit was not a waste. Standing in the trauma bay—among beeping machines and very young doctors darting in New Balance running shoes—Kouri and Levant were approached by a stocky patrol officer with sideburns.

Officer John Tumino had been looking for them. A witness had left a note with her phone number on the ground for the police guarding the crime scene. But the officers there had failed to pick it up. Tumino, who had come to the scene later, had somehow learned about this and tracked the woman down. He now handed Kouri her number. Kouri stared, astonished. "You know, thank you! *Thank you!*" he exclaimed. He glanced away, laughing, with a small shake of his head. A patrol officer providing a lead. So simple. So rare.

Kouri and Levant took an elevator from the trauma bay and exited into a hall painted turquoise blue and decorated with illustrations of penguins and storks.

At the desk, a nurse shook her head, "He didn't even make it up here," she said. She sent Kouri and Levant back the way they came, past the painted storks and penguins—the children's intensive care unit that thirteen-year-old Da'Quawn had not lived long enough to see.

They found the doctor who had treated the boy, who gave the time of death: 2:14 P.M. Da'Quawn had been shot five times.

Next was the morgue. At the front desk, the attendant's eyes went from Kouri to Levant, then back. "I pity y'all," she said. She led them to a pair of double doors. Levant made a weak joke about not going in, then followed Kouri inside.

The morgue was cold, with little white and gray tiles on the floor like a locker room. Five enormous stainless steel doors lined the wall, each with a number at the top. "He on the bottom," the attendant said. Kouri plucked a pair of plastic gloves from a box on the wall, opened one of the doors, and pulled on the handle of a bottom drawer.

It rolled out, a zippered white bag, the lump of a small figure within. Kouri bent down, stepping gingerly around the drawer to pull down the zipper. Levant drew back, a wincing hesitation in his eyes.

Da'Quawn's body was wrapped in a sheet soaked with light pink blood. Kouri plucked at the sheet, and a corner fell away. The mask of the ventilator still covered the lower half of his face, its tubes twisted around his limp frame. Kouri worked quickly, touching only the sheet, searching for tattoos. He tugged a fold, and the sheet slid fully off the head.

On the back of Da'Quawn's head, soft fine curls tapered into light brown skin at the base of the neck. Kouri flipped another fold and exposed the thirteen-year-old's arms and chest, padded with a childish layer of fat. Last came the legs, skinny and coltish. No tattoos. Levant watched silently. Kouri replaced the sheet, pushed the drawer back in, and locked it.

They went outside. The sun was setting into a gray sea mist at the horizon, fading instead of flaring down, throwing the palm trees into silhouette. The air had a peculiar chill. They talked about other cases. Kouri brought up a witness on another of his cases, a woman nicknamed "Chocolate" who had run into the killer while waiting in line for county benefits. They praised Tumino. "That cop's pretty good," Kouri said. He had fallen into the homicide detectives' habit of referring to uniformed officers as "cops," as if they were a species apart.

Neither detective spoke of Da'Quawn. But when Levant's wife rang his cell phone, he told her he'd be late and explained, using delicate, uncoplike phrasing, that "a young man passed away."

They interviewed witnesses. They walked from house to house, past chain-link fences, graffitied couches. A gleam of orangey twilight played over the parked cars. Levant, with no flashlight, delivered painful bare-knuckled knocks on the screens of steel security doors.

Darkness fell, and they returned to the crime scene. A cluster of candles threw a white glow on the feet of about twenty mourners, stunned teenagers with their hands jammed in their pockets. A gray-haired man who described himself as a gang intervention worker carried a poster with Da'Quawn's photo—a sweet picture taken perhaps a few years before. He asked Kouri for masking tape. Only in South Bureau do people know that police carry tape. Kouri gave him some.

Back in the office much later, Kouri flipped through a stack of photos of recent graffiti, coded boasts, declarations of grief, and avowals of revenge. "We got a war here!" he exclaimed. His phone went off. A shooting in the Seventy-seventh Street Division. Retaliation for Da'Quawn, already.

Kouri took Levant back out to the sedan. They drove through dark streets under the pale gray sky: night is never black in L.A. Kouri leaned out the window into the cold air, talking casually to passersby. To a father in a front yard with children, Kouri called out, "You guys doing all right?" and the father grinned and pointed at his sons: "They don't gang-bang or nothin'! I don't let 'em get into anything!"

They knocked on more doors, Kouri calling out "It's the *po*-lice," using the ghettoside pronunciation without affectation.

They found Da'Quawn's house. The living room was a mess. A Lakers clock on the wall, a lampshade teetering on a shelf, a stack of *Ebony* magazines sliding across the coffee table, children's bicycles on the floor.

The boy's grandmother sat in the midst of the clutter, gap-toothed with a spray of curly brown hair framing a tired face, dressed in a shift. She sat with bare feet splayed in front of her. Near her, Da'Quawn's little brother, ten years old, leaned in the arms of an aunt, tears streaming down his face.

Kouri gave his condolences and talked about the case. A ceiling fan rattled overhead. On the couch, the little brother kept sobbing. It wasn't childish crying. It was convulsive, involuntary, uninhibited anguish. The boy wept as though he were being turned inside out. He stared with unseeing eyes.

As Kouri talked, Levant's gaze returned again and again to this boy. At last, the boy's aunt wrapped the child in her arms, lifted him like an infant, and carried him outside.

Da'Quawn's mother was incarcerated, so his grandmother had been caring for him. She confided that she had been worried about

Da'Quawn's joining a gang. She had "been trying to get the hell out of here."

She was unusually frank about gangs. A cousin interjected: "But an adult killed a *kid*!" she snapped, looking hard at Kouri. She was annoyed. Uniformed officers had been jamming up young men on their block all evening, part of the LAPD's "saturation" response to the homicide. Fifteen young men were spread-eagled against a wall down the street as she spoke. The cousin dangled her keys and was caustic: Were they going to look for the killers, or just harass the victims?

Kouri and Levant bade her goodbye and walked out. The aunt was sitting on the front porch, cradling the brother, as they walked past. The boy turned his brimming eyes toward the detectives and, as if yielding to a reflex, Levant reached out. He laid a hand on the boy's head. Then he hurried after Kouri.

Police would later piece together that Da'Quawn Allen's killing was part of a tit-for-tat retaliation cycle. When it finally quieted a week later, the spasm of reciprocal violence had cost the lives of three black men and two black teenage boys and had left three people wounded. Two gangs were involved—a clique on Main Street in the Southeast Division and the 8-Trey Hoover Criminals in the Seventy-seventh Street Division.

Several other unrelated homicides happened in South Bureau the same week, and two officer-involved shootings. Homicide detectives were so swamped that one of the murder cases was assigned to a pair of trainees with only a couple of months' experience between them.

The cycle had begun with a Saturday night house party on the Eastside. Hoovers and Main Street gang members were socializing together. Then a brawl had broken out among the women there. Several hours later, the argument spilled over into the street. A car drove by. There was "chipping" between its occupants and some pedestrians. The car left and returned. Then shots. A young woman on foot was struck in the leg. She was Main Street. It was *on*.

Early that Sunday, Main Street assailants hit back at the Hoover neighborhood, shooting into a car where a couple sat at Eighty-ninth and Broadway. They missed. Main Street struck again that afternoon, this time hitting and killing Da'Quawn, with his orange bandana—Hoover gang attire.

That night, Hoover suspects struck back, killing twenty-one-year-old Christopher Lattier, who happened to be walking on Eighty-fourth and Main. Lattier was a school district employee with no criminal record. He had nothing to do with it. He was simply a convenient target because he was young, black, and male.

Shortly after that, Hoover suspects threw a glass beer bottle with a wick full of gasoline through the window of a home in their own neighborhood. An older Main Street gang member had been living there on a "pass." The "pass" had been revoked.

Nathan Kouri worked continuously through Sunday night and Monday. He had good leads, thanks in part to "friendlies" who had fed information to John Skaggs. Then Kouri got lucky. Cruising down dark alleys where homeless men lurked with ice picks, he came across a rental Pontiac driven by a man "on disability" because of injuries from a previous shooting. A clerk at the employment office had told him disability was "the best thing going." It turned out to be the suspect car, though the driver was not a suspect. The car had been passed around.

In the midst of this, Kouri got a call. An officer alerted him that county Children and Family Services workers were on their way to Da'Quawn's grandmother's house to take the remaining children into foster care. There had been no report of abuse, the officer said, just questions about Da'Quawn's death.

"DCFS," Kouri muttered, hanging up the phone. *"Oh my fucking God."*

An image rose before his eyes: social workers yanking Da'Quawn's sobbing brother from the arms of his aunt. Kouri turned the sedan around and intercepted the caseworker—a harried man in a polo shirt and dress shoes—on a dark street. Kouri planted himself on the sidewalk, stared at the sky for a moment, then spoke: "I know you are just doin' your job—"

The caseworker thought he knew what Kouri was going to say: "I know you don't want to be involved," he interrupted.

But Kouri shook his head and corrected him. "No, no!" he said. "We *are* involved."

Nothing could be more obvious to Kouri. Involvement was the heart of his job. It was what made homicide work different—that intimate *involvement* with people, with their problems, quarrels, and grievances.

Up at headquarters, where crime was all maps, numbers, and abstractions—"policing by the dots," one detective said—the enforcement of law was essentially about prejudgment. But down around Eighty-ninth and Broadway, where Nathan Kouri plied his trade, crime was what happened to individuals—real people—who were now his own. Kouri was not, like the LAPD airship, an instrument of law that hovered at such heights that those below were rendered an indistinguishable blur, victims and perpetrators blended into one mass of "at risk" inner-city blackness. Kouri had learned to wade among the inhabitants of the "desperately helpless community" and look into their faces, to choose a side and throw his weight behind it. He made individual injuries his own. His job was to anchor the law in the suffering of real human beings, to bring it down from on high and straight into the living rooms of Watts.

Nathan Kouri did not have a muddled mission like so many others in the police force. He knew exactly what he was fighting for, and for whom. His job was taking sides—always the same side, always without reservation. "The victims' side," Camus had written. "In every predicament, the victims' side." Now one of his victims' families faced calamity. Kouri *was* involved. Profoundly.

As the caseworker talked, Kouri scrunched his face and kicked a toe on the pavement. Cars roared by on the boulevard beside them.

At length, Kouri cut in. Alienating the family could jeopardize the investigation, he suggested. "What's the bigger picture here? Taking two kids? Or solving a murder?"

The caseworker, a young black man, met Kouri's troubled gaze.

"Solving the murder," he said. DCFS backed off. Kouri swung back to work.

In the office the next morning, Da'Quawn's face appeared on the television behind Kouri's desk. His murder had qualified for media coverage because of his age. "Police say the victim is a known gang member," the newscaster said. This was consistent with the way LAPD brass had described the killing. One captain had gone so far as to call Da'Quawn "a hard-core gang-banger."

La Barbera was disgusted. Da'Quawn had just turned thirteen and had not a single tattoo. Gang involvement for such a child was "like playing cops and robbers," La Barbera thought. Da'Quawn's preposterous orange bandana, so outré and out-of-date, was like a cap gun and costume cowboy hat.

Nearby, Kouri picked up his cell phone to update Marullo on the case. This was typical. Though he remained in a gang unit, Marullo called constantly, wanting details on each new case. La Barbera cast a sour glance at Kouri. He had long abandoned his notion of Marullo as Li'l Skaggs. "Tell 'im if he wants to work homicide to come back here," he groused. "If he wants to run his numbers game, stay over there. If he wants to work fucking *homicide*, come back!"

La Barbera was especially annoyed at the uniforms that week. He was furious at the way they had handled the crime scene, not bothering to talk to the dying boy, shooing his relatives away, then failing to pick up a phone number left by a witness. He'd been promised searches that hadn't materialized. Gang and narcotics officers were running around acting important, busily visiting what La Barbera called "proactive harassment" upon the people of Southeast. But they'd brought no leads. "I hate cops," La Barbera grumped. "I fuckin' *hate* cops."

Late Sunday, long after the murders of Da'Quawn and Christopher Lattier, LAPD commanders had decided to mount a targeted "saturation" response. But the designated units had scheduled days off. So it took two days for the "surge" to hit the streets.

By then, another black man had died and two more people were injured.

Early Tuesday morning, in Main Street territory near Eighty-second Place and Main, forty-nine-year-old Thaddeus Risher was sitting in a car when Hoover suspects shot and killed him. Near the same time, two blocks away, candles in glass holders were smashed at the shrine for Christopher Lattier. Risher was an ex-convict and "straight hustler," according to his daughter, who loved him dearly. But he had nothing to do with this quarrel either. He was just out late in the Main Street 'hood. That same night, Main Street vandals struck back, smashing the candles at Da'Quawn's street shrine.

As the retaliations played out, a meeting was convened between gang leaders from both sides who wanted to quash the feud. These men considered the killing of a thirteen-year-old boy out-of-bounds, and they knew it would bring out the heat. But it didn't work. Younger gangsters either didn't know about the meeting or didn't care. They kept fighting.

By Tuesday afternoon, the LAPD surge was finally in full swing. Patrol cars passed every few minutes in the twelve-block area where the feud was playing out.

Officers bird-dogged Da'Quawn's sidewalk shrine, at one point "hemming up" four young mourners in their early twenties. They put them against the wall next to the balloons, candles, and white teddy bears. Uncuffed at length, the young men turned around to argue with the officers. One officer was scolding and contemptuous. But the other, in a reasoning voice, told the four to "be careful . . . There's been a lot of shooting." The young men seemed to hear only the contemptuous officer.

A watching crowd was angry. Why weren't police out catching the killers? "People are being shot, and what are they doing? Just jacking people up!" one woman said. "Their priorities are mixed-up," said a man nearby. "You should be out looking for *them*!" a woman yelled at the departing officers. A young man rejoined that this wasn't likely. Police wouldn't bother to solve the murder: "They put less effort on gang members than on others," he said. "It's like we are second-class citizens."

Later that night, when only a few mourners lingered, a car pulled up, and a youth in dark clothes jumped out with an AK-47. He opened fire, swinging the weapon around. A man at the shrine was grazed, and a young woman was hit in the leg. By Tuesday night, between fifty and seventy-five additional officers had been redeployed from other areas of the city to the twelve blocks, which commanders called "the box."

LAPD brass used a vocabulary their underlings did not. They spoke of "victimology," and of "biasing" and "stacking" resources, of responding "surgically." Mostly it meant deploying lots of cops to stop and search people and to conduct parole and probation searches. The surge brought in everyone from elite Metro platoons to Harbor Division traffic cops—the latter none too pleased to have been pulled from their regular duties.

South Bureau commanders were sensitive to the impact of this onslaught and genuinely concerned about the toll of the violence. But they had no other ideas, and in this as in everything else, they were compelled to adhere to civilian oversight, honor public expectations, and respond to political direction, which meant that "proactive" policing and crime "suppression" ruled the day. "I don't want to be perceived as an invading force," said Capt. Thomas McDonald, of Southeast patrol. "But at the end of the day, we just want it to stop."

La Barbera, like many homicide detectives in the south end, was skeptical. In October 2003, six-year-old D'Angelo Beck was killed by a bullet intended for someone else near Avalon and Eighty-seventh Place, after a patrol car had passed the scene seconds before. Skaggs, monitoring the retaliations by phone from Olympic, agreed: "If they don't see the black-and-white, they'll do it," he said.

But what really bothered La Barbera was that the saturation did not include detectives. Fresh officers in uniforms adorned every corner. But every member of his squad was exhausted, and they'd busted through overtime limits. Nathan Kouri had been living out of his sedan for days; the unit had lost the "salvage" cars they'd hoarded, so two detectives were bumming rides from colleagues to help out.

Still, if the saturation produced clues, La Barbera could get behind it. The brass had promised "task forces." There was always the possibil-

ity all those searches could produce a gun or a rumor. "You want to talk
to people!" La Barbera said. "Use the laws to get into their cars—then
talk. I tell these cops all the time: Be a salesperson. We don't need the
Gestapo stuff."

But several days of the surge had produced not a single report to
homicide detectives. Despite numerous arrests and citations, not one
witness had been identified. Not one rumor. Not one gun. There was
always this disconnect between so-called proactive policing and detective work.

It was late the following week when La Barbera finally got a report
of the arrests made by a special narcotics buy team that was part of the
surge. He scanned it, appalled.

The team was supposed to advance the investigations. Instead, it had
gone to a parking lot where crack addicts camped in plain sight and
picked up some sickly middle-aged addicts including several women
on minor possession charges involving twenty- and thirty-dollar rocks of
crack cocaine. La Barbera's crew knew that parking lot well: they had
recently recruited a homicide witness from there, a homeless man who
burst into tears when they tried to interview him. It turned out his
daughter had been murdered.

The addicts had no part in the youthful violence; they weren't even
in the territory of either suspect gang. "You gotta be kidding me," La
Barbera muttered as he read. "The fucking *parking lot*!"

The surge had occasioned a modified tactical alert requiring the detectives to don their ill-fitting blue uniforms. Even mild Rick Gordon
rebelled. Murders were happening, and "the department's reaction is to
put detectives in uniform!" he exclaimed.

Detectives disliked looking like patrol officers, since people were then
less likely to talk to them. The uniforms added to the sense that the
neighborhood was under siege, but did nothing to insert justice into it.
The spectacle of Rick Gordon, one of the city's most effective investigators, compelled to play the role of blue scarecrow at the very moment
when his craft mattered most was a microcosm of how police had long
functioned in the United States: preoccupied with control and preven-

tion, obsessed with nuisance crime, and lax when it came to answering for black lives.

The following Tuesday, despite the massive deployment, two more black people were killed in a double homicide related to the retaliation. They were Drayvon James, twenty-nine—a gang member who had tried to escape the life but had returned to visit with family—and his cousin, Robert Lee Nelson, Jr., sixteen, a student with no criminal record.

To La Barbera, this meant the saturation hadn't worked. To those above him, it could be argued that things would have been worse without it. At a "crime control" meeting after the double homicide, commanders talked of "decoy" vehicles and personal theft statistics.

South Bureau chief Kirk Albanese praised the surge: "We put a stop to some issues that had a chance to be more explosive." When one supervisor cited his division's success in clearing backlogged cases, allowing detectives to attack new ones more aggressively, Albanese interrupted him with an old canard: "So you have a faster response from detectives!" he said. "But that doesn't lower crime!"

The LAPD called a press conference on the killing cycle. Nathan Kouri was ordered to speak, since his investigation was the most advanced. The other cases had stalled. Keep it short, he was told.

Kouri was miserable. Waiting for the press conference to start, stripes of sunshine cutting through the vertical blinds in the Seventy-seventh Street Division community room, he sat in a corner, ignoring the press release someone had placed in his hands.

As the cameras rolled, Kouri found a hiding place behind Albanese, a tall man. Albanese talked of "senseless violence" and remarked that when a suspect is sent to prison "nobody wins—we have to find another way." When it was Kouri's turn, Kyle Jackson had to push him forward with a hand on his back.

Kouri changed color twice, looked sick, then fell silent before the microphone. Sweat glistened on his upper lip. At last, prompted by a reporter, he spoke in a barely audible voice. He credited everybody else for things he had done almost entirely alone over his days of skipping sleep and living on Nutri-Grain bars. "We used numerous resources throughout the department," Kouri intoned, staring at the back wall. "Surveillance. ATF task force. Parole Probation. Various uniform entities."

Afterward, La Barbera was beside himself. Kouri had recently canceled his vacation to compensate for the overtime restrictions. Seeing Kouri, of all people—possibly the hardest-working cop in South Bureau—praise a useless and mostly theoretical "task force" for his own work was almost too much for La Barbera. But Kouri was just relieved to get through it. Fifteen minutes later, the press had packed up their cameras and his complexion had returned to normal.

During the press conference, Kouri had discovered that one of the reporters, Leo Stallworth, had grown up in Nickerson Gardens. Kouri sat down with Stallworth as the rest departed, relaxed, hands clasped on his head, quizzing the reporter about growing up in the Nickersons. "I fought every day! I remember that. I lived in total fear!" Stallworth told Kouri. It was the early seventies, and the gangs were thick there—"You join or you die," Stallworth said. Kouri was delighted—how he loved getting information from a good source. "How'd you get out?" he asked. "Football, man!" Stallworth said.

The five victims of retaliation that week in August fell across a spectrum. Their profiles exposed the falseness of the public's conception of "innocent victims." A thirteen-year-old boy with no tattoos. A twenty-one-year-old working man, clean-cut and decent. A forty-nine-year-old hustler with an old bank robbery rap living off girlfriends. A twenty-nine-year-old gang member trying to get out of the life. His sixteen-year-old cousin, full of promise.

"All those innocent people," Skaggs had once said. In this case, they all were, in a sense. Da'Quawn was the most likely of the five to have been killed for more than his skin color, since he was wearing the bandanna. The others, like Bryant Tennelle, were just unlucky.

And there was no difference in the grief left behind.

Thaddeus Risher's daughter frankly admitted her father's flaws and addictions —"He was a professional hobo!" she said. Even so, she sobbed talking of his murder. She had visions of his body slumped in the car. Tears streamed down her cheeks. She was astonished by the pain. "Does it ever stop?" she pleaded.

At Da'Quawn Allen's funeral, men in double-breasted suits, sunglasses, and earrings sat up front and wept. There was talk of the gang members who had recruited Da'Quawn. One rose to speak: "For him to look up to us—it ain't the way to be," he said. "We gotta give these babies a chance to live."

After the service, teenagers streamed by Da'Quawn's open casket—kissing his corpse, shaking their heads with eyes full of rage, then jamming on caps and stalking away.

At the double funeral for Robert Nelson and Drayvon James, a relative held James's toddler son so that his mother could view James. The mother wept over the open casket. The toddler, held high behind her, stared at his murdered father over her shoulder. His eyes were wide and confused. At last they bore him away. But the toddler twisted and looked back, eyes still fixed on his father's face.

At Christopher Lattier's funeral, a young black man took the podium. "This hurts me and scares me," he rambled, speaking quickly while staring at a point in space. "I'm afraid I'm gonna die."

Outside, the sky was brown from wildfires and the smell of smoke filled the chapel. A second young man rose. "I'm trying to live," he said. "At least to see twenty-one. That's a lot." A stir went through the crowd. A youth pastor sprang to his feet and called the young men back. He placed his hands on their shoulders. "We want better for you than just twenty-one! Understand?" His voice was thick. *"It is possible in our community to live on for a full life!"*

The pastor then called on all the young people present to stand. He told the crowd to place hands on them. *"Protect them from the evil thing that lurks in our community!"* he cried. "Amen! Amen!" the crowd shouted. The young men for whom they prayed wept like children.

Hordes of cops patrolled "the box" for a week or so. Eventually,

Metro officers barged into a Hoover party, arrested several people, and seized some guns. Sal La Barbera considered it the only "good caper" of the surge. But it generated no leads on any homicides.

By fall, his squad had exceeded the overtime allotment and he was sending detectives home to take unplanned days off. La Barbera was feeling moody and pessimistic. His squad too inexperienced. Resources still scarce. Two years since they'd moved to this office, yet the phones still didn't work. His personal problems were mounting. Cases were going unsolved or falling apart.

The suspect in Marullo's case from in front of Barbara Pritchett's house—the killing of Henry Henderson—had been tried unsuccessfully three times without being convicted. The suspect was back in Pritchett's neighborhood. She'd heard rumors he'd been involved in more shootings.

But Pritchett had her own worries. Carlos, her thirteen-year-old brother, had been "hit up" by men down the block. The men belonged to the same gang as the suspects in La'Mere Cook's killing, which remained unsolved. After the hit-up, Dovon's older brother had confronted the men, telling them to leave Carlos alone. Pritchett, learning of this later, was cold with fear. What if her surviving son were also killed? She would lose her mind, she thought. She might even retaliate.

That fall, after all the months of hard work, a mistrial had also been declared in the double-murder case on Laconia. This had been a complete surprise. After seemingly endless relocations, Kouri and Eiman had succeeded in forcing, coaxing, and physically carrying all of the terrified Laconia witnesses into the courtroom. One teenager had pulled the hood of his sweatshirt entirely over his face as he testified, but the marijuana dealer had been impressive on the stand—though she shook so violently that the hem of her T-shirt flapped against her chest.

In the end, however, jurors said they couldn't continue. Four of them said the defendants had mad-dogged them in the courtroom and corridor outside it. A fifth wrote a note saying he'd seen a defendant's relative at his local grocery store and felt menaced.

For the first time, Tom Eiman, Kouri's partner, still new to homicide, felt bad about being a police officer. He felt protective of the marijuana dealer. She was the sort of person he might have arrested in his old narcotics cop job. Now Eiman considered her principled and brave.

She and the other witnesses would have to testify again. "This is asking way too much of them," Eiman seethed. "How can you allow an environment like that and do a mistrial? You leave those jurors in the hallway . . . ?"

To La Barbera, things were not much better than in his early days at Southeast. He had a sense of disintegration: Skaggs bored in Olympic, Marullo bored in his uniform, his own grand project thwarted. Retirement was inching up on him, but La Barbera had no legacy.

He had one consolation. Shortly after Da'Quawn Allen's murder, La Barbera had noticed Kouri at his desk, bent over the case file. La Barbera had given up communicating with Kouri, Marullo's introverted sidekick. But this time, Kouri glanced up and read his mind.

"I got this," he said.

22

THE OPENING

It was cold and sunny the day the Bryant Tennelle murder trial opened.

The decor of Department 105 at the Clara Shortridge Foltz Criminal Justice Center reflected the modern era of public sector economy. Harsh strips of fluorescents overhead threw a dull oatmeal sheen over the courtroom and bounced a metallic glint off the judge's microphone. Slippery blue seat cushions were too short to cover the length of the wooden benches. Oily dark blotches left by weary jurors' heads stained the wall behind the jury box. On the witness stand, a box of tissues stood ready.

There was no one in the courtroom except lawyers and cops. The lawyers looked nervous—no matter how many years in, they never got over the pretrial butterflies. Stirling was flying around the room, tripping over things. His suit jacket was crooked, his hair askew. Colello paced, then sat, hunched. His eyes were red and watery, his skin pale and blotchy. He'd come down with the flu, and the combination of illness and anxiety had reduced him to a ball of misery.

The defense attorneys, Zeke Perlo and Seymour Applebaum, were better at playing it cool. Perlo, who would retire from trial work after this case, ending a forty-six-year career, was wearing a stylish pin-striped suit. Applebaum—not one to overlook such a transgression—flipped over the lapel to expose an Armani label. Perlo protested weakly: "It was on sale!"

But even Perlo and Applebaum's usual enjoyment of the courtroom scene was muted. Applebaum tightened his tie more than was necessary. Perlo jiggled. Only Skaggs seemed unperturbed. He was in a smart gray suit, watching Stirling's antics and shaking his head. His cheekbones were burned from a weekend in the sun; lifelong fair-skinned Californians get sunburned once a year, on the first hot weekend in March, caught slipping after a winter without sunscreen. Balanced in Skaggs's lap was the big blue binder, divided by neat yellow tabs.

Skaggs had faith in Stirling, though the two men were forged from different elements. Once Skaggs had described to Stirling a scene he loved from Steinbeck's *Cannery Row* in which Mack and the boys, "healthy and curiously clean," in Doc's description, keep their backs turned to the Fourth of July parade. The scene appealed to Skaggs—the image of men so immune to popular taste that they were not tempted by the spectacle. But Steinbeck's lyricism, so resonant to Skaggs, was lost on Stirling, who wrinkled his face and asked such obtuse and literal questions ("Well, why were they *there*, then?") that Skaggs grew irritated and cut the conversation short. "You don't get it!" he said. Skaggs and Stirling did not quite interact on the same plane. But Skaggs respected Stirling and they worked well together.

A door on one side of the courtroom opened and all four attorneys subsided into silence, taut and ready, as if awaiting the starter's gun. Devin Davis's round eyes wheeled around the room in a futile search for his mother as he was led in, handcuffed in blue fatigues. His body had finally grown in proportion to his large head; he looked like a man now. But his eyes were as childlike as ever. Derrick Starks entered next, massive shoulders stretching the yoke of an orange jumpsuit.

Judge Bob S. Bowers was tall and lean, with deep furrows on each side of his mouth. His dour expression was lightened only by an occasional glimmer of humor. Everyone stood. Court was in session.

There were some issues to be decided outside the jury's presence.

The testimony of the two witnesses who had disappeared—the man in the wheelchair and the young probationer who had told Skaggs, "Everybody know"—would be read into the record. But first prosecutors had to prove they had done everything possible to find them. In Los Angeles Superior Court, AWOL witnesses were as much a part of the culture as Scotch tape and mismatched furnishings.

Corey Farell took the stand to discuss the disappearance of the man in the wheelchair. Colello questioned him. Stirling sat at his side, anticipating his opening statement with such anxiety that he was bent double, hands over his eyes. Farell told Colello that detectives had tracked the man to another California city, then lost the trail. Farell had checked death records but found nothing to indicate the man had been killed. Perhaps he had finally "gotten out" and put his gang ties behind him, as he had long claimed he wanted to do.

Next Colello brought up the young probationer. Farell recited the nine visits detectives had made to the house, the long discussions with the boy's father. They thought the relationship was going well, he said. Then came an unexpected twist: another Seventy-seventh Street detective, Refugio Garza, had contacted the father, also trying to find his probationer son. It seemed the youth was a witness in yet *another* homicide case.

The story was like so many others: Two years before Bryant Tennelle was shot, the probationer and his friends had crossed into rival gang territory over on the Eastside to visit a girl. They had stopped at a liquor store and exchanged words with a man inside who had ties to the Swans, a Blood gang. The quarrel ended in gunfire. The victim, Marquise Burnett, thirty-four, hadn't been an active gang member in years; he had been working in construction. The probationer had agreed to testify against the shooter, telling Garza that he didn't even know he'd had a gun. But as it became clear that the youth would be taking the stand in not one but *two* homicide trials, his father balked. The young man fled, and the more detectives pressed his father for his whereabouts, the less cooperative he became.

Stirling moved successfully to admit Bryant's photograph, the one

with his jacket thrown over his shoulder. Applebaum then moved successfully to redact "sexually explicit talk" from Starks's letters to Jessica,
prompting Starks to laugh silently and blush lightly.

The discussion was routine. But it kept getting sidetracked because
Stirling introduced arguments where there were none. He rose several
times, moving his hands around, sprinkling his remarks with the phrase
"If I may."

Stirling had a distinct way of gesturing. He framed his hands in front
of him and moved them from side to side as if placing each point he
made in space. Once placed, the various points remained in their places
until finally they were all suspended somewhere in front of his nose. He
would then rearrange them to make his arguments. It was as if he were
stocking shelves with invisible shoeboxes.

Listening to him, Judge Bowers veered between amusement and impatience and at last grimaced, staring balefully as Stirling shuffled his
imaginary shoeboxes. Finally, Bowers chided Stirling for creating confusion and needlessly repeating things. Stirling agreed heartily, repeating
to Bowers exactly what Bowers had just said about repeating. Bowers
glared. Farell, in back of the courtroom, suppressed a laugh. The morning's session was over.

In the afternoon the trial finally began in earnest. By 1:25 P.M., the
hall in front of the courtroom was packed. Rick Gordon was there,
along with half a dozen RHD detectives in natty RHD suits. And a
surprise visitor: Skaggs's wife, Theresa. All week Skaggs had assured her
that this trial was no big deal. Theresa knew him better than that. After
watching Skaggs sweat over every detail of the case all weekend, she
had bidden him goodbye, then dressed nicely and followed him to court.
It was the first of his trials she had attended. Skaggs was clearly pleased.

A few Tennelle family members had arrived: Wally's mother, Dera,
balancing on a cane, and Wally's sister. And then there was Wally Tennelle himself, occupying a halo of empty space in the crowded hallway.
Yadira was not with him. Tennelle was thrumming with tension, his eyes
brimming.

A few months before, Tennelle had dismissed questions about Bryant with a wave of his hand, saying that his grieving was over and he was moving on. But the approach of the trial had stripped him of his defenses. For days he had barely slept. He stood slightly stooped, embarrassed by his tears.

The RHD detectives fell back. But Skaggs walked right up to Tennelle. He clapped him on both shoulders in a hail-fellow-well-met spirit, then turned quickly away, lighthearted, shaking hands all around. Skaggs behaved as if he had not noticed Tennelle's tears. Experience had made him deft with homicide grief: his hearty handshakes, his whole manner lowered the tension palpably.

After the courtroom doors were flung open, the RHD detectives, eleven in all, filled the mismatched office chairs in back of the courtroom. Tennelle composed himself. He dragged a lip balm across his lips, then hunched over, staring at the floor, hands over his mouth.

There were two juries, one for each defendant. As the members filed in, Skaggs adjusted his jacket and studied their faces. In front of him, Starks was doing the same thing.

Perlo put on his glasses and moved his Vitamin Water bottle around on the defense table. Colello performed the same motions at the People's table, using an Arrowhead water bottle. Stirling looked as if he was playing giant solitaire: he had six notepads spread out in front of him and was arranging and rearranging them, leaving no surface of the desk uncovered. When he finished, he sat still, looking slightly nauseated.

Even Skaggs was showing the pressure. His small frown was pulled a little tighter than usual. He sat stock-still.

After the judge delivered his instructions to the jury at agonizing length, Stirling rose. A pause, and the room held its breath. Stirling played with his sleeve. Colello grinned nervously and took a sip from his red plastic cup. Then, as if on cue, the two prosecutors inhaled, and Stirling began.

He started by noting the disappointment on the faces of the jurors when they had been chosen for this trial, and he urged them to make the experience worthwhile. Then he launched into his statement, and it was suddenly clear why Stirling had his job. Gone were the neurotic tics, the

Laurel and Hardy bumblings. His presentation was disciplined and exhaustively thorough, as if he were reading the table of contents of an academic treatise. Perhaps this was why Stirling laughed at himself so easily. There was at least one arena in which he excelled, and he knew it.

He told the jurors they needed a "historical backdrop" to the crime. "You have all heard of the Crips and the Bloods," he said. He launched into the oversimplified version of gang life in L.A. favored by the media and prosecutors. He talked of gangs as though they were rival governments, highly organized and bent on warfare.

By many accounts, the so-called Rollin' Hundreds were a relatively small, inconsequential, disorganized gang whose members were largely blood relations from a single family. But Stirling called it "a conglomerate." Kicking a chair aside to get to the overhead projector, he displayed a map with gang territories blocked out in lavender. It looked like an L.A. version of the board game Risk. The Rollin' Hundreds and the 8-Trey Gangster Crips "are mortal enemies, they hate each other," he said.

Privately, John Skaggs could have done without the gang enhancement legislation and the courtroom gymnastics it required. He thought that if appropriate sentences had been handed down all along for murder the system wouldn't need gang statutes. He wasn't even a big fan of life sentences. Forty years in prison for the killing of another human being—whatever the motive—and be done with it. The sentence wasn't as important as the fact that the killer was caught.

Stirling flipped through one transparency after another like a schoolteacher, his red laser pointer dancing over the screen. Then he introduced the victim, Bryant Tennelle. "He wasn't one to pay much attention to the politics of gang violence," he said. He flashed Bryant's graduation photograph on the screen. The soft smile. The curls. The jacket thrown over his shoulder. Tennelle, who had been sitting with his head down, raised his eyes and stared. A juror noticed and pressed a finger to his lips.

Stirling moved on to the next slide: graffiti, tattoos—Starks's arm tats, the name "Rollin' 100's" and hands forming the letters *b* and *c* for Blocc Crip.

Then Stirling said: "Friday, May 11." Behind him, Wally Tennelle's dress shoes began to tap the vinyl floor. Stirling picked up a paper bag and drew from it a faded black Houston Astros hat, a dry pinkish tint on it. He told the jury, incorrectly, that Wally Tennelle was the first officer on the scene. "The paramedics came, and"—Stirling paused for a long moment, took a sip of water—"he dies."

The prosecutor hadn't told the jurors which of the somber, suit-clad detectives crowding the courtroom was the victim's father. But some seemed to have guessed. They kept glancing toward Tennelle. Bryant's likeness to his father was most plain in the smile. But Detective Tennelle had not smiled. More likely, the jurors were tipped off by the tender grief that clung to him like a cloud.

Stirling talked and talked, methodically chronicling the seizure of the gun and its identification. Derrick watched him closely. Perlo made occasional pro forma objections. But for the most part, the trial seemed to unfold on cruise control. Stirling concluded with a terse admonition: "Keep an open mind, everybody."

Zeke Perlo rose. He spoke softly, plainly, extemporaneously, barely glancing at his notes. Unlike Stirling, Perlo was the same in front of a jury as he was on the street. He struck a reasonable, confidential tone that conveyed to jurors that he wouldn't try to put anything over on them. He didn't speak for long. He didn't need to prove guilt beyond a reasonable doubt, as Stirling did. He had only to show the weaknesses in Stirling's case. He told the jurors that the defense would concede much of the evidence but would call into question the credibility of the man in the wheelchair, who he said was pressured by police, and of Jessica Midkiff. He pointed out that she hadn't come forward on her own, and she had reason to be angry at Starks. Starks sat with arms folded as his lawyer talked, looking over the jury. The judge rose; the day in court was over. As they exited the courthouse, a cold hard wind hit the jurors.

By the second day of the trial, the wind had died and the first orange

California poppies were blooming on roadway medians. Devin Davis's mother appeared in a gray suit, and one of his sisters also came. Davis, at the defendant's table in tie and slightly rumpled white shirt, smiled at them.

It was time for the second jury to hear the opener. Throughout the trial, the dance of the two juries would make life complex for bailiff Dontae Hardy. Both juries were present for some testimony, but were separated for other portions. When both were in court, a section of the audience benches was marked off with police tape to accommodate them all. It made for close quarters. One day, Wally Tennelle sat elbow to elbow with Starks's mother, Olitha.

Stirling gave the Davis jury the same treatment the Starks jury had received the previous day.

This time he left Bryant's picture—the soft lips, the jacket thrown over the shoulder—up for a while. Wally Tennelle pulled his eyes away with effort, then kept glancing back at the photo.

Arielle Walker, as pretty and fluttery as ever, was a swirl of blond extensions and big swingy earrings on the witness stand. She declared that she had been dating Bryant for four and a half months. This absurdly meticulous timekeeping reminded everyone in the courtroom that these were just a bunch of teenagers, after all.

Arielle pursed her lips and began to cry when Stirling showed her Bryant's senior picture, and she cried through the rest of her testimony, sniffling and squeaking and wiping a tissue theatrically across her face, long orange fingernails flashing.

Arielle's testimony had the feel of a performance that, though entwined with authentic grief, was so saturated with adolescent self-regard that it negated all emotion. The jury seemed unmoved.

Bryant's friend Walter Lee Bridges was next, looking right at Phil Stirling with his solemn dark brown eyes, the tattoo on his neck plainly visible. Stirling asked him to step down from the witness stand to show where he was when the shots were fired. Walter, with a bearing far be-

yond eighteen, detached the microphone and raised it to his lips me-
chanically to answer Stirling's questions.

Stirling was finding his rhythm. He was a blur of horizontal and,
strangely, vertical motion. He questioned and pointed, bobbing up and
down and tugging his jacket. His movements were part of the courtroom atmosphere by then. At a couple of points, he even knelt on the
floor. But because it seemed such a natural extension of all his other
absurd tics, no one batted an eye.

Walter's testimony describing the shots was the third time that Bryant's death had played out in court that afternoon. Wally Tennelle
kneaded his hands.

Next on the stand was Josh, describing Bryant's injuries in detail, as
Wally Tennelle covered his mouth. Josh was the fourth of the teenagers
who had been at the scene to testify that day. All of them spoke as if they
still saw an image hovering somewhere just beyond their vision—that
image of Bryant, his head blown open, dying on the grass before their
eyes. The submerged horror in their faces made their testimony crush-
ingly credible. As Josh walked out of the courtroom, Skaggs laid an
approving hand on his shoulder.

The night before the third day of the trial, Skaggs was out on a homicide that had "broken open" in the middle of the night. A car had
been found. Leads were suddenly pouring in. The suspect was the son
of a Superior Court judge.

But Skaggs did not look tired when he arrived in court in his dapper
gray suit. He sat down in his usual spot in the first row behind Starks
and Davis, chewing gum, and studied his black leather notebooks filled
with little jottings in black ink.

Starks was in one of the two pullover sweaters he wore each day of
the trial. Davis, in his tie, was sitting nervously with a fist over his mouth,
the proceedings suddenly real.

Tennelle appeared, smiling and relaxed. His brother had come up
from San Diego for the trial, and the whole family had gone to supper
at a super-trendy downtown restaurant called Palm the night before.

Tennelle had eaten nearly nothing and was still grousing about the high prices, drawing good-natured ribbing from his mother and sister.

Judge Bowers entered and Stirling stood. "The people call Wallace Tennelle," he said.

Tennelle rose with a frozen, intent look on his face, walked to the witness stand, and sat.

Stirling asked him to spell his name.

Tennelle began crisply. "W-a-l-l-a-c-e." But then he faltered. "T-e," he said, and broke off. A pause. No one seemed to breathe.

"T-e," Tennelle began again. But tears flowed and he could not continue. Jurors, attorneys—everyone froze. The seconds ticked by. Tennelle sat, in the dark blue RHD suit he had clearly chosen for the occasion, fighting for composure. In the jury box, hands clenched and lips tightened.

He wept. Then he recovered, straightened, and broke down again, conducting an excruciating battle with himself in front of a room full of people, unable to spell his own last name. "T-e-n-n-e-l-l-e," he fought out at last in a broken voice, barely audible.

Skaggs, his face impassive, knotted his fingers together. Tennelle's effort at self-control was wrenching, more thunderous than any of Arielle's histrionics. Having finally spelled his name, he dabbed his eyes with a tissue and returned Stirling's gaze with effort.

"How many children do you have?"

"Three," Tennelle said. "Well—" He caught himself. "Two, now."

He looked shrunken in the chair. In the jury box, no one moved.

"Did you have a son named Bryant?"

Tennelle emitted a tiny gasp. "Yes—yeah. Yes."

Stirling asked him what he did for a living. Tennelle raised his chin.

This time, his voice came clear and strong: "I am a detective for the City of Los Angeles."

Stirling walked the witness through the events of May 11. Tennelle gave weary answers in his quick-paced Alabama lilt. But as the narrative drew closer to the actual bullets—and the image of his son on the ground—he began to rock back and forth. He sighed deeply between phrases and pressed on, soldiering past the baseball cap, the blood—speaking, despite the rough emotion in his voice, with a detective's precision in that strange cop language of street numbers, picayune detail, and direction, easts and wests. He told of parking the car, securing the witness, and proceeding eastbound on Eightieth to reach "my boy."

Tennelle got through all of this. Then Stirling asked why he didn't go with Bryant in the ambulance. Tennelle said it was because—and here was the part that always blasted him—because, he said, choking with sobs, he had to go back home and "tell my wife."

The defense attorneys had no desire to prolong this. They asked no questions. Tennelle reeled from the witness stand.

Most of the spectators were teary-eyed. Stirling, who never seemed to make any effort to hide his emotions, retreated to the back of the courtroom to blow his nose.

But the jurors were not crying. They were stone-faced, focused on their job. Skaggs had never found a jury so hard to read.

Slides of the crime scene flashed by on the screen. Palm trees against the sky. Blood on the ground.

At the defense table, Davis's mother fussed over her son's attire, frequently appealing to Applebaum about some detail of his appearance. Almost every day, sheriff's deputies would deliver a coat hanger with a dress shirt on it for Devin. Inevitably, they carried the hanger carelessly, and the shirt arrived askew and wrinkled. Their indifference must have felt like the sharpest contempt to the always proper and neatly dressed Sandra James.

On the fifth day of the trial, Yadira Tennelle appeared in the courtroom, a heart-shaped locket at her throat.

Yadira remained stock still as the recorded sound of Davis's sniffling voice flooded the courtroom: "I didn't want to hurt nobody! I was just trying to fit in!" Davis shook his head violently as the tape rolled. A juror placed a hand on his forehead. Yadira kept her head up, arms folded, the sadness in her face so deep it seemed ancient.

Skaggs's turn on the stand came that day, too.

The chair seemed too small for his knees and elbows, an effect heightened by the giant blue binder he gripped in his hands. He half turned toward the jurors so they could see his face, fixing them with the blue eyes under the blond eyebrows, and he used a pointer and map as a teacher would. He was in command, calm and pleasant. Only once did Applebaum succeed in rattling him.

Applebaum was trying to make the case that Skaggs had overpowered the vulnerable and confused teenager Devin Davis. Under his questioning, Skaggs acknowledged that he sometimes lied to suspects to extract the truth. And, yes, he sought to manipulate them.

"You are a very persistent investigator, aren't you?" Applebaum demanded. Skaggs hesitated. But his confusion quickly passed. A half smile flickered across his face and his features resolved into their usual self-assurance. He returned Applebaum's gaze with conviction. "Yes!" he said.

There was no room for false modesty in Skaggs's world. He was, in truth, a very persistent investigator.

23

"WE HAVE TO PRAY FOR PEACE"

"Salvation, not retaliation!" cried a voice outside the unit in Nickerson Gardens.

Inside, curled on the beige-specked linoleum floor, lay the body of a young man. He lay half rolled on his side, almost on his stomach, eyes closed, a sleepy, comfortable position like that of a napping child. One of his arms was stretched out straight along the floor. A hand clutched a few bills, tens and fives—a total of forty-five dollars. He had brown hair, grown out a little, and brown skin, and he was neither tall nor short, thin nor fat. Rather, he had that perfect, fully formed middle build, the birthright of healthy young men of his age, which was twenty-nine—that moment in men's lives when adolescence is fully shed and age not yet visible. A mazy web of faded tattoos covered his naked back. From under his torso seeped a large amount of blood, so much that it had pooled on the linoleum. There was a single sweeping brush-stroke through it, perhaps from paramedics, or a last sweep of the young man's outstretched arm in death.

The room was empty except for a green Schwinn bicycle on its side, the upholstery torn from the seat, a blue Calypso soda on the counter-top, and a shell casing on the floor. It was early in the morning. Somehow, the pallid California light streaming through the half-open door and the steel grates of the window above had washed away the shabbiness of this unit in the Nickerson Gardens public housing project, with its tan walls, peeling paint, and huge institutional fire alarm on the wall. The light had transformed architect Paul Revere Williams's small apartment unit into a bright and peaceful country cottage, its rays settling softly over the contours of the murdered young man's smooth skin like a baby's blanket, the most pitiful sight in the world.

Nathan Kouri was moving in and out of the room in a dark suit, a black leather notebook clutched to his chest, an intent wrinkle shaped like a little *v* in his forehead. He was processing the crime scene. The cries of "Salvation!" were coming from a knot of people outside. A woman in Ugg boots was preaching: "We have to pray for peace!"

Michael Scott had been shot inside unit 88 of the project at 115th and Success Avenue early in the morning of March 13, 2010. His body had been found by the woman he called his wife. The sun was just beginning to burn through the night's mist as a crowd gathered to watch the police investigate.

The crowd coalesced into little knots among the geraniums, wafts of marijuana smoke drifting between them, the preacher's voice rising over murmurs and the thwack of pigeon wings in the wires overhead. Southeast patrol and gang officers were out in force for this emotional crowd with its rows of haunted eyes—stunned-looking eleven-year-old boys with earrings, weeping fifteen-year-old girls with Rococo cell phones.

Scott's family sat outside the unit on white plastic chairs, his grieving mother hunched in slippers, a pack of Aquafina water bottles at her feet. Her eyes were closed. Her head tilted skyward, her chest heaving. Off to one side, a man sat on a curb, head in his hands, shaking with sobs.

A woman appeared at the mother's side and embraced her: it was Barbara Pritchett. The mother was a dear friend. Barbara remained by her side throughout the morning, stroking her hair, watching the cops.

Nate Kouri had been scurrying out of sight, pen on his lapel, jacket askew over his gun. He was deep in thought, juggling too many objects at once—yellow plastic placards, notebook, manila envelopes, plastic bags. At last he emerged to talk to Scott's mother. Pritchett saw him.

She threw her arms around him—right there, in front of everyone in the projects. She knew people from her neighborhood might look askance at her for embracing a cop. But she didn't care. "Nathan!" she cried. "You tied to this?"

Twenty-eight uniformed cops formed a skirmish line so that Scott's body could be brought out to the waiting coroner's van. They stayed far back: "friendlies" in the crowd had promised the cops they would keep the crowd from rushing the corpse, a common hazard. A few officers chafed at the liberties being granted to the emotional Nickerson crowd. "They ought to be pushed back to a hundred and fourteenth," one grumbled, eyeing the knots of teenagers.

The coroner's van with its blue lettering pulled up, orange lights flashing. A stretcher rolled out of the unit, bearing the corpse in a blue body bag. Emotion caromed through the crowd at the sight of it. Someone cried out. A few people pressed forward. The friendlies hollered at them. "Stay calm!" As her son's body passed her, the mother cried out and collapsed. "*Oh no, no, no!* Mikey, oh Mike!" she gasped. Her head lolled to the side with grief as the officers, watching from afar, drew in their lips, their faces betraying a trace of the anguish unfolding before them.

Scott had been in a gang. His rap sheet was almost twenty pages long. His murder was related to drug dealing, or some arcane argument within the gang. But there was more to the story, as always. Scott had almost escaped the life. He had fallen in love with a girl. They had fled to Bakersfield, where he got a good job in a glass molding plant and for a while was earning thirty bucks an hour. Then the recession hit. He lost his job. The couple had moved back to Los Angeles. They were just moving into the empty unit when he was killed.

Scott had a number of friends and relatives who were also in the gang. When Kouri and a detective named Gerry Pantoja sat down with one of them for an interview after the murder, he was frank about what was on his mind: "I hound this stuff myself . . . I'll kill that 'un myself," he told them. The man was almost apologetic about it.

"Don't do that," Kouri counseled quietly. "You all don't get 'em."

Kouri was by now running crime scenes with a sure hand. He had always insisted that he could never be as natural as his mentor, John Skaggs. So he had sought to make up for his supposed deficiencies by working harder than anyone else.

It turned out that his ability to work hard was its own brand of genius. Through endurance, focus, and sheer earnest effort, Kouri had found in himself his own version of Skaggs's relentlessness.

Kouri worried less about not being able to talk to people. He had discovered he could be effective simply by trying to reason with people without affectation, using the manner that came most naturally to him, stumbling over his words if he had to. He was not smooth. But he was sincere and nonadversarial, and people trusted him.

More important, Kouri's commitment to the craft had deepened with every case. This was really the key to his success: his emotional response to working homicide. He was open and sensitive enough to take in the misery of the people involved in his cases. He allowed their pain and terror to rework his understanding of the work he did.

Like Skaggs, like Skaggs's father before him, Kouri had found nothing was the same after working homicide. He could no longer invest any other type of police work with the same conviction. Homicide investigations had opened his eyes. Before, he hadn't understood the depths of grief and trauma in Watts—never comprehended the pain set in motion by each murder. In all his years in uniform, "I never saw it. Then you do these interviews. It's a whole 'nother world," he said.

His cases had shifted his allegiances. He had come to sympathize with the same people against whom he had directed the harshest doubts when he wore a blue uniform. Hustlers, drug dealers, prostitutes, probation violators had become his witnesses, his suffering family members, all united with him against the Monster. "I don't care who they are. It impacts them," he said.

Kouri no longer shared the views of some of his uniformed colleagues, who parroted the clichés insisting that the people of Watts lacked "values" and didn't value life. "Until you live it, you can't fully understand it."

Far from his commanders' assertions that detective work was "reactive," or that faster response from detectives would not lower crime, Kouri had become quietly convinced that solving ghettoside homicide cases was worth almost any price.

He believed in his heart that violence comes first—that law is built on the state's response to violence—and that responding was better than preventing. It was more true to the spirit of the law—and in the long run, more effective. This belief, more than anything else, made an ordinary investigator into a great one. Earlier that year, the Laconia case had finally concluded. It had been more than eighteen months since the murders. After the mistrial came a new trial. All of the witnesses were dragged through the ordeal of testifying again. This time, all four defendants were convicted.

As usual, by the end, the only people watching in the courtroom were parents. The mother of one defendant ran out just before the verdicts were read—just the sight of the manila envelope in the judge's hand was too much for her. When the judge said "guilty," victim Raymond Requeña's mother dropped her head and covered her eyes.

But the costs were great. One witness had been a promising high school student. Over the course of two trials, and various threats and relocations, he dropped out. The marijuana dealer ended up living far from the 'hood, where she had no means of support, and was beaten up at least twice. After one incident, Kouri came to see her and found her with a row of blue stitches across her forehead. She was relocated far from her family and her customers, and she continued calling Kouri for help with various personal problems for years after the trial.

Asked later why she had agreed to cooperate in the case, enduring threats and beatings for the sake of justice in the state courts, she gave a short answer. "I trust Nate," she said.

Kouri ended up handing off the Michael Scott case to Pantoja, who solved it, and the killer was convicted.

Unbeknownst to the detectives, Barbara Pritchett spent hours as the case unfolded arguing and pleading with various friends and acquaintances. They wanted to retaliate. Pritchett begged them not to. They did not believe the police would solve it. *Give the cops a chance*, Pritchett countered. Over and over, she invoked the name of Nathan Kouri, whom she had hugged at the crime scene. Kouri was one of the good ones, Pritchett assured her friends. There was no need to strike back; they could trust him. She no longer talked of the need for John Skaggs to come back.

By that spring, in the closing days of the Tennelle case, La Barbera had to finally admit that Kouri was the talented apprentice he had so long hoped to find. He'd been their man all along, the real Li'l Skaggs, the personification of vigor in the face of societal indifference. Kouri was now what Seymour Applebaum had accused John Skaggs of being: "a very persistent investigator." In Skaggs's world, there was no higher compliment.

Daylight savings time arrived over the second week of the trial, so working days now ended in sunlit evenings. Perlo and Skaggs both now had the flu that had started with John Colello. It had made the rounds of the courtroom. Perlo joked that his coughing would win sympathy from the jurors.

It was Jessica's turn. Stirling had never had the faith in her that Skaggs had. She remained for him ever a prostitute, a street person, and, after all, the driver of a murderer's car. Midkiff offered the defense so many opportunities to discredit her. Even her repeated relocations might be portrayed in court as prosecutorial favors.

Stirling also feared the case being hurt should Midkiff grow testy or temperamental under defense questioning. The prosecution's theory that Starks had directed the murder relied heavily on her account. The cell phone records, the Suburban, and the many independent points of corroboration between Midkiff's and Davis's testimony amounted to quite a bit of evidence. But without Midkiff testifying well, the case would be much weaker.

Stirling had devoted much of the work of preparing for this trial to Jessica—asking her questions, allowing her to read her prior statement. He and Colello had met with her until late the previous night. Still, Stirling remained nervous. Her performance at the preliminary hearing had not reassured him, and this time, he worried, the high-pressure conditions of trial could push her over.

Skaggs, too, appeared uncharacteristically edgy. Later he would blame it on the discomfort of the flu. But it was also true that much of his work on this case rode on Midkiff's performance.

But this Jessica Midkiff was not the same chain-smoking, girlish young woman of two years ago. She was twenty-five now, seeing her daughter regularly, and she was within ten points of passing her GED exam—she had only to boost her math score. Her handsome new boyfriend was kind and decent. He had a job. It was miraculous, given where Jessica had been not so long before.

But what most impressed Skaggs was not the educational gains, not the sobriety, not the boyfriend, but the fact that Jessica had taken to *working out at a gym.* She was learning kickboxing. This fit well with Skaggs's notions of a wholesome life.

Jessica walked in all in black, long sleeves and high heels, with a gold cross around her neck. The dyed streak in her hair was gone. Her dark locks were pulled into a tight braid down her back. The braid plus her plucked eyebrows made a sharp, pious contrast with her vanilla complexion. On the stand, she heaved a sigh, lifting her shoulders once and dropping them. Then she leaned forward into the mike, her face serious and sad. This time, there were no opportunities for the discomforting sexual energy that had unnerved her at the preliminary hearing; she did not glance at Starks. Stirling began.

Jessica answered Stirling's questions one after another. There was no repeat of the dramatics of her earlier appearance, the tears or the temper. Instead, with a serious delivery and a small frown, Jessica plodded through her story, pausing now and then to look at the ceiling, or scooch up her mouth, trying to remember details now dim, admitting it readily when she couldn't recall them. Slowly, methodically, Stirling elicited all the details that Skaggs had first drawn out at the Seventy-seventh Street station so long ago, on the night when the Tennelle case "broke open." Matching Stirling's methodical tone, she related her story, the antithesis of the alternatively weeping and cutesy probationer Skaggs had first met in a jail cell in December 2007. In the back of the courtroom, Olitha Starks listened with her face twisted in skeptical disgust. She had been accompanied this day by a woman who sat next to her and regarded Midkiff with a look of blank hostility. Midkiff did not look back.

Skaggs gripped his hands together or played with his pen. Once, Jessica tilted her head up to view some point on the map, and her neck tattoo became fully visible to the jury. As the testimony wore on, she looked cold, sinking in her chair and drawing in her shoulders. But she missed no cue.

She was perhaps just a little too affectedly ladylike (she made an unnecessary show of delicacy when Stirling asked her if she'd been "intimate" with Starks), but apart from that, Stirling could not have asked for a better witness. He sat down and braced himself.

But neither Applebaum nor Perlo went after Midkiff. They cross-examined her in a perfunctory, careful manner, Perlo trying to build a case that Midkiff also knew the man in the wheelchair's cousin Bobby Ray Johnson, twenty-six, nicknamed "Gutta," whom investigators believed had been stabbed to death by one of his own comrades from the Bloccs in 2008. Perlo was planning to try to pin the murder on Johnson later in the trial.

Applebaum did manage to summon a little of Midkiff's old combativeness when he asked why she had at first hidden from police. "You didn't want to get caught?" he asked. "No," Midkiff snapped. "Who would?" But the cross-examination Stirling dreaded never materialized. Good defense attorneys know that if a witness is telling the truth, it can only hurt their case to attack. Midkiff stepped down without having lost an ounce of self-possession. As she passed the bench where Tennelle sat on her way out of the courtroom, he whispered to her, "Thank you."

.   .   .

On what was supposed to be the last day of testimony, an earthquake hit. People across the region were awakened at 4:30 A.M. by a 4.4 temblor under Pico Rivera.

John Skaggs, of course, was already awake. Further rattled was Arielle Walker, who was by then complaining to Skaggs about what she said were cars with tinted windows parking in front of her house since her testimony. She was convinced she was being threatened. Skaggs was not so sure.

Half of the jury, it seemed, was coughing and sneezing. The lineup offered no relief: a coroner's investigator and Rubin, the weapons analyst. Numbing talk of "muzzle climb" and "lead cores." The state patrol officer who arrested Starks in the Suburban testified. Then came the "gang expert," Sheriff's Detective Daniel Leon of the Lennox station, a crew cut and a chin in a light beige suit clutching an attaché case by the handle.

Leon spoke with confidence of the gangs' undying hatred of each other and the brazenness of their face tattoos as if he were describing some exotic tribe. They lived for "putting in work," he said. Leon's testimony was supposed to back up the gang enhancement charges in the prosecution's case. But when Stirling showed Leon graffiti of a downpointing arrow—perhaps the most universal bit of gang shorthand in L.A., it means "this is our turf"—Leon could not tell him what it meant. Skaggs, watching, looked pained. Later, again, Leon failed to recognize graffiti containing the initials "S.C." Stirling had to tell him the obvious: "South Central."

A state-ordered furlough day due to budget cuts would put off the trial's conclusion for one more day. The defense felt the walls closing in. A glum Zeke Perlo summed up week two: the prosecution, he said, "was building a monster of a case."

But Phil Stirling was still nervous. The central problem—proving Starks's culpability—remained elusive. Everything, including Midkiff's testimony, had gone as well as possible for the prosecution. But there was no telling how the jury saw it. Like Skaggs, Stirling was unnerved by the stony faces in the jury box. If the jurors thought Jessica was more involved than she let on, or that Davis had taken the initiative to kill on his own, the case against Starks could still be weakened. The long, hot furlough day fell on a Wednesday and prolonged the suspense.

On Thursday, when the trial resumed, Devin Davis initially refused to come out of his cell. He was despondent. Five deputies were stationed in the courtroom to watch him in case he misbehaved.

Then Perlo stood and delivered a thunderbolt.

"The defense calls Derrick Starks," he said.

Perlo had spent the previous day and night pleading with his client not to take the stand. Perlo had a plan. It was not to tear apart the prosecution's case—he had gone through the pages and pages of Skaggs's investigation without spotting a hole—but rather to build a credible alternative theory of the murder, enough to sow doubt and confusion in the jury's mind. If Jessica's testimony could be called into question, there were plenty of other ways that the car and the gun and Bryant Tennelle might have come together without Derrick Starks. Chiefly, he planned to show that Bobby Ray Johnson, the cousin of the man in the wheelchair, had had access to all of them. He did not want any facts to come out that would conflict with the alternate theory, a strong possibility if the prosecution got hold of Starks.

He saw another danger: that Starks's testimony could open the way to the admission of evidence the judge had excluded. He hadn't had high hopes for the case before this. But at least he had a defense. An argument. Starks's testimony could ruin it.

But nothing he said made any difference. Starks, watching the prosecution take shape before him, had decided his attorney was incompetent. So now he swung his way into the stand, scooted around a little in the chair to get comfortable, and took a deep breath. Perlo, questioning him, did his best to conceal his dismay from the jury.

Starks had been working on a goatee during the trial. It was brown and neatly trimmed, with a little peak that ran up the middle of his chin. He wore a tan shirt, a maroon tie, and a small, self-confident smile. His mustache clung to the corners of his lips and his collar did not quite lie flat. His eyes had deep shadows above and below. From where the jury sat, the little tattoo under his eye looked like a birthmark. His face softened for an instant when his eyes fixed on his mother.

"Are you a member of the Blocc Crips?" Perlo asked. "Yes," Starks said, and they were off.

Starks was taking the "I'm no angel but I didn't do it" tack. He was all that the gang "experts" alleged, he said, but he had been out of town in North Carolina at the time of the murder. He had left a week before Bryant's death and heard about the murder after he returned. He had gone east to help a cousin move. She lived near Charleston, was pregnant, he said, and needed his truck. He was not in the Suburban when Jessica had the accident, he said. He had come running to see what had happened and got arrested.

Perlo took his time between questions, his expression flat. Starks rocked and swung slightly in the chair as he answered. At the noon break, Starks walked away from the stand with a little rolling step.

After the break, Devin Davis sauntered into court. His shirt was untucked, and now he was joking with bailiff Hardy and with Applebaum. Perlo resumed, and Starks offered the version of the case that Perlo had hoped to make plausible: *Johnson had sold his cousin the gun. Johnson had been running with Jessica at the time of the murder.* Starks was still swinging slightly, as if he heard music in his head. He seemed relaxed, rocking his head back and forth between questions, glancing periodically at the clock. Perlo finished and bowed his head.

Phil Stirling stood up. He crumpled a piece of paper in his hand and flung it down with a flourish.

Then he pounced.

Everything was fair game. He brought up Starks's recent criminal history—robbery, attempted burglary—and then laid into his story. He forced Starks to recount every detail of the trip to North Carolina, what he'd done every day, what he had eaten, whom he had stayed with. Starks grew noticeably tense. He pressed his lips together between answers, and he stopped swinging in his chair.

Stirling had calculated distances and driving times. He asked Starks how much gas his tank held and tested him on when and where he had stopped for gas. Starks was trapped into insisting he had driven at eighty miles per hour all the way to Baton Rouge, Louisiana barely stopping, amped up on energy drinks and NoDoz before heading up to North Carolina. Stirling asked about people he had seen on the way. Starks recalled some relatives but said he couldn't remember others.

The situation played to Stirling's strengths. He barely glanced at his notes. He did not bother to point out that Charleston was in South Carolina, that no one could drive that fast, that a man facing murder charges might be expected to at least try to corroborate his alibi. He didn't need to.

Starks said a cousin picked him up for the last leg of the journey from Louisiana to North Carolina. Stirling prodded. Starks said he couldn't recall in what type of car they rode. He mentioned another passenger. Stirling pressed. "I can't recall his name," Starks said. "You have been in jail two and a half years. Have you made an effort to learn that person's name?" Stirling asked.

By the end, Starks was asserting that he had stayed in houses in places he couldn't remember, occupied by people whose names he didn't know. He couldn't say who he was carpooling with, he said, because "I was pretty much inebriated through the whole way," drinking Courvoisier and smoking marijuana. He said he couldn't recall whether it was day or night when he departed.

Starks was stiff, but he faced Stirling squarely. Once, between answers, he drew a hand over his forehead in a gesture of exhaustion. Perlo suffered silently through his client's self-destruction, a finger over his lips, one leg jiggling.

Davis, watching from the defense table, appeared relaxed and jovial, as if he had given up. Skaggs went out to take a phone call and returned smiling a little irrepressible smile. A bunch of DAs had filed into the courtroom. Something was up.

But first, Stirling took Starks to task on all the recorded material from jail that up until now had been kept out of court. He was now able to introduce Starks's jailhouse reproach to Davis that "you should have kept your mouth shut," and his "bitch be squealing" remark in reference to Midkiff. "I was talking about somebody else," Starks said. But his voice was weak.

Finally, Stirling introduced Starks's threat against Skaggs on the jail tape. He displayed the transcript and asked Starks to confirm that he had said, "If I were to kill a copper, it'd be Detective Skagg"—the "tall white boy" he described as wearing only a shirt and a tie but no jacket.

"I don't recall," Starks said. Through it all, Olitha Starks kept gazing at the ceiling, a trace of a wan smile on her face.

The Starks jury at last betrayed a faint emotion: impatience with Starks's routine. Perlo noted it. The defense disaster was nearly complete.

Stirling returned to Starks's alibi, got him to insist again that he had been out of town on the night before the killing when Midkiff said they had stayed at the Desert Inn.

Then, without fanfare, Stirling laid a small slip of blue paper on the overhead projector.

It was rectangular and lined—an old-style motel receipt. It bore the Desert Inn logo, the hotel's name in a retro font with a palm tree. And it was dated 5-10-07. Also on the receipt were the printed name D. Starks, a driver's license number, and a signature.

The jurors peered. Stirling pointed to the slip and forced Starks to admit that it was his driver's license number and, grudgingly, that "it looks like my signature."

"Nothing further," Stirling said, and sat down.

After court adjourned, John Colello couldn't contain himself. "That's it!" he cried, rising from his seat and turning toward his fellow DAs in back. In the corridor, Stirling gave John Skaggs one of his awkward hugs. "A seven-year-old could have done that," he said. "A seven-year-old could have tried that case!"

The motel receipt was Skaggs's final contribution to the case. Prompted by Starks's testimony, he had sent Matt Gares, one of his young detectives from Olympic, down to the Desert Inn at the break. Gares had driven the length of the city in search of the receipt. Skaggs had given Gares no particular instruction for this assignment, except the usual one: "Do whatever you have to do."

Gares did. It meant searching through scores of tiny, flimsy receipts in the back office of the motel.

The management bundled the receipts in little stacks for each day. But when Gares looked, there was no stack from May 10, 2007.

So he went through the next day's receipts, and then the next. No luck. He went back in time. It was like the way Skaggs went back to knock on a door again and again. Just keep going, keep pushing, until that door opens. In the end, Gares resigned himself to searching randomly through box after box.

At length, he found the missing receipts. They had been filed by mistake under May 27. Gares pulled out what he was looking for: the little blue slip marked "D. Starks."

Court convened that Friday, the nineteenth of March, a cloudy, cool day. Stirling sported a shiny yellow tie that looked like trim from a bridesmaid's dress, and Colello was finally healthy. For the first time since the trial began, the pair appeared relaxed. Devin Davis had spent Starks's time on the stand nudging Applebaum over and over to confirm his suspicion that Starks was badly muffing it—"That's bad, right?" Now he, too, seemed relaxed, ready for it to be over. Even Starks seemed looser than usual, smiling at his family in the back, as if relieved.

Skaggs was called to confirm that he was likely the "tall white boy" wearing a shirt and a tie but no jacket that Starks had mentioned. Yes, he said, that's how he dressed on the job. Yes, he said, he did wear a jacket sometimes: for court appearances and always at the scene of a murder. His face was grave: to Skaggs the homicide dress code was a serious matter.

By 10:45 A.M., it was over, except for closing arguments. Yadira Tennelle looked exhausted.

• • •

Closing arguments stretched over two days, since each of the two juries got a separate rendition. John Colello closed the prosecution's case against Davis. He had a touch of color in his neck and cheeks, heightening the emotion in his delivery as he pounded home to the jury, once again, each and every element of the prosecution's massive case. He was a tad bathetic and indulged in prosecutorial clichés. He held up an imaginary gun and yelled *"bam, bam, bam"* to reprise Davis's motions.

Applebaum rose, stroked his beard, and leaned on his beloved lectern. He began speaking, his hands in his pockets, a watercooler pose, jiggling coins or keys in one pocket as he talked. He sought to address the emotion of the case, acknowledging how charged it was to be defending Devin Davis in sad circumstances such as this, and he deftly sought to neutralize the trial's most affecting moment. "It's hard," he said. "John Colello here was almost in tears. All of us were almost in tears. Including me! Nothing worse than to see a hardened RHD detective . . . up here with tears running down his face." But he begged the jurors to be dispassionate.

He argued for second-degree murder on the basis of intent. Starks's intent had been to kill, but Davis, Applebaum said, had no idea of what he had gotten himself into until the last instant. He proceeded to hammer at what points he could. There weren't many—that Midkiff had testified to Starks's controlling ways, that nothing about the shooting suggested that Davis was particularly intentional or focused, and that much of the evidence suggested he was drugged out of his mind, terrified of Starks, and acting under pressure.

Applebaum mentioned that "Devin had snot coming out of his nose" and was crying for his mother during the confession. The image effectively reminded jurors of Davis's age. Applebaum used John Skaggs's relentlessness against him. "Because he was a police officer's son, they are not holding back," he said. Finally, Applebaum attacked Stirling's tedious use of clicking slides, a point guaranteed to be a crowd-pleaser, since the jurors had endured two weeks of remorseless PowerPoint torture at the hands of the prosecution. "I don't need to show you a slide show," Applebaum said contemptuously. "I want to *talk* to you about this."

But for all his skills, Applebaum's most effective argument was sitting at the defense table. Jurors had watched the big-eyed, moon-headed, overweight Devin Davis fidget, fuss, yawn, and chuckle throughout the trial. The prosecution was trying to portray him as "sophisticated, smart," Applebaum said. As he spoke, Davis sat back, his legs stretched out, feet poking out from under the defense table like a bored schoolboy. Applebaum motioned toward him once or twice. "If he is so smart, why would he put the tattoos on after he is in jail?" More likely, he was just trying to survive, Applebaum said.

The unspoken implication was clear: to suggest that Davis was a calculating criminal capable of premeditated first-degree murder was ridiculous; *just look at the kid.*

Phil Stirling's rebuttal was so repetitive—he even reprised the panto-mime of gunfire, *"boom-boom-boom!"*—that the judge chastised him for being redundant.

So much talk. John Skaggs had work to do. Forced to sit still through these overly long closing arguments was the worst kind of punishment imaginable for him. As the long day in court wore on, Skaggs had gone from irritated to seething without moving any part of his body except his mouth, which had grown steadily tighter. Wasting time appeared to affect even his circulation: his skin had grown pale.

The next morning, the Starks jury got their closings. Stirling stood up, his voice ragged and hoarse. He adjusted his jacket, yanked his chair around, and began by saying that he would try not to be too redundant, then was, repeating the prosecution's case once again, giving due spot-light to what he called the "Perry Mason moment" when the D. Starks motel receipt had gone up on the screen.

Then Zeke Perlo stood to give the last closing of his career under circumstances that could only be described as a defense rout. He had been unusually quiet all morning.

Maybe the jurors felt for his predicament, for they seemed especially attentive. Like Applebaum, Perlo was relaxed, mature, conversational. His pen in one hand, folded glasses in the other, he gestured naturally. He began his attempt at damage control by saying, "I wouldn't expect you to believe Derrick Starks's testimony—but don't decide based on that."

He argued that the jurors needed to evaluate how much of the mountain of evidence that had been heaped on them really pertained to Starks's presence at the scene. This critical point, he said, was thin. The man in the wheelchair had reason to lie. Midkiff was not the innocent she pretended to be, he said. Was she an accomplice? He methodically sifted through the eyewitness testimony, noting the inconsistencies. Applebaum, who had come in late to observe, wore a look of quiet sympathy. Perlo was making the best of it.

When it was over Perlo walked out of the courtroom into the half sunlight, his forty-six-year career as a trial lawyer over.

Throughout the trial, the prosecutors had worried most about the case against Starks. But in the end, the case against Starks was concluded faster than the one against Davis. His jury deliberated only two days. With the Davis jury still out, they came back at 3:25 P.M. that Thursday with a verdict.

The afternoon was moist and cool. Wally Tennelle was on a training day. He came in response to the call wearing a Hawaiian shirt, the lone member of the family to appear to hear the verdict. Sixteen RHD detectives also showed up. "The question arises, who is patrolling the streets of L.A.?" Perlo murmured, surveying the phalanx of business suits milling in the courtroom.

His coworkers had come to support him, but Wally Tennelle did not mingle with them. He sat off to the side, an invisible wall around him, one arm draped along the back of the bench in a casual pose contradicted by the tension in his face. As the judge called the court into session, the prosecutors sat hunched together, flushed with emotion, Colello with a fist in his mouth. Skaggs did not attend, but Farell did.

Skaggs never went to hear verdicts, on principle: it was not part of his job. To attend would be a waste of time.

The jury filed in. As Judge Bowers began to read, Tennelle lifted his chin with an effort.

"Guilty," Bowers said. "Murder in the first degree . . ."

Starks stared straight ahead. His rib cage expanded with a deep breath followed by a heavy sigh. Tennelle swallowed hard. His eyes reddened. He appeared swept with weariness, holding himself up with effort, tired, sad, and hollowed out. The jurors were polled in turn, every one of them wearing an expression of profound seriousness. None showed relief, or triumph. None so much as glanced at Wally Tennelle.

Olitha Starks did not get to the courtroom in time to hear the verdict. She arrived at the courthouse door with her husband just after the rest had gone. Told that her son had been found guilty, she nodded, her face full of resignation and disgust.

Corey Farell sent a text message on his cell phone to John Skaggs to apprise him of the verdict that Skaggs had refused to come and hear. Farell's phone buzzed immediately with a blasé response. It was vintage Skaggs—one word: *sweet*.

The Davis jury came back the next morning. This time the courtroom was empty except for a gaggle of prosecutors, friends of Stirling and Colello. Wally Tennelle did not attend. Davis watched the envelope intently as it traveled across the courtroom in the clerk's hands from the jury to the judge. When the guilty verdict was announced, he put a hand over his mouth, swung his head upward, and stared at the ceiling as the long list of findings was read. As court adjourned, Davis sat shaking his head.

Corey Farell did not attend because he had been called in early to his new job with the Foothill Division in the San Fernando Valley. His new station had seen two homicides in a week, the victims a Latino man and a young black woman. The cases were problematic: none of the witnesses wanted to cooperate. But Farell kept tabs on the court proceedings by phone and notified Skaggs of the guilty verdict. This time, his text message prompted an even more laconic answer from the cop with a tie and no jacket: *Rog,* for "Roger that."

24

THE MISSING

Jurors reported being exhausted and emotionally spent. Several were terrified of retribution. Waiting to be escorted into the courtroom for the reading of the verdict, one juror admitted his hands were shaking. Despite their appearance of stoicism, several said that they had been churning inside and choking back tears.

Some thought the defense competent, others found it hopelessly passive. Some wondered why the defense had not gone more aggressively after Midkiff. A few thought the prosecutors' open expression of emotion during the trial was overkill. A couple of jurors said they did, indeed, feel sorry for Zeke Perlo.

Several also thought Stirling's cross-examination of Starks and the prosecution's closing arguments were excessive: the problems with Starks's deceptiveness didn't need to be belabored. Similarly, the drama of the hotel receipt was impressive, but apparently not game-changing. The reference to a "Perry Mason moment," however, elicited a spirited discussion in the jury room when it turned out a younger juror did not know who Perry Mason was.

The Davis jurors had more disagreements and prolonged discussions. They scrutinized the physical evidence closely to arrive at the con-

clusion that Davis had not been shooting randomly. All said they had
taken their duties seriously. "I'm not going to forget any day of this,"
one said.

The defense attorneys, noting that the jurors were mostly white, had
speculated that they could not relate to the circumstances of the case.
But at least one juror was not as far from the ghettoside world as they
thought. This was the Davis foreman, forty-four, a white man with
blond hair and blue eyes who worked as an upper-level manager of a
chain of local fast-food restaurants. His job often took him to Compton
and other neighborhoods south of the Ten. He lived in the suburbs, but
he had grown up in military housing in Washington, D.C., and attended
schools that drew from the city's black neighborhoods. He had been in
many a street fight. As an adolescent, he had learned the rules of the
black inner city—learned that when it came to fighting in a lawless
place, "if you back down, you back down forever," he explained.

Commenting on the Tennelle case, this juror proved more perceptive than some of the professional cops who had trailed in and out of
the courtroom. He knew Midkiff had been a prostitute. He suspected,
without its ever coming out at trial, that Starks had pimped her out. He
was astounded by fellow jurors who couldn't understand why Bryant
was wearing what he called the "stupid hat." "It's to feel safe in his environment!" he said.

Speaking of Bryant, the foreman seemed to comprehend the place
the struggling eighteen-year-old had occupied among his friends. Told
that Bryant's friends had thrown play punches, he nodded knowingly.
They had to teach him to fight in order to risk hanging out with him, he
remarked. A friend who was seen as weak could jeopardize one's respect
and status and therefore one's safety.

Like many Angelenos, the foreman knew black-on-black homicide
south of the Ten was deeply entrenched. He had picked up on Tennelle's choice to live in the Seventy-seventh Street Division, "trying to
do good, and trying to be a role model," and realized that the killing had
gotten little public attention. It bothered him.

"There is a perception that blacks are doing it to blacks, and if I'm white, it doesn't affect me," said the white jury foreman. His eyes flashed with sudden anger. "Well, get over it. *It does.*"

The story of the lives of these two ghettoside craftsmen—Tennelle and Skaggs—converging in the death of a son seemed to deserve a dramatic ending. But in truth, the trial of Derrick Starks and Devin Davis was not even very suspenseful. The case that had gone unsolved for so long proved to be about as formidable as a sand castle on the beach. As the last waves of Skaggs's persistence washed over it, the defense crumbled.

For years, politicians on the right and left had been building the notion of "gang violence" in the public's mind as some kind of implacable social disease, springing from a deeply rooted moral crisis or from some kind of complicated family, economic, or cultural pathology.

But the Tennelle trial suggested a different idea: that it was really not so hard to insert legal authority into the chaos of extralegal violence among the young men of South Central, and that the state's monopoly on violence could be established fairly easily, after all.

But you had to be willing to pay the cost, to put in the effort. You had to be *very persistent.*

The Tennelle case wasn't just solvable. It was friable, breaking open so dramatically in the end that, as Stirling said, a seven-year-old could have tried it. Many people had heard about what Devin Davis and Derrick Starks had done. Rumors had flown freely. The suspects themselves had talked about it. They had made little effort to cover their tracks. They had brought a young woman with them and assumed she would obey the rules and regulations and keep their secret—assumed that she would not be as brave as she turned out to be, determined to stand up, change her life, and, as she put it later, "be a testament." They had assumed the attack would be just another barely noted, barely investigated skirmish in South Central—in short, a typical gang case—until word got back to them that they had killed a police officer's son. The case was eminently solvable—once the right kind of pressure was applied. In Skaggs's hands, the murders were elevated in law to what they were in fact: atrocities that must be answered for every single time.

The world wasn't watching. The public, his superiors, and a large share of the country's thinking classes gave only glancing notice to the battle Skaggs had devoted his life to. But Skaggs didn't care; Skaggs turned his back to the parade.

And just as it is impossible to imagine that things in the South would not have been different if the legal system had operated differently—had black men's lives, for example, been afforded profound value as measured by the response of legal authorities—it is impossible to imagine that the thousands of young men who died on the streets of Los Angeles County during Skaggs's career would have done so had their killers anticipated a "John Skaggs Special" in every case.

If every murder and every serious assault against a black man on the streets were investigated with Skaggs's ceaseless vigor and determination—investigated as if one's own child were the victim, or as if we, as a society, could not bear to lose these people—conditions would have been different. If the system had for years produced the very high clearance rates that Skaggs was so sure were possible—if it did not function, in the aggregate, as a "forty percenter"—the violence could not have been so routine. The victims would not have been so anonymous, and Bryant Tennelle might not have died in the nearly invisible, commonplace way in which he did.

The Tennelle case stood for all of them. Yes, certainly, sometimes, as the detectives said, the cases *were what they were*—a few casings on the ground and no willing witnesses. But the Tennelle case strongly suggested that many more of these murders were solvable than the dismal clearance rates suggested, the assaults as much as the homicides, and that the Monster Skaggs had been chasing his whole career could be beaten.

It was an *evil thing*, as the pastor had said. The Monster arose from what was meanest and most vicious in human nature. But the dark swath of misery it had cut across generations of black Americans was a shadow thrown on the wall, a shape magnified many times the size of its source because of a refusal to see the black homicide problem for what it was: a problem of human suffering caused by the absence of a state monopoly on violence.

The Monster's source was not general perversity of mind in the population that suffered. It was a weak legal apparatus that had long failed to place black injuries and the loss of black lives at the heart of its response when mobilizing the law, first in the South and later in segregated cities. The cases didn't get solved, and year after year, assaults piled one upon another, black men got shot up and killed, no one answered for it, and no one really cared much.

Starks's defense attorney Ezekiel Perlo had never heard of John Skaggs before the Tennelle case. He walked out of the courthouse on the last day of his trial career overpowered on every front by the evidence that had been assembled against his client and assuming that Skaggs must have been handpicked from the elite RHD unit to solve this case.

Later, when Perlo found out that that was not so—that Skaggs was a mere divisional detective who had spent his whole career in the backwater unit of Watts and whose name had been unknown to the homicide lieutenant from headquarters—he shook his head in surprise. If the police department had any sense, Skaggs "should be training people," he said.

And then, without prompting, Perlo made the observation that is the point of this account:

"If all these cases were investigated like Tennelle," he remarked, "there'd be no unsolved cases."

Both Starks and Davis were sentenced to life without parole.

Afforded the privilege granted to victims' families to speak in court, Yadira Tennelle stood up to speak at the sentencing of Devin Davis.

She bade Davis to look at her.

Then she forgave him.

But the signature image of these events was not that of Yadira standing alone and facing Davis, but rather of Wally Tennelle, alone and in tears after the reading of the Starks verdict.

It came after his colleagues had filed out of court in their suits without him. Tennelle, rather too deliberately, lingered behind, congratulated the two prosecutors in his gracious way, then putzed about for a few moments more until the courtroom was nearly empty and the hall outside quiet. The coast clear, Tennelle made his way to the slow, creaking, roaring elevators, rode down, and walked out briskly into the cool, moist afternoon.

A wind was rippling through downtown Los Angeles, and an evening mist was just beginning to drift toward the ground. It was getting late, and small knots of office workers were starting to exit buildings and trickle through the streets on their way home.

As he walked down Spring Street from the Clara Foltz Center in the cool spring air, Tennelle sought to return to business. All signs of his earlier weeping had vanished from his face. Except for a trace of that haunted look, the "homicide eyes" of all the bereaved, he was as matter-of-fact as ever, a professional man of duty, headed back to his counterterrorism training session, one of the many obligations of his job as "a detective for the City of Los Angeles."

That city, rustled by a wet wind that evening, was incomplete. It was missing a son—for Bryant Tennelle was a native son if there ever was one, a young man who personalized all the city's best qualities, its beauty, its practical, hardworking, enterprising spirit, its relaxed generosity, its artistic whimsy—the child of a family of municipal workers, half black, half Latino, with the name *Los Angeles* tattooed on his back. Bryant Tennelle would have been just fine had he made it past the rough adolescent stage in which death took him. There was too much good in him, too much of the sheer force of the Tennelle family wholesomeness in his nature, for any other outcome to be conceivable. He should have been among the movements in the drawing dusk that night—should have been out there somewhere, advancing through his life. The fact that he wasn't stood as a reproach.

As Wally Tennelle disappeared into a city without Bryant, the gathering clouds and erratic wind had a haunted quality. They seemed to buttress Joyce Cook's view that there should be no more candles on the streets of L.A., since too many spirits of the murdered lingered there already. Tennelle went back to his job serving a city that did not deserve him—a city that rolled on indifferently, barely seeming to notice all the people missing from the crowd.

And even if, in the future, some of the lessons of Bryant's death are absorbed and something is learned from the John Skaggs Special that was applied to his case, those people will still be missing. The losses will still be incalculable. We will still be less than we might have been.

"All those innocent people!" Skaggs had lamented. So many of them—it was true. Bryant Tennelle murdered, and so many more. So many black men down.

EPILOGUE

After two prison transfers and a spell in solitary confinement, Derrick Starks ended up for a time at Pelican Bay State Prison near the Oregon border, a spot so remote that even his mother went months without visiting him. The prison lies alongside a desolate, windswept coastal lagoon called Lake Earl, about ten miles northeast of the small town of Crescent City. For anyone used to Los Angeles, it is a cold place. Starks spent days there alone in a cell, looking out at a concrete wall. At the base of the wall, yellow dandelions sprouted. The flowers fascinated Starks. They closed at night, opened in the morning, and turned their faces to the sun throughout the day. How did they do it? An answer came to him: "They're alive!" His voice was freighted with awe. Starks spent most of his time alone in a cell without roommates because he was considered dangerous. He had been in various scraps and fights in prison. He said he liked to be in the cell alone—liked being in solitary confinement, in fact—because it was better than the alternative. His fellow inmates made for stressful companions. According to prison policy, he was being held in the same area as other Blocc Crips, including some men he had known in the neighborhood. He disliked this. Infighting among fellow gang members held more potential for violence than rivalry between men of different gangs, he remarked. He feared the former more.

Often, he wished he were dead. But then again, he added, glancing up at the gray Northwest sky over the prison yard, he had often wished that when he was still free; life outside had been its own kind of prison. So many neighborhoods he couldn't go to safely, and no way to escape his gang associations. He had learned to be "down" whether he felt like shooting or not, he said—"You make it look good." Early on, he said, an older gangster had pressed a gun in his hand and driven home the point with just one word: "Here." He loved his family's ancestral home near Baton Rouge. It was peaceful and far from any street violence, but his people there did not accept him. They found him too rough, too gangster, as he put it. He came back.

Starks readily admitted that he had lied on the stand. He said he did so out of desperation. He insisted on his innocence. He said that Devin Davis had committed the murder with Bobby Ray Johnson, "Gutta," the cousin of the man in the wheelchair, and that Jessica Midkiff was there, too, and that, afterward, his friends had conspired to falsely accuse him. He had been in the 'hood at the time, he said, hanging out, but couldn't remember what he had been doing. He said he was determined to get out of prison—somehow. He said it several times. "I *will* get out." He expressed sympathy for Tennelle in court, though he remembered his name with difficulty. "Wallace?" he asked.

Starks was angry toward Skaggs. But he seemed to bear no ill will toward Phil Stirling, the prosecutor whose work had imprisoned him. He had grown to like Stirling, he admitted.

Devin Davis drew a better card. He ended up serving his life sentence at California State Prison, Los Angeles County, in Lancaster, the closest prison to L.A. He opted for protective custody in prison, severing his gang ties (a status Starks, too, would later choose), and described his environment as safe and peaceful. Davis had become a Muslim and appeared much healthier in prison than during the trial. He had lost weight and was down to about 160 pounds. He did not complain about prison at all, and he appeared trim, energetic, and relaxed. He said he was taking medication regularly for his various conditions, including bipolar disorder. His eyes still wheeled around, however, and he moved jerkily and spoke quickly. Face-to-face, Davis appeared more agitated and unpredictable than Starks, and was much less coherent.

Davis talked of the gang fights he'd been in before prison. He defended his role. "Gotta police ourselves," he explained. When it was suggested to him that gang members usually do not make very good police, he laughed and agreed. "Yeah, gangs shoot everyone," he said. "If you're black."

Davis, too, denied involvement in the killing, but gave a different account than Starks. He said that Starks, Midkiff, and Bobby Ray Johnson had taken him in the car with them, but that he had not known of their plans and never got out. In one regard, his account harmonized with that of Starks: like Starks, he claimed that Johnson was a fourth in the car, and like him, he claimed that Johnson was the real murderer. Otherwise, their two accounts bore little resemblance. Davis said he had confessed to Skaggs purposefully. He said he had earlier agreed to take the fall for Johnson and thought that, because he was a juvenile, the sentence would be light. But for all that he insisted he was innocent, Davis said he planned no further efforts to seek release. He said he didn't know what he would do if he got out of prison—didn't know how he would survive. "It's okay," he repeated when pressed. He mentioned the Tennelles. "They lost his life, I lost mine. So it's okay," he said.

Skaggs continues to work for the LAPD as a homicide detective and has occasional lunches with Jessica Midkiff, who works full-time and continues to make progress toward her goals, her previous life now behind her. Frustrated with his exile to the Olympic Division, Skaggs made some efforts to get himself transferred back to South Bureau after the Tennelle case concluded. But before he succeeded, he became annoyed at what he considered a deficient administrative structure in his new bureau. It struck him as flawed—not as efficient as it should be, detrimental to certain investigative best practices.

Without pausing to consider what might happen, Skaggs shot off a blunt memo to his commander criticizing the existing organization and arguing that, given the scant number of cases, the West Bureau homicide investigation function should be centralized. He spelled out how such a centralized unit would work. Among other benefits, he argued, a change would ensure that young detectives would get consistent caseloads. They would learn better, he wrote. Getting enough cases had never been a problem in South Bureau, but in West Bureau, detectives went months between callouts.

The commander liked the memo. Before Skaggs knew what had happened, he was being asked to head up a new centralized West Bureau homicide squad along the lines he'd suggested. Skaggs realized belatedly that he couldn't back out. He remains in West Bureau. He is in the spotlight a little more. But he says the pace is slow. He misses the south end. He is nearing retirement, however, and he is unlikely to return.

As Barbara Pritchett's little brother neared his high school graduation, she looked forward, for the first time since she was very young, to freedom from child care. Then one of her sisters died of complications of childbirth. The baby survived. Pritchett took the new infant home, fed him and cared for him. She is raising him now—starting over with one more baby in her late forties. She still weeps about Dovon every time this writer calls on her. She remains in Watts. One of her nephews was recently murdered.

Sam Marullo decided he could no longer stand being a gang officer. He shed his blue uniform for a tie and returned to working homicide. He is assigned again to South Bureau homicide squad, and has resumed being one of its most effective practitioners. He has finally been granted the lowest detective rank, D-1.

Nathan Kouri works in the same unit. Pritchett offered a description of him that perhaps best describes his present status. "Nate," she said, "is always Nate." His boss is Rick Gordon, who calls Kouri one of the strongest investigators in the group. Sal La Barbera shifted jobs in the homicide group, working under the lieutenant and planning retirement. The "retal" cycle pitting Main Street Crips against Hoovers that began with events the week of Da'Quawn Allen's killing continues as of this writing. A subsequent victim was Harold Germany, twenty-one, one of the young men hemmed up at Da'Quawn's shrine in this narrative. That murder has not been solved. Another recent victim was Jarret Crump, twenty-one, a janitor on his way to dinner, mistaken for a Main Streeter because of the car he drove.

Wally Tennelle continues to work at RHD and still solves cases with regularity. The Tennelles now have several grandchildren and are very involved in their lives. They remain in the same house where Bryant grew up.

The motive for Bryant's murder remains unclear. Skaggs believes that Starks and Davis may have been targeting Bryant's friends down the block, and that Davis shot Bryant by mistake or as a proxy. Skaggs said that the details of the case suggest a personal grudge, not mere gang rivalry. It's significant, he said, that in both Davis's and Midkiff's accounts, Starks's recital of directions seems to indicate that he sought a remembered spot—a specific street. If Skaggs is right about this, it means that, like so many "gang" murders, this one was actually related to an argument, maybe a previous fight. And it means that Skaggs is probably also right about another point: Bryant's hat didn't matter much. Davis shot him because of where he was.

It is difficult to gain more insight from Starks's and Davis's divergent accounts. However, Starks offered a version that, though unverifiable—and offered chiefly to underscore what he said was his minor role—has the sound of authenticity.

He said that Bobby Ray Johnson, though well loved by some, was at times an obnoxious drunk. Before the murder, Johnson had punched an older, respected fellow member of the Bloccs while drinking. Powerful members of the gang plotted to kill him in revenge. Johnson needed to prove his loyalty, Starks said. This, he claimed, was the backdrop to the hit. Asked if these events led to Johnson's murder months later, Starks shook his head. That was separate, he said—that fight involved a woman. As for who committed the still unsolved in-house killing of Bobby Ray Johnson, Starks grimaced: "Everybody knows, *everybody* knows!" he said.

• • •

At this writing, homicides in Los Angeles County have fallen to levels that would have been unimaginable to Skaggs at the turn of the century, when he came to Southeast. By 2010, the year Starks and Davis were tried, homicide death rates for black men ages twenty to twenty-four had fallen to about 158 per 100,000, or less than half their peak in the Big Years, though of course this figure is still twenty or thirty times higher than the national mean. Killings have gone down further since. In the city of Los Angeles, the drop has been especially dramatic. There were 297 homicides in the city in 2011. By 2013, there were 251, a breathtaking decline. But the figures had a similar tilt as in years past: Three high-crime station areas—Southeast, Southwest, and Seventy-seventh—accounted for 109 homicides, or 43 percent of the city's total. Nearly all the victims in the three divisions were men, more than three quarters of them were black (double the proportion of black people in the area's population)—and 84 percent of the killings with known suspects were intrarace. Still, the slack has allowed LAPD investigative units to breathe a little—to better archive and investigate cold cases and to clear more new ones. Caseloads are falling. Detectives have more time and clearance rates are rising. There is no longer a need for the trailer behind the Southeast station: the LAPD at long last has been entering those cases into computer databases. The firearms laboratory recently adopted new technology to allow better, faster matches of bullets to revolvers.

Some neutral factors, a few positive ones, and at least one negative one have helped drive the decline in murders. For the city of L.A., it is clear that demographic change is an important driver. The city's black population is fast disappearing: black Angelenos were once nearly a fifth of the city's population, but they made up a scant 9 percent in the 2010 census. Their numbers have been dropping steadily each year as the city's black residents scatter to the exurbs. To some extent, their high homicide rates travel with them. But the change has also coincided with—at long last—a dramatic easing of the residential hyper-segregation that set the conditions for sky-high inner-city murder rates. As black people finally begin to integrate into more mobile and mixed communities, the Monster is in retreat.

That change perhaps has been aided in part by a related development—an increase in public benefits paid to poor black people, particularly men, primarily in the form of SSI (Supplemental Security Income, a payment available to people with disabilities). One reason for this is prison reforms. The federal Second Chance Act in 2005 inspired new efforts to provide SSI to prisoners upon reentry; many prisoners qualify, since a third of the state's inmates have been diagnosed with mental illness. As we have seen, autonomy counters homicide. Cold cash paid out to individuals is a powerful thing: this author has watched SSI transform many aspects of life in South Central Los Angeles over about a decade, but the change for indigent black men has been especially dramatic. Statistics reinforce these observations: enrollment of working-age African Americans in SSI in 2009 was nearly twice their representation in the population, and African American children made up nearly one-third of SSI recipients age fifteen to seventeen. African American recipients of SSI are more likely to be poor and less likely to be college educated than SSI recipients generally, suggesting this money is indeed finding its way into the hands of the urban poor—including adult men who historically have been cut out of social welfare programs.

Money translates to autonomy. Economic autonomy is like legal autonomy. It helps break apart homicidal enclaves by reducing interdependence and lowering the stakes of conflicts. The many indigent black men who now report themselves to be "on disability"—many of them with mental disabilities, such as ADD and bipolar disorder—signal an unprecedented income stream for a population that once suffered near-absolute economic marginalization. An eight-hundred-dollar-a-month check for an unemployed black ex-felon makes a big difference in his life. The risks and benefits of various hustles surely appear different to him. He can move, ditch his homeys, commit fewer crimes, walk away from more fights. Doubtless many people will criticize this trend and decry the expense of SSI. But this author can't condemn a program that appears to have saved so many from being murdered or maimed.

For those not convinced by humanitarian arguments, it's worth noting that homicide is expensive, too. Health insurance for these same indigent black men through the new Affordable Care Act may change the picture further. Another factor reducing murder rates is a bleak one—large numbers of black men in prison. Imprisonment brings down homicide rates because it keeps black men safe, and they are far less likely to become victims in prison than outside it. California's rate of imprisonment increased fivefold between 1972 and 2000. Homicide deaths among this largely black and Latino population of tens of thousands number just a handful per year. But this is, it need hardly be said, a rotten—and expensive—way to combat the problem. Other factors, such as the shift to cellphone sales of drugs, the abuse of legal pharmaceuticals, computer games that keep adolescents indoors, and the improved conduct of police (former chief Bernard Parks deserves much credit for the latter in L.A.), probably count, too.

People are much safer, on the whole, in America than they used to be, and this is good. But anyone who tracks homicide in L.A. County and elsewhere still can't escape the obvious: black men remain disproportionately victimized. Solving this problem deserves every honest effort. People may disagree about the remedies—particularly the balance between preventive and responsive measures—but they should not disagree about the problem's urgency.

The homicide problem lost two of its great intellectual prophets in the course of the events described in this book—William J. Stuntz and Eric Monkkonen. Both scholars believed that an understanding of violence must proceed from a study of the structure of law and the working of formal legal institutions. Both died young, of cancer. It remains for others to do the considerable work required to turn back the plague. Stuntz died in 2011. His pithy summation of the problem still applies: "Poor black neighborhoods see too little of the kinds of policing and criminal punishment that do the most good, and too much of the kinds that do the most harm." Monkkonen, a professor at UCLA, died in 2005. He did not live to see the recent, stunning homicide declines here in L.A. But he left these lines for the future: "The challenge for the twenty-first century," he wrote, "is to keep pushing for lower rates even when it seems as though this is happening automatically."

AUTHOR'S NOTE

This book grew out of reporting on homicide in Los Angeles extending from late 2001, when the *Los Angeles Times* put me on the police beat, to 2012, when I wrapped up the field research for this book.

A year or two into the beat, I sought the LAPD's permission to "embed" at its Seventy-seventh Street Division and was given a desk in the detectives' squad room on the second floor of the station house. From then on, I focused on the streets of South Bureau and the squad cars and roll calls of the Seventy-seventh and neighboring Southeast stations, reporting on homicides and other crimes, talking to witnesses, bystanders, suspects, and families of victims. I first met Sal La Barbera during that period, and also John Skaggs and Chris Barling. Around that time, I began assembling the data used in these pages with the help of analysts within the LAPD, epidemiologists at the Injury and Violence Prevention Program at the Los Angeles County Department of Health Services, and the staff of the Los Angeles County coroner's office.

In late 2006, I launched "The Homicide Report" on the *Los Angeles Times* website. This was an attempt to provide a comprehensive, day-by-day accounting of every homicide in the county. I reported about a thousand homicides for The Homicide Report over the course of the next two years, working mostly out of my car—a 2001 Ford Escort. I carried a police radio, went to crime scenes, talked up people I met on the street, and got to know police officers. By the time I started compiling the blog, I had already covered many homicides and was familiar with homicide statistics. Still, I found the project to be profoundly revealing. Suddenly, I was watching the statistics unfold in real time— living the data, not just reading it on a page. Every corpse, every weeping relative, and every sleep-deprived detective was linked to a data point in my hard drive, as if—in traversing the county's four thousand square miles—I was guiding my Escort across a vast Excel file. I saw patterns I hadn't seen before and found myself inventing new categories to keep my charts organized. "Group home." "Party." "Hangfire" (sheriff's shorthand for cases in which victims linger in hospitals or in nursing homes). I will never look at statistics quite the same way again. I wrote briefly about Bryant Tennelle in 2007, and also about Dovon Harris, whose mother, Barbara Pritchett, I met when I knocked on her door a few days after his death.

In mid-2008, the Times suspended The Homicide Report, and I began working on this book, researching and writing it in intervals over the next five years, between hiatuses to meet other work or personal obligations. Beginning in June 2008, I embedded myself once again in the Seventy-seventh, shadowing homicide detectives as I had in the early 2000s. Sam Marullo and Nathan Kouri had joined La Barbera's squad by then, now working under the same roof with the Seventy-seventh and Southwest's squads. For more than a year, I accompanied Southeast detectives to crime scenes, court hearings, and interviews, peeling off in the evenings and on weekends to visit victims' families, attend funerals, or walk the streets. I spent subsequent months in follow-up interviews and library research.

The events, scenes, and details described in this book were, in all cases, either directly observed by me or reconstructed after the fact using interviews with participants. Wherever possible, court documents, police reports, and other official records were used to verify particulars. All names are real names; some names were withheld due to safety considerations, with particular care extended to witnesses possibly facing reprisal.

I have consistently had problems reconciling reported homicide data with my own data collected through real-time reporting. Officially reported clearance rates, as this book suggests, are frequently at odds with the data reported by detectives when they are asked, point-blank, "Were charges filed?" But to a surprising extent, straight tallies of homicides vary, too. There are unappreciated complexities involved in counting homicides, and these have caused me no small share of headaches.

For this book, I have largely relied on lists of homicides assembled by the coroner's office, cross-checked with police data, detective-squad tallies, and my own reporting, as this is the most immediate, detailed, and directly sourced information I could come by. The tables I've compiled include names of victims, circumstances of deaths, and, in many cases, observations made at crime scenes and funerals and information provided by families and detectives. Over the years, in search of clarity on clearance rates, I have conducted surveys of case outcomes by calling or visiting the assigned detectives or their field supervisors and asking for updates.

For years now, I have tried to penetrate the mystery of disproportionate black homicide. Correlation is not causation. I wanted to know exactly what was happening and why. I've sought answers in reported facts and observations, and tried to avoid pat speculation and received wisdom. Mostly, I've relied on what I have myself seen or heard directly from those who are close to homicide. I have made deliberate efforts to listen to the bereaved—to seek out the parents, siblings, spouses, and children of black homicide victims, whose viewpoints are under-represented in our national debates over criminal justice. I tried to discipline myself to find people in great pain, from a sense that the sad and disturbing nature of this subject matter is one of the reasons it is avoided and under-emphasized. These interviews, in particular, led me to consult scholarly research on the history of black homicide and the attitudes and policies of legal authorities toward it. So, although statistics are important—the high homicide rate for black men is, after all, the reason I wrote this book—I am with John Skaggs in his preference for the field and the unmediated detail of lived experience. This book is my attempt to relate what I've learned—a circumstantial case, to be sure, but the one I saw.

ACKNOWLEDGMENTS

This book would not have happened without the faithful and keenly intelligent efforts of my brother, Steven Leovy, who read every draft, checked facts, and advised and argued with me through every stage, despite his own full-time career and duties. My brother, an engineer, was an unlikely participant in this. But he contributed on every level, from deep issues of writing and story-telling to small matters of jargon and typos, and also provided moral support and every manner of practical assistance. I cannot thank him in any manner that would equal his contribution. I can only reiterate that his commitment to this project is the reason it exists.

Many other people helped in ways great and small. I will not name all of them here, but they include my editors and colleagues at the *Los Angeles Times*, who launched and supported the efforts that supplied the context for this book. They include John Spano, Sam Enriquez, Miriam Pawel, Doug Smith, Sandi Poindexter, and especially Gale Holland, one-of-a-kind editor and friend, who oversaw the Homicide Report blog and also read drafts of this book. I owe gratitude to scores of people in the LAPD, many of whose names do not appear here but who brooked my intrusions for the best of reasons—to make sure I got it right. A short list must include Matt Mahoney, Glenn Krejci, Pat Gannon, Dorayya Dasari, Gerry Pantoja, Roger Allen, Rick Gordon, David Garrido, Carlos Velasquez, Kyle Jackson, Paul Vernon, Mike Owens, Brent Josephson, and especially Kerri Potter and Mark Hahn. Very special thanks to Tom Eiman, whose brief mention in this book belies his selfless, thoughtful contributions. Thanks also to William Bratton, Charlie Beck, Earl Paysinger, Andy Smith, Rick Jacobs, Jim McDonnell, and Willie Pannell for access, multiple interviews, and general transparency, and also to the crew of South Bureau Criminal Gang Homicide. Special appreciation to Bernard C. Parks, who has generously enlightened me for years with his unmatched knowledge of the LAPD. Finally, I must recognize the late Kenneth O. Garner, who died midway through my work. Garner believed in truly open public institutions and was of great assistance.

Boundless thanks to Farley Chase, who saw the potential of this work when there was no reason to, and to Cindy Spiegel and Julie Grau and their colleagues at Spiegel & Grau, who embraced its complexities and stuck by it through difficulties. To my genius editor, Chris Jackson, whose work transformed this book, I am not just indebted but in awe. Thanks also to W. Fitzhugh Brundage, who kindly reviewed historical portions of this manuscript, Grace Rai, La Wanda Hawkins, Douglas Lee Eckberg, Carter Spikes and Butch Lemon of the Businessmen, eyewitness expert Steven E. Clark for research help, Ben Adair, Brian Vander Brug, Jill Connelly, Craig Harvey, Tom Dotan, Jeffrey Adler, Douglas Massey, Luis Montes and his colleagues at Rancho Los Amigos National Rehabilitation Center, Timothy Tyson and the staff of L.A. City Street Trees, Monique Jordan, Ferroll Robins of Loved Ones Victims Services, and many other family members of victims who courageously chose to speak out. Apologies to the hundreds whose loved ones' names did not appear here; you are the reason for this book. Deep thanks to my friends and family, who buoyed me through years of sometimes trying work—my parents, both of whom passed away during its research, my steadfast sisters, and my husband, Marc, incomparable journalist, editor and friend.

NOTES

vii **The Plague** The name "The Plague" is borrowed from Albert Camus, as are various themes in this book. The opening quote and subsequent ones are drawn from both Stuart Gilbert's and Robin Buss's translations of his 1947 novel *The Plague* (in French, *La Peste*).

6 **Most had been killed by other black men and boys who still roamed free** Analysis by the author, LAPD homicide data. Characteristics and status updates of 16,435 homicides in the city of Los Angeles from 1986 to the first quarter of 2009 were provided by the LAPD at the author's request. To reach this conclusion, 3,333 killings of black males were considered, committed between 1991 and 2006. Thirty-eight percent were cleared by arrest in this period. The clearance rate presented here is calculated differently than the federal rate. It represents the outcome of each case, not the sum total of cases cleared each year measured against new homicides, and it excludes cases "cleared by exceptional means," that is, cases closed with no arrest made. (In recent years, the LAPD has balked at providing this data and said it would no longer update the status of cases or release information more than six months old.) As in the rest of the country, homicide in Los Angeles occurs mostly between people of the same race. In 2006, for example, just 22 of 236 LAPD South Bureau homicides—or ten percent—crossed racial lines.

6 **"Nigger life's cheap now"** Leon F. Litwack, *Been in the Storm So Long: The Aftermath of Slavery* (New York: Vintage Books, 1980), p. 275

6 **"a simple mention is made of it"** Gilles Vandal, *Rethinking Southern Violence* (Columbus: Ohio State University Press, 2000), p. 180.

6 **"Providence has chosen to exterminate them in this way"** Vandal, *Rethinking Southern Violence*, p. 159.

7 **"This is a case of one negro killing another"** Douglas A. Blackmon, *Slavery by Another Name: The Re-Enslavement of Black Americans from the Civil War to World War II* (New York: Doubleday, 2008), p. 305. Governor Cole Blease provided the lyrics to this "song" in his explanation: "Hot supper; liquor; dead negro."

7 **"complaisance toward violence among the Negroes"** Hortense Powdermaker, *After Freedom: A Cultural Study in the Deep South* (New York: Viking Press, 1939) p. 173.

7 **"One less nigger"** Edward L. Ayers, *Vengeance & Justice: Crime and Punishment in the 19th Century American South* (New York: Oxford University Press, 1984), p. 231. The full quote offered by the anonymously cited Southern police officer is as follows: "If a nigger kills a white man, that's murder. If a white man kills a nigger, that's justifiable homicide. If a nigger kills another nigger, that's one less nigger." It would seem to have folkloric status. Black sources interviewed in Los Angeles rendered it various ways, including, "One less of 'em to deal with" and "one less gang member."

7 **"if a black man kills a black man,"** *Report of the National Advisory Commission on Civil Disorders* (New York: Bantam Books, 1968), p. 308.

8 **what Max Weber called a *state monopoly on violence*** Max Weber, *The Vocation Lectures: Science as a Vocation, Politics as a Vocation* (Indianapolis: Hackett Publishing Company, 2004), p. 33.

Here and throughout this book, I am indebted to the work of legal scholar Markus Dirk Dubber for articulating the problems of legal theory inherent in preventive policing. For a fuller exploration of the connection between legal autonomy, violence, and what Dubber terms the policing of "inchoate" crimes, that is, crimes that have not yet been committed, see Markus Dirk Dubber, *Victims in the War on Crime: The Use and Abuse of Victims' Rights* (New York: New York University Press, 2002).

9 **In Jim Crow Mississippi** Mississippi figures from Powdermaker, *After Freedom*, pp. 173, 395. Los Angeles figures based on Fredric N. Tulsky and

Ted Rohrlich, "And Justice for Some: Solving Murders in L.A. County," *Los Angeles Times*, Dec. 1, 1996, and Dec. 3, 1996.

Tulsky and Rohrlich's in-depth analysis of 9,442 cases found less than one-third of reported killings resulted in conviction for murder or manslaughter, and that black- and Hispanic-victim cases were less likely to result in charges and brought lighter penalties than white-victim cases. (The study found that cases involving white victims were 40 percent more likely to be solved than those involving black or Hispanic victims.) But Tulsky and Rohrlich did not include in their findings the 7 percent of all cases that remained to be adjudicated. So the percentage presented here for blacks in the early 1990s is the author's estimate. It takes into account lower clearance rates for black victims but adds pending cases to the count, adjusted for average conviction rate. It is compared against the author's analysis of LAPD homicide case data for those years and reported conviction rates published by the California Department of Justice, which yield a similar result. See also Catherine Lee, "The Value of Life in Death: Multiple Regression and Event History Analysis of Homicide Clearance in Los Angeles County," *Journal of Criminal Justice*, 33, no. 2 (November–December 2005): pp. 527–34. Lee analyzed the *Times* data and arrived at similar conclusions.

9 **"which places the Negro outside the law"** Powdermaker, *After Freedom*, p. 173. She expands elsewhere, saying: "Since no Negro can expect to find justice by due process of law, it is better in the long run to suffer one's loss—or to adjust it oneself. From this angle, the 'lawlessness' sometimes ascribed to the Negro may be viewed as being rather his private individual 'law enforcement' "(p. 126).

10 **black-on-black homicide is much of the reason** Blacks, who make up about 12 percent of the county's population, account for nearly half of its homicide victims. Homicide data from several sources, including the FBI data and James Alan Fox and Marianne W. Zawitz, "Homicide Trends in the United States" *Bureau of Justice Statistics* (2007); see "Trends by Race, 1976–2005." A total of 186,807 people died from homicides in the United States between 1995 and 2005, according to Fox and Zawitz. Of these victims, 89,991 were black, or 48 percent.

Homicide numbers reported by the U.S. Centers for Disease Control and Prevention are consistently a little higher that the FBI's because they are drawn from a different data set—mortality records. But the racial disparity is similar. For example, between 2005 and 2010, the agency reported that about 47 percent of U.S. homicide victims were non-Hispanic blacks. (See "Fatal Injury Reports").

10 **But historians have traced** For example, historian Eric Henry Monkkonen found that disproportionately high black rates emerged in the last decades of the nineteenth century in his study of New York (Eric H. Monkkonen, *Murder in New York City* [Berkeley and Los Angeles: University of California Press, 2001], p. 164.). Vandal found the same in his study of Louisiana, and Lane in his study of Philadelphia (Roger Lane, *Roots of Violence in Black Philadelphia 1860–1900* [Cambridge: Harvard University Press, 1986]). Explaining why high black murder rates should not be attributed to developments in black industrial "inner cities" of the twentieth century, Vandal wrote: "The first signs of this even predated the great migration. . . . It was in the political and economic conditions of the Reconstruction era that the roots of modern African American violence can be traced" (*Rethinking Southern Violence*, p. 208). The gap between black and white rates in New York is distinct by the late 1880s, Monkkonen found. It grew wider and became a chasm as early as the 1930s. "The twentieth-century difference in black and white rates is so large as to cry out for explanation and understanding," he wrote (p. 139).

Historians once talked about a U-curve in homicide rates over time, based on research that suggested that homicide in the United States fell to comparatively low levels in the late nineteenth and early twentieth centuries, then rose sharply after. This is incorrect. Work by Douglas Lee Eckberg and others has shown that homicides were almost certainly undercounted in the decades at the bottom of the U-curve. The omission of Southern homicides and the large number of killings classified as justifiable—up to 50 percent in some cities—led to the error. We now know there was probably no turn-of-the-century dip, and that Americans have been fairly murderous all along. See Douglas Lee Eckberg, "Estimates of Early Twentieth Century U.S. Homicide Rates: An Econometric Forecasting Approach," *Demography*, vol. 32, no. 1: pp. 1–16.

10 **black death rates from homicide nationwide** H. C. Brearley, "The Negro and Homicide," *Social Forces* 9, no. 2 (1930): pp. 247–53.

10 **Southern observers also noticed startling rates of black violence** All the great social scientists of the South in that era—Powdermaker, Charles S. Johnson, John Dollard, and Davis/Gardner/Gardner—remarked on the phenomenon. Later studies echoed their findings. One found that

85 percent of homicide victims in Birmingham, Alabama, were black, though blacks were less than half the city's population. Howard Harlan "Five Hundred Homicides," *Journal of Criminal Law and Criminology* 40, no. 6 (1950): pp. 736-52.

10 **in the 1940s, a Philadelphia study found** Marvin E. Wolfgang, *Patterns in Criminal Homicide* (Philadelphia: University of Pennsylvania Press, 1958; 1975 reprint), pp. 33, 223, 84. Interestingly, Wolfgang also found that those black Philadelphians used guns far less than they used pen knives, ice picks, and various blunt instruments, yet they maintained death rates similar to today's. This reinforces the conclusion that guns are not a root cause of black homicide. Wolfgang examined the years 1948 to 1952 and found that nonfirearm killings such as stabbings and beatings were 61 percent of black male homicides in Philadelphia in that era, and this mix of weapons produced an overall black homicide death rate of 23 per 100,000 per year. Nationally, in recent years about 67 percent of homicides nationally were committed with guns, and the black rate of death from homicide was about 21 per 100,000. In L.A. in the 2000s, guns were used in 70 percent of black homicides, and the black rate of death was probably in the low thirties per 100,000. (FBI Uniform Crime Reports and Mary-Ann Hunt, "2007 Homicide Analysis," Los Angeles Police Department Robbery-Homicide Divison, Powerpoint presentation, slides 13, 15).

10 **remained as much as ten times higher** *Health, United States,* National Center for Health Statistics (Hyattsville, Md.: 2005, etc.), Mortality trend tables. See also Henry Allan Bullock, "Urban Homicide in Theory and Fact," *The Journal of Criminal Law, Criminology, and Police Science* 45, no. 5 (1955): pp. 565–75; U.S. Census statistics; and A. Joan Klebba, "Homicide Trends in the United States 1900–1974," *Public Health Reports* 90, no. 3 (1975): pp. 195–204.

10 **five to seven times higher** Fox and Zawitz, "Homicide Trends in the United States." According to them, the black rate was six times that of whites in 1980; five times in 1985; seven times in 1990; nearly seven times in 1995; six times in 2000; and six times in 2005. More recent crime data is not available, but 2010 mortality data from NCHS Vital Statistics System shows black rates were eight times white rates, though, as noted above, this figure is not comparable to the previous ones.

10 **young black men are murdered two to four times more frequently** Mortality file data was analyzed at the author's request by the

Injury and Violence Prevention Program of the Los Angeles County Department of Health Services and the county's Department of Public
Health, Data Collection and Analysis Unit. Many thanks to epidemiolo-
gist Isabelle Sternfeld for years of help with these records.

10 **violent crime was plummeting in Los Angeles County** Countywide homicides reached a high of 2,113 deaths in 1992 and had fallen to
1,085 in 2006, according to statistics provided at the author's request by
Craig Harvey, Los Angeles County coroner's office. Crime would, of
course, fall much lower after that.

11 **"progressives tend to avoid or change the subject"** James Forman, Jr., "Racial Critiques of Mass Incarceration: Beyond the New Jim
Crow," *Faculty Scholarship Series* 3599 (2012): p. 128.

12 **"The familiar dismal statistics"** Randall Kennedy, *Race, Crime and the
Law* (New York: Vintage, 1998), p. 145.

CHAPTER 2

16 **such calls, at least in this year, came more than once a day, on
average** There were 835 shooting victims in South Bureau in 2007, and
1,016 in 2006—Los Angeles Police Department, *Crime and Arrests Weekly
Statistics,* Dec. 31, 2007.

CHAPTER 3

24 **Los Angeles's nineteen police precincts were called divisions**
There were eighteen LAPD divisions for most of Skaggs's career. By
2014, there were twenty-one. This point in the narrative takes place after
the LAPD's nineteenth police station, Mission, was opened in the San
Fernando Valley. LAPD officers don't like the word "precinct" and it has
no official use, but it is sometimes used here for clarity.

26 **One of Skaggs's colleagues picked up a word** Detective Roger
Allen.

CHAPTER 4

34 **exceeded nine hundred per hundred thousand people** Various,
including Fox and Zawitz, "Homicide Trends in the United States"; Alexa

Cooper and Erica L. Smith, "Homicide Trends in the United States" (Bureau of Justice Statistics, 2011); FBI Uniform Crime Reports.

34 **similar to the per capita rate of death for U.S. soldiers deployed to Iraq** County mortality data; Iraq data from Samuel H. Preston and Emily Buzzell, "Service in Iraq: Just How Risky?" *The Washington Post,* Aug. 26, 2006. Preston and Buzzell calculated a military death rate of about 392 deaths per 100,000 among American troops deployed to Iraq 2003-2006. According to their figures, if only combat deaths are considered, the military rate in Iraq would total about 309 deaths per 100,000. For twenty- to twenty-four-year-old black males, the homicide death rate in Los Angeles County hit a high of 368 per 100,000 population in 1993.

36 **striking several with batons** Homicide of Stephanie Smith, Dec. 7, 2008, 546 W. 102nd St. Smith was thirty-seven.

39 **the constitution places many constraints on legal procedure** Carol S. Steiker, "The Limits of the Preventive State," *The Journal of Criminal Law and Criminology* 88, no. 3 (1988): pp. 771–808.

39 **LAPD's South Bureau and Central Bureau "homicide experts"** This term was technically applied within the LAPD to denote working D-3s in RHD. There were very few working D-3s in South Bureau, although such a position was badly needed to counter the chronic inexperience that hampered homicide units there. Skaggs and other south-end cops who were promoted to the D-3 supervisory rank liked the term and used it, however. The reason is obvious: They were, indisputably, homicide experts. For a long time, Skaggs hoped to devise a permanent working D 3 slot in South Bureau—solving cases, not overseeing people—but apart from his brief stint in Southwest, it never happened.

40 **"Women work through men by agitating them to homicide"** June Nash, "Death as a Way of Life: The Increasing Resort to Homicide in a Maya Indian Community," *American Anthropologist* 69, no. 5 (1969): p. 462.

40 **Canadian Inuits . . . Jim Crow blacks** E. Adamson Hoebel, "Law-Ways of the Primitive Eskimos," *Journal of Criminal Law and Criminology* 31, no. 6 (1941): p. 677; M.A.O. Malik, "A Profile of Homicide in the Sudan," *Forensic Science* 7 (1976): p. 143; Powdermaker, *After Freedom,* p. 164. See also John Dollard, *Caste and Class in a Southern Town* (Garden City, New York: Doubleday Anchor, 1937; 1949 reprint), p. 278.

40 **"touts" kneecapped in Northern Ireland, informants necklaced**

in South Africa See Rachel Monaghan, "Not Quite Lynching: Informal Justice in Northern Ireland," in *Globalizing Lynching History: Vigilantism and Extralegal Punishment from an International Perspective*, Manfred Berg and Simon Wendt, editors (New York: Palgrave Macmillan, 2011), pp. 157–58; also Colin Knox and Rachel Monaghan, *Informal Justice in Divided Societies: Northern Ireland and South Africa* (New York: Palgrave Macmillan, 2002).

40 **murderous neighborhood-watches of Ghana** Mensah Adinkrah, "Vigilante Homicides in Contemporary Ghana," *Journal of Criminal Justice* 33 (2005): p. 423

40 **grabbing one's friends from police** Lars Buur, "Democracy and its Discontents: Vigilantism, Sovereignity and Human Rights in South Africa," *Review of African Political Economy* 35, no. 118 (2008): p. 580.

41 **They fixate on honor and respect** John Dollard, discussing the premium Jim Crow black men placed on aggressive, boastful posturing, compared it to the "admiration felt on the frontier for the individual who is physically and morally competent to take care of himself." The reason it arose, he said, was that "the formal machinery of the law takes care of the Negroes' grievances much less adequately than of the whites', and to a much higher degree the Negro is compelled to make and enforce his own law with other Negroes." Dollard, *Caste and Class in a Southern Town*, p. 274.

41 **arson, for some reason, gets a starring role** E.g., Stephen P. Frank, *Crime Cultural Conflict, and Justice in Rural Russia 1856–1914* (Berkeley and Los Angeles: University of California Press, 1999), p. 19; Michael Schwaiger, "Salmon, Sagebrush, and Safaris: Alaska's Territorial Judicial System and the Adventures of the Floating Court, 1901–1915," *Alaska Law Review* 26, no. 1 (June 2009): p. 97; E. M. Beck and Stewart E. Tolnay, "When Race Didn't Matter: Black and White Mob Violence Against Their Own Color," in *Under Sentence of Death: Lynching in the South*, W. Fitzhugh Brundage, editor (Chapel Hill: University of North Carolina Press, 1997), p. 140; Manfred Berg, *Popular Justice: A History of Lynching in America* (Lanham, Md.: Ivan R. Dee, 2011), p. 113.

See also Julia Eichenberg, "The Dark Side of Independence: Paramilitary Violence in Ireland and Poland after the First World War," *Contemporary European History* 19, no. 3 (August 2010): pp. 231–48.

41 **"individuals willingly give up their implicit power to the state"** Monkkonen, *Murder in New York City*, p. 164.

41 **High homicide rates have also been recorded among hunter-**

gatherer peoples E. Adamson Hoebel, "Law-Ways of the Primitive Eskimos," *Journal of Criminal Law and Criminology* 31, no. 6 (1941): pp. 662–83; Bruce M. Knauft, "Reconsidering Violence in Simple Human Societies: Homicide Among the Gebusi of New Guinea," *Current Anthropology* 28, no. 4 (1987): pp. 457–500, p. 458; Richard Borshay Lee, *The !Kung San: Men, Women, and Work in a Foraging Society* (Cambridge: Cambridge University Press, 1979; 1984 reprint), p. 398; Wilfred T. Masumura, "Law and Violence: A Cross-Cultural Study" *Journal of Anthropological Research* 33, no. 4 (1977): pp. 388–99.

41 **Thus, some Indian tribes in Canada and the U.S.** Anthony N. Doob, Michelle G. Grossman, and Raymon P. Auger, "Aboriginal Homicides in Ontario," *Canadian Journal of Criminology* 36, no. 29 (1994): pp. 29–35; Steven W. Perry, "American Indians and Crime: A BJS Statistical Profile," U.S. Department of Justice, Office of Justice Programs, Bureau of Justice Statistics, *BJS Profiles 1992–2002* NCJ 203097 (December 2004).

41 **as do ethnic and immigrant enclaves** See Roberta Belli and William Parkin, "Immigration and Homicide in Contemporary Europe," p. 253, and Nora Markwalker and Martin Killias, "Homicide in Switzerland," p. 351, in Marieke C. A. Liem and William Alex Pridemore, editors, *Handbook of European Homicide Research: Patterns, Explanations, and Country Studies* (New York: Springer, 2012). See also Patsy Richards, "Homicide Statistics, Research Paper 99/56," House of Commons Library, May 27, 1999: pp. 20–21. (This paper further notes that in only 40 percent of those black-victim cases in England and Wales was a suspect identified, compared to 90 percent in cases involving white victims.)

41 **non-Dutch ethnics suffer many times the homicide rate** Soenita M. Ganpat and Marieke C.A. Liem, "Homicide in the Netherlands," in Liem and Pridemore, *Handbook of European Homicide Research*, pp. 329, 336.

41 **Eighteenth-century rates among settlers** Randolph Roth, *American Homicide* (Cambridge: The Belknap Press, 2009), p. 162. Rates among black people in South Los Angeles ranged from 20 to 40 per 100,000 in the period discussed in this book, according to the analysis by the Los Angeles County Department of Public Health, Data Collection and Analysis Unit; Roth reports that homicide-death rates for white adults were 25–30 per 100,000 from the Georgia Piedmont to the Ohio River Valley, 1760–1812.

42 **"As long as it's Arabs killing Arabs"** Edmund Sanders, "Arab Citi-

zens Call for More Israeli Police," *Los Angeles Times,* Oct. 30, 2012. Estimated rate computation by the author.

42 **The ancient Greeks wrote of the Furies** Aeschylus, *The Eumenides.* In
the play, Athena convinces the Furies to surrender the power to adjudi-
cate wrongs to her formal court. Thus, "the shackles of the primitive ven-
detta lend their rigor to the lasting bonds of law," said classicists Robert
Fagles and W. B. Stanford. *The Oresteia: Agamemnon, the Libation Bearers, the
Eumenides,* translated by Robert Fagles (New York: Penguin Books, 1966;
1977 reprint); quote is from the introduction by Robert Fagles and
W. B. Stanford, p. 22.

CHAPTER 5

47 **only about a tenth of all murders resulted in a conviction** Monkkonen, *Murder in New York City,* p.167.

47 **Less than half did in Philadelphia and Chicago** Chicago data for
1875 to 1920 kindly provided at the request of the author by Jeffrey S.
Adler of the University of Florida. Adler found that about 41 percent of
black-on-black murders involving men resulted in a conviction, and that
rates for other groups were not much different. Philadelphia figures are
from Roger Lane, *Roots of Violence,* p. 89. Lane notes only that fewer than
half of homicide offenders arrested were convicted of any offense; convictions relative to all homicides committed were probably even lower.
Also see William J. Stuntz, *The Collapse of American Criminal Justice* (Cambridge: The Belknap Press, 2011), p. 137.

47 **a suspiciously large percentage of homicides** Author's computation based on LAPD annual reports. The reports reinforce Eckberg's
conclusions about uncounted homicides, noted above. For example, in
fiscal year 1932–1933, the city reported 107 homicide deaths but called
eight of these justifiable and twenty-one "killed while committing a
crime." An additional twenty remaining cases were reported closed because the suspects committed suicide—a much higher proportion than is
typical today. In six cases, the suspects escaped, but, oddly enough, these
were categorized separately from unsolved cases.

In another forty-two cases, police declared the investigation closed because suspects had been "arrested or killed"—they didn't specify which.
Thanks to so many justified killings, mysteriously vanished suspects, and un-
timely deaths, the LAPD's investigative results that year looked pretty good:

the department reported that only ten cases were "unsolved." Reports from the late twenties and thirties reports also mention a handful of homicides classified as "mercy killings." They do not elaborate on what this meant.

48 **"had merely taken the law into their own hands"** June 17, 1925, "Screen Writer Bandit Killed," *Los Angeles Times.* The victim was a black man.

48 **But California prison rolls tell a different story** These proportions were computed by the author based on statewide criminal-homicide data reported by the California Department of Justice, compared against historic censuses published by what is now the California Department of Corrections and Rehabilitation. The relevant tables contain tallies of felons newly committed to California institutions by offense. Women and juvenile offenders were included and vehicular manslaughter felons excluded. The analysis used ten-year increments to capture the lag time between killings and the time it takes for police to catch suspects and courts to process them. See, California Department of Corrections, "Summary Statistics of Felon Prisoners and Parolees," "California Prisoners," and "California Prisoners and Parolees," and related reports; tables are titled "Felons Newly Received from Court." Also, California Department of Justice, *Homicide Crimes in California 2004*, p. 14.

Obviously, a better way to measure the vigor of criminal justice in response to murder would be to track individual case outcomes and assemble conviction rates from these. But there are problems in state justice department data in this area, so the prison reception counts were used instead. The downside of using these prison counts is that there is no way to differentiate between cases involving a single victim and suspect and those involving multiple victims or multiple suspects. However, studies suggest that one-on-one cases predominate among murders, and multiple suspects of single victims are more common than the reverse. Given this, these ratios perhaps understate the number of homicide cases in which no one went to prison.

48 **Killers of whites received the harshest penalties** Tulsky and Rohrlich.

48 **people who kill blacks get lighter penalties** David C. Baldus, *Equal Justice and the Death Penalty: a Legal and Empirical Analysis* (Boston: Northeastern University Press, 1990), pp. 185, 401.

49 **a suspect was arrested in 38 percent of 2,677 killings** Author's computation from LAPD files, as above.

49 **In L.A. County, a much larger area, similar patterns prevailed** A suspect was in custody six months later in only 38 percent of killings involving black victims countywide in 2007. This finding, for the entire county, which is more than twice as populous as the city of L.A. alone, is based on the author's interviews, six months later, of investigating officers involved with 710 homicide cases across all major police agencies in the county, excluding the city of Pomona's. The survey eliminated murder-suicides from consideration and counted double and triple homicides as single cases. Cases in which the suspect remained outstanding on a warrant were counted as cleared, since they represent well-advanced investigations.

49 **an average of more than 40 per square mile** Jill Leovy and Doug Smith, "Getting Away with Murder in South L.A.'s Killing Zone," *Los Angeles Times*, Jan. 1, 2004. Mapping and data analysis by Smith, a colleague to whom the author owes thanks for his careful work on homicide statistics over many years.

49 **four or five injury shootings for every fatal one** Various, including, Los Angeles Police Department "Weekly Crime and Arrest Comparison Report," Dec. 25, 2004. The number of reported "shooting victims" investigated by police exceeded the number of people killed by four and a half times in 2002, 2003, and 2004. The Centers for Disease Control and Prevention puts the ratio of assault firearm injuries versus deaths at about five times.

49 **A waggish colleague of Skaggs** Detective Gerry Pantoja.

49 **Some thirty almocides occurred each month** On average, Southeast Division had thirty-two cases per month involving nonfatal shooting victims in 2002, 2003, and 2004. Los Angeles Police Department, "Weekly Crime and Arrest Comparison Report, Dec. 25, 2004.

49 **only about 17 percent ended with an assailant convicted** Official numbers are from LAPD Statistical Digests. The conviction rate here was calculated by detective-supervisor Lou Leiker of Southeast Division at the request of the author. Leiker considered 234 Southeast category-one assault cases that his "table" of detectives had handled in 2004. Category one cases include those involving serious injuries and those with strong leads.

49 **hundreds of arsons a year in Los Angeles** Les Wilkerson, Los Angeles city fire investigator, interview by the author, Aug. 31, 2009. Wilkerson said about half were gang-related Molotov cocktail cases—"message-

sending" arsons, he called them, aimed at intimidating people, and very difficult to solve. "No one wants to talk," he said.

50 **When the Swedish social scientist Gunnar Myrdal** He further concluded that "leniency toward Negro defendants in crimes involving other Negroes is actually a form of discrimination." Gunnar Myrdal, *An American Dilemma: The Negro Problem and Modern Democracy* (New York: Harper and Row, 1944; 1962 reprint), pp. 542, 551.

50 **"the principal injury suffered by African-Americans"** Kennedy, *Race, Crime and the Law*, p. 19.

CHAPTER 6

55 **and for years, the cops declined to do so** In 2001, an LAPD press release reported that twenty-three percent of officers lived in the city. The release hailed this as progress, citing housing incentives. Los Angeles Police Department news release, March 8, 2001.

CHAPTER 7

61 **the nine square miles of Watts were home to about 130,000 people, 39 percent of them black** Los Angeles City Planning Department, Southeast Area population and housing study.

61 **they got the City of Los Angeles to annex it instead** Douglas Flamming, *Bound for Freedom: Black Los Angeles in Jim Crow America* (Berkeley and Los Angeles: University of California Press, 2005), p. 264.

61 **"An infected pocket of misery"** Theodore H. White, "Lesson of Los Angeles: A Call for New Thinking About Race Relations in the Big City," *Los Angeles Times*, Aug. 22, 1965.

62 **George Kelling and James Q. Wilson's famous essay** James Q. Wilson and George L. Kelling "Broken Windows: The Police and Neighborhood Safety," *The Atlantic* (March 1982), pp. 29–38.

66 **Southeast led the city in killings** LAPD figures; race breakdown by Southeast detectives.

69 **So there was little political pressure to address them** Police agencies are subject to civilian control, and in Skaggs's time the Los Angeles police chief answered to the city's elected mayor. So police executives could not responsibly enact any dramatic structural realignment of resources without some public backing even if they saw the need for it,

which they frequently did. There is a tendency for critics of the criminal-justice system to lay blame on police professionals generally for failings that should more fairly be placed at the feet of political leaders and the voters who elect them.

CHAPTER 8

74 **the "colossal" problem of ghettoside homicide cases** Halim Dhanidina, now a Los Angeles superior court judge.

74 **40 percent of all cases in which witnesses played any role** Survey conducted by the author. Findings are based on interviews with investigating officers involved in 381 L.A. homicides in 2008. Investigators were asked to give case details and prioritize reasons they remained unsolved.

76 **the real figure was probably at least a dozen** Witness murder counts are based on the number of homicide defendants charged with a special allegation of witness murder—PC 190.2(a)(10)—in Los Angeles County Superior Court from 1999–2004. "Known" cases include those in which the killer of a witness was charged, not cases that remain unsolved. Report prepared by officials with the Los Angeles County District Attorney's Office at the author's request. Thanks to Sandi Gibbons.

76 **rewards offered for help on cases were virtually never collected** See Susannah Rosenblatt, "Crime Rewards Net Few Payoffs," *Los Angeles Times*, Nov. 23, 2007; Jill Leovy, "Rewards Fail to Lure Witnesses," *Los Angeles Times*, Aug. 25, 2003; Nicholas Riccardi, "Rewards for Crime Tips Rarely Help," *Los Angeles Times*, Oct. 18, 1995; Hugo Martin, "Most Rewards for Crimes Go Unclaimed," *Los Angeles Times*, May 29, 1994.

79 **They bartered goods, struck deals, and shared proceeds** For this wording and these insights—as applicable to L.A. as to Chicago—I'm indebted to Sudhir Alladi Venkatesh, and particularly his groundbreaking work in *Off the Books: The Underground Economy of the Urban Poor* (Cambridge: Harvard University Press, 2006).

79 **an East Coast Crip gang member** The name of this gang is said to refer to the old restrictive-covenant boundary along Main Street, not to the Atlantic coast of the United States. "East Coast" was a lyrical version of "eastside," that is, the east side of Main Street, to which black people were effectively confined in the midcentury period. Main Street runs north-south behind Seventy-seventh Street Station.

80 **moonshiners who intimidated people and killed snitches** Frank,

pp. 124, 126; Lane, *Roots of Violence in Black Philadelphia*, p. 9; Monkkonen, *Murder in New York City*, p. 73; W. Fitzhugh Brundage, *Lynching in the New South: Georgia and Virginia, 1880–1930* (Urbana and Chicago: University of Illinois Press, 1993), p. 23.

80 **"sown in the nature of man"** Quoted from the Federalist Papers in Cass R. Sunstein, "The Enlarged Republic—Then and Now," *The New York Review of Books*, March 26, 2009.

81 **so few gang homicides stemmed from drug deals** Later, a Centers for Disease Control and Prevention study would confirm what LAPD homicide detectives already knew—that very few street homicides directly involve drug deals. The study found that less than 5 percent of all homicides in Los Angeles and Long Beach involved the drug trade. See Arlen Egley, Jr., et al., "Gang Homicides, Five U.S. Cities, 2003–2008," *Morbidity and Mortality Weekly Report*, Jan. 27, 2012. For a fascinating discussion of the idea that gangs are protective agencies, see Russell S. Sobel and Brian J. Osoba, "Youth Gangs as Pseudo-Governments: Implications for Violent Crime," *Southern Economic Journal* 75, no. 4 (2009): pp. 996–1018. The authors argue that gangs may exist to compensate for the absence of a state monopoly on violence by providing people alternate means of protection, and so could actually serve to *lower* crime rates, not the reverse.

82 **"They have their own business"** Porras is now a Los Angeles County superior court judge

82 **"there's *rules and regulations* behind living there"** This witness spoke at trial in the killing of Rendell Woods, age twenty-four, April 24, 2008, 1471 E. 109th St. Woods was an acquaintance of Barbara Pritchett.

82 **"the law to her is a vague and sinister force"** Powdermaker, *After Freedom*, p. 190.

85 **"moral comfort" to people who didn't want to testify** James Q. Whitman, *The Origins of Reasonable Doubt: Theological Roots of the Criminal Trial* (New Haven: Yale University Press, 2008).

CHAPTER 9

91 **"Murderers are mean"** Monkkonen, *Murder in New York City*, p. 56

94 **the name of a typical seminar** California Homicide Investigators Association, 35th Annual Conference and Golf Tournament, March 3–5, 2004, agenda, p. 7.

CHAPTER 10

103 **the homicide death rate for San Bernardino's young black men**
Centers for Disease Control and Prevention, National Center for Health
Statistics, Compressed Mortality File 1999–2010 on CDC WONDER
Online Database, January 2013.

CHAPTER 14

141 **"proxy crimes" to substitute for more difficult** William J. Stuntz
singled it out as a particularly damaging trend. Stuntz, *Collapse of American
Criminal Justice,* pp. 270, 269-274.

142 **a man in a wheelchair from a gunshot injury had been murdered** Akkeli Hollie, twenty-nine, killed July 4, 2003, on 114th Street.

143 **The high-tech NIBIN system** NIBIN is administered by the U.S.
Bureau of Alcohol, Tobacco, Firearms and Explosives. In an interview,
ATF spokesmen Tim Graden and Chris Amon said that, although they
did not know the specifics of the events described in this narrative,
they had no reason to doubt Hudson's account. They confirmed that
NIBIN has had difficulty with revolver matches for the reasons she
described, and the system mostly matches semiautomatic pistols to casings. It would therefore not be surprising that the LAPD, though a large-
scale user of the system, had made no revolver matches as of 2007, they
said.

146 **one of the most dangerous tasks a state can perform** From
Stuntz: "Enforcing criminal law is one of government's most important
tasks, yet also among the most dangerous." *Collapse of American Criminal
Justice,* p. 63.

152 **a gang called the Rollin' Sixties** This style of gang names reflect
L.A.'s grid geography. "Rollin'" refers to the gangs associated with blocks
north and south of streets bearing that number. Thus, the sets of the Rollin' Thirties are associated with South 30th through 39th streets, sets of
the Sixties with South 60th through 69th streets (roughly), and so on. The
fact that numbers grow bigger as streets move south often added a few
killings to the official tallies every summer and fall. Numbered gangs celebrated their "birthdays" on corresponding calendar days. The 8-9 Family Bloods from South 89th Street, for example, gathered on August 9;

the 9-7 Gangster Crips from South 97th Street gathered on September 7, and so forth. Such gatherings could lead to violence.

154 **Vigilantism and vendettas flourished** For an extraordinarily thorough description of violence in America before and after the revolutionary war, see Randolph Roth, *American Homicide* (Cambridge: The Belknap Press, 2009). See also Stuntz, *Collapse of American Criminal Justice*, p. 68; Monkkonen, *Murder in New York City*, pp. 162, 167; and Berg, *Popular Justice*.

154 **roughing up people to teach them lessons** Monkkonen quotes a popular refrain: "More justice in a nightstick than in a statute book." Monkkonen, *Murder in New York City*, p. 166.

154 **their work consisted largely of rounding up drunks in paddy wagons** As late as 1956, Los Angeles police arrested more than two hundred thousand people yearly for "drunkenness" and various municipal code violations, a number equal to nearly a tenth of the city's population. Police today don't arrest nearly so many people—Los Angeles Police Department statistical digests (population figures from historic U.S. census data, 1950 and 1960).

154 **long, painful history of caste domination and counterrevolution** The emphasis here on the counterrevolutionary foment in the south is not accidental. First, conservatives opposed Reconstruction; then blacks and dissenting whites occasionally challenged and, more often, surreptitiously resisted the ruling order of the Redemption period. This culminated, eventually, in the second Reconstruction. All this upheaval in the decades following the Civil War leads the author to conclude that the legitimacy of the state was never really a settled question in the South, creating a situation that inevitably fuels high rates of personal violence. Civil wars and revolutions are homicide engines, said homicide historian Randolph Roth. Just as homicide exploded in the South after the Civil War, Roth noted, it surged among the French following the French Revolution, the Germans in the Weimar period and the Italians and Belgians after World War II. Nothing fuels homicide quite so well as what Roth calls "an unending series of revolutions and counter revolutions." (Roth, pp. 243, 146, 436–43.) For an eye-opening exploration of the patterns of intra- and interracial violence before Redemption, and the change after former Confederates regained power, see Vandal, *Rethinking Southern Violence*.

154 **the racist atrocities of Southern law** Powerfully catalogued by

Blackmon in *Slavery by Another Name*, a story of law gone very wrong. Blackmon noted, incidentally, that black people in the early twentieth century were sometimes punished severely for murdering other black people, and the murder of a single black person could result in the arrest of many others (p. 334). This runs counter to the observations of other Jim Crow sociologists and anthropologists, who emphasized the leniency of the southern system on black-on-black violence. But to this author, it does not seem a contradiction. No one has asserted that black people weren't punished for murder—they were, and still are, in significant proportion. But the picture Blackmon paints of a system corrupted by the need to conscript black men as labor fits with a larger picture of law rendered plastic and meaningless, which was also the conclusion of many contemporary observers. Whether lax or excessive, law in the south was twisted to serve a shadow state; the fact that it functioned partially—arresting some killers, some of the time—gave the whole system plausible deniability and a staying power that it would not have had if southern authorities had refused to prosecute any black killers. This situation of law-as-window-dressing is perhaps even more conducive to homicide than outright lawlessness.

154 **black people dismissed the whole framework** E.g., Leon F. Litwack, *Trouble in Mind: Black Southerners in the Age of Jim Crow* (New York: Alfred A. Knopf, 1998), p. 278.

154 **a "winking" system** Mark Schultz, *The Rural Face of White Supremacy: Beyond Jim Crow* (Urbana and Chicago: University of Illinois Press, 2005), p. 135.

155 **real power was upheld outside the law** This section owes much to the work of Christopher Waldrep, *Roots of Disorder: Race and Criminal Justice in the American South, 1817–80* (Urbana and Chicago: University of Illinois Press, 1998).

155 **that historian Mark Schultz dubbed "personalism"** Schultz, *Rural Face of White Supremacy*, p. 37. See also Kennedy, *Race, Crime and the Law*; Litwack, *Trouble in Mind*; and Eric Foner, *Reconstruction: America's Unfinished Revolution, 1863–1877* (New York: Harper and Row, 1988; 1989 Perennial Library edition). Also Vandal, *Rethinking Southern Violence*.

155 **"shot down for nothing"** 1899 black tenant farmer reporting from Mississippi, quoted in Terence Finnegan, "Lynching and Political Power in Mississippi and South Carolina," in W. Fitzhugh Brundage, editor,

Under Sentence of Death: Lynching in the South (Chapel Hill: University of North Carolina Press, 1997), p. 205.

155 **"so much cutting and killing going on"** Charles S. Johnson, *Shadow of the Plantation* (Chicago: University of Chicago Press, 1934; 1966 Phoenix Books edition), p. 190.

155 **In Atlanta in 1920 . . . In Memphis in 1915** "Mortality Statistics reports, 1921 and 1920, Twenty-First Annual Report," U.S. Department of the Census. Thanks to Douglas Eckberg. These are astoundingly high rates for a general population—much higher than on tough streets of LAPD's South Bureau—because women and children dilute the count. One can assume the rates for adult men, who always dominate among homicide victims, were much higher. It's not clear what was happening in these places, but whatever it was, it must have been horrible for those who lived through it.

155 **Black people even lynched each other** We know details of this thanks to Stewart E. Tolnay and E. M. Beck's astonishing study: *A Festival of Violence: An Analysis of Southern Lynchings, 1882–1930* (Urbana and Chicago: University of Illinois Press, 1995).

155 **White people "had the law"** E.g., "They got the law," in Litwack, *Trouble in Mind,* p. 278. Also, interviewed in Schultz, a black sharecropper from Hancock County, Georgia who said: "What little you made, they'd take it . . . They'd say they had the law" (Schultz, *Rural Face of White Supremacy,* p. 34).

155 **"serve the ends of the white caste"** Dollard, *Caste and Class in a Southern Town,* p. 280.

156 **together just because they were the same color** The anthropologist Bruce M. Knauft has suggested that, contrary to what is sometimes assumed, egalitarian societies whose members share power evenly may be more, not less, likely to have high personal homicide rates. A scholar of the traditional Gebusi people, who were extraordinarily homicidal, Knauft identified the group's reliance on consensus, not headman or elders, as one of the conditions for violence. This is not to overstate the similarities: Gebusi killings often had to do with witchcraft, and their homicide rate has plummeted since Knauft first wrote about it. But his suggestion that equality disperses violence among individuals, resulting in more argument deaths, remains relevant. Black people in the Jim Crow south must have been similarly leaderless and disorganized, thrown to-

gether in conditions of chaotic equality. They were subject to social restrictions that did not permit even the minimal stratification that would
produce class structure. Knauft, "Reconsidering Violence," p. 476. For
the lack of class distinctions among black southerners, see Allison Davis,
Burleigh B. Gardner, and Mary R. Gardner, *Deep South: A Social Anthropological Study of Caste and Class* (Chicago: University of Chicago Press, 1941;
reprint University of South Carolina Press, 2009), p. 241.

156   **They enlisted blacks as spies** Mention of spies and informants
      crops up in many accounts of the Jim Crow south—for example, Powder-
      maker's description of a "mulatto man who acts as a 'go-between' for the
      white and colored people and who is something of a spy, with an unsavory
      reputation" (Powdermaker, *After Freedom*, p. 184), and also Gunnar Myr-
      dal's mention of the use of black "informers, spotters, and stool pigeons"
      by police (Myrdal, *An American Dilemma*, p. 541). But one of the most vivid
      examples was offered to this writer by Ray Knox, a retired L.A. County
      Youth Authority counselor born in 1951, who is black and was a frequent
      childhood visitor to his family's native McComb, Mississippi. "If someone
      was lynched, or shot, killed, or whatever . . . and if you knew what hap-
      pened, you couldn't talk about it among other black people," Knox said.
      "There was always someone there that was receiving something from
      people in charge: white people."

156   **favored "their Negroes"** Dollard, *Caste and Class in a Southern Town*,
      p. 283. Southern history offers many examples of how white patrons and
      protectors placed some black people at an advantage over their fellows in
      criminal and business matters, including the white practice of obtaining
      leniency for black criminals who worked for them. Reports Dollard, "If a
      white man gets a Negro off on a murder charge because he 'needs him on
      the plantation,' that Negro is indebted to him." Interestingly, Dollard
      compares this unofficial system to premodern legal settings. He called it
      "a feudal protectoral relationship." Dollard, *Caste and Class in a Southern
      Town*, pp. 282–85. See also Davis, Gardner, and Gardner, *Deep South*,
      pp. 520–23; Schultz, *Rural Face of White Supremacy*, p. 152.

156   **and used them as pawns in their battles** The many incidents when
      southern white police, and occasionally white civilians, challenged and
      fought mobs in an effort to protect black people from lynching come to
      mind here. At least half of threatened lynchings failed because they were
      averted in this manner. Brundage's finding that many lynchings were
      committed furtively, as if the perpetrators could not trust other whites to

back them, also hints at the degree of white division in the south. In courtrooms, white people also sometimes saw to it that black people they liked were given an advantage over whites held in low esteem. See Larry J. Griffin, Paula Clark, and Joanne C. Sandberg, "Narrative and Event: Lynching and Historical Sociology," in Brundage, *Under Sentence of Death*, pp. 26, 24–47. See also Davis, Gardner, and Gardner: They describe a case in which a black woman, considered a "'good nigger,' deferential and hardworking," prevailed in a court case over a white "young city man" whom locals disliked and viewed as arrogant. *Deep South*, pp. 524–26.

156 **a contested prize in a low-level, unfinished revolution** For good reason, this phrase finds its way into the subtitle of Eric Foner's history of Reconstruction. Eric Foner, *Reconstruction: America's Unfinished Revolution 1863–1877*.

156 **as a systematic extension of the campaign of terrorist violence** For example, in Litwack, *Trouble in Mind:* "When whites after Reconstruction moved on every front to solidify their supremacy, nowhere was the reassertion of power over black lives more evident than in the machinery of the police and the criminal justice system" (p. 247).

156 **"submit to . . . arrest by any damned rebel police!"** Howard N. Rabinowitz, "The Conflict Between Blacks and the Police in the Urban South 1865–1900," in *Black Southerners and the Law, 1865–1900*, Donald G. Nieman, editor, African-American Life in the Post-Emancipation South, volume 12 (New York: Garland Publishing, 1994), p. 292.

156 **they wrested friends from police hands** Rabinowitz, "Conflict Between Blacks and the Police," pp. 292–98.

156 **Nashville's "Black Bottom," Atlanta's "Darktown"** Rabinowitz, "Conflict Between Blacks and the Police," p. 297.

156 **"but rather stayed on the main thoroughfares"** Mydral, *An American Dilemma*, p. 1341.

156 **"at least to some extent, self-policing"** Harlan Hahn and Judson L. Jeffries, *Urban America and Its Police: From the Postcolonial Era Through the Turbulent 1960s* (Boulder: University Press of Colorado, 2003), p. 125.

156 **They brought with them their high homicide rates** In Los Angeles, the black homicide problem clearly predated the rise of crack cocaine and modern gang organizations, such as Crips and Bloods. As early as 1941, twenty-one percent of homicide victims in the city were black, although blacks made up less than 5 percent of the population, and all but one of these victims was killed by a black suspect. Similarly, in 1952, mostly black

Newton Division—the original "South Central" since it lies along South Central Avenue—the homicide rate was shockingly high: more than 80 deaths per 100,000. Most people don't associated the fifties with high crime, but this rate of killing in what would come to be known as L.A.'s "Negro Community" was much higher than the citywide black rate in the 2000s. (LAPD annual reports and historic U.S. Census data).

Older black men in Los Angeles are often the strongest proponents of the idea that black homicide is a new phenomenon, created by a vicious young upstart generation. They insist that they fought with fists not guns, and that the new gangs are more lethal than the old. But statistics suggest otherwise, and, as the Philadelphia study quoted earlier found, a lot of people end up dead even when guns are not the weapon of choice. Shane Stringer, a member of an old-style L.A. gang called the Businessmen, active in the 1960s and 1970s, offered a typical view: "In my time, it was ninety percent fistfights," he insisted. "Very seldom would we see gunplay. Stabbings, yes. We had the normal stabbings." And of course, he admitted, the "fistfights" included assaults with "bumper jacks and ties—they'd hurt 'em bad."

157 **the LAPD spent four times as much per capita in Newton Division** Los Angeles Police Department, 1961 *Annual Report,* author's computation.

157 **remains a cherished template for left-leaning critics of criminal justice** I'm indebted to James Q. Whitman for a version of this wording.

157 **It practiced victim-discounting on a mass scale** The scale of the Monster swiftly swamped the deployment formulas mentioned above. By 1975, LAPD's mostly black Southwest Division had more than six times the murder rate of West Los Angeles Division, but only one and a half times as many police per capita. (Los Angeles Police Department, *Statistical Digest 1975*).

157 **making this country one of the world's most lenient** Mark A. Kleiman, *When Brute Force Fails: How to Have Less Crime and Less Punishment* (Princeton, N.J.: Princeton University Press, 2009), pp. 8–15; Stuntz, *Collapse of American Criminal Justice,* pp. 2, 34, 246.

157 **only a third of California's convicted homicide perpetrators** "California Prisoners, 1977 and 1978: Summary Statistics of Felon Prisoners and Parolees," *State of California Health and Welfare Agency, Department of Corrections* (table 30a), p. 79.

157 **seemingly blind to the ravages of underenforcement** Two recent exceptions: Forman, cited above, and Alexandra Natapoff, "Underenforcement," *Fordham Law Review* 75 (2006); *Loyola Law School Los Angeles Legal Studies Paper No. 2006-44.*

157 **the largest single category of new prison arrivals** California State Department of Corrections and Rehabilitation, *Prisoners and Parolees* (2007), p. 3 (Arrivals). They churned in and out and ended up comprising about one-sixth of all incarcerated inmates.

157 **In fact, homicide solve rates dropped** From 79 percent to 62 percent nationally between 1976 and 2005 (including cleared other), according to Fox and Zawitz, "Homicide Trends in the United States."

158 **not the harshness of punishment but its swiftness and certainty** Kleiman, *When Brute Force Fails,* p. 23.

158 **homicide rates for all Americans still lag behind those of the safest European nations** Aki Roberts, "Predictors of Homicide Clearance by Arrest: An Event History Analysis of NIBRS Incidents," *Homicide Studies* 11 (2007): p. 82.

CHAPTER 17

211 **He never expressed resentment of Miranda** Skaggs may have not minded all those procedural reforms, but the legal scholar Stuntz wrote provocatively about what he said was America's misplaced focus on them. He found fault with Supreme Court Justice Earl Warren for not seeing that violent crime is a civil-rights issue, too, and suggested that it's unjust for black people to suffer disproportionately. There's an alternate interpretation of the Fourteenth Amendment, Stuntz suggested—that "equal protection" could imply a right to an equal measure of safety. In the murderous early days of the amendment, he wrote, the idea might have spawned more robust violent-crime prosecutions, and even a federal homicide law (Stuntz, *Collapse of American Criminal Justice,* pp. 104–22, 232–33).

CHAPTER 18

215 **One detective coined a noun in the aftermath of the arrests— a "John Skaggs Special"** Bill Ritsch.

CHAPTER 19

223 **Felony conviction rates in California were much higher** California Department of Justice, *Crime in California 2007*, p. 149. The agency's
adult felony arrest disposition data shows that 48.4 percent of felony cases
ended in conviction in 1975, and an average of 56 percent of cases in the
subsequent five years. By 2005, conviction rates for felony arrests had
reached 71 percent.

CHAPTER 20

240 **At the same time, homicides had plummeted** Jill Leovy, "A Complex Portrait of Rampart's Redemption," *Los Angeles Times*, July 13,
2006.

240 **poverty does not necessarily engender homicide** Monkkonen
makes this point forcefully. He singles it out as one of the chief lessons of
the history of homicide. "In some of New York City's most miserable
periods, murder rates were at their lowest," he writes (Monkkonen, *Murder
in New York City*, p. 8). Nor was there a homicide spike during the Great
Depression.

241 **nearly 40 percent of Rampart residents remained below the
poverty line** Data from the Los Angeles City Planning Department
based on 2000 U.S. Census figures.

241 **recent immigrants tend to have lower homicide rates** Ramiro
Martinez, Jr., *Latino Homicide: Immigration, Violence, and Community* (New
York: Routledge, 2002), pp. 105–8.

241 **Instead, they were stopovers** For demographic studies indicating that
Hispanics were dispersing, see Philip J. Ethington, William H. Frey and
Dowell Myers, "The Racial Resegregation of Los Angeles County," Pub-
lic Research Report 2001-04, *Race Contours 2000 Study* (University of
Southern California–University of Michigan, 2001).

241 **an "unabashed preference" for Hispanic labor** Josh Sides, *L.A. City
Limits: African American Los Angeles from the Great Depression to the Present* (Berkeley and Los Angeles: University of California Press, 2003), pp. 4, 6, 14,
25, 33, 60, 65–74, 80–88, 94.

242 **"Black segregation was permanent, across generations"** Douglas S. Massey, interview with the author, March 8, 2012.

242 **No one else had it as bad** Douglas S. Massey and Nancy A. Denton,

American Apartheid: Segregation and the Making of the Underclass (Cambridge: Harvard University Press, 1993).

242 **black people were no more likely to have white neighbors** Ethington, Frey and Myers, pp. 8, 14.

242 **Indices of residential segregation are strong homicide predictors** E.g., Ruth D. Peterson, Lauren J. Krivo, "Racial Segregation and Black Urban Homicide," *Social Forces* 71, no. 4 (June 1993): pp. 1001–26; and Matthew R. Lee, "Concentrated Poverty, Race and Homicide," *The Sociological Quarterly* 41, no. 2 (Spring 2000): pp. 189–206

252 **Prison was safer than freedom** The overall homicide death rate for black, white, and Hispanic men over eighteen in California in 2009 and 2010 was two and a half times greater than the corresponding death rate in the prison population. Men outside prison suffered a much higher homicide death rate even though they are, on average, older than the prison population, and so should be at lower risk.

The safety benefit of prison for the highest-risk group—young black men—is probably even greater than these figures suggest. Prison homicide victims are nearly always older men. Press releases on homicides during the year above, nearly all of which list the age of the victim, mention only one inmate victim who was in his twenties, a twenty-six-year-old, and nearly all the rest were in their forties or even sixties. Given the very high death rates of black men in their early twenties outside prison, the absence of any victims in this age category inside prison walls is especially noteworthy. This is not to dispute that there are a lot of nonfatal assaults in prison—fistfights and worse—but simply to note that the lethality is on a much lower scale than outside. (Computation by the author. Prison population statistics and homicide releases are published by the California Department of Corrections and Rehabilitation. Homicide counts to verify them were provided by CDCR at the request of the author; thanks to Bill Sessa. California homicide death rates for adult males are from the Centers for Disease Control and Prevention, Injury Prevention and Control: Fatal Injury Reports. Demographic age data provided at the request of the author by Jonathan Buttle, California State Census Data Center, Demographic Research Unit, California State Department of Finance.)

253 **estimated as high as one in thirty-five** "The 1997 Chances of Lifetime Murder Victimization," Section V, in *Crime in the United States, 1999*, Uniform Crime Reports, U.S. Department of Justice, Washington, D.C.

The figure used here is for a black male of the prisoner's age by five-year interval. The corresponding chance for a white male was 1 in 251.

CHAPTER 21

258 **545 black men and boys had been killed in Los Angeles County** Files provided by the Los Angeles County Coroner's office. Thanks to Craig Harvey for years of assistance with this data.

EPILOGUE

316 **a dramatic easing of the residential hyper-segregation** Thanks to demographer William H. Frey for help in interpreting segregation patterns.

317 **enrollment of working-age African Americans in SSI in 2009** See Patricia P. Martin and John L. Murphy, "Research and Statistics Note, No. 2014-01: African Americans: Description of Social Security and Supplemental Security Income Participation and Benefit Levels Using the American Community Survey" (Social Security Administration, Official of Retirement and Disability Policy, Office of Research, Evaluation and Statistics, January 2014), p. 13.

SELECT BIBLIOGRAPHY

Alexander, Michelle. *The New Jim Crow: Mass Incarceration in the Age of Color Blind ness.* New York: New Press, 2010. 2012 edition.

Anderson, Elijah. *Code of the Street.* New York: W.W. Norton, 1999.

Ayers, Edward L. *Vengeance and Justice: Crime and Punishment in the 19th Century American South.* New York: Oxford University Press, 1984.

Berg, Manfred. *Popular Justice: A History of Lynching in America.* Lanham, Md.: Ivan R. Dee, 2011.

Berg, Manfred, and Simon Wendt, editors. *Globalizing Lynching History: Vigilantism and Extralegal Punishment from and International Perspective.* New York: Palgrave Macmillan, 2011.

Black, Donald. *The Behavior of Law.* New York: Academic Press, 1976.

Blackmon, Douglas A. *Slavery by Another Name: The Re-Enslavement of Black Americans from the Civil War to World War II.* New York: Doubleday, 2008.

Bodenhamer, David J., and James W. Ely, Jr., editors. *Ambivalent Legacy: A Legal History of the South.* Jackson: University Press of Mississippi, 1984.

Brearley, H. C. *Homicide in the United States.* Chapel Hill: University of North Carolina Press, 1932.

Brundage, W. Fitzhugh. *Lynching in the New South: Georgia and Virginia, 1880-1930.* Urbana and Chicago:University of Illinois Press, 1993.

Brundage, W. Fitzhugh, editor. *Under Sentence of Death: Lynching in the South.* Chapel Hill: University of North Carolina Press, 1997.

Butterfield, Fox. *All God's Children*. New York: Alfred A. Knopf, 1995; 2002 reprint.

Davis, Allison, Burleigh B. Gardner, and Mary R. Gardner. *Deep South: A Social Anthropological Study of Caste and Class*. Chicago: The University of Chicago Press, 1941; reprint University of South Carolina Press, 2009.

Dollard, John. *Caste and Class in a Southern Town*. Garden City, N.Y.: Doubleday Anchor, 1937; 1949 reprint.

Dubber, Markus Dirk. *Victims in the War on Crime: The Use and Abuse of Victims' Rights*. New York: New York University Press, 2002.

Flamming, Douglas. *Bound for Freedom: Black Los Angeles in Jim Crow America*. Berkeley and Los Angeles: University of California Press, 2005.

Foner, Eric. *Reconstruction: America's Unfinished Revolution, 1863–1877*. New York: Harper and Row, 1988; 1989 Perennial Library edition.

Frank, Stephen P. *Crime, Cultural Conflict, and Justice in Rural Russia, 1856–1914*. Berkeley and Los Angeles: University of California Press, 1999.

Grossman, Dave. *On Killing: The Psychological Cost of Learning to Kill in War and Society*. New York: Back Bay Books, 1995, 1996.

Hahn, Harlan, and Judson L. Jeffries *Urban America and its Police: From the Postcolonial Era Through the Turbulent 1960s*. Boulder: University Press of Colorado, 2003.

Hawkins, Darnell F., editor. *Homicide Among Black Americans*. Lanham, Md.: University Press of America, 1986.

Johnson, Charles S. *Shadow of the Plantation*. Chicago: University of Chicago Press, 1934; 1966 Phoenix Books edition.

Kennedy, Randall. *Race, Crime and the Law*. New York: Vintage Books, 1998.

Kleiman, Mark A. *When Brute Force Fails: How to Have Less Crime and Less Punishment*. Princeton, N.J.: Princeton University Press, 2009.

Knox, Colin, and Rachel Monaghan. *Informal Justice in Divided Societies: Northern Ireland and South Africa*. New York: Palgrave Macmillan, 2002.

Lane, Roger. *Roots of Violence in Black Philadelphia, 1860–1900*. Cambridge: Harvard University Press, 1986.

———. *Murder in America: A History*. Columbus: Ohio State University Press, 1997.

Langer, Lawrence L. *Admitting the Holocaust: Collected Essays*. New York: Oxford University Press, 1995.

Lemann, Nicholas. *The Promised Land: The Great Black Migration and How it Changed America*. New York: Alfred A. Knopf, 1991; 1992 reprint.

Litwack, Leon F. *Trouble in Mind: Black Southerners in the Age of Jim Crow*. New York: Alfred A. Knopf, 1998.

————. *Been in the Storm So Long: The Aftermath of Slavery*. New York: Alfred A. Knopf, 1979; 1980 reprint.

Martinez, Ramiro, Jr. *Latino Homicide: Immigration, Violence, and Community*. New York: Routledge, 2002.

Massey, Douglass S., and Nancy A. Denton. *American Apartheid: Segregation and the Making of the Underclass*. Cambridge: Harvard University Press, 1993.

Monkkonen, Eric H. *Murder in New York City*. Berkeley and Los Angeles: University of California Press, 2001.

Myrdal, Gunnar. *An American Dilemma: The Negro Problem and Modern Democracy*. New York: Harper and Row, 1944; 1962 reprint.

Nieman, Donald G., editor. *Black Southerners and the Law, 1865–1900*. African-American Life in the Post-Emancipation South, volume 12. New York: Garland Publishing, 1994.

Powdermaker, Hortense. *After Freedom: A Cultural Study in the Deep South*. New York: Viking Press, 1939.

————. *Stranger and Friend: The Way of an Anthropologist*. New York: W. W. Norton, 1966.

Redfield, H. V. *Homicide, North and South: Being a Comparative View of Crime Against the Person in Several Parts of the United States, 1889*. Ithaca, N.Y.: Cornell University Law Library, 1893.

Report of the National Advisory Commission on Civil Disorders. Otto Kerner, chairman. New York: Bantam Books, 1968.

Roth, Randolph. *American Homicide*. Cambridge: The Belknap Press, 2009.

Rubinstein, Jonathan. *City Police*. New York: Farrar, Straus and Giroux, 1973; 1985 reprint.

Schatzberg, Rufus, and Robert J. Kelly *African-American Organized Crime: A Social History*. New York: Garland Publishing, 1996; reprint New Brunswick, N.J.: Rutgers University Press, 1997.

Schultz, Mark. *The Rural Face of White Supremacy: Beyond Jim Crow*. Urbana and Chicago: University of Illinois Press, 2005; 2007 paperback edition.

Sides, Josh. *L.A. City Limits: African American Los Angeles from the Great Depression to the Present*. Berkeley and Los Angeles: University of California Press, 2003.

Skaggs, William H. *The Southern Oligarchy*. New York: The Devin-Adair Company, 1924.

Steinberg, Allen. *The Transformation of Criminal Justice: Philadelphia, 1800–1880*. Chapel Hill: University of North Carolina Press, 1989.

Stuntz, William J. *The Collapse of American Criminal Justice*. Cambridge: The Belknap Press, 2011.

Tolnay, Stewart E., and E. M. Beck. *A Festival of Violence: An Analysis of Southern Lynchings, 1882–1930*. Urbana and Chicago: University of Illinois Press, 1995.

Vandal, Gilles. *Rethinking Southern Violence*. Columbus: Ohio State University Press, 2000.

Venkatesh, Sudhir Alladi. *Off the Books: The Underground Economy of the Urban Poor*. Cambridge: Harvard University Press, 2006.

Waldrep, Christopher. *Roots of Disorder: Race and Criminal Justice in the American South, 1817–80*. Urbana and Chicago: University of Illinois Press, 1998.

Weber, Max. *The Vocation Lectures: Science as a Vocation, Politics as a Vocation*. Indianapolis: Hackett Publishing Company, 2004.

Whitman, James Q. *Harsh Justice: Criminal Punishment and the Widening Divide Between America and Europe*. New York: Oxford University Press, 2003.

———. *The Origins of Reasonable Doubt: Theological Roots of the Criminal Trial*. New Haven: Yale University Press, 2008.

Wolfgang, Marvin E. *Patterns in Criminal Homicide*. Philadelphia: University of Pennsylvania, 1958; reprint Montclair, N.J.: Patterson Smith, 1975.

Woodward, C. Vann. *The Strange Career of Jim Crow*. New York: Oxford University Press, 1955; 2002 reprint.

INDEX

ABOUT THE AUTHOR

JILL LEOVY is an award-winning reporter for the *Los Angeles Times*. She lives in Los Angeles.